People, Planet and Profit

People, Planet and Profit

Socio-Economic Perspectives of CSR

Edited by

SAMUEL O. IDOWU
London Metropolitan University, UK

ABUBAKAR S. KASUM
University of Ilorin, Nigeria

ASLI YÜKSEL MERMOD
Marmara University, Turkey

Routledge
Taylor & Francis Group

LONDON AND NEW YORK

First published in paperback 2024

First published 2014 by Gower Publishing

Published 2016 by Routledge
4 Park Square, Milton Park, Abingdon, Oxon OX14 4RN

and by Routledge
605 Third Avenue, New York, NY 10158

Routledge is an imprint of the Taylor & Francis Group, an informa business

Publisher's Note
The publisher has gone to great lengths to ensure the quality of this reprint but points out
that some imperfections in the original copies may be apparent.

Gower Applied Business Research
Our programme provides leaders, practitioners, scholars and researchers with thought
provoking, cutting edge books that combine conceptual insights, interdisciplinary rigour and
practical relevance in key areas of business and management.

British Library Cataloguing in Publication Data
A catalogue record for this book is available from the British Library.

The Library of Congress has cataloged the printed edition as follows:
People, planet and profit : socio-economic perspectives of CSR / [edited] by Samuel O. Idowu,
Abubakar S. Kasum, Asli Yüksel Mermod.
    pages cm
 Includes bibliographical references and index.
 ISBN 978-1-4094-6649-9 (hardback) – ISBN 978-1-4094-6650-5 (ebook) – ISBN 978-1-4094-6651-2
(epub) 1. Social responsibility of business. 2. Corporations – Social aspects. I. Idowu, Samuel O.

 HD60.P387 2014
 658.4'08–dc23
                                                                                    2013037634

 ISBN: 978-1-4094-6649-9 (hbk)
 ISBN: 978-1-03-283695-9 (pbk)
 ISBN: 978-1-315-59991-5 (ebk)

DOI: 10.4324/9781315599915

Contents

List of Figures

List of Tables

About the Editors

Samuel O. Idowu is Senior Lecturer in Accounting at the city campus of London Metropolitan University Business School, where he has also held the positions of Course Organizer for Accounting Joint degrees, Course Leader/Personal Academic Adviser (PAA) for students taking Accounting Major/Minor and Accounting Joint degrees and he is currently Course Leader for the Accounting and Banking degree. Samuel is a Professor of CSR and Sustainability at Nanjing University of Finance & Economics, China. He is a Fellow of the Institute of Chartered Secretaries and Administrators, a Fellow of the Royal Society of Arts, a Liveryman of the Worshipful Company of Chartered Secretaries and Administrators and a named freeman of the City of London. Samuel has published some 40 articles in professional and academic journals and has contributed chapters to edited books. He is the Editor-in-Chief of two major global reference books – *The Encyclopedia of Corporate Social Responsibility* (ECSR) and *The Dictionary of Corporate Social Responsibility* (DCSR); and a Series Editor for Springer's CSR, Sustainability, Ethics and Governance books. Samuel has been in academia for 25 years and in 2008 won one of the Highly Commended awards of the Emerald Literati Network Awards for Excellence. In 2010, one of his edited books was placed in 18th position out of 40 top sustainability books by the Cambridge University Programme for Sustainability Leadership. He has examined for The Chartered Institute of Bankers (CIB) and The Chartered Institute of Marketing (CIM); and has marked examination papers for the Association of Chartered Certified Accountants (ACCA). His teaching career started in November 1987 at Merton College, Morden, Surrey; he was a Lecturer/Senior Lecturer at North East Surrey College of Technology (Nescot) for 13 years, where he was the Course Leader for BA (Honours) Business Studies, ACCA and CIMA courses. He has also held visiting lectureship posts at Croydon College and Kingston University. He was a Senior Lecturer at London Guildhall University prior to its merger with the University of North London, when The London Metropolitan University was created in August 2002. He has served as an external examiner to a number of UK universities, including the University of Sunderland, the University of Ulster, Belfast and Coleraine in Northern Ireland, and Anglia Ruskin University, Chelmsford. He is currently an External Examiner at the University of Plymouth and the Robert Gordon University, Aberdeen, Scotland and Teesside University, Middlesbrough, UK. He was also the Treasurer and a Trustee of Age Concern in Hackney, East London, from January 2008 to September 2011. Samuel is on the Editorial Advisory Board of the *Management of Environmental Quality Journal* and *The International Journal of Business Administration* and *Amfiteatru Economic* Journal. He has been researching in the field of corporate social responsibility since 1983 and has attended and presented papers at several national and international conferences and workshops on corporate social responsibility.

Abubakar Sadiq Kasum is a Lecturer in the Department of Accounting, University of Ilorin, Ilorin, Nigeria, where he has taught accounting courses at undergraduate and postgraduate levels since 2001. He has supervised student projects at undergraduate and Master's levels and he is currently supervising a PhD candidate, in addition to many other MSc Accounting and MSc Finance students in the university. He also services other departments and faculties in the university and he is an associate/adjunct lecturer to other universities in Nigeria. He holds a BSc in Accounting (1999), an MSc in Accounting (2005), and a PhD in Accounting and Finance (2010) and was elected Associate Member of the Institute of Chartered Accountants of Nigeria (ACA) in 2005. He has conducted research in the areas of financial reporting, corporate social responsibilities, sustainable development and environmental accounting, and forensic accounting. He has presented his research report at various international conferences around the world and has published them in refereed journals, book chapters and conference proceedings. He has served on conference organizing committees of various Northern Nigeria Regional Districts of Accountants Conferences and on the Member's Education and Training Committee of the Institute of Chartered Accountants of Nigeria. He is the Editor of the *Ilorin Journal of Accounting*, a journal of the Department of Accounting, University of Ilorin, Nigeria. He is currently serving on the editorial boards of *The International Journal of Critical Accounting*, *Contemporary Management Research*, *The European Journal of Business and Management* and *The Research Journal of Accounting and Finance*. He is a Member of the American Accounting Association (AAA), the American Taxation Association (ATA), the Global Entrepreneurship Monitor (Nigeria Team), The Sustainable Development Research Society, The Social Responsibility Research Network, The Standing Conference on Organizational Symbolism, The International Group on Governance, Fraud, Ethics and Social Responsibility, and The International Critical Accounting Society. He is a resource person for training in IFRS/IPSAS and pension/post-retirement plans in Nigeria. In addition to teaching, student supervision and research he has also served his university of primary employment as the Coordinator of The Department of Accounting, Chairman of the Departmental Undergraduate Curriculum Review Committee, and Faculty Representative on The University Computer Services Management Committee and The Business Committee of Faculty of Business and Social Sciences. As community service, he is currently serving as the Treasurer of the Academic Staff Union of Universities (ASUU), University of Ilorin Chapter, and the Unilorin Business Community Multi-purpose Co-operative Society. He is an associate in a firm of accountants, Olaiya Oludare Balogun and Co., and he is a Financial Analyst with the Primace Consulting Group.

Asli Yüksel Mermod is Professor of Finance in the Faculty of Economics and Administrative Sciences at Marmara University Business Administration Department, Istanbul, Turkey. She started her academic career in 1996 after moving from a professional business career where she worked as a public relations manager in Istanbul Convention and Exhibition Center and as editor, copywriter and accounts director in the Mediart and Sanatevi advertising agencies. Dr Yüksel Mermod also taught at Webster University in Geneva, Switzerland, from 2004 to 2006 and she still teaches as visiting professor at Bahcesehir University,in the International Finance Department, and Okan University, in the Social Sciences Institute as adjunct faculty. She studied Economics (Volkswirtschaftslehre) at Konstanz University in Germany and graduated from Marmara University Economics Department. She completed her MSc and PhD in Finance from Marmara University Banking and Insurance Institute and is fluent in Turkish, English and German. She is currently at intermediate level in French.

Dr Asli Yüksel Mermod's research areas cover bank management, CSR, socially responsible investing, brand equity, electronic finance and financial services marketing. She teaches undergraduate courses in International Banking, International Finance, Project Finance, Bank Management, Principles of Finance, and Financial Markets and Institutions; and MBA, PhD and Executive MBA classes in Bank Funds Management, Project Finance and Management, and Risk Management in Banking. She has supervised four PhD theses and fourteen master theses to date. She has published books on bank management, service marketing, brands and measuring brands' equity, electronic banking and risks, and banking law and management in Turkey and in Germany. She has also published in several national and international journals, including *Internationale Wirtschafts-Briefe*, *The Journal of Business Economics and Management*, *The Journal of Internet Banking and Commerce*, *The International Journal of Energy Sector Management* and *The Journal of Business and Economics Research*. Dr Yüksel Mermod has also contributed chapters to many internationally published books. In addition to her research and teaching responsibilities, Dr Yüksel Mermod has been actively involved in administration at Marmara University. She was the Vice Director of Marmara University Institute of Social Sciences and Erasmus–Socrates Program Coordinator for postgraduate students. She holds key positions in some international scientific conference organizations in organization and scientific committee membership and board of referees, and she has taken part in a number of book projects about CSR with internationally esteemed scholars.

Notes on Contributors

Adewale Abideen Adeyemi is currently an Assistant Professor of Finance, Kulliyyah of Economics and Management Sciences, International Islamic University Malaysia, and a Research Fellow at the Accounting Research Institute, Universiti Teknologi Mara, Malaysia. He is also an Associate Member of the Chartered Institute of Bankers of Nigeria. He holds a PhD degree specializing in finance from the International Islamic University Malaysia, where he also did a Postdoctoral Fellowship. His Bachelors and MSc degrees were in the areas of finance from the University of Ilorin, and University of Lagos, Nigeria, respectively. DrAdewale's current research interests are in the areas of responsible finance, livelihood finance, Islamic microfinance, financial inclusion, financial literacy and payment systems. In addition to consultancy services experience, he has also taught, published and presented papers in these areas at international conferences.

Dr Maria Aluchna is an Associate Professor in the Department of Management Theory, Warsaw School of Economics, Poland. She specializes in corporate governance (ownership structure, board, executive compensation, transition economies) and in strategic management. She also researches in the field of corporate social responsibility. She was awarded the Deutscher Akademischer Austauschdienst (DAAD, 2001/2002)) a study visit research scholarship by the Universität Passau, and a Polish–American Fulbright Commission scholarship to Columbia University in the US. Since 1998 she has been working at the Department of Management Theory of the Warsaw School of Economics, where she obtained her PhD degree (2004) and completing habilitation procedure (October 2011). She was also awarded the Polish Science Foundation for young researchers for two consecutive years (2004 and 2005). Recently, within a grant financed by the European Union, she completed a visiting scholar's stay at London Metropolitan Business School in the UK and at the University of Sydney Business School in Australia. Maria Aluchna teaches Corporate Governance (in Polish and English), Strategic Management (in English) and Transition in Central and Eastern Europe (in English). She is the author of a number of articles in national and international journals, as well as conference papers. She served on two editorial boards in 2008 and was the Editor-in-Chief of the Warsaw Stock Exchange portal on corporate governance best practice. Currently, she is a consultant to law firm Głuchowski, Siemiątkowski i Zwara and conducts research projects for the Capital City of Warsaw, Poland.

Taiwo Olufemi Asaolu is a professor and holds a BSc Accounting degree, a PGD Computer Science, and MBA, MPhil and PhD degrees in Accounting. He is a Fellow of the Institute of Chartered Accountants of Nigeria (FCA), and a Deputy Chairman of the Examination Committee of the Institute. He has attended and presented papers at several international and national conferences and has published several articles in refereed academic journals. He is the author of many textbooks, including *Cost and Management*

Accounting, Quantitative Techniques in Management Accounting, etc. He is currently the head of the Department of Management and Accounting at Obafemi Awolowo University, Ile-Ife, Nigeria and the coordinator, MBA (Executive) Program of the same University.

Tajudeen John Ayoola is a lecturer and holds a BSc Accounting degree (1996), MBA (2004), MPhil Accounting (2011), and is currently on a PhD programme. He holds several professional qualifications, including an Associateship of the Institute of Chartered Accountants of Nigeria (ACA–2001), Certified Information Systems Auditor (CISA–2008), Certified Information Security Manager (CISM–2009), and Certified Ethical Hacker (CEH–2009). He was a Principal Accountant in the Bursary Department of OAU Ile-Ife before he took up his teaching appointment at the Department of Management and Accounting, Obafemi Awolowo University in 2008. His research interests focus on corporate social responsibility, corporate governance issues (such as fraud and earnings management) and the application of forensic accounting techniques. He has written many papers in reputable journals and presented papers at national and international conferences.

Gülcan Çağil graduated in Business Administration from the Faculty of Management of Istanbul University in 1999. She completed her Master's degree in Banking from The Institute of Banking and Insurance, Marmara University, in 2001. She has a PhD in Banking from Marmara University. She has been employed by the School of Banking and Insurance at Marmara University, Istanbul, Turkey, since 2001 as a lecturer. She has attended and presented several papers at national and international conferences and has published several articles in academic journals. She has also published a number of books in the areas of energy finance and risk management in the Turkish banking sector.

Matthias S. Fifka is Professor for Business Administration and Business Ethics at the University Erlangen-Nuerrnberg. He is also a visiting professor at the University of Dallas (USA), the Nanjing University of Finance and Economics and the Shanghai Jiao Tong University (China), the École Supérieure des Sciences Commerciales d'Angers (ESSCA) (France), and the Maastricht School of Management (Netherlands). From 2011 until September 2013 he held the Dr Juergen Meyer Endowed Chair for International Business Ethics and Sustainability at Cologne Business School (CBS).

His research and teaching focuses on sustainability, corporate social responsibility/corporate citizenship, corporate governance and business ethics, but also on the business–government relationship, international and strategic management as well as on the economic and political system of the United States.

Moreover, he has published more than 40 articles in renowned journals and books, and serves as member of the editorial board and reviewer for several journals. He frequently contributes articles and interviews to a variety of international media.

Siriyama Kanthi Herath is an Associate Professor of Accounting at Clark Atlanta University. She earned her PhD in accounting and a Master of Accountancy (Honors) degree from the University of Wollongong in Australia. She received an MBA degree and a BCom (Honors) degree from the University of Colombo in Sri Lanka. She is the author or co-author of over 40 publications. She serves on the editorial boards of the *International Journal of Electronic Finance*, the *International Journal of Accounting and Finance* and the *African Journal of Accounting, Auditing and Finance* (AJAAF). Dr Herath has worked at the

University of Ruhuna, University of Colombo, University of Wollongong, University of Western Sydney, Lynchburg College, Georgia State University, Pittsburg State University and Georgia Institute of Technology.

Laksitha Maheshi Herath holds a High School Diploma from North Atlanta High School, where she was in the International Baccalaureate Program. She has attended schools in Australia and the US. She is currently working on earning her BA in Accounting at Clark Atlanta University in Atlanta, US. She has published a poem, 'Stolen Property' and has won several awards in writing competitions. She serves as the secretary in the Honors Program of Clark Atlanta University and is a member of Toastmasters.

Dr Manoj Joshi is a Professor of strategy, Entrepreneurship and Innovation with Amity Business School, Amity University; he has more than 22 years of experience. Passionate about entrepreneurship and innovation, he has assisted business institutions in launching entrepreneurship electives, besides mentoring budding entrepreneurs globally and helping them in crafting and executing startup strategy. Prior to being in research he was with the engineering industry in the area of designing screw pumps and loading arms and heading business development for international markets. Professor Joshi has a PhD in the area of Strategy Innovation; he is a Fellow of the Institution of Engineers, holds an MBA and has over 30 publications in International peer reviewed journals and conferences. His focus area is around creating and managing entrepreneurship strategy, family business entrepreneurship, innovation and innovative practices, business modeling, etc. Professor Joshi is the Asia Editor for the *International Journal of Entrepreneurship and Innovation*; regional Editor India, *Journal of Family Business Management*; Editor, *Amity Business Journal*; and he is an editorial board member of some 12 international peer-reviewed journals on entrepreneurship such as *JSBM, WREMSD, IJGSBM, JCE, JEBE, Business Strategy and Environment*; *Reveue 2000*aand *Foundation and Trends in Entrepreneurship*.

Vindhyalaya Joshi is a retired Senior Research Professor with the Department of Education, Uttar Pradesh, India. He is a Philosopher with an interest in areas such as Political Science, Economics and General Management. He has worked for more than 35 years with the Department of Education of the government of Uttar Pradesh and has contributed to rural progress by channelling education for all through various government schemes. He is a philosopher, thinker and an avid reader on issues connecting economics, political science, history, management, etc.

Maria Lai-Ling Lam has been a Professor of Business Administration at Malone University, Canton, Ohio, since 2001. She holds a PhD in Marketing and Organization Behavior from George Washington University, an M.A. degree in Religion Studies focusing on Christianity and Chinese religions, a MBA degree in Marketing and International Business, and a BBA degree in Marketing from the Chinese University of Hong Kong. She has published a book entitled *Working with Chinese Expatriates in Business Negotiation: Portraits, Issues and Application*, and has also authored more than 60 peer-reviewed journal articles, book chapters and proceedings published in refereed academic and professional outlets. She is a fellow of the International Academy of Intercultural Research, and a member of the editorial review boards of business journals and several professional organizations. She received the Distinguished Faculty Award in Scholarship and Creative

Expression in 2011. Her joint paper with Dr Georgia Eshelman and Dr Martha Cook, entitled 'Three contributing factors to effective utilization of technology in management education and practice: Personhood, mindfulness, and meditation', and her paper, 'An alternative paradigm of managing sustainability in the global supply chain', have won Distinguished Paper and the Best Research Paper award respectively at national conferences.

Sarah Lauwo is a Faculty Member of the Essex Business School, University of Essex, UK. She holds a PhD in accounting from the University of Essex, UK. She is a qualified chartered accountant who worked as an auditor 10 years ago, before moving to the higher education arena. Her research is into corporate social responsibility with a particular focus on the mining sector in Tanzania. Her research interests are Social and Environmental Accounting, Corporate Social Responsibility, Corporate Governance, Accounting issues in Developed and Developing countries, Corporate Regulation and Accountability and Accountability in the Public Sector. Sarah has presented her research at national and international conferences and seminars. She has also contributed a number of articles to highly ranked academic journals and to edited books.

Zororo Muranda is currently an Associate Professor and Dean of the School of Business Sciences and Management at Chinhoyi University of Technology in Zimbabwe. He teaches Research Methods, Entrepreneurship and Strategic Management at undergraduate and postgraduate levels. He previously taught at the University of Zimbabwe, the Midlands State University and the University of Botswana. His research interests are in youth and female entrepreneurship, corporate governance and corporate social responsibility.

Olatunde Julius Otusanya is a Senior Lecturer in Accounting and currently the Acting Head of the Department of Accounting, the University of Lagos, Nigeria. He obtained his Master's and Doctoral degrees in Accounting from the University of Lagos and the University of Essex respectively. He has published a number of articles and monographs. His research interests include financial crime, tax evasion and tax avoidance, the role of professionals in antisocial practices, and corporate social responsibility. He is an Associate Member of the Institute of Chartered Accountants of Nigeria, the Chartered Institute of Taxation of Nigeria, the Nigerian Institute of Management (Chartered) and the British Accounting and Finance Association (BAFA). He is currently the Editor of the *Nigerian Journal of Management Studies*, member of the editorial board of the *African Journal of Economics and Sustainable Development* and the *Global Journal of Accounting*, and a reviewer for a number of local and international journals. He has received several research grants and awards.

Mia Mahmudur Rahim is a lecturer at QUT Business School at the Queensland University of Technology, Australia. He obtained his LLB with Honours and LLM from Dhaka University; LLM in International Economic Law from Warwick University as a Chevening Scholar; MPA from LKY School of Public Policy with an NUS Graduate Scholarship; and PhD from Macquarie University with a Research Excellence Scholarship. Before he joined academia, he was a lawyer and a Deputy District and Sessions Judge in Bangladesh. He also worked for the Law Commission and the High Court of Bangladesh. He is a member of the Center for Legal Governance of Macquarie University and Technical

Committee for Asian Consumer Protection Research Network. His interests include research and consultancy, particularly on issues related to state, market and regulation.

Ioana Teodoreanu is currently a PhD student at Gheorghe Asachi University, Iași, Romania, and Cologne Business School, Germany. Her thesis is concerned with the implementation of sustainability in universities. The focus of the study rests on the design and integration of CSR in curricula and the resulting potentials. From 2002 to 2007 she specialized in management and engineering at Gheorghe Asachi University and obtained a Master's degree from ISTIA, Angers University, France,in 2009. From 2008 to 2010 she worked as a teaching assistant at the Department of Management and Engineering at Gheorghe Asachi University and did research in various areas of management (environmental, strategic, performance and production).

S.P. Tiwari holds a PhD in Economics and he is a Professor, Head of the Department of Economics and Dean of the Faculty of Arts with Dr R.M.L. Avadh, at Faizabad University. He is an avid researcher with a specialization in Rural Economics. He has been a prolific teacher and mentor to students in the area of economics and has guided several PhD projects. He is an active member of the Indian Economic Association and has presented several papers at national and International conferences.

Sibel Yilmaz Türkmen has been part of the academic staff of the Faculty of Business Administration at Marmara University in Turkey since 2000. She gained her Bachelor's degree from Istanbul University Faculty of Business Administration in 1999. She received her Master's degree (MA) and Doctorate (PhD) in Accounting and Finance in 2001 and 2006, respectively, both from Marmara University. She has published a book and written articles in national and international journals. She has also attended and presented papers at several international and national conferences. She teaches finance courses at graduate and undergraduate levels and her research interests are in the areas of corporate finance, financial markets and institutions and international finance.

Rodica Milena Zaharia holds a BA in Economics (1988), a PhD in Economics (1999) and she is currently a Professor at the Bucharest University of Economic Studies, Romania. She has been a faculty member of the International Business and Economics Department since 1993. She is the author or co-author of articles in peer-reviewed journals, books and book chapters published in Romania and abroad. She has coordinated several research grants and she is a member of international research teams. Rodica Milena Zaharia is PhD coordinator and she has successfully supervised three PhD candidates since 2009. She is also a member of the scientific board of the International Business and Economics Research Center at Bucharest University of Economic Studies and the editor in chief for the peer-reviewed *European Journal of Interdisciplinary Studies*. She is a member of the editorial boards of peer-reviewed journals in Lithuania, Romania, the US, the UK and Ukraine. Her research interests are in the areas of social responsibility, globalization, international business and international political economy.

Foreword

This publication has not only proved that Corporate Social Responsibility (CSR) has the potential to become a global success story but has also shown how people from different countries are already joining a mutual belief that business can make the world better for us all if economic, social and ecological challenges are strategically addressed. In every corner of the world leading business people, academics as well as politicians, continue to debate the new role of business in society. International standards have been developed in addition to corporate entities exchanging best practices.

CSR will not only be implemented on the micro-level by multinational corporations (MNCs) and many regional small and medium sized enterprises (SMEs) – but also on a macro-level – in terms of new institutional governance structures and international agreements. Looking at the speed of progress as well as the learning curve of CSR, it looks glaringly clear that a deeper understanding about the current developments is urgently needed. Especially in terms of how international frameworks and collaboration are affecting the development of CSR as well as institutional arrangements which are appropriate to foster the expansion and development of the field of CSR. Most of the questionable aspects of CSR can only be answered by a sound understanding of the socio-economic dimensions of the current development practices.

This publication provides important socio-economic perspectives and in-depth insights into the link between the micro and macro perspective through these diverse contributions of pioneering academics in their respective countries. This information will not only be useful for further research but will also provide useful tools required by business leaders and politicians worldwide in their attempts to implement effective CSR strategies in their own organizations.

These examples from different countries make it also clear that there is no one size fits all strategy to CSR. The cultural and institutional contexts which frame business activities play an important role. Thus, CSR has to be developed individually and from the bottom up in every country and enterprise. Nevertheless one can learn a lot from the different experiences in other countries and organizations. We are all in an open-search process, required in order to find sustainable answers to our most pressing challenges. It helps a lot to see people all over the world having the same goal and vision.

Through the immense effort of these editors as well as the authors our mutual search and innovation process in the field of CSR now has another milestone. All those who are genuinely striving to be socially responsible will appreciate the important contribution provided by this book in order to better understand the socio-economic dimension of CSR. It is hoped that all the efforts of this publishing venture pay off by helping to make the world a better place for all of us, especially for our children and their own children, to whom the future of our world belongs.

René Schmidpeter
Head of Research, Centre for Humane Market Economy, Salzburg, Austria

Preface

Corporate social responsibility (CSR) has impacted on our world positively in such an unprecedented manner that many countries around the world continue to feel these positive impacts of CSR (even during a period of global financial meltdown) from all angles, including their social and economic well-being. The 8 United Nations Millennium Development Goals adopted by 189 countries, signed by 147 country leaders in New York in September 2000 during the Millennium Summit, are a precursor of the further social and economic development of our world. It is hoped that by 2015, despite the many impediments the current global financial crisis has put in the way of progress, significant progress will have been made by all countries in all areas of the eight pillars that constitute the Development Goals. Two of these, 'to eradicate extreme poverty and hunger' and 'to develop a global partnership for development' are examples of what all countries need to put in place in order to function effectively in the twenty-first century, not least the poorer nations of the world.

The drive for socio-economic well-being of the 196 nation states that make up our world requires that governments, corporations and individual citizens should be CSR-conscious; in other words, they should be socially responsible in all the ramifications of that concept. Responsibility is demonstrated by actions and deeds, not by words or information inserted in glossy magazines called 'CSR Reports', or on corporate websites. As a matter of fact, remarkable progress has been made around the world in corporate social responsibility. There is compelling evidence to support this claim. For example, it has been manifested from the number of issues in the field that we debate, research, write about and hold conferences and workshops on today, which were never on any research or practitioners' agenda some 50 or so years ago. By way of further examples, 50 years ago no one talked about global development, climate change, corporate and individual impacts on the rainforest, extreme poverty in faraway places, depletion of man's natural resources or sustainable development, but today these are issues we debate and talk about freely and with passion. This can only be attributed to the coming of age of CSR.

It is believed that a book on socio-economic development perspectives of CSR would provide us with a framework for a better understanding of how the field of CSR is contributing to development as it continues to evolve in many countries around the world. Our world continues to be radically different from what it used to be as a result of many factors, including socially responsible actions by every corporate and individual citizen. We all need to understand the developmental perspectives of CSR and how this is happening and being recognized in different places around the globe.

This book has therefore been fortunate in its ability to have attracted interest from scholars writing about socio-economic development perspectives of CSR from ten countries' experiences, namely Australia, Botswana, China, India, Nigeria, Poland, Romania, Tanzania, Turkey and the USA. It is therefore hoped that the information it contains will be useful to our readers from any sector of society, for example education, industry and commerce, practitioners, international organizations, governments, non-governmental organizations and those who are enthusiastic about the developmental impacts of CSR.

Samuel O. Idowu, UK
Asli Yüksel Mermod, Turkey
Abubakar S. Kasum, Nigeria

Acknowledgements

Publishing an edited book by several contributors spread around the globe is definitely a team effort of several committed professionals; the putting together of this book is no exception to that general belief and understanding. Our first 'thank you', therefore, goes out to all our fantastic contributors who are located in 11 countries around the world; without whose hard work and professionalism; there would have been no edited book to publish on how CSR in contributing to socio-economic development around the world. The three Editors appreciate these individuals' hard work and will remain indebted to them all for a very long time – if not forever – for making the publication of this book a reality.

There are also some individuals we want to thank:

Samuel O. Idowu would like to thank the following friends and colleagues who have assisted him either directly or indirectly in ensuring the publication of his eleventh book in the series of books, Richard Ennals, Pat Wood, David Ogunlaja, Samuel Ogunlaja, Edward O. Akintaro, Jeremiah O. Akintaro, Michael Soda, Timothy Ogunyale, Julius O. Olanrewaju, Christopher Soyinka, Adebayo Idowu, Paul Idowu, Samson Nejo, and Samson A. Odugbesi. His thanks are also due to his brother and sister; Michael A. Idowu and Elizabeth A.A. Lawal, the same are also due to members of his direct clan – his wife – Olufunmilola O. Idowu and their young children – Josiah Opeyemi Idowu and Hannah Ayomide Idowu who continue to support him during the entire process of managing this volume, others in his book series and who have once again shared with him both the pleasures and travails of his publishing venture.

Abubakar S. Kasum would like to acknowledge Professors M.L. Nassar, H.A. Saliu, A.A. Aderinto, T.O. Asaolu and Dr A.A. Owolabi, for the different roles played by them in his academic career. He would also like to thank Dr A. Abdulraheem and his other colleagues in the Department of Accounting and Finance, University of Ilorin. His thanks also go to members of his family: Hamidat A. Abu-Kasum – wife; Nahima Bidemi Abu-Kasum and Zainab Kemisola Abu-Kasum – children; Alhaja Salamat I. Kasum – Mum; and Rafiat, Falilat, Bashir and Kasum (Jr) – siblings. Specific thanks also go to Dr M.S. Ajao of The Department of Anatomy, University of Ilorin.

Asli Yüksel Mermod would like to thank all her friends and colleagues who have encouraged her in her academic career and studies at Marmara University Department of Business Administration; Profs Ercan Gegez, Suat Oktar, Jale Oran, Cemal Ibis, Kiymet Caliyurt and Ayten Cetin; and for their patience and support, especially to her husband Philippe, son Atakan, mother Nuran Yuksel, sister Ulku Yuksel and all the members of her family. She would also like to remember and send her gratitude to heaven to her dear Father Professor Dr Ali Sait Yuksel who had always been her role model in her life.

The three Editors would like to thank two colleagues at Gower Publishing Company: their Publishing Editor, Martin West, and his Assistant, Donna Shanks, for their professional support during the process of putting together the bits and pieces that make up the book.

Finally, we would like to apologize for any errors and omissions which may appear anywhere in this book, no harm or displeasure was intended to anyone.

Developmental Perspective of CSR: An Introduction

SAMUEL O. IDOWU AND ASLI YÜKSEL MERMOD

Corporate Social Responsibility (CSR) has impacted on us from different directions and has been linked to enabling us to understand better some of the biggest challenges which have ever faced man during his existence on planet Earth. For example CSR has enabled us to respond to climate change, address the consequences of globalization, increase the effectiveness of internal corporate governance, uphold international human rights, increase justice and equity, especially in the poorest parts of the world, fight corruption and poor governance and achieve stable and sustainable economic growth (Blowfield and Murray, 2011). Our understanding of these issues has provided us with the opportunity to break these complex challenges down into addressable pieces.

The Editors of *People, Planet and Profit: Socio-economic Perspectives of CSR* believe that while corporate social responsibility is by no means a new concept, neither to academics nor practitioners, insufficient attention has thus far been paid to the end product of CSR in practice, which they define in terms of social and economic developmental effect.

The contributions in this edited volume therefore serve to explain the developmental aspect of CSR from a conceptual perspective and to provide empirical evidence of the impact of CSR delivery on stakeholders in different corners of the world. Many studies examine the relationship between good governance within corporations and socially responsible behaviour. In this book the emphasis is on what corporations take from and give back to their stakeholders when ostensibly behaving in a corporately responsible fashion.

Stakeholders, including employees, customers, host communities, governments and non-governmental organizations (NGOs) have diverse interests and expectations of CSR. This gives rise to questions about whether the CSR activities which corporate entities support are the ones today's stakeholders need; about whether the CSR programmes being delivered are adequate; and about the relationship between the corporations' view of what constitutes CSR and that of the supposed beneficiaries.

The chapters in this book provide thoughtful answers to these questions and help to assess the outcomes of corporate activities both in developed and developing countries and regions, in terms of economic progress and social and political advancement.

Samuel O. Idowu (2010) argues that societies around the world are gradually coming to terms with the understanding that we all have to behave responsibly and change all our socially unacceptable and irresponsible behaviours in dealing with certain issues which affect mankind, regardless of whether we live in an advanced or less advanced part of the world. Some of the consequences of past corporate actions are gradually unfolding and being felt with similar or the same levels of intensity by us all in terms of climate change or global warming, food crisis (even in the First World, which was considered unthinkable a few years ago; this is now almost a reality in all parts of the world) and several other socio-economic challenges. We need to act to deal with all these issues; and CSR has acted and continues to act as the required vehicle to use to address them.

Interestingly, the global community has taken the issues relating to the world's social and economic development very seriously for over a decade – as is evidenced by the common development objectives adopted in New York in September 2000 by 189 world leaders, set out in the 8 United Nations Millennium Development Goals (MDGs). These world leaders resolved in September 2000 to meet these 8 MDGs, a project they hope to achieve by 2015:

1. Eradicate extreme poverty and hunger;
2. Achieve universal primary education;
3. Promote gender equality and empower women;
4. Reduce child mortality;
5. Improve maternal health;
6. Combat HIV/AIDS, malaria and other diseases;
7. Ensure environmental sustainability;
8. Develop global partnerships for development.

A cursory look at these eight goals suggests that they are all inherently socio-economic development goals which are necessary for global development and could only be achieved through CSR-related actions. The goals were designed to provide the directions to be followed by the nations of the world in order to ensure our world's socio-economic development, as they would help to reduce poverty, improve health and promote peace, human rights, gender equality and environmental sustainability (Liimatainen, 2013). One must not lose sight of the fact that the recent global financial crisis could have seriously affected the chances of meeting the 2015 achievement date, but one hopes that a United Nations (UN) audit of progress between 2000 and 2015 will tell us what development progress we will have made by 2015 in achieving the eight goals and look at what needs to be done to address those goals which have fallen short of expectations.

Liimatainen (2013) has also argued that to ensure the measurability of the eight MDGs, they have been broken down into 21 targets that can be measured using 60 indicators, see Table 1.1 for a better understanding of the measurable targets and their indicators.

To assess how our world is faring in terms of these development goals is perhaps a reason for putting together a book on socio-economic development perspectives of CSR covering roughly two years to 2015.

This book, *People, Planet and Profit: Socio-economic Perspectives of CSR*, provides an insight into how CSR has helped different countries around the world to develop in terms of the triple bottom line – *social, economic and environment* or, alternatively, in terms of the 3Ps – *People, Planet and Profit*. The book is fortunate in the sense that its contributors, who are actively working in the field of CSR, have provided information on how CSR has contributed to their countries' focus on socio-economic development.

Table 1.1   Millennium Development Goals (MDGs), targets and indicators

MDGs	Targets	Indicators
Goal 1 Eradicate extreme poverty and hunger	1a Reduce by half the proportion of people living on less than $1 a day	**1.1** Proportion of population below $1 (PPP) a day **1.2** Poverty gap ratio **1.3** Share of poorest quintile in national consumption
	1b Achieve full and productive employment and decent work for all, including women and young people	**1.4** Growth rate of GDP per person employed **1.5** Employment-to-population ratio **1.6** Proportion of employed people living below $1 (PPP) per day **1.7** Proportion of own-account and contributing family workers in total employment
	1c Reduce by half the proportion of people who suffer from hunger	**1.8** Prevalence of underweight children under five years of age **1.9** Proportion of population below minimum level of dietary energy consumption
Goal 2 Achieve universal primary education	2a Ensure that all boys and girls complete a full course of primary schooling	**2.1** Net enrolment ratio in primary education **2.2** Proportion of pupils starting grade 1 who reach last grade of primary **2.3** Literacy rate of 15–24 year-olds, women and men
Goal 3 Promote gender equality and empower women	3a Eliminate gender disparity in primary and secondary education preferably by 2005, and at all levels by 2015	**3.1** Ratios of girls to boys in primary, secondary and tertiary education **3.2** Share of women in wage employment in the non-agricultural sector **3.3** Proportion of seats held by women in national parliament
Goal 4 Reduce child mortality	4a Reduce by two-thirds the mortality rate among children under five	**4.1** Under-five mortality rate **4.2** Infant mortality rate **4.3** Proportion of 1 year-old children immunized against measles
Goal 5 Improve maternal health	5a Reduce by three-quarters the maternal mortality ratio	**5.1** Maternal mortality ratio **5.2** Proportion of births attended by skilled health personnel
	5b Achieve, by 2015, universal access to reproductive health	**5.3** Contraceptive prevalence rate **5.4** Adolescent birth rate **5.5** Antenatal care coverage (at least one visit and at least four visits) **5.6** Unmet need for family planning
Goal 6 Combat HIV/AIDS, malaria and other diseases	6a Halt and begin to reverse the spread of HIV/AIDS	**6.1** HIV prevalence among population aged 15–24 years **6.2** Use of condoms has reduced new incidence of HIV/AIDS **6.3** Proportion of population aged 15–24 years with comprehensive correct knowledge of HIV/AIDS **6.4** Ratio of school attendance of orphans to school attendance of non-orphans aged 10–14 years
	6b Achieve, by 2010, universal access to treatment for HIV/AIDS for all those who need it	**6.5** Proportion of population with advanced HIV infection with access to antiretroviral drugs
	6c Have halted and begun to reverse the incidence of malaria and other major diseases	**6.6** Incidence and death rates associated with malaria **6.7** Proportion of children under 5 sleeping under insecticide-treated bed nets **6.8** Proportion of children under 5 with fever treated with appropriate anti-malarial drugs **6.9** Incidence, prevalence and death rates associated with tuberculosis **6.10** Proportion of tuberculosis cases detected and cured under directly observed treatment short course

Table 1.1   Millennium Development Goals (MDGs), targets and indicators
Continued

MDGs	Targets	Indicators
Goal 7 Ensure environmental sustainability	7a Integrate the principles of sustainable development into country policies and programmes; reverse loss of environmental resources 7b Reduce biodiversity loss, achieving, by 2010, a significant reduction in the rate of loss	**7.1** Proportion of land area covered by forest **7.2** CO_2 emissions, total, per capita and per $1 GDP (PPP) **7.3** Consumption of ozone-depleting substances **7.4** Proportion of fish stocks within safe biological limits **7.5** Proportion of total water resources used **7.6** Proportion of terrestrial and marine areas protected **7.7** Proportion of species threatened with extinction
	7c Reduce by half the proportion of people without sustainable access to safe drinking water and basic sanitation	**7.8** Proportion of population using an improved drinking water source **7.9** Proportion of population using an improved sanitation facility
	7d Achieve significant improvement in lives of at least 100 million slum dwellers by 2020	**7.10** Proportion of urban population living in slums
Goal 8 Develop a global partnership for development	8a Develop further an open, rule-based, predictable, non-discriminatory trading and financial system 8b Address the special needs of the least developed countries 8c Address the special needs of landlocked developing countries and small island developing states 8d Deal comprehensively with the debt problems of developing countries through national and international measures to make debt sustainable in the long term	Some of the indicators listed below are monitored separately for the least developed countries (LDCs), Africa, landlocked developing countries and small island developing states' official development assistance (ODA) **8.1** Net ODA, total and to the least developed countries, as percentage of OECD/ DAC donors' gross national income **8.2** Proportion of total bilateral, sector-allocatable ODA of OECD/DAC donors to basic social services (basic education, primary healthcare, nutrition, safe water and sanitation) **8.3** Proportion of bilateral official development assistance of OECD/DAC donors that is untied **8.4** ODA received in landlocked developing countries as a proportion of their gross national incomes **8.5** ODA received in small island developing states as a proportion of their gross national incomes Market access: **8.6** Proportion of total developed country imports (by value and excluding arms) from developing countries and least developed countries, admitted free of duty **8.7** Average tariffs imposed by developed countries on agricultural products, textiles and clothing from developing countries **8.8** Agricultural support estimate for OECD countries as a percentage of their GDP **8.9** Proportion of ODA provided to help build trade capacity Debt sustainability: **8.10** Total number of countries that have reached their HIPC decision points and number that have reached their HIPC completion points (cumulative) **8.11** Debt relief committed under HIPC and MDRI Initiatives **8.12** Debt service as a percentage of exports of goods and services

MDGs	Targets	Indicators
	8e In cooperation with pharmaceutical companies, provide access to affordable essential drugs in developing countries	**8.13** Proportion of population with access to affordable essential drugs on a sustainable basis
	8f In cooperation with the private sector, make available the benefits of new technologies, especially information and communications	**8.14** Telephone lines per 100 population **8.15** Cellular subscribers per 100 population **8.16** Internet users per 100 population

Source: Liimatainen (2013). Based on: http://www.undp.org/mdg/.

DAC: Development Co-operation Directorate of the OECD; GDP: gross domestic product; HIPC: heavily indebted poor countries; MDRI: Multilateral Debt Relief Initiative; OECD: Organisation for Economic Co-operation and Development; PPP: Purchasing Power Parity.

The book is divided into three parts, each part focusing on different dimensions of CSR which have been grouped together for convenience. Part I: Multinational Corporations and CSR – which encompasses six chapters – addresses the contributions of multinational corporations (MNCs) to socio-economic development in different countries around the world. Part II: CSR and Socio-economic Progress – explores in three chapters how CSR has been used as a vehicle for socio-economic development; and Part III: CSR in the General Environment – in six chapters – looks at different dimensions of CSR in global development. Let us now look in turn at each of the 15 chapters that make up the book.

The first chapter, entitled 'Multinational Corporations and CSR in the Nigerian Oil and Gas Sector' by Dr Taiwo Olufemi Asaolu and Dr Tajudeen John Ayoola assesses the CSR activities of MNCs in the Nigerian oil and gas sector using international standards such as the Global Reporting Initiative (GRI), the UN Global Compact Ten Principles, ISO 26000, Accountability AA 1000 Standards, and the OECD Guidelines for Multinational Enterprises. The results of the study by these two scholars in this sector of the Nigerian economy showed a substantial variation in the level of attention and extent of disclosure on CSR by the MNCs operating within the borders of Nigeria. The study notes that the prevailing approaches to CSR were seen as fragmented, cosmetic and disconnected from business strategy. These variations, they argue, could be resolved by the institution of a mandatory CSR framework in the Nigerian oil and gas sector.

In Chapter 2, 'CSR and the Enterprise Culture of Multinational Corporations in Developing Countries', Olatunde Julius Otusanya notes that the bourgeoning CSR literature rarely examines the predatory enterprise culture of many MNCs, even though practices have real consequences for the life chances of millions of people. Dr Otusanya argues that MNCs are increasingly willing to increase their profits through indulgence in some socially unacceptable practices such as price fixing, tax avoidance/evasion, bribery and corruption, money laundering and practices that show scant regard for social norms and even laws. Many MNCs legitimize their social credentials by making promises of responsible and ethical conduct, but organizational culture and practices have not necessarily been aligned with publicly espoused claims, the chapter argues. Dr Otusanya also exposes some MNCs' antisocial behaviour, suggesting that the area lends itself to the possibilities of further research in social and business culture, ethics, social disorder and crime.

Chapter 3 by Maria Lai-Ling Lam, entitled 'CSR of Foreign Multinational Corporations in China', is based on a six-year field study, carried out between 2006 and 2012 in China, on the perceptions of 30 Chinese executives from 20 different foreign multinational enterprises of their CSR programmes in China. Professor Lam examines the CSR practices of foreign MNCs in a state-driven CSR with emerging non-governmental organizations (NGOs) in the context of China. The chapter notes that the scope of CSR activities in China is, as in many other emerging nations, still narrowed down to charity, internal economic efficiency and political visibility. The results of the study note that only four exemplars learned about how to provide public services through their CSR programmes to complement the needs of the Chinese government. These companies have learned how to institutionalize their CSR programmes through industry associations, self-regulated industry codes of conduct and collaborations with selected NGOs in China. The four exemplars did not follow the institutional norms and the existing efficiency paradigm. They were exemplars owing to the moral consciousness of their leaders and the persistence, compassion and humility of their dedicated CSR officers, Professor Lam notes.

Matthias S. Fifka and Ioana Teodoreanu in Chapter 4, 'The Economic and Social Impact of Multinational Corporations in Romania', note that the role that MNCs can play in the social and economic development of developing and emerging countries especially, has been controversial in discussions since the 1970s. The advent of CSR has consequently given the debate new input, they argue. This was the context under which the provision of information on the economic and social impact of the CSR activities of MNCs in Romania as a transition country was considered necessary. The chapter analyses the specific national political and socio-economic background to CSR and its development in the country. It also investigates CSR activities of MNCs using three case studies. The results show that the understanding of CSR in Romania is mostly reduced to philanthropy and does not encompass other core business activities. Moreover, governmental and civil society initiatives to promote CSR in the country are very weak. The chapter concludes that the potential of CSR to contribute to economic and social development in Romania is still not being used.

Chapter 5 was provided by Abubakar Sadiq Kasum and Asli Yüksel Mermod and is entitled 'A Comparative Study of CSR Practices of Multinational Corporations in their Operations in Developed and Developing Economies'. These authors compare how CSR is practised by MNCs in developed countries with that of developing countries, with the ultimate aim of understanding how influential the CSRs of these entities are in contributing to the socio-economic development of their host countries. The study observes that MNCs, just like all other business entities, are essential to the development stages of every country and it has ben argued that some developmental gains accrue from them. It also confirmed that MNCs are known to be engaging in CSRs as one of the ways to give back to the communities in which they operate some of the wealth made from them. It observes, however, that there is a big gap when a comparison is made between MNCs' operations in developed and in developing countries. Problems such as lower education levels, general awareness of CSR issues, and bad leadership in developing countries are noted to be responsible for the high level of ignorance on the part of citizens of many of the emerging countries.

In Chapter 6, 'CSR of Multinational and Indigenous Corporations in Romania', Rodica Milena Zaharia argues that the role of MNCs in the development process continues to be a hotly debated issue. The chapter on the one hand discusses the benefits that MNCs bring to a country's economy through Foreign Direct Investments (FDI), especially in developing economies; for instance, Professor Zaharia lists the following benefits: efficiency and modern technologies, job creation, increased opportunities to export goods and services out of the host country, higher wages and taxes, and product diversification. She also notes that there is another side to these benefits, arguing that MNCs have been under severe criticism for their exploitation of poorer and less educated labour forces, their disregard for national and local values, unbalanced competition against local companies, environmental irresponsibility, bribery, corruption and other socially irresponsible practices.

Part II begins with Chapter 7, 'The Diamond-shaped Socio-economic Development of Botswana', in which Zororo Muranda studies the CSR of Botswana's largest diamond-mining company, Debswana. The chapter adopts a historical analysis to the case by first introducing the country's historical and economic background in order to give context to the study. Professor Muranda demonstrates that CSR in Debswana is not just a result of philanthropy, but is influenced by the structure of shareholding in the mining company. Botswana's socio-economic development has largely been financed through diamond-mining. Debswana's participation in CSR and the country's socio-economic development is intertwined in the country's development trajectory, argues Professor Muranda.

Sarah Lauwo and Olatunde Julius Otusanya examine the political economy perspective of CSR in Tanzania in Chapter 8. They argue that the role of MNCs in fostering socio-economic development in developing countries has been the subject of considerable debate by civil society organizations, academics and practitioners. Dr Lauwo and Dr Otusanya assert that, by working closely with host governments, MNCs have a role to play in alleviating poverty and stimulating economic development, particularly in poverty-stricken developing countries. To achieve this requires a strong commitment on the part of both corporations and their host governments. But in the context of the contemporary global economy, the ability of governments in developing countries to demand accountability, responsibility and transparency from modern corporations has remained questionable, they argue. The reason for this is due in part to the fact that governments in developing countries are desperate to attract foreign investment in order to deal with their socio-economic problems, including and in particular, poverty. Thus, a tension exists between encouraging foreign investment and issues associated with promoting socio-economic order. This chapter adopts a political economy perspective to consider how neo-liberal ideologies adopted in the global capitalist economy have been manifested within institutional structures as well as in CSR practices; and to show how this has serious implications for the socio-economic development of many developing countries, as is the case in Tanzania. The two authors argue that any attempts to change CSR practices and their potential to promote socio-economic development in Tanzania need to be accompanied by changes in the governance structures at both domestic and global levels.

In Chapter 9, 'CSR and Energy Investments in Turkey', Sibel Yilmaz Türkmen and Gülcan Çağil argue that in a globalized world, the importance of CSR is further increased and becomes a significant part of sustainable development (SD) when corporate entities are demonstrably responsible. While enhancing the benefits of firms, CSR does not have a high cost, the authors note. Corporate responsibility practices affect society and other related parties not only in the short run but also in the long run. Many financial organizations in Turkey and around the world support efforts for CSR. Accordingly, this has been the reason why socially responsible investment has been of considerable interest to investors and has attracted their attention. Green investments and investments in renewable energy are examples of tools of these efforts. These two scholars note that the perception of CSR is improving in areas such as education, healthcare, environment and technology use.

In Chapter 10, entitled 'Corporate Social Responsibility to Small and Medium-sized Enterprises: Extending Sustainable Development in Society', Dr Mia Mahmudar Rahim describes how SD and CSR could together act as a 'meta-fix' whose ideas and philosophies have evolved from an objective perspective to one which is process-focused. He argues that while SD aims to sustain economic growth with the required maintenance and protection of the environment, CSR is a long-term business strategy that balances corporate rights with economic, environmental and social obligations towards their stakeholders. The semantics of these two terms have changed over time to a point where the concepts they express have come to signify interrelated processes for ensuring a long-reaching goal of development. The chapter posits that the notion of SD can contribute to integrating the objective of development to a reasonable extent in society Small and medium-sized enterprises (SMEs) could be sensitized to the core concepts behind CSR.

In Chapter 11, entitled 'The Effectiveness of CSR Initiatives and their Impact upon Stakeholders', Dr Maria Aluchna argues that CSR is a concept that describes the practice whereby companies integrate social and environmental concerns into their business operations. Businesses' interactions with stakeholders on a voluntary basis aims to achieve long-term sustainable growth and development. Thus the concept of CSR is a spin-off from the social model of a corporation and emphasizes social performance as the additional dimension for the evaluation of a company's operational well-being. Stakeholder groups include shareholders, employees, suppliers, customers, local communities and management. On the operational level, CSR refers to a set of different initiatives undertaken in various spheres of social and economic lives (environmental protection, national heritage, social programmes, sports, education, etc.) in order to solve social, economic and environmental problems, provide for stakeholder management and social dialogue and minimize the negative impact of corporate actions on society and the environment, argues Dr Aluchna.

The twelfth chapter, by Dr Adewale Abideen Adeyemi, 'Livelihood Assets Financing as a CSR Initiative of Microfinance Banks in Nigeria', provides a theoretical model that accentuates the imperatives of Nigerian microfinancial institutions' CSR activities aimed at ensuring that access to and use of financial services are maximized by the unbanked. The chapter demonstrates that enormous opportunities, which transcend philanthropy, exist, through which the Nigerian microfinance banks can be socially responsible. Dr Adeyemi's conclusion and recommendations elicit the need for empirical studies that investigate the implications of the apparent social mission drift of the Nigerian microfinance banks for the accumulation of the livelihood assets needed by the poor for a sustainable livelihood.

Chapter 13 by Professor Siriyama Kanthi Herath and Lakshida Maheshi Herath, entitled 'Environmental Management Accounting: An Overview' argues that environmental reporting as an important element of CSR has received much attention in recent years and many companies have in fact attempted to adopt practices that promote SD. The chapter notes that organizations should align their economic development activities with CSR behaviour. The authors, who note that the decision to research this area for the book emanated from the lack of research into environmental management accounting, examine the development of environmental management accounting research and discuss several empirical research studies.

In Chapter 14, 'CSR: Global Perspective, Competitiveness, Social Entrepreneurship and Innovation', Dr Manoj Joshi, Dr S.P. Tiwari and Professor Vindhyalaya Joshi provide a series of quotations on profit and social responsibility, state, city state, quality in work, life, liberty, etc. and argue that there should be continuous efforts to reduce economic disparity among citizens. These authors argue that it is ironic that the state is unable to execute its primary duties in the form of social responsibilities, for the following possible reasons: the state is not able to mobilize funds; funds available are not adequate against requirements; the state is not able to utilize the funds and/or there is lack of governance and will power. As a result, the entrepreneurs in the microcommunity or corporate community emerge as 'an entrepreneur consortium' to carry out this critical task, using innovative methods. They participate as 'social entrepreneurs' and emerge as drivers of the engine of economic and social growth.

In Chapter 15, 'Corporate Social Responsibility: A Modern Tool for Building Social Capital', the final chapter of the book, Samuel O. Idowu provides a set of concluding remarks which sum up the book. He traces CSR back to Howard Bowen's 1953 book, *Social Responsibilities of the Businessman*, which is generally considered the genesis of modern CSR. Samuel O. Idowu notes the importance of *social capital* in the modern debate on CSR and how CSR has contributed in many different ways to the transformation of our world.

A careful read through the issues explored in this introductory chapter to each of the 15 chapters featured in this book should hopefully reveal that they have one common theme and message: that CSR has several critical roles to play in the socio-economic development of any nation state. Modern corporate entities have come to realize that long-term economic growth and sustainable success would be far too difficult to achieve if they were perceived by all and sundry to be socially irresponsible and not weaving the triple bottom line ethos into their strategies. Success is no longer measured only in terms of the bottom line or share prices on the stock markets; in any case a company that is perceived to be socially irresponsible would have a poor bottom line result and a lower share price at the stock exchange. It is now no longer the case (as was previously believed) that it is only society that benefits from a corporate entity's CSR actions, but rather that the entity actually helps itself to operate sustainably and consequently does well because of its triple bottom line actions (Idowu, 2010).

References

Blowfield, M. and Murray, A. (2011). *Corporate Responsibility*. 2nd edition. Oxford: OUP.

Idowu, S.O. (2010). Professionals' perspectives of CSR: An introduction, in S.O. Idowu, and Leal Filho, W. (eds), *Professionals' Perspectives of Corporate Social Responsibility* Heidelberg, Germany: Springer.

Liimatainen, A. (2013) Millennium Development Goals, in S.O. Idowu, N. Capaldi, L. Zu, and A. Das Gupta (eds), *Encyclopedia of Corporate Social Responsibility*, 3, 1682–1689.

Multinational Corporations and CSR

1

Multinational Corporations and CSR in the Nigerian Oil and Gas Sector

TAIWO OLUFEMI ASAOLU AND TAJUDEEN JOHN AYOOLA

Abstract

This study assesses the corporate social responsibility (CSR) activities of multinational corporations (MNCs) in the Nigerian oil and gas sector using international standards such as the Global Reporting Initiative (GRI), the UN Global Compact principles, ISO 26000, the Accountability AA 1000 Standards, and the Organisation for Economic Co-operation and Development (OECD) Guidelines for Multinational Enterprises. The study adopted the use of secondary data in its scope. All companies operating in the oil sector of the Nigerian economy constituted the population, while the sample consisted of the six major oil multinationals which account for over 50 per cent of the oil exploration in Nigeria. Content analysis of CSR documents and established scoring criteria were adopted for the analysis of data. The results show a substantial variation in the level of attention and extent of disclosure of CSR by the multinationals. The prevailing approaches to CSR are seen as fragmented, cosmetic and disconnected from business strategy. These variations could be resolved by the institution of a mandatory CSR framework in the Nigerian oil and gas sector.

Introduction

A conventional view held by advocates of corporate business is that the purpose of the corporation is to make a profit for its shareholders (Minch, 2011; Friedman, 1962), so that traditional financial statements principally report to shareholders, to the detriment of other stakeholders (such as environmentalists, non-governmental organizations, immediate community, etc.). In the past decade however, there has been a consistent pressure from other stakeholders from the standpoint that traditional financial reporting which focuses on shareholders' interests does not adequately represent the multiple dimensions of corporate value today (Simnet, Vanstraelen and China, 2009). Pressure as a result of concern for environmental degradation, social ills and global financial crisis has resulted in a call for better corporate governance, transparency, accountability and shareholder value creation situated within new financial and non-financial measures of corporate performance appraisal. This call has justified the need for interdisciplinary reporting that reflects a simultaneous integration of economic, environmental and social factors into corporate behaviour with the aim of sustaining resources for future generations (Quick, 2008). Corporate Social Responsibility (CSR) has emerged in an attempt to respond to the demands for interdisciplinary reporting.

The concept of CSR is associated with other terms such as 'corporate responsibility', 'corporate citizenship', 'responsible business' and 'corporate social performance'. Despite a growing body of CSR literature, no definition has been universally accepted (Matten and Moon, 2008). The absence of a widely agreed framework on CSR which specifies minimum outcome-based standards of social performance has created an enabling milieu for socially harmful companies which externalize many of their costs to pass themselves off as socially responsible (Fooks et al., 2013). Even though there is no legally binding obligation for companies to report on their social responsibilities, more and more companies publish reports that address these issues under wide-ranging names such as 'social responsibility report', 'sustainability report', and 'environmental, health and safety report'. This social report states what contributions companies have made to the society or what efforts they have taken to protect the environment (Gossling and Vocht, 2007). CSR means different things in different places to different people at different times (Campbell, 2007), and this is as a result of national divergence and cultural divergence perspectives on the CSR diffusion process around the globe (Yin and Zhang, 2012). The concept refers to organizational conduct that proactively integrates the voices of parties affected by business activities in corporate decision-making. This type of conduct typically reaches beyond the firm's economic and legal obligations in order to satisfy and sometimes exceed its stakeholders' expectations (Heugens and Oosterhout, 2002; McWilliams and Siegel, 2001; Husted, 2000).

CSR is evolving into a core business function, central to a firm's overall strategy and vital to its success. Specifically, CSR addresses the question of whether companies can perform better financially by addressing both their core business operations and their responsibilities to the broader society (Basu and Palazzo, 2008; Vogels, 2005). Consequently, many companies have realized that having a socially responsible corporate image is a valuable strategic asset. Several studies have shown that firms that perform socially responsible activities enjoy benefits such as customer satisfaction and favourable customer and positive community evaluations (Carroll, 2004; Luo and Bhattacharya, 2006).

In Nigeria, the oil and gas industry is critical to the survival of the country, as it accounts for over 95 per cent of the country's foreign exchange earnings, 40 per cent of her gross domestic product (GDP) and 85 per cent of the Federal Government's collectable revenue (Uwakonye, Oshoand Anucha, 2006; Aghalino, 2004). The government charges a flat-rate 50 per cent tax on profits and a royalty of 0–12 per cent depending on the location (OECD/AFDB, 2009). The major oil companies operating in the Nigerian oil and gas sector are Shell Petroleum Development Company of Nigeria Ltd., Mobil Producing Nigeria Unlimited, Chevron Nig. Ltd., Nigerian Agip Oil Company Ltd. Elf Petroleum Nig. Ltd. and Texaco Overseas Petroleum Company of Nigeria Unlimited. These multinationals participate in the petroleum industry in joint ventures with Nigeria National Petroleum Corporation (NNPC), as operators/contractors in the deep water under production-sharing contracts (PSC). All of the crude oil comes from numerous small producing fields located in the swamps of the Niger Delta region. According to the Ministry of Niger Delta Affairs (2009),the region comprises nine states: Delta, Rivers, Bayelsa, Cross Rivers,

Akwa Ibom, Edo, Imo, Abia, and Ondo state, with a total of 185 local government areas. The region hosts a population of approximately 30 million, settled in around 13,000 small communities. The region covers a land area of approximately 75,000 square kilometres, making up 12 per cent of Nigeria's landmass. There are about 600 oilfields producing from around 5,000 wells, and although production is focused in limited areas, the region is criss-crossed by approximately 10,000 kilometres of pipelines.

These multinationals have initiated, funded and implemented community development schemes in the name of CSR, such as schools, hospitals, microcredit schemes, scholarships, etc.; however, the effectiveness of such CSR initiatives is being increasingly questioned, and there is mounting evidence of a gap between the stated intentions of the multinationals and the impact on the communities where their operations are domiciled (Frynas, 2005). The relationships between the multinationals and their host communities have been affected by the degradation of the environment through oil spillage, gas flaring and pollution. The relationship has been unfriendly owing to different perceptions of the role that multinationals are expected to play in the development process of their host communities. On the one hand, the host communities claim that the multinationals are not doing enough considering the amount of oil wealth taken away from their lands; while the multinationals, on another hand, believe that they have gone even beyond the realm of normal CSR. In the face of conflicting perceptions of the issues in contention, crises have erupted in the oil-producing region (Alabi and Ntukekpo, 2012; Aghalino, 2004). It is in the light of the above that it has become imperative to examine the claims of the multinationals with regard to CSR efforts, using internationally acclaimed corporate, social, and environmental performance indicators. Thus, the objective of this study is to attempt to examine the CSR of the multinational firms in the Nigerian oil and gas sector using international accepted standards.

Review of the Literature

CSR

CSR has been broadly defined as the responsibilities of a business towards the economic and social development of the communities where they operate, which are affected by its corporate policies and practices (Brown and Forster, 2012; Lahdesmaki and Suutari, 2012; Smith, 2003). It enables organizations to take responsibility for the impact of their activities on their shareholders, society and the environment. This ensures that organizations behave ethically and responsibly in improving the quality of life for the stakeholders. It is of increasing concern and holds strategic implications for companies across industry, as it helps a company to differentiate its product and service by creating a positive brand image and this safeguards the firm's reputation (Hsu, 2012; Ketola, 2005). The essence and manifestation of CSR lies at the discretion of each business, thus depending not only on the core competencies and stakeholder interests but also on the cultural and institutional context of the business (Crane and Matten, 2004). The business case for CSR argues that there are legitimate reasons for a corporation to invest in CSR activities. From an economic standpoint, there is theoretical logic and some inconclusive empirical evidence that engaging in socially responsible activities can reduce costs and risks to the firm, build firm competitive advantage, enhance reputation and legitimacy, and create synergies (Salazar and Husted, 2008, quoted in Brown and Forster, 2012). However, CSR cannot be seen solely through the lens of the business case, as the expectations of what CSR could potentially accomplish are much broader. From society's point of view, it is important to assess the contribution that companies can make to development (Frynas, 2005). CSR has been variously conceptualized: Schwartz and Carroll (2003) posit economic, legal and ethical obligations, collapsing the fourth dimension of philanthropy into the ethical component. Windsor (2006) delineates it into ethical, economic and corporate citizenship.

The increased industry attention and researchers' enthusiasm for CSR led to the development of fragmented theories and approaches aimed at understanding how, and with what impact, CSR strategies can contribute in creating competitive advantage and superior performance (Torugsa, O'Donohue and Hecker, 2012; Porter and Kramer, 2006). The three common approaches are: stakeholder-driven approach; performance-driven approach; and motivation-driven approach (Hsu, 2012; Basu and Palazzo, 2008). The stakeholder approach is the extent to which businesses meet the economic, legal, ethical and discretionary responsibilities placed on them by their various stakeholders (Maignan, Ferrel and Hult, 1999). CSR is seen as a response to the demands of external stakeholders about general social concerns for the firm's operations. Without CSR activities, this group might withdraw their support from the firm (McWilliams, Siegel and Wright, 2006). The performance-driven approach concerns the link between CSR, corporate strategy and requisite performance. These led scholars to focus on determining activities to implement CSR and then measuring their effectiveness. CSR activities include incorporating social concerns into products, adopting progressive human resource management practice, focusing on environmental performance and advancing the goals of community organizations (McWilliams, Siegel and Wright, 2006; Amit and Schoemaker, 1993). The motivation-driven approach examines the extrinsic reasons for a firm's CSR engagement or the intrinsic rationale to advance notions of its obligations and responsibilities (Basu and Palazzo, 2008). While the extrinsic reasons concern favourable outcomes towards the focal company, such as enhancing reputation, consumers' resilience to negative information and managing risk, the intrinsic rationale draws on philosophical concept (Hsu, 2012). CSR has also been viewed from other angles: one is CSR as integrated into business strategy. If CSR is accepted as embedded in everything a company does, then CSR is part of good business strategy, thus, embedding socially responsible principles in corporate management is called 'before-profit' obligation (McElhaney, 2007). A second view sees CSR as a residual, that is, an add-on set of projects that are not part of the core business strategy. CSR is thus seen as an 'after-profit' obligation. The consequence is that if companies are not profitable, they do not have to behave responsibly (Hopkins, 2004; Kang and Wood, 1995).

INTERNATIONAL CSR PERFORMANCE INDICATORS

UN Global Compact principles

The United Nations Global Compact is a voluntary initiative to encourage businesses worldwide to adopt sustainable and socially responsible policies, and to report on them. The ideology is built on the following four areas and ten principles of global compact:

1. Human rights
   - Principle 1: Businesses should support and respect the protection of internationally proclaimed human rights; and
   - Principle 2: make sure that they are not complicit in human rights abuses.
2. Labour standards
   - Principle 3: Businesses should uphold the freedom of association and the effective recognition of the right to collective bargaining;
   - Principle 4: the elimination of all forms of forced and compulsory labour;
   - Principle 5: the effective abolition of child labour; and
   - Principle 6: the elimination of discrimination in respect of employment and occupation.
3. Environment
   - Principle 7: Businesses should support a precautionary approach to environmental challenges;
   - Principle 8: undertake initiatives to promote greater environmental responsibility; and
   - Principle 9: encourage the development and diffusion of environmentally friendly technologies.
4. Anti-corruption
   - Principle 10: Businesses should work against all forms of corruption, including extortion and bribery.

ISO 26000

ISO 26000 provides practical guidelines to implement social responsibility, identify and engage stakeholders, and enhance credibility of reports and claims made about social responsibility. It contains:

a) A definition of social responsibility.
b) Seven principles, which are: accountability for the organization's impacts on society and the environment; transparency in the organization's decisions and activities that have an impact on society and the environment; ethical behaviour at all times; the obligation to respect, consider and respond to the interests of the organization's stakeholders; accept that respect for the rule of law is mandatory; respect international norms of behaviour, while adhering to the principle of respect for the rule of law; and respect human rights and recognize both their importance and their universality.
c) Seven core subjects which should be addressed in order to identify the issues and priorities that are relevant for the organization. They are: organizational governance; human rights; labour practices; environments; fair operating practices; consumer issues; and community involvement and development.

ACCOUNTABILITY AA 1000 STANDARDS

Accountability's AA 1000 series are principles-based standards to help organizations become more accountable, responsible and sustainable. They address issues affecting governance, business models and organizational strategy, as well as providing operational guidance on sustainability, assurance and stakeholders' engagement.

OECD GUIDELINES FOR MULTINATIONAL ENTERPRISES

These guidelines are recommendations addressed to multinationals for the provision of voluntary principles and standards for responsible business conduct in a variety of areas including employment and industrial relations, human rights, environment, information disclosure, competition, taxation, science and technology. The guidelines are:

a) Concepts and principles: set out the principles which underlie the guidelines such as their voluntary character, their application worldwide and the fact that they reflect good practice for all enterprises.

b) General policies: contain the first specific recommendations, including provisions on human rights, sustainable development, supply chain responsibility, and local capacity-building, and more generally call on enterprises to take full account of established policies in the countries in which they operate.

c) Disclosure: recommend disclosure in all material matters regarding the enterprise such as its performance and ownership; and encourages communication in areas where reporting standards are still emerging such as social, environmental and risk reporting.

d) Employment and industrial relations: address major aspects of corporate behaviour in this area including child and forced labour, non-discrimination and the right to bona fide employees' representation and constructive negotiation.

e) Environment: encourage enterprises to raise their performance in protecting the environment, including performance with respect to health and safety impacts.

f) Combating bribery: cover public and private bribery and addresses passive and active corruption.

g) Consumer interest: recommend that enterprises should act in accordance with fair business, marketing and advertising practices and take all reasonable steps to ensure the safety and quality of goods or services provided.

h) Science and technology: aim to promote the diffusion by MNCs of the fruits of research and development activities among the countries where they operate.

i) Competition: emphasize the importance of an open and competitive business climate.

j) Taxation: call on enterprises to respect both the letter and spirit of tax laws and to co-operate with tax authorities.

GLOBAL REPORTING INITIATIVE (GRI)

The GRI sets out the principles and indicators organizations can use to measure and report their economic, environmental, and social performance. The GRI is currently the industry leader in providing a set of voluntary principles for companies in the area of CSR. Impetus was given to its set of voluntary principles when GRI formally launched its report at the World Summit on Sustainable Development in Johannesburg in 2002 (Hopkins, 2004).

Research Methodology

This study examined the CSR of the MNCs operating in the Nigerian oil sector in line with international standard and best practices. The oil sector was chosen because of the strategic role of oil in the sustenance of the Nigerian economy. It is the mainstay of the economy and any action in the sector will impact positively or negatively on the economy.

SAMPLE

The sample used in the study consisted of the six major MNCs and this choice was driven by the finding that they account for over 50 percent of the oil drillings in the Niger Delta. In 2008, two of the MNCs, Exxon Mobil and Royal Dutch Shell, each has revenue in excess of $350 billion (Winston, 2011), which is far above the GDP of Nigeria as at the same year. MNCs generally account for over 70 percent of world trade (Hopkins, 2004), and control over 25 percent of global commerce (Winston, 2011). The MNCs are international firms and are open to international CSR influences.

MEASURES OF CSR DISCLOSURE

There is no single way of assessing CSR performance, as different rating organizations are available (Wolfe and Aupperle, 1991); ditto for the measurement approaches, some of which are survey methodology, reputation index and rating, and content analysis of documents (Hino, 2006). This study adopted the content analysis method. This is a common technique in CSR research (Gray, Kouhy and Lavers, 1995), and it is a line of research widely adopted to ensure reliability and valid inference from narrative data in accordance with their context (Mallin, Michelon and Raggi, 2013; Krippendorff, 2004; Hackston and Milne, 1996). It is a systematic, replicable technique for compressing many words of text into fewer content categories based on explicit rules of coding (Weber, 1990), and has been verified as an appropriate technique for making deductions by using systematic methods for the analysis of texts and other messages (Gossling and Vocht, 2007; Stemler, 2001). Content analysis was performed using CSR documents created by oil multinationals, including their websites, company reports, press releases, codes of conduct/ethics, performance indicators, declarations of compliance, case studies, etc., for the financial year 2011 (Bondy, Moon and Matten, 2014).

Items for assessing CSR for the relevant stakeholder group were developed after examining the issues covered under various global standards such as UN Global Compact Principles, ISO 26000, Accountability AA 1000 standards, OECD Guidelines for Multinational Enterprises, and the GRI. While the standards applied extensive ranges of evaluation criteria, this study uses only limited criteria from all the standards deemed relevant and which have been the subject of controversy between the MNCs and all stakeholders in the Nigerian oil and gas sector. The MNCs were rated in six areas, namely: strategic CSR and stakeholders' engagement shareholders, government, employees, surrounding community and the environment. CSR was measured separately for each of these six areas (see Appendix).

The scoring criteria of Zeng, Xu, Yin, and Tam (2012) and Wiseman (1982) were adopted and each area was scored according to the level of disclosure. The scores range between 0 and 3, and were determined as follows:

✓ When no information is available   0
✓ For general non-monetary information   1
✓ For concrete non-monetary information   2
✓ When monetary information is available   3

Monetary-related and non-monetary-related CSR disclosures are effective tools to gauge the levels of corporate CSR activities (Cho and Patten, 2007, as quoted in Zeng, Xu, Yinand Tam, 2012). The key difference between 'concrete non-monetary information' and 'general non-monetary information' is that the former includes a goal statement, while the latter only talks about environmental concerns in very general terms. Percentages were used in the analysis of data.

Analysis of Findings

CRITERION 1: STRATEGIC CSR AND STAKEHOLDERS' ENGAGEMENT

CSR is now seen from the lens of corporate strategy. Strategic CSR is a business strategy that is integrated with core business objectives and core competencies to create business value and positive social/environmental value. While in the sampled statements from the multinationals' chief executive officers (CEOs) there is fairly general non-monetary information about the relevance of CSR, there was neither a documented process for evaluating the performance of the organizations in respect of CSR,nor the alignment of CSR with the companies' strategic plans. Existing independently of such plans, CSR can yield no more than a drop in the ocean of developmental efforts. As Frynas (2005) notes, '[m]any of the CSR projects embarked upon by the multinationals were fragmented and driven at too low a level of management rather than at the strategic level'; therefore, there may be little co-ordination in determining which areas should benefit and how projects can be put together to contribute to a greater whole. The multinationals identified with the need for stakeholder group engagement, but the basis for identification and selection of the stakeholders were not disclosed, nor the disclosure of the mechanism for such stakeholders to provide recommendations to the highest governance body responsible for CSR.

CRITERION 2: CSR AND SHAREHOLDERS

The multinationals were committed to fairly adequate shareholders' disclosure. Information regarding dividends paid and total new investments made by them were disclosed in monetary terms. Information about local purchasing was documented also.

CRITERION 3: CSR AND GOVERNMENT

A recurring criticism of the oil multinationals has been their lack of transparency about oil revenues, which makes it difficult to fully understand the potential economic benefits of the sector and to hold government accountable for how the money was spent (Baumuller, Donnelly, Vines and Weimer, 2011). It is in the public domain that revenue from oil has been non-transparent and under-reported in fiscal accounts. The introduction of the Nigerian Extractive Industry and Transparency Initiative (NEITI) has not brought about the required transparency. The initiative has been criticized for inefficiency, although a 2005 NEITI audit report released in 2009 highlighted unprecedented financial discrepancies among the multinationals, the Federal Inland Revenue Service (FIRS), the Central Bank of Nigeria (CBN), the Nigerian National Petroleum Corporation (NNPC), and the Ministry of Finance. Although the multinationals reported income tax paid to government, the volume and type of estimated proven reserves and productions, and a disclosure of the specific policies adopted for the promotion of transparency of payments to government, were both unavailable.

CRITERION 4: CSR AND EMPLOYEES

Higher CSR towards employees in terms of the existence and implementation of an occupational health and safety management system, employee policies and practices, etc., were disclosed. Multinationals have successfully integrated various employee-related CSRs, such as workplace safety and benefit plans, into their companies' functions. However, some other critical issues such as the existence of programmes to understand the general health risks; the description of programmes to gauge employees' satisfaction; the percentage of employees covered by collective bargaining agreements, etc. were largely unavailable, or very general in description.

CRITERION 5: CSR AND SURROUNDING COMMUNITIES

While the multinationals in their various reports affirmed their responsibilities to the surrounding communities' welfare, the findings showed contrary views. Information relating to the surrounding communities where the operations of the multinationals were domiciled were largely unavailable or barely general. The description of processes to engage with and address the needs of indigenous communities, the percentage of operations which implemented the engagement of local communities, operations with significant potential or actual negative impacts on local communities and processes for managing such impact, etc., were largely unavailable. This corroborated earlier findings that CSR initiatives have often been conceived in the air-conditioned offices of the multinationals with selected local chiefs rather than the ordinary members of the communities (e.g., Baumuller et al., 2011; Frynas, 2005). Effective stakeholders' identification and selection based on internationally recognized standards could be adopted by these multinationals, as this will result in the participation of local, indigenous people in genuine self-help initiatives using local knowledge, skills and tools.

CRITERION 6: CSR AND THE ENVIRONMENT

Oil production in Nigeria has had a significant environmental impact; although data on environmental degradation (specifically oil spills) has been a subject of controversy among stakeholders, worst-case figures put the daily average loss of oil at 712 barrels per day. In sub-Saharan Africa, Nigeria ranks highest in gas flaring. Consequences attributed to environmental degradation include the collapse of local fishing and farming, loss of habitat and biodiversity, acid rain damage, health-related problems such as skin cancer and respiratory ailments, and other health impacts of air and noise pollution (Baumuller et al., 2011; Maass, 2009; Clarke, 2008). Multinationals differed greatly in their reports of the effects of their operations on the environment. Generally, concrete non-monetary information was not available on spills and annual emissions by type; quantities of waste and toxic releases; the impact of operations on biodiversity; and strategies for managing the impact. A favourable CSR towards the preservation of the environment is essential to the loyalty of the stakeholders towards the multinationals, as it will result in fewer lawsuits and less unrest and criticism associated with their operations.

Conclusion

This study has assessed the CSR activities of multinational firms in the Nigerian oil and gas sector using international standards such as the GRI, the UN Global Compact Principles, ISO 26000, Accountability AA 1000 Standards, and the OECD Guidelines for Multinational Companies. The study concludes that there is a substantial variation in the level of attention and extent of disclosure of CSR by the multinationals. The prevailing approaches to CSR are fragmented, cosmetic and disconnected from business strategy, and the current CSR agenda is inappropriate for addressing social and environmental problems occasioned by the activities of the oil multinationals. It is believed that if the multinationals were to analyse their CSR activities using the same frameworks that guide their core business choices, then CSR would become more than a charitable deed but rather a source of opportunity to showcase their responsibility to all stakeholders. CSR is not currently being embedded in the day-to-day business activities of the multinationals, as their strategy does not recognize CSR as central to creating social, environmental and business values.

The multinationals do not disclose adequate information in line with international best practices, especially in the area of the environment. The level of environmental degradation and pollution as a result of the activities of the multinationals was found to be monumental, with little or no disclosure about its extent, impact and strategies in combating the menace in concrete monetary terms. The absence of a uniform framework of reporting has resulted in the varying degree of information provided by the multinationals despite their allegiance to international CSR standards. This study therefore advocates a mandatory CSR framework for the multinationals and other operators in the Nigerian oil and gas sector.

Appendix

S/No	Code	Variables
STRATEGIC CSR AND STAKEHOLDERS' ENGAGEMENT		
1	ST1	Statement from CEO and/or chairman about the relevance of CSR to the organizational strategy
2	ST2	Governance structure of the organization, including major committees under the BODs that are responsible for setting strategy or organizational oversight
3	ST3	Procedure of the highest governance body for overseeing the organization's identification and management of economic, environmental and social performance including relevant risks and opportunities, and adherence or compliance with internationally agreed standards, codes of conduct and principles
4	ST4	Process for evaluating the highest governance body's own performance, particularly with respect to economic, environmental and social performance
5	ST5	Description of key impacts, risks and opportunities

S/No	Code	Variables
6	ST6	Externally developed economics, environmental, and social charters, or other initiatives to which the organization subscribes or endorses
7	ST7	Internally developed statements of mission or value, codes of conduct and principles relevant to economic, environmental and social performance and the status of their implementation
8	ST8	List of stakeholder groups engaged by the organization
9	ST9	Basis for identification and selection of stakeholders with whom to engage
10	ST10	Approaches to stakeholder engagement, including frequency of engagement by type and by stakeholder group
11	ST11	Key topics and concerns that have been raised through stakeholder engagement, and how the organization has responded to those key topics and concerns, including through its reporting
12	ST12	Mechanism for stakeholders to provide recommendations or direction to the highest governance body
SHAREHOLDERS		
13	SH1	Dividend paid
14	SH2	Total revenues
15	SH3	Value of imports and exports
16	SH4	Total new investments
17	SH5	Local purchasing
GOVERNMENT		
18	GT1	Income tax
19	GT2	Volume and type of estimated proven reserves and production
20	GT3	Policies or advocacy programmes for the promotion of transparency of payments to host government
EMPLOYEES		
21	EM1	Implementation and coverage of an occupational health and safety management system for employees
22	EM2	Participation of employees in safety and health dialogues
23	EM3	Existence of programmes and practices to understand the general health risks and experiences affecting the local workforce
24	EM4	Description of a system for recording occupational injuries and illness and reporting them as total injury rate, total illness rate, lost time injury rate and fatality rate
25	EM5	Total hours of employees' training on issues of human rights relevant to operations
26	EM6	Policies/procedures to address human rights as relevant to operations including implementation progress
27	EM7	Total number of incidents of discrimination against employees and actions taken
28	EM8	Policies/procedures preventing discrimination among employees in operations, including a description of equal opportunity practices
29	EM9	Description of programmes to gauge employees' satisfaction
30	EM10	Total workforce by employment type, contract, region, and gender
31	EM11	Average hours of training per year per employee category
32	EM12	Policies/procedures for hiring and training local employees including at senior levels
33	EM13	Total employees' payroll and benefits with breakdown by employment type and gender for the current reporting period
34	EM14	Organization's defined benefit plan obligations for employees' procedure for local hiring and proportion of senior management hired from the local community at locations of significant operations

S/No	Code	Variables
35	EM15	Total number, rate, and reason of employee turnover broken down by gender
36	EM16	Percentage of employees covered by collective bargaining agreements
SURROUNDING COMMUNITIES		
37	CO1	Percentage of operations with implemented local community engagement, impact assessments, and development programmes
38	CO2	Operations with significant potential or actual negative impacts on local communities
39	CO3	Processes for assessing and managing positive and negative impacts on communities in area affected by core business activities
40	CO4	Prevention and mitigation efforts implemented in operations with significant potential or actual negative impacts on local communities
41	CO5	Number and description of significant disputes with local communities and indigenous peoples
42	CO6	Total number of legal actions against the organization and their outcomes
43	CO7	Policies/procedures to address resettlement and land rights of impacted communities
44	CO8	Description of processes to engage with and address the needs of indigenous communities
45	CO9	Number of sites that have been decommissioned and sites that are in the process of being decommissioned
46	C10	Number of process safety events, by business activity
ENVIRONMENT		
47	EV1	Number and volume of hydrocarbon liquid spills greater than 1 barrel that reach the environment
48	EV2	Quantities of hydrocarbons present in controlled or regulated discharges to a water environment (to inland waterways or to the sea)
49	EV3	Quantities of permitted or controlled discharges of chemicals or materials other than hydrocarbons
50	EV4	Significant non-hydrocarbon spills and accidental releases from operational upsets
51	EV5	Annual emissions of greenhouse gases (GHG) reported as total CO_2 equivalent and as individual types, from facilities managed and/or owned by the company
52	EV6	Total mass or volume of hydrocarbon gas both vented and flared to the atmosphere from operations and reported separately
53	EV7	Individual quantities of emissions by type released to the atmosphere from oil and natural gas operations during routine and non-routine processing
54	EV8	Total amount invested in renewable energy
55	EV9	Benzene, lead, and sulphur contents in fuels
56	EV10	Quantities of regulated hazardous wastes disposed
57	EV11	Quantities of non-hazardous wastes disposed
58	EV12	Total quantity of materials recycled, reused or reclaimed that would otherwise have been considered hazardous or non-hazardous wastes
59	EV13	Toxic releases
60	EV14	Quantity of primary energy consumed in oil and natural gas operations including the primary energy that is generated on site or imported
61	EV15	Fresh water consumed in oil and gas operations where availability is a significant issue
62	EV16	Initiatives to develop, produce or use alternative or renewable energy sources

S/No	Code	Variables
63	EV17	Location and size of land owned, leased, managed in, or adjacent to protected areas of high biodiversity value outside protected areas
64	EV18	Description of significant impacts of activities, products, and services on biodiversity in protected areas of high biodiversity value outside potential areas
65	EV19	Habitats protected or restored
66	EV20	Strategies (current and future plans) for managing impacts on biodiversity associated with activities in terrestrial, freshwater and marine environments
67	EV21	National conservation list species with habitats in areas affected by operations by level of extinction risk
68	EV22	Implementation and coverage of an environmental management system

BOD: Boards of Directors.

References

Aghalino, S. (2004). Oil firms and corporate social responsibility in Nigeria: the case of Shell Petroleum Development Company. *Ayebaye Babcock Journal of History and International Studies*, 2, 1–17.

Alabi, O.F. and Ntukekpo, S.S. (2012). Oil companies and corporate social responsibility in Nigeria: an empirical assessment of Chevron's community development projects in the Niger Delta. *British Journal of Arts and Social Sciences*, 4(2), 361–74.

Amit, R. and Shoemaker, P.J.H. (1993). Strategic assets and organisational rent. *Strategic Management Journal*, 14(1), 33–46.

Basu, K. and Palazzo, G. (2008). Corporate social responsibility: a process model of sensemaking. *Academy of Management Review*, 33(1), 122–36.

Baumuller, H., Donnelly, E., Vines, A. and Weimer, M. (2011). *The Effects of Oil Companies' Activities on the Environment, Health and Development in Sub-Saharan Africa*. Brussels: Directorate-General for External Policies, Policy Department.

Bondy, K., Moon, J. and Matten, D. (2014). An institution of corporate social responsibility in multinational corporations: form and implications. *Journal of Business Ethics*, forthcoming.

Brown, J.A. and Forster, W.R. (2012). Corporate social responsibility and stakeholder theory: a tale of Adam Smith. *Journal of Business Ethics*, 112(2), 301–12.

Campbell, J. (2007). Why would corporations behave in socially responsible ways? An institutional theory of corporate social responsibility. *Academy of Management Review*, 32(3), 948–67.

Carroll, A.B. (2004). Managing ethically with global stakeholders: a present and future challenge. *Academy of Management Executive*, 18(2), 114–20.

Cho, C.H. and Patten, D.M. (2007). The role of environmental disclosures as tools of legitimacy: a research note. *Accounting, Organisations, and Society*, 32(7–8), 639–47.

Clarke, D. (2008). *Crude Continent: The Struggle for Africa's Oil Prize*. London: Profile Books.

Crane, A. and Matten, D. (2004). *Business Ethics: A European Perspective. Managing Corporate Citizenship and Sustainability in the Age of Globalisation*. Oxford: Oxford University Press.

Fooks, G., Gilmore, A., Collin, J., Holden, C. and Lee, K. (2013). The limits of corporate social responsibility: techniques of neutralisation, stakeholder management, and political CSR. *Journal of Business Ethics*, 112(2), 283–99.

Friedman, M. (1962). *Capitalism and Freedom*. Chicago, IL: The University of Chicago Press,

Frynas, J. (2005). The false developmental promise of corporate social responsibility: evidence from multinational oil companies. *International Affairs*, 81(3), 581–98.

Gossling, T. and Vocht, C. (2007). Social role conceptions and CSR policy success. *Journal of Business Ethics*, 74, 363–72.

Gray, R., Kouhy, R. and Lavers, S. (1995). Methodology themes constructing a research database of social environmental reporting by UK companies. *Accounting, Auditing, and Accountability*, 8(2), 78–101.

Hackston, D. and Miline, M. (1996). Some determinants of social and environmental disclosures in New Zealand. *Accounting, Auditing and Accountability*, 77–108.

Heugens, P.P.M. and Oosterhout, J.V. (2002). The confines of stakeholder management: evidence from the Dutch manufacturing sector. *Journal of Business Ethics*, 40(4), 387–403.

Hino, K. (2006). *Corporate Social and Financial Performance: An Empirical Study on a Japanese Company*. IFSAM 8th World Congress (Berlin), 28–30.

Hopkins, M. (2004). *Corporate Social Responsibility: An Issue Paper*. Geneva: World Commission on the Social Dimension of Globalisation, Policy Integration Department.

Hsu, K. (2012). The advertising effects of corporate social responsibility on corporate reputation and brand equity: evidence from the life insurance industry in Taiwan. *Journal of Business Ethics*, 109(2), 189–201.

Husted, B. (2000). A contingency theory of corporate social performance. *Business and Society*, 39(1), 24–48.

Kang, Y.C. and Wood, D.J. (1995). *Before-Profit Social Responsibility: Turning the Economic Paradigm Upside Down*. Proceedings of the 6th Annual Meeting of the International Association of Business and Society (Vienna), 408–418.

Ketola, T. (2006). From CR-psychopaths to responsible corporations: waking up the inner sleeping beauties of companies. *Corporate Social Responsibility and Environmental Management*, 13(2), 98–107.

Krippendorff, K. (2004). *Content Analysis*. Thousand Oaks, CA: Sage.

Lahdesmaki, M. and Suutari, T. (2012). Keeping at arm's length or searching for social proximity? Corporate social responsibility as a reciprocal process between small business and the local community. *Journal of Business Ethics*, 108(4), 481–93.

Luo, X. and Bhattacharya, C.B. (2006). Corporate social responsibility, customer satisfaction, and market value. *Journal of Marketing*, 70(4), 1–8

Maass, P. (2009). *Crude World: The Violent Twilight of Oil*. London: Allen Lane.

Maignan, I., Ferrel, O.C. and Hult, G.T.M. (1999). Corporate citizenship: cultural antecedents and business benefits. *Journal of the Academy of Marketing Sciences*, 27(4), 455–69.

Mallin, C., Michelon, G. and Raggi, D. (2013). Monitoring intensity and stakeholders' orientation: how does governance affect social and environmental disclosures? *Journal of Business Ethics*, 114(1), 29–43.

Matten, D. and Moon, J. (2008). Implicit and explicit CSR: a conceptual framework for a comparative understanding of CSR. *Academy of Management Review*, 33(2), 404–424.

McElhaney, K. (2007). Strategic CSR. *Sustainable Enterprise Quarterly*, 4(1), 1–8.

McWilliams, A. and Siegel, D. (2001). Corporate social responsibility: a theory of the firm perspective. *Academy of Management Review*, 26(1), 117–27.

McWilliams, A., Siegel, D.S. and Wright, P.M. (2006). Corporate social responsibility: strategic implications. *Journal of Management Studies*, 43(1), 1–18.

Minch, M. (2011). Corporate Social Responsibility. *Encyclopedia of Global Justice*. Berlin: Springer.

OECD/AfDB (2009). *African Economic Outlook 2009*. Organisation for Economic Co-operation and Development and African Development Bank.

Porter, M. and Kramer, M. (2006). Strategy and society: the link between competitive advantage and corporate social responsibility. *Harvard Business Review*, 78–92.

Quick, R. (2008). Voluntary sustainability reporting practices in Germany: a study on reporting quality. *Portuguese Journal of Accounting and Management*, 5, 7–35.

Salazar, J. and Husted, B. (2008). Principals and agents: future thoughts and the Friedmanite Critique of corporate social responsibility, in Crane, A.M. (ed.), *The Oxford Handbook of Corporate Social Responsibility*, Oxford: Oxford University Press.

Schwartz, M.S. and Carroll, A.B. (2003). Corporate social responsibility: a three-domain approach. *Business Ethics Quarterly*, October, 503–530.

Simnet, R., Vanstraelen, A. and Chua, W.F. (2009). Assurance on sustainability reports: an international comparison. *Accounting Review*, 84(3), 937–67.

Smith, C. (2003). Corporate social responsibility: whether or how? *California Management Review*, 45(4), 52–76.

Stemler, S. (2001). An overview of content analysis. *Practical Assessment, Research and Evaluation*, 7(17), 1–7.

Torugsa, N.A., O'Donohue, W. and Hecker, R. (2012). Capabilities, proactive CSR and financial performance in SMEs: Empirical evidence from an Australian manufacturing industry sector. *Journal of Business Ethics*, 109(4), 483–500.

Uwakonye, M.N, Osho, G.S. and Anucha, H. (2006). The impact of oil and gas production on the Nigerian economy: a rural sector economic model. *International Business and Economics Research Journal*, 5(2), 61–75.

Vogel, D. (2005). Is there a market for virtue? The business case for corporate social responsibility. *California Management Review*, 19–45.

Weber, R. (1990). *Basic Content Analysis*. Newbury Park, CA: Sage

Windsor, D. (2006). Corporate social responsibility: three key approaches. *Journal of Management Studies*, 43(1), 93–114.

Winston, M. (2011). Multinational corporations. *Encyclopedia of Global Justice*. Springer-Verlag, 1–5.

Wiseman, J. (1982). An evaluation of environmental disclosure mode in corporate annual reports. *Accounting, Organisations and Society*, 7(1), 53–63.

Wolfe, R. and Aupperle, K. (1991). Introduction to corporate social performance: methods for evaluating an elusive construct, in Post, J. (ed.), *Research in Corporate Social Performance and Policy*. Greenwich, CT: JAI Press, 12, 265–68.

Yin, J. and Zhang, Y. (2012). Institutional dynamics and corporate social responsibility in an emerging country context: evidence from China. *Journal of Business Ethics*, 111(2), 301–16.

Zeng, S.X., Xu, X.D., Yin, H.T. and Tam, C.M. (2012). Factors that drive Chinese listed companies in voluntary disclosure of environmental information. *Journal of Business Ethics*, 109(3), 309–21.

2 CSR and the Enterprise Culture of Multinational Corporations in Developing Countries

OLATUNDE JULIUS OTUSANYA

Abstract

The bourgeoning literature on corporate social responsibility (CSR) rarely examines the predatory enterprise culture of multinational corporations (MNCs) even though the practices have real consequences for the life chances of millions of people. Corporations and MNCs are increasingly willing to increase their profits through indulgence in price fixing, tax avoidance/evasion, bribery and corruption, money laundering and practices that show scant regard for social norms and even laws. MNCs legitimize their social credentials by making promises of responsible and ethical conduct, but organizational culture and practices have not necessarily been aligned with publicly espoused claims. The chapter locates business behaviour within the broader dynamics of global capitalism to argue that the desire of MNCs for higher profits and at almost any cost is not constrained by rules, laws or even periodic regulatory action. The chapter seeks to bring the antisocial behaviour of MNCs under scrutiny and thus extend the possibility of research into social and business culture, ethics, social disorder and crime. Publicly available evidence is used to provide case studies to show that MNCs engage in bribery, corruption, money laundering and tax evasion/avoidance in developing countries, as against their claims of responsible social conduct. The chapter also encourages reflections on MNCs' endemic antisocial and predatory practices and offers some suggestions for reform.

Introduction

Over the last 150 years the corporations have systematically increased their reach, scope and influence so that they are now the dominant social institution anywhere in the world (Bakan, 2004; Porritt, 2005; Sikka, 2008). Increasingly, corporations dictate the decisions of their supposed overseers in government and control domains of society once firmly embedded within the public sphere. For instance, Anderson and Cavanagh (2000) noted that the combined sales of the top 200 corporations were bigger than the combined economies of all countries minus the big ten, and accounted for over a quarter of the world's economic activity. Sikka (2008) therefore notes that despite this huge clout and power, enterprise culture has not necessarily been used in the wider social interest. It has been argued that long before Enron's scandalous collapse, the corporation, a fledgling institution, was engulfed in corruption and fraud (Bakan, 2004; Sikka, 2008; Otusanya, 2011b), tax evasion/avoidance and money laundering (Sikka, 2008; Otusanya, 2011a; 2011b).

The growth of global capitalism may produce enormous economic activity, trade and wealth, but it is also accompanied by extreme poverty, social exclusion and huge inequalities in the distribution of income, wealth, and the quality of life for many people (Sikka and Hampton, 2005). The rapid pace of globalization and the concomitant increase in the volume of international trade and investment, coupled with recent corporate scandals, have heightened the importance of issues relating to politics, corruption and corporate social responsibility (CSR) (Rodriguez et al., 2006). Thus, with the assistance of information technologies, networking, globalization and tax havens, many companies devise strategies to opt out of their social obligation to pay democratically agreed tax (Desai and Dharmapala, 2006; Sikka and Willmott, 2010) and have indulged in a number of predatory activities that affect the life chances of millions of citizens (Baker, 2005; Christensen, 2007; Sikka, 2008; Otusanya, 2011a; 2011b).

As foreign firms expanded into, and new firms were born within, developing and transition economies, governments, managers and scholars grew more aware of the magnitude of tax evasion, tax avoidance, corruption, money laundering and the need to understand and address these issues (Cobham, 2005; Johnston, 2005; Sikka, 2008; Otusanya, 2010; Palan, Murphy and Chavagneux, 2010). This is because the outcomes of these practices are associated with loss of taxes, public revenues, economic devastation, lack of investment in public goods, the emergence of gangs and private armies, loss of faith in law and institutions, a poor quality of life and even decline in average life expectancy (Christian Aid, 2005, Sikka and Hampton, 2005; AAPPG, 2006; Sikka, 2008; Otusanya, 2010).

It has been argued that developing countries, often some of the poorest, receive around $120 billion in foreign aid from G20 countries, but are estimated to be losing between $858 billion and $1 trillion illicit financial outflows each year (Kar and Cartwright-Smith, 2008; Sikka, 2010). The World Bank estimates that between $1 trillion and 1.6 trillion is lost each year to various illegal activities, including corruption, criminal activities and tax evasion (World Bank, 2007). Tax evasion, tax avoidance and corrupt practices are continually depriving the developing economies of sums large enough to make a real difference in social investment in education, transport, pensions, housing, health care and for freeing people from poverty and squalor (Oxfam, 2000; Filling and Sikka, 2004; Sikka, 2008). A large body of literature has shown the huge involvement and the role played by MNCs in facilitating these practices, which are detrimental to the socio-economic development of the economies of the South (Baker, 2005; Sikka, 2008; 2010; Sikka and Wilmott, 2010; Otusanya, 2010).

It has been shown in the literature that corporations increasingly produce brochures and reports containing statements in which they profess to be acting in a socially responsible way, but at the same time, somewhat contrarily, corporations engage in large-scale antisocial strategies, such as tax evasion, tax avoidance and corruption (Sikka, 2010; Otusanya et al., 2012). In other words, corporations are merely 'window dressing' in order to appear to be socially responsible, and have double standards when they profess to be promoting CSR initiatives while simultaneously engaging in antisocial financial practices to minimize their fiscal and social obligations (Bakan, 2004; Riesco, Lagos and Lima, 2005). National and international evidence continues to put MNCs in a contradictory position in respect of their pronouncements and the reality of their predatory enterprise culture, particularly in developing countries.

In recent years, there has been considerable increase in the volume of research and scholarship on the issue of CSR reporting in the accounting literature (Sikka, 2010; Otusanya et al., 2011; Otusanya et al., 2012). This literature is informed by a variety of theoretical perspectives which seeks to address issues about governance, accountability, ethics, pollution and gender and human rights (Okafor et al., 2008; Obalola, 2008; Adewuyi and Olowookere, 2010; Sikka, 2010). While there is considerable research on a number of aspects, broader accounts of the corporate socio and economic claims of social responsibility and their practice of tax evasion, tax avoidance, offering bribes and engaging in other corrupt practices as impediment for sustainable socio-economic development in developing countries are scarce. Thus there is a little research on the contradictions which exist between the professed claims of MNCs to be acting in a socially responsible way and the fact that they engage in antisocial tax strategies (Sikka, 2008; 2010; Otusanya, 2010; Sikka and Willmott, 2010; Otusanya et al., 2011) and corrupt practices through a variety of business vehicles (US Senate Sub-Committee on Investigations, 2005; AAPPG, 2006; Otusanya et al., 2012).

This chapter seeks to contribute to the debate on the consequences of unethical enterprise culture as an aspect of CSR because the public revenue going untaxed and being paid as bribes can make a difference to the quality of life of millions of people. Corporate claims of socially responsible conduct and obedience to local laws are difficult to reconcile with MNCs tax avoidance and corrupt practices such as illegally securing competitive advantages to increase profits. This chapter examines the antisocial practices (tax evasion, tax avoidance, bribery and corruption) of some MNCs which increase profits but harm citizens and generate huge social consequences.

This chapter is divided as follows. The next section provides a framework for exploring CSR and its relationship with the antisocial enterprise culture of MNCs. It is argued that the policy of ethical conduct of socio-economic dimensions of CSR does not stymie the MNCs from engaging in predatory practices in pursuit of corporate profits and ever-rising return to capital. The section following examines the literature on the various studies and cases that have implicated MNCs and their managers in antisocial tax practices (including tax evasion and tax avoidance) and corrupt practices, which shows considerable disparity between corporate talk and corporate action. The subsequent section provides extracts from a number of CSR statements from MNCs and their activities. It is argued that despite the laws and regulations of the countries in which they operate, and the MNCs' claims of social responsibility and codes of ethical business conduct, MNCs have been implicated in antisocial tax practices and in facilitating bribery and corruption in developing countries. The final section discusses the significance of tax evasion, tax avoidance and corruption as aspects of CSR and their implications for economies and social development in developing countries.

Multinationals and the Pathological Pursuit of Profit

CSR from the socio-economic dimension involves promises of ethical and socially responsible conduct on the part of companies, and its scope is increasingly being broadened. In the contemporary market society, corporations, particularly MNCs, are the motor of capitalism. Although they created by national laws and numerous social contracts, when in pursuit of profit, corporations do not owe allegiance to any nation, community or locality (Bakan, 2004). From the economic standpoint, they are essentially 'private' organizations and are required by law to prioritize the welfare of shareholders (capital) above other stakeholders (Sikka, 2008). Markets place pressure on companies to generate ever-increasing profits and returns, and capitalism provides no guidance on the upper limits of capital accumulation. Despite the claimed advances in transparency, accountability and CSR, large tracts of business activity remain relatively opaque (Levitt, 2002; Bakan, 2004). The resulting vacuum has created space for a variety of questionable practices that increase corporate profits but also undermine the social fabric and welfare of citizens.

Therefore, to legitimize their social power, corporations may acknowledge some social responsibilities, but they cannot buck the systemic pressure to increase profits and dividends for their shareholders (Sikka, 2008). In order to do so MNCs may engage in novel strategies to reduce or avoid the payment of democratically agreed taxes. Taxation and transfer pricing arrangements provide one such example for MNCs today, posing a challenge to both equity and transparency ground. A narrow interpretation of a company's traditional fiduciary duties to its shareholders means that it should be doing everything in its power, within the law, to reduce the amount of tax it pays to any government and to maximize the financial benefits to be had from juggling prices, revenue and currency exchange across different markets (Porritt, 2005). This is the general belief, as is expressed by Henderson (2001: 21): 'some are inclined to endorse tax avoidance with the claims that company directors' prime legal responsibility is to promote the success of the company for the benefit of the shareholders and their interest must somehow override the interests of other stakeholders'.

Some have argued that such a claim should be scrutinized because there are no laws which required directors to specifically increase profits by avoiding taxes, or by eroding returns on the investment of social capital and engaging in bribery and corruption (Sikka, 2010; Otusanya et al., 2012). Porritt (2005) notes that CSR sceptics have rightly pointed out that they could be much more of a 'force for good' if they simply paid over all the taxes owed in any particular country, rather than relying on quasi-philanthropic handouts. Therefore, CSR activists argue that taxation policy should now be included as a critical indicator of responsible and ethical business behaviour and the regulators should insist on far greater transparency in the way in which multinationals account for tax payments and transfer pricing arrangements. It has been argued from a radical rationale that tax avoidance should be seen not just in legal terms, but in terms of morality and corporate responsibility (Porritt, 2005; Sikka, 2008; 2010). Corporations may regard tax evasion and strategic tax avoidance practices merely as 'cost reduction' exercises, rather than as practices which have the effect of undermining the social fabric and the development of a just and fair society. As Bakan notes: 'The corporation too is all about creating wealth, and it is a highly effective vehicle for doing so. No internal limits, whether moral, ethical, or legal, limit what or whom corporations can exploit to create wealth for themselves and their owners' (2004: 111–12).

Therefore, Bakan (2004) emphasizes the need for caution in believing the claims of business leaders today, who say that their companies care about more than profit and loss, that they feel responsible to society as a whole, not just to their shareholders.

CSR is their new creed, a self-conscious corrective to earlier greed-inspired versions of the corporation. Despite this shift, the corporation itself has not changed. It remains as it was at the time of its origins as a modern business institution in the middle of the nineteenth century, a legally designated 'person' designed to valorize self-interest and invalidate moral concern (Bakan, 2004). Bakan notes that:

> Corporate social responsibility is like the call boxes. It holds out promises of help, reassures people, and sometimes works. We should not, however, expect very much from it. A corporation can do good only to help itself do well, a profound limit on just how much good it can do. [...] The benevolent rhetoric and deeds of socially responsible corporations create attractive corporate images, and likely do some good in the world. They do not, however, change the corporation's fundamental institutional nature: its unblinking commitment to its own self-interest. (Bakan, 2004: 50)

The people who run corporations are, for the most part, good people, moral people. Despite their personal qualities and ambitions, however, their duty as corporate executives is clear. They must always put their corporation's best interests first and not act out of concern for anyone or anything else (unless the expression of such concern can somehow be justified as advancing the corporation's own interests) (Bakan, 2004). This means that certain values get emphasized, while others get de-emphasized. And the ones that get emphasized are those that promote what is going to raise the bottom line. Bakan suggests that as pressure builds on chief executive officers (CEOs) to increase shareholder value, corporations are doing anything and everything they can to be competitive: 'If you are a CEO, do you think your shareholders really care whether you are Billy Buttercup or not? Do you think that they really would prefer you to be nice guy over having money in their pocket? I do not think so. I think people want money. That is the bottom line' (2004: 55).

This therefore illustrates how an executive's moral concerns and altruistic desire must ultimately succumb to her corporation's overriding goals. Greed and moral indifference define the corporate world's culture. The use of bribery and inducement to secure competitive advantages is primarily a matter of executive discretion rather than any legal or moral compulsion. This discretion may be used to enrich directors, since their remuneration is influenced by the level of profits and return to capital. According to Sikka: 'Such practices seem to be part of the 'enterprise culture' that persuades many to believe that 'bending the rules' for personal gain is a sign of business acumen' (2008: 270).

It has been argued that corporations are irresponsible because in an attempt to satisfy the corporate goal, everyone else is put at risk. A lack of empathy and asocial tendencies are also key characteristics of corporations. Their behaviour indicates that they do not really concern themselves with their victims. 'If [corporations] get caught [breaking the law], they pay big fines and they [...] continue doing what they did before anyway. And in fact in many cases the fines and penalties paid by the organisation are trivial compared to the profits that they rake in' (Bakan, 2004: 57). Hence, corporations are not democratic institutions – their directors and managers owe no accountability to anyone but the shareholders that employ them.

Corporations' codes of business conduct include statements rejecting the payment or acceptance of bribes, collusion, pressure or illegitimate favour, either directly or through third parties, whether public officers or private individuals. Yet their involvement in corrupt practices and other antisocial tax practices means that they cannot be reconciled with their business codes of conduct (Christensen and Murphy, 2004; Sikka, 2008; 2010; Otusanya et al., 2011; Otusanya et al., 2012). This therefore highlights the review of corporate policies and compliance which manifests itself in hypocrisy, emphasizing the gap between the promise to act responsibly by not taken unfair advantage through manipulation, concealment and abuse of privileged information. Since policies and actions may not easily be reconciled, corporations develop dual strategies to manage conflict. It has been suggested that such codes of business conduct and statements of responsible and ethical conduct are used as strategic resources to mould public opinion and shield businesses from a hostile and turbulent external environment and to disarm critics (Bakan, 2004; Unerman and O'Dwyer, 2007; Sikka, 2010; Otusanya et al., 2012).

Review of Related Cases

This section of the chapter examines the literature on the role of MNCs in tax evasion, tax avoidance, bribery and corruption, a role which seems to deviate from the espoused claim of most corporations to be protecting the public interest. The subsection below reviews the involvement of MNCs in tax evasion and tax avoidance.

THE INVOLVEMENT OF MULTINATIONAL COMPANIES IN TAX EVASION AND TAX AVOIDANCE

Under pressure to compete with other companies and to increase profits, capitalist organization constantly seek new ways of boosting their earnings by devising complex structures and novel ways of increasing profits. The availability of taxation revenues is crucial to any attempt by the state to redistribute wealth, alleviate poverty and provide a variety of social goods. Yet corporations often see tax evasion and tax avoidance as business strategies for creating wealth for capital rather than practices that undermine social development in developing countries and the development of a just and fair society. Tax evasion and tax avoidance are considered by most governments to be serious threats to the integrity of tax systems in democratic society. According to Spicer:

> Tax evasion and tax avoidance result in loss of tax revenue, impair the chances of realising the distributional or equity goal of taxation, and, if they become widespread, as they have in recent times, then more taxpayers may lose faith in the tax administration system and be tempted to join the ranks of tax evaders. (1975: 152)

The collapse of Enron drew attention to the gap between corporate talk and action. Enron, the largest US energy company, was ranked seventh on the Fortune 500 list of the country's largest companies. An investigation by the US Senate Joint Committee on Taxation into Enron tax affairs reported that for the period 1996–1999 the company reported a net income of $2.3 billion, but claimed tax losses of $3 billion. For the year 2000, Enron reported in its financial statement a net income of $1 billion and a taxable income of $3.1 billion, subject to utilization of tax losses brought forward (US Senate Joint Committee on Taxation, 2003). WorldCom, a US telecommunications company that collapsed amidst allegations of fraud in 2002, was also reported to have made extensive use of tax avoidance schemes to increase its accounting earnings (see Sikka, 2010).

In 2005, Chevron Nigeria Limited was also alleged to have used petroleum profit accounting technology, such as fictitious qualifying capital expenditure, reserve additional bonus, intangible drilling cost, in order to evade sums of petroleum profit tax payable in Nigeria (Otusanya et al., 2011). Technical fees and royalties can also be used as a tax avoidance strategy for moving taxable profits from subsidiaries to the parent company in tax havens under the pretence that the company is a non-resident company. Between 1995 and 2003, Cadbury Nigeria plc. and its parent company, Cadbury Schweppes Overseas Limited, based in the UK, was indicted for using technical fees to evade taxes in Nigeria (Otusanya et al., 2011).

The gap between corporate talk and action was also documented in the study by Sikka (2010) that illuminates the role of MNCs, their managers and the accountancy firms in tax evasion and tax avoidance. A number of episodes were presented in which the companies examined claimed to be socially responsible and promised high standards in serving communities, and of accountability and transparency, yet they simultaneously indulged in tax avoidance and in some other cases tax evasion. Some other studies have also documented the role of MNCs in tax evasion and tax avoidance in both developed and developing countries and the use of transfer pricing schemes to shift profits abroad (Sikka, 2008; Otusanya, 2010; Otusanya, 2011; Sikka and Willmott, 2010; Otusanya, forthcoming). It has therefore been argued that the corporate claim of serving the public, behaving ethically and socially should translate to payment of taxes. The tax revenue would help countries – and developing countries in particular – to provide education, healthcare, security, transportation and pensions.

THE INVOLVEMENT OF MULTINATIONAL CORPORATIONS IN BRIBERY AND CORRUPTION

Though somewhat contentious to define, bribery and corruption remain major features of the world economy. Bribery and corruption are often disguised in the financial reports as legitimate expenses. It has been argued that market forces through greater competition will lead to less, rather than more, corruption (Rose-Ackerman, 1996; Ades and di Tella, 1999; World Bank, 1997).

In contrast to the above, globalization and free market ideology has further contributed to corruption globally. The literature has indicated that Western countries have often provided the infrastructures that facilitates corruption in developing countries (Kapoor, 2005; AAPPG, 2006; Martens, 2007; Sikka. 2008; Otusanya, 2010). A number of studies have argued that companies, especially MNCs, use a sophisticated network of notional companies and corporate structure to facilitate corruption, and so are the biggest perpetrators of corrupt practices in developing countries (Sikka, 2008; Otusanya, 2010).

The corporate hand in corrupt practices is sometimes given visibility by regulatory reports such as the US Securities and Exchange Commission (SEC), the US Department of Justice, the UK Special Fraud Office, and the former UK Financial Services Authority (FSA). A number of related cases have also been reported in the UK. For example, Balfour Beatty, a leading UK-based construction company, agreed to pay a penalty of £2.25 million in relation to certain payments irregularities in respect of a major project in Egypt. It was also reported that, Aon, an insurance company, made suspicious payments to third parties amounting to approximately $2.5 million and €3.4 million. The company was fined £5.25 million by the UK's FSA, for failing to establish and maintain effective systems and controls to counter the risk of bribery and corruption. In addition, the famous case prosecuted against the French oil company, Elf, by Eva Joly clearly shows that Transnational Corporations (TNCs) had engaged in corrupt practices in developing countries (WSWS, 2004).

Since the enactment of the Foreign Corrupt Practices Act (FCPA) of 1971 in the US there has been a series of revelations about US corporations making corrupt payments to foreign government officials to win business (Earle, 1989; Kim and Kim, 1997; Vanasco, 1999; Wallace-Bruce, 2000). For example, in 1975, *The Wall Street Journal* documented a number of cases; The United Brands Corporation made payments to high foreign officials to obtain a banana tax reduction in Honduras; and The Ashland Oil Company bribed foreign officials to obtain an oil drilling permit in Gabon. The Lockheed Aircraft Corp. bribed lower and middle bureaucrats in 36 countries. It was disclosed at a Senate hearing in 1975–76 that Lockheed had paid more than $106 million in secret 'commissions' to promote foreign sales, including $7 million to a well-connected Japanese agent who was also the head of a right-wing youth movement (Tinker, 1985). The Lockheed Corporation pleaded guilty and was fined $24.8 million, a figure representing double the amount it made on the transaction. One of the corporation's executives pleaded guilty and was fined $125,000 and jailed for 18 months' (see Wallace-Bruce, 2000).

The Exxon Corporation offered kickbacks more than $50 million to the Italian political parties and government officials in order to secure a natural gas contract and to buy favourable tax and energy legislation (Vanasco, 1999; Tinker, 1985). In 1976, the US Senate Committee on Banking, Housing, and Urban Affairs' hearings on illicit payments further revealed that several American concerns were engaged in bribing foreign officials or political parties to secure contracts abroad:

> *Northrop Corporation paid foreign agents/consultants inflated fees or commission to pay officials in Saudi Arabia, NATO, and the Common Market countries. Lockheed Aircraft Corporation reportedly made payoffs in Germany, Italy, Turkey, Columbia, Nigeria, Greece, South Africa, Japan, Saudi Arabia, Indonesia, and the Philippines. Gulf Oil Company made illegal Payments in South Korea, and Mobil Oil Corporation made illicit payments to Italian government officials. (Vanasco, 1999: 162)*

These include Boeing ($500 million), General Tire and Rubber ($41 million), Northrop ($34 million), and many others (Tinker, 1985). In addition, the US Conglomerate Baker Hughes Incorporated pleaded guilty to three charges of corruption and was fined $44 million for hiring agents to bribe officials in Nigeria, Angola, Indonesia, Russia, Uzbekistan and Kazakhstan. It was reported that Baker Hughes paid approximately $5.2 million to two agents while knowing that some or all of the money was intended to bribe government officials of state-owned companies in Kazakhstan (US SEC, 2007). In 2007, three wholly owned subsidiaries of Vetco International Ltd. plead guilty to violating the foreign bribery provisions of FCPA in connection with the payment of approximately $2.1 million in bribes. The company agreed to pay a total of $26 million in criminal fines. IBM and Boeing, and more than 400 other US corporations, including 117 Fortune 500 companies, had made corrupt payments in their global business transactions (see Salbu, 1997; Wallace-Bruce, 2000).

Reflecting the contemporary enterprise culture, many MNCs aggressively sought to increase their profits through financial engineering and corruption. It was reported in these cases that companies devised several schemes to make illicit payments to foreign officials and political parties which included cash and non-cash transactions. The expenses were accounted for under a variety of false and financial headings such as 'publicity' and 'promotional expenses', 'fees paid to agents', or as consulting agreements advances to the corporation's foreign subsidiaries. This highlights the inconsistencies in organization talk, decisions and actions which manifest themselves in hypocrisy.

Some Evidence

This section draws attention to a number of cases where MNCs had pledged to behave ethically and in socially responsible ways, but simultaneously indulged in antisocial criminal practices. All the entities discussed in this section have claimed to be observing high standards of ethics and responsibility, and there is no reason to doubt the applicability of these claims to what these corporations actually do. They claimed to be observing the code of business conduct, integrity, ethical standards and social responsibility, but the cases illuminate the gap and contradictions between corporate anti-tax and corruption policy and their activities.

This section does not rely on a statistical sample in any positivistic sense because corporations and perpetrators of these acts rarely provide information about their anti-tax practices, bribery and corruption. Therefore, the size of the appropriate populations cannot be determined in any meaningful way. For this reason, this chapter does not pretend to offer any comprehensive analysis, but instead details some cases in order to show that tax evasion, tax avoidance, bribery and corruption by MNCs are some of the significant examples of irresponsible business behaviour in developing countries which often contradict their claims of CSR and good conduct. The data was obtained from archival documentation from media, documents published by regulators, court judgements and other documentary sources, in order to provide evidence of MNCs' involvement in anti-tax, bribery and corrupt practices in developing countries.

CSR AND THE TAX EVASION AND TAX AVOIDANCE PRACTICES OF MNCS

The cases chosen and described in this section provide evidence of predatory practices which have acted as impediments to development. The entities examined claim to be observing the code of business conduct, integrity, ethical standards and social responsibility, but the analysis illuminate the gap and contradictions between corporate anti-tax policy and their activities.

With global revenue of $1.34 billion, Bristow is a Delaware corporation with its headquarters in Houston, Texas. It provides helicopter transportation services and operates oil and gas production facilities. Other entities within the group are: AirLog International, a wholly owned subsidiary of Bristow based in New Iberia, Louisiana; PAAN, its subsidiary in Nigeria; Bristow Aviation; Bristow Helicopters; and Bristow Nigeria (US SEC Administrative Proceedings, 2007). Bristow's Code of Business Integrity states that 'it is the policy of the Company to pay all applicable taxes levied against the Company or its operations. Employees are prohibited from assisting any person or company, including the Company's customers, joint venture partners, or employees, from evading any applicable taxes' (Bristow, 2013: 7). Furthermore, the Code of Business Integrity states that:

It is the policy of the Company that all employees maintain the highest ethical standards and comply with all applicable laws and regulations when conducting Company business. Employees are prohibited from assisting any person or company, including customers and joint venture partners, in any activity which assists such person or entity in violating any law or regulation. (Bristow, 2013: 8)

Such statements may help to mould public opinion, but they are also economical about enterprise culture and practices. Despite the corporation's claims, PAAN conducted a tax evasion plan involving the interface between its company executives and the Internal Revenue Service officials in Delta State and Lagos State, the two Nigerian states where PAAN operated. PAAN under-reported its employees' payroll expenses, which involved deliberately claiming a deduction to which it knew it was not entitled and which was conducted through inducements (in other words, bribes) made to tax officials. Poor internal controls in the Bristow Group enabled the tax fraud and the illegal payments to tax officials to go undetected (US SEC Administrative Proceedings, 2007).

In 2007, the US SEC indicted the Bristow Group for inducing state officials in Nigeria to evade payment of PAYE tax for 2002 and 2003 which was owed to Delta State and Lagos State. The investigations show that the Bristow Group, through its Nigeria subsidiary PAAN, evaded the payment of $873,940 (₦121.38 million) for 2002 and 2003 in employees' personal income tax. According to the SEC, the payment amounts were approximate and were based on a conversion rate of ₦139 to the US$ (US SEC Administrative Proceedings, 2007: 4). The implication is that PAAN therefore knew that it was likely to be able to negotiate a deal with the revenue authorities to settle the matter. Thus, the tax officials in Delta State had caused the government to lose $793,940 in PAYE tax for 2002 and 2003, and $325,440 payable to tax officials. In Lagos State, the government also lost $80,000 in 2002, an unknown amount for 2003, and $97,860 to tax officials. As a consequence, the state was able only to collect $121,700 from the negotiated sum of $545,000, with the remainder being used for personal payments (unreceipted cash) (US SEC Administrative Proceedings, 2007).

During investigations, Bristow admitted that it had under-reported the expatriate payroll expenses of PAAN and Bristow Nigeria in Nigeria (US SEC Administrative Proceedings, 2007). PAAN had concealed the improper payments through inappropriate recording in AirLog's books. The Bristow's affiliate in Nigeria disregarded its internal controls despite the institution of internal controls in its subsidiaries. This case provides an insight into the use of inducements and tax negotiations to save almost $1 million of PAYE tax in just two years in order to enhance company profits, which has a huge social consequence. Despite claims of instituting sound 'internal control systems' and implementing the corporation's Code of Business Integrity, none of the illegal payment and tax avoidance strategies were explained in the company's report. The Code of Business Integrity report proclaimed that Bristow and its employees are dedicated to transparency and social business conduct.

The inconsistencies between its talk of ethical and responsible conduct and enterprise culture geared to increase profits were highlighted in the above investigation. The above example draws attention to the role of MNCs in facilitating tax avoidance and tax evasion. The company generally shelters under claims of codes of ethics and double taxation. The following section explores the role performed by MNCs in bribery and corrupt practices in developing countries.

CSR AND THE BRIBERY AND CORRUPTION PRACTICES OF MNCS

A large amount of bribery and corruption is associated with looting of countries by the rulers, a process that frequently carries the fingerprints of corporation. Yet a number of corporations claim that they are socially and ethically responsible and their activities are committed to public interest. This contradiction is illuminated in the following cases.

In 2010, the US SEC charged six oil services and freight forwarding companies (GlobalSantaFe Corp., Noble Corporation, Transocean Inc., Tidewater Inc., Pride International Inc., Royal Dutch Shell plc., and Panalpina Inc.) for widespread bribery of customs officials and tax officials to receive preferential treatment and improper benefits during the customs process and tax assessment in a number of developing countries including Nigeria. These cases are fully discussed below to show the involvement of MNCs in corrupt practice, despite their claims of behaving and conducting their business ethically in their host countries.

The GlobalSanteFe Corp. was incorporated in the Cayman Islands and had its headquarters in Texas. GlobalSanteFe provided offshore oil and gas drilling services for oil and gas exploration companies. Acting through its direct subsidiary, Global Offshore Drilling Ltd., the company engaged in activity in West Africa (Nigeria, Gabon, Angola and Equatorial Guinea). In 2010 GlobalSanteFe was alleged to have made illegal payments through customs brokers to officials of the Nigerian Customs Service (NCS) from approximately January 2002 through July 2007, in order to obtain preferential treatment during customs processes for the purpose of assisting the company in retaining business in Nigeria (US District Court Southern District of Columbia, 2010a). The US SEC report noted that: 'By making the payments GlobalSanteFe profited in the amount of approximately $2.7 million by avoiding customs-related costs, including those associated with actually physically moving the rig out of Nigerian waters, and gaining revenue from not interrupting its drilling operations during a move' (US District Court Southern District of Columbia, 2010a: 2).

It was further alleged that GlobalSanteFe, through its customs brokers, also made a number of other payments during the relevant period totaling approximately $300,000 to government officials in Gabon, Angola and Equatorial Guinea. The US SEC complaints to the US District Court of Columbia noted that GlobalSanteFe disguised these illegal transactions as legitimate transactions. Following the US SEC investigations, GlobalSanteFe admitted to criminal wrongdoing and submitted to an injunction to pay disgorgement of $3,758,265 and a criminal penalty of $2.1 million (US SEC, 2010).

Noble Corporation is a Swiss company whose common stock is registered on the New York Stock Exchange under the symbol 'NE'. Prior to March 2009 and during the relevant period, the parent company of Noble Corporation was a Cayman Islands corporation with headquarters and principal executive officers in Sugar Land, Texas, but the place of incorporation of the parent of the Noble group of companies later changed and was established in Switzerland in March 2009. Noble reported a net revenue of $3.6 billion and a net income of $2 billion in 2009 (Noble Corporation, 2009). The Noble Corporation operates in Nigeria through its wholly owned subsidiary Noble Drilling (Nigeria) Ltd., 'Noble-Nigeria'. The corporation's Code of Conduct states that:

We seek to outperform our competition fairly and honestly. We seek competitive advantages through working smarter and harder than our competition, never through unethical or illegal business practices [...]. No employee should take unfair advantage of anyone through manipulation, concealment, abuse of privileged information, misrepresentation of material facts, or any other intentional unfair dealing practice. (Noble Corporation, 2013: 3)

The code of business conduct and ethics states further that 'if a law, local custom and policy conflict with the code, the employee must comply with the code. The code shall serve as a touchstone for every employee in the conduct of his or her day to day work activities' (Noble Corporation, 2013: 1). Yet Noble-Nigeria authorized its customs agent to submit false documents to the NCS to reflect physical export and re-import of its drilling rigs when in fact the rigs never moved (referred to below as the 'paper process'). The US SEC alleges that:

Noble-Nigeria obtain Temporary Importation Permits (TIPs) with paper process exports and re-imports of rigs eight times from January 2003 through May 2007, and made a total of at least $79,026 in payments to the customs agent that were designated by the agent as 'special handling charge' on invoices associated with the paper process TIP renewals. Noble also made payments in 2005 and 2006 to obtain two discretionary extensions. (US District Court Southern District of Texas, 2010a: 5)

The SEC further noted that: 'Although Noble had an FCPA policy in place, Noble lack sufficient FCPA procedures, training and internal controls to prevent the use of paper process and making of payment to Nigerian government officials to obtain TIPs and TIPs extensions' (US District Court Southern District of Texas, 2010a: 6).

Through the alleged bribery scheme, Noble Corporation wrongfully obtained profits and avoided a cost of at least $4,294,933. After investigations by US SEC into this corrupt allegation and its subsequent indictment, Noble agreed to pay a disgorgement and prejudgment interest of $5,576,998 and a criminal fine of $2.59 million for hiring agents to bribe officials in Nigeria (US SEC, 2010).

Pride International, Inc. is one of the world's largest offshore drilling companies. Pride is a Delaware corporation headquartered in Houston Texas. The corporation operated its global business through more than 100 subsidiaries that employed as many as 14,000 people and operated more than 300 rigs in approximately 30 countries (US District Court Southern District of Texas, 2010c). The corporation's code of conduct states that:

Pride is committed to conducting its business in an open, vigorous and competitive manner. The United States, the European Union and many other countries regulate and some instances prohibit certain types of anticompetitive behaviour. The Company's policy is to comply with both the letter and the spirit of the antitrust and competition laws of the jurisdictions where it operates. Violations of the law can result in severe penalties, including personal criminal liability. (Pride International, n.d.: 1)

Despite Pride's anti-corruption commitment as extracted from its report, US SEC alleges that: 'Pride and its subsidiaries paid approximately $2 million to foreign officials in eight countries from 2001 through 2006 in exchange for various benefits related to oil services' (US SEC, 2010).

For example, Joe Summer, Pride's former country manager in Venezuela authorized bribes of approximately $414,000 to a state-owned oil company to secure extensions of drilling contracts. The finance manager of the US-based Eastern Hemisphere, India, made three payments totaling $500,000 to an administrative judge to favourably influence an ongoing customs litigation relating to the importation of a rig to India. Bobby Benton, Pride's Vice President, Western Hemisphere operation, also authorized $10,000 to a third party to be paid to customs officials in Mexico (US District Court Southern District of Texas, 2010c). In addition, Pride paid $150,000 to customs and $204,000 to a Kazakh tax consultant. $10,000 was paid in Saudi Arabia for clearance of a rig, $8,000 in the Republic of the Congo for maritime certification, and $116 was paid in Libya for INAS assessment (US District Court Southern District of Texas, 2010c).

Pride Forasol Drilling Nigeria Limited and Somaser S.N.C., majority-owned subsidiaries of Pride Forasol, which operated in Nigeria (hereinafter collectively 'Pride Forasol Nigeria'). The SEC report noted that Pride Forasol Nigeria played a key role in the bribery scheme designed by Pride's managers by authorizing illegal payment through agents and tax consultants. Pride Forasol Nigeria through its agent paid between $15,000 and $93,000 for Temporary Importation permits (TI), $15,000 for new TI intervention and $35,000 for importation of rigs without completing certain legally required steps. In addition, Pride Forasol Nigeria also paid $55,000 and $65,000 to Rivers State Internal Revenue and Bayelsa State Internal Revenue tax officials to reduce the amount of its PAYE taxes. The sum of $52,000 was also paid to the Federal Inland Revenue Service of Nigeria (FIRS) for resolution of VAT tax audit (US District Court Southern District of Texas, 2010c).

The document examined by US SEC showed that Pride's Managers in Nigeria knew the nature of the transaction but still chose to engage the services of the agent and tax consultant in funnelling the bribes to government officials, which contradicts their corporate claims of social responsibility. Through these several bribery practices, Pride was reported to have obtained improper benefits totalling approximately $19.3 million. Pride was later indicted by US SEC, for violating the provisions of FCPA. As a consequence, Pride agreed to pay disgorgement and prejudgment interest of $23,529,719 and Pride and its subsidiary Pride Forasol agreed to pay a criminal fine of $32.625 million (US SEC, 2010).

Tidewater Inc. is a US company based in New Orleans, Louisiana, that operates offshore service and supply vessels designed to support all phases of offshore energy exploration, and the development and production industry. Tidewater Inc. operates through its wholly owned subsidiary Tidex Nigeria Limited. Tidex provided agency and operational support for all vessels that Tidewater Marine L.L.C. operated in Nigeria. The code of business conduct and ethics of Tidewater states: 'The company shall comply with applicable laws, rules and regulations. Full, fair, accurate, timely and understandable disclosure in reports and documents that the company files with, or submits to SEC and in other public communications made by the company, and accountability for compliance with the code' (Tidewater, 2009: 1).

The company through its code of business conduct and ethics promised to behave ethically and to observe all laws, rules and regulations, but in 2010 the US SEC alleges that:

In 2002 through March 2007, Tidewater, through its subsidiaries and agents also authorized the reimbursements of approximately $1.6 million to customs broker in Nigeria used, in whole or in part, to make improper payments to Nigerian Customs Services (NCS) employees to induce them to disregard certain regulatory requirements in Nigeria relating to the temporary importation of company's vessels into Nigeria waters. (US District Court of the Eastern District of Louisiana, 2010: 2)

As a consequence of the violation of the provisions of US FCPA, Tidewater agreed to pay $8,104,362 in disgorgement and a $217,000 penalty and Tidewater Marine International agreed to pay a criminal fine of $7.35 million (US SEC, 2010).

Transocean Inc. is a Cayman Islands corporation with its principal offices in the Cayman Islands and Houston, Texas. Transocean is the world's largest international provider of offshore drilling services and equipment. Its clients are leading international oil companies as well as many government controlled and smaller independent oil companies. Transocean has offices throughout the world, including Nigeria and the United States (US District Court Southern District of Columbia, 2010b). Transocean global revenue for the year 2010 was $9.58 billion, and its operating income was $1.89 billion (Transocean, 2010). The company Code of Integrity states:

> *In accordance with the expansive scope of global anti-corruption laws, including the FCPA and the U.K. Bribery Act, Transocean's policy prohibits all bribes from being paid or promised, regardless of whether the recipient is a foreign government official or a private individual (commercial bribery). Transocean personnel are also prohibited from accepting or agreeing to accept improper benefit or bribe. (Transocean Inc., 2011: 9)*

Specifically, Transocean does not permit its funds, assets or property to be used in an illegal manner and therefore does not permit bribery, any form of money laundering or the support of terrorism. The US SEC alleges that: 'Transocean made illicit payments through its custom agent to Nigerian government officials in connection with paper moves, thus avoiding moving cost approximately $1,008,985 and gaining profit of approximately $3,172,378. The reported gain made from the illicit payments amounted to $4.2 million' (US District Court Southern District of Columbia, 2010b: 6). Despite the company's claims and commitment to the global anti-corruption laws and code of integrity, 'Transocean's management failed to stop the illicit conduct and in some cases even approved it' (US District Court Southern District of Columbia, 2010b: 6). After the investigations into the role Transocean has played in bribing government officials in developing countries, particularly in Nigeria, and for violating the US FCPA, Transocean agreed to pay disgorgement and prejudgment interest of $7.27 million and Transocean Ltd. and Transocean Inc. agreed to pay criminal fine of $13.44 million (US SEC, 2010).

Royal Dutch Shell plc., an English-chartered company headquartered in The Hague, The Netherlands, focuses, through its subsidiaries, on oil, gas and power production and exploration. Shell reported a net revenue of $368.056 billion and a net income of $20.47 billion in 2010 (Shell Global, 2010a). The code of conduct of Royal Dutch Shell plc. states that: 'Shell does not tolerate bribery, insider dealing, market abuse, fraud or money laundering. Facilitation payments are bribe and must not be paid. You must also avoid any real or potential conflict of interest (or the appearance of a conflict) and never offer or accept inappropriate gifts or hospitality' (Shell Global, 2010b: 10).

In 2010 the US SEC alleged, through the administrative proceedings instituted against Shell International Exploration and Production Inc. (SIEP), a Delaware company with headquarters in Houston, Texas, and a wholly owned indirect subsidiary of Shell:

> *From September 2002 through November 2005, SIEP on behalf of Shell, authorized the reimbursement or continued use of services provided by a company acting as a customs broker that involved suspicious payments of approximately $3.5 million to officials of the Nigerian*

Customs Service in order to obtain preferential treatment during the customs process for the purpose of assisting Shell in obtaining or retaining business in Nigeria on Shell's Bonga Project. (US SEC Administrative Proceedings, 2010: 2)

The US SEC Administrative Proceedings (2010: 2) further states that 'as a result of these payments, Shell profited in the amount of approximately $14 million. None of the improper payments was accurately reflected in Shell's books and records, nor was Shell's system of internal accounting controls adequate at the time to detect and prevent these suspicious payments'. The illegal payments violate the FCPA and contradict the Shell code of conduct, which forbids payment of bribery and facilitation payments. In anticipation of the institution of the proceedings, Shell and SIEP submitted an offer of settlement to the US SEC and the US Department of Justice, and agreed to pay disgorgement and prejudgment interest of $18,149,459; and Shell Nigeria Exploration and Production Co. Ltd. agreed to pay a criminal fine of $30 million (US SEC, 2010). It was also reported that in February 2007, one of the Bonga Project Contractors pleaded guilty to violations of the FCPA and agreed to pay $26 million in criminal fines in connection with the payments to Nigerian customs officials through Courier Subcontractor to obtain preferential treatment during the customs process (see US v. Vetco Gray UK Ltd., 2007).

The gap between the anti-corruption policies and the actions of MNCs is not just confined to the oil and gas industry, as is illustrated in the above cases. Panalpina, Inc., a freight forwarding company, is a New York corporation with its principal place of business located in Morristown, New Jersey. Panalpina, Inc. is a wholly owned subsidiary of Panalpina World Transport (Holding) Ltd. (PWT), a global holding company located in Basel, Switzerland, whose subsidiaries and affiliates (collectively called the Panalpina Group) provides global freight forwarding and logistics services in approximately 160 jurisdictions through a network of local affiliates (US District Court Southern District of Texas, 2010b: 3–4). Panalpina reported a net revenue of $5.96 billion and a gross profit of $1.38 billion in 2009 (Panalpina, 2009). The Panalpina Inc. Code of Conduct of states that:

Panalpina employees do not give any undue advantage to influence the judgment or behaviour of a person in a position of trust whether in government or in private business. Similarly, Panalpina employees do not accept or solicit such undue advantages. This applies regardless of the geographical location and also includes undue advantages directed to or coming from a foreign government official or a foreign business partner. (Panalpina, 2013)

Despite the company's claims to have followed an ethical code of conduct, the US SEC alleges that:

Between 2002 and continuing until 2007, Panalpina, Inc. engaged in a series of transactions whereby it directed business to affiliated companies within the Panalpina Group, which then used part of the revenues generated from this business to pay a significant number of bribes running to hundreds of thousand dollars to government officials in countries including Nigeria, Angola, Brazil, Russia, and Kazakhstan. (US District Court Southern District of Texas, 2010b: 1)

Panalpina, Inc. was also reported to have obtained improper benefits totaling at least $11, 329,369 from the illegal conduct. The US SEC reports show that these companies specifically provide false invoices with line items to mask the nature of the bribes. The illegal payments were made to government officials in a number of countries, which contradicts the company claim that it does not give undue advantage to influencing the behaviour of people in positions of trust. As a consequence of the violation of anti-corruption provisions of FCPA, Panalpina, agreed to pay disgorgement of $11,329,369; and PWT and Panalpina agreed to pay a criminal fine of $70.56 million (US SEC, 2010).

Conclusion

This chapter has sought to stimulate debates about the contemporary enterprise culture and corporate claims of socially responsible conduct by examining corporate tax, bribery and corruption practices. The cases described in this chapter show that there is a considerable gap between corporate talk and corporate action in respect of tax-saving strategies, bribery and corrupt practices. Tax evasion, tax avoidance, bribery and corruption are carefully structured schemes which are concealed in company reports. Corporations have developed two cultures within the socio-economic dimension of CSR: one promises ethical conduct and commitment to public interest, and this is decoupled from the enterprise culture, which is geared to improving profits by avoiding and evading taxes and engaging in corrupt practices. Despite the claims of transparency, integrity and ethical business conduct, none of the corporations examined in this chapter communicated their anti-tax and corrupt practices to stakeholders or explained the possible social consequences of evading and avoiding taxes and engaging in bribery and corrupt practices.

The cases show how MNCs can use a variety of tax and bribery schemes and novel practices to reduce taxes payable, as well as bribery and corrupt practices, as a way of gaining competitive advantages, but that these practices have huge social consequences. MNCs involvement in these practices seems to contradict their professed corporate social obligations to the societies in which they operate. The chapter has drawn attention to a variety of strategies and processes (such as the use of subsidiaries and offshore entities and agents) used by MNCs to advance their business agenda in developing countries. The limited cases provided in this chapter illustrate the politics of international business, the drive for profit and the opportunities created by globalization. In addition, it provides an insight into the loopholes in the tax laws and the inadequate institutional structures in developing countries which facilitate antisocial tax and corrupt practices. It is submitted that MNCs are key actors in these antisocial practices in developing countries, which conflict with their acclaimed adherence to codes of conduct and claims to conduct their business according to the highest ethical standards.

Despite MNCs' appeals to their codes of conduct, the cases illustrate how an executive's moral concerns and altruistic desires must ultimately succumb to the corporation's overriding goals. MNCs and the culture they create do more than just stifle good deeds – they nurture, and often demand, bad ones. The underlying reasons for an MNC's enterprise culture could be traced to characteristics common to all corporations: obsession with profits and share price, greed, lack of concern for others, and a penchant for breaking legal rules. These traits are, in turn, rooted in an institutional moral concern. This is because there is no legal or moral compulsion for company directors to indulge in tax evasion, tax avoidance, bribery and corruption.

It has been argued that it is a choice that they themselves have made in pursuit of higher profits, remuneration, status and media accolades (see Sikka, 2010). As long as business executives are rewarded for increases in profits there may be economic incentives to engage in predatory behaviour.

Behind the wall of secrecy, some firms have devised aggressive tax avoidance and tax evasion schemes, and engaged in bribery and corruption. These practices are, therefore, carefully crafted, researched and documented and sanctioned at the highest levels in these organizations; and this demonstrates that the recurring enterprise culture has little regard for the consequences of these practices for citizens, local laws and economic development. Therefore, organized tax avoidance has real human consequences, even though MNCs' CSR reports remain silent. The payment of democratically agreed taxes represents a litmus test for claims of social responsibility. Taxation provides the most durable resource to finance social infrastructure and provide much-needed economic and social development to improve the quality of life of millions of people. The state can only provide support if it collects sufficient tax revenue and corporations live up to their promises of responsible and ethical conduct.

The chapter has argued that these companies have boosted their profits by abandoning their tax contribution and have engaged in bribery and corruption to gain competitive advantage. Therefore, the study of corruption and anti-tax practices offers rich possibilities for interdisciplinary research as it provides a window for studying some of the problems facing the world today. The possibilities of CSR rest with the alignment of corporate culture with the social expectations that corporations or MNCs will honour their publicly espoused goals. MNCs have embraced CSR to show their commitment to the national and local economies, yet they have been implicated in a number of antisocial practices. In order to understand the claim of managers to be following ethical codes of conduct and to be serving the public interest, further research could be conducted by examining micropractices such as accounting technology and processes that are embedded in the enterprise culture of most companies, and how this shapes the behaviour of corporate managers and employees. Another area for future research may be the consideration of why such hypocritical practices flourish.

References

AAPPG (2006, March). *The Other Side of the Coin: The UK and Corruption in Africa. A Report by the Africa All Party Parliamentary Group*. London: UK Government. Available at: http://www.taxjustice.net/cms/upload/pdf/other_side_of_the_coin_PDF.pdf.

Ades, A. and Di Tella, R. (1999). Rent, competition and corruption. *American Economic Review*, 89(4), 982–93 [Online: dio: 10.1257/aer.89.4.982].

Adewuyi, A.O. and Olowookere, A.E. (2010). Corporate social responsibility of a Nigerian polluter: The West African Portland Cement (WAPCO) Nigerian PLC's case. *Social Responsibility Journal*, 6(1), 108–125 [Online: dio: 10.1108/17471111011024586].

Anderson, S. and Cavanagh, J. (2000). *The Rise of Corporate Global Power*. Washington, DC: Institute for Policy Studies. Available at: http://www.ips-dc.org/files/2452/top200.pdf.

Bakan, J. (2004). *The Corporation: The Pathological Pursuit of Profit and Power*. London: Constable and Robinson.

Baker, R.W. (2005). *Capitalism's Achilles Heel*. New York: John Wiley.

Bristow Group (2013). *Code of Business Integrity*. Revised edition, June. Houston, TX: The Bristow Group. Available at: http://www.bristowgroup.com/_assets/filer/2013/07/22/cobi_june2013.pdf [accessed: 23 November 2013].

Christensen, J. (2007). The corruption interface: tax havens, bankers and dirty money flows. *Accountancy Business and the Public Interest*, 6(1), 215–27.

Christensen, J. and Murphy, R. (2004). The social responsibility of corporate tax avoidance: taking CSR to the bottom line. *Development*, 47(3), 37–44.

Christian Aid (2005). *The Shirt off their Backs: How Tax Policies Fleece the Poor. Christian Aid Report*. [Online.] Available at: http://www.globalpolicy.org/nations/launder/havens/2005/09shirts.pdf.

Cobham, A. (2005). *Tax Evasion, Tax Avoidance and Development Finance*. QEH Working Paper Series – QEHWPS 129. Oxford: University of Oxford. Finance and Trade Policy Research Centre Queen Elizabeth House. Available at: http://www3.qeh.ox.ac.uk/pdf/qehwp/qehwps129.pdf [accessed: 18 July 2008].

Desai, M.A. and Dharmapala, D. (2006). CSR and taxation: the missing link. *Leading Perspectives*, (Winter), 4–5. Available at: http://www.people.hbs.edu/mdesai/D+D_BSR.pdf.

Earle, B. (1989). Foreign corrupt practices act amendments: the Omnibus Trade and Competitiveness Act's focus on improving investment opportunities. *Cleveland State Law Review*, 37, 549–56.

Filling, S. and Sikka, P. (2004). Taxing the boundaries of corporate social reporting. *In the Public Interest*, 33(1). Available at: http://aaahq.org/PublicInterest/newsletr/Fall04/item09.htm.

Henderson, D. (2001). *Misguided Virtue: False Notions of Corporate Social Responsibility*. London: The Institute of Economic Affairs.

Johnston, M. (2005). *Syndromes of Corruption: Wealth, Power, and Democracy*. Cambridge, UK: Cambridge University Press.

Kapoor, S. (2005). *Plugging the Leaks: A Very Short Paper on Curbing Capital Flight, Tax Avoidance and Tax Evasion for International Policy Dialogue*. Organized by InWEnt and the Federal Ministry for Economic Cooperation and Development (BMZ). Available at: http://www.new-rules.org/docs/kapoor4.pdf [accessed: 28 March 2006].

Kar, D. and Cartwright-Smith, D. (2008). *Illicit Financial Flows from Developing Countries: 2002–2006*. Washington, DC: Global Financial Integrity. [Online.] Available at: http://www.gfintegrity.org/.../economist%20-%20final%20version%201-2-09.... [accessed: 23 November 2013].

Kim, J. and Kim, J.B. (1997). Cultural differences in the crusade against international bribery: rice-cake expenses in Korea and the Foreign Corrupt Practices Act. *Pacific Rim Law & Policy Journal*, 6, 549–67.

Levitt, A. (2002). *Take on the Street: What Wall Street and Corporate American Don't Want you to Know*. New York: Random House.

Martens, J. (2007). *The Precarious State of Public Finance; Tax evasion, Capital Flight and Misuse of Public Money in Developing Countries – and What can be done about it*. New York: Global Policy Forum, 1–54. Available at: http://www.globalpolicy.org/eu/en/publ/martens_precarious_finance_%20 207.pdf [accessed: 23 May 2008].

Noble Corporation (2009). *Annual Report*. London: Noble Corporation. Available at: http://phx.corporate-ir.net/phoenix.zhtml?c=98046&p=irol-reportsAnnual [accessed: 23 November 2013].

Noble Corporation (2013). *Code of Conduct*. London: Noble Corporation. Available at: http://www.noblecorp.com/governance [accessed: 23 November 2013].

Obalola, M. (2008). Beyond philanthropy: corporate social responsibility in the Nigerian insurance industry. *Social Responsibility Journal*, 4(4), 538–48.

Okafor, E.E., Hassan, A.R. and Doyin Hassan, A. (2008). Environmental issues and corporate social responsibility: the Nigeria experience. *Journal of Human Ecology*, 23(2), 101–107.

Otusanya, O.J. (2010). *An Investigation of Tax Evasion, Tax Avoidance and Corruption in Nigeria*. Unpublished Doctoral Thesis, University of Essex, UK.

Otusanya, O.J. (2011a). The tale of multinational companies in tax evasion and tax avoidance: the case of Nigeria. *Critical Perspectives on Accounting*, 22(3), 316–32.

Otusanya, O.J. (2011b). The role of multinational companies in corrupt practices: the case of Nigeria. *International Journal of Critical Accounting*, 3(2/3), 171–203.

Otusanya, O.J. (Forthcoming). The role of inter-company transfers of intangible assets in tax avoidance practices in Nigeria, in Leaman, J. and Waris A. (eds), *Tax Justice and the Political Economy of Global Capitalism, 1945 to the Present*. Oxford and New York: Berghahn Publishers.

Otusanya, O.J., Adeyeye, G.B. and Arowomole, S.S.A. (2011). Talk and action: corporate social responsibility and multinational companies' tax practice in Nigeria. *The Nigerian Journal of Risk and Insurance*, 7(1), 26–46.

Otusanya, O.J., Lauwo, S. and Adeyeye, G.B. (2012). A critical examination of the multinational companies' anti-corruption policy in Nigeria. *Journal of Accountancy Business and the Public Interest*, 11, 1–52.

Oxfam (2000). *Tax Heaven: Releasing the Hidden Billions for Poverty Eradication. Oxfam GB Policy Paper*. Available at: http://www.oxfam.org.uk/what wedo/issues/debt-aid/tax-heaven.htm [accessed: 25 November 2010].

Palan, R., Murphy, R. and Chavagneux, C. (2010). *Tax Havens: How Globalisation Really Works*. Ithaca, NY: Cornell University Press.

Panalpina (2009). Annual Report. Basel: Panalpina World Transport (Holding) Ltd. Available at: http://www.panalpina.com/content/www/global/en/home/investor_relations/annual_report/_jcr_content/contentParSys/download_0/downloadList/_2009.spooler.download/panalpina_ar09_web_complete_small.pdf [accessed: 23 November 2013].

Panalpina (2013). Code of Conduct. Basel: Panalpina World Transport (Holding) Ltd. Available at: http://www.panalpina.com/content/www/global/en/home/AboutPanalpina/ethics-and-compliance/CoC/_jcr_content/contentParSys/download/downloadList/panalpina_code_of_co.spooler.download/Code%20of%20Conduct%2006%2013%20English.pdf [accessed: 23 November 2013].

Porritt, J. (2005). *Capitalism: As if the World Matters*. London: Earthscan.

Pride International (n.d.). *Code of Business Conduct and Ethical Practices*. Houston, TX: Pride. Available at: http://public.thecorporatelibrary.net/ethics/eth_14033.pdf [accessed: 23 November 2013].

Riesco, M., Lagos, G. and Lima, M. (2005). *The 'Pay Your Taxes' Debate: Perspectives on Corporate Taxation and Social Responsibility in the Chilean Mining Industry*. Geneva: United Nations Research Institute for Social Development.

Rodriguez, P., Siegel, D.S., Hillman, A. and Eden, L. (2006). *Three Lenses on the Multinational Enterprise: Politics, Corruption, and Corporate Social Responsibility*. Rensselaer Working Papers in Economics, No. 0608. New York: Rensslaer Economics Institute.

Rose-Ackerman, S. (1996). *Redesigning the State to Fight Corruption: Public Policy for Private Sector*. World Bank, Note 75. Washington DC: World Bank.

Salbu, S. (1997). Bribery in the global market: a critical analysis of the Foreign Corrupt Practices Act. *Washington & Lee Law Review*, 54: 229–62.

Shell Global (2010a). *Annual Report*. Houston, TX: Shell Global. Available at: http://www.shell.com/global/aboutshell/investor/financial-information/annual-reports-and-publications/archive/2010.html [accessed: 23 November 2013].

Shell Global (2010b). *Shell Code of Conduct*. Houston, TX: Shell Global. Available at: http://s06.static-shell.com/content/dam/shell/static/aboutshell/downloads/who-we-are/code-of-conduct/code-of-conduct-english2010.pdf [accessed: 23 November 2013].

Sikka, P. (2008). Enterprise culture and accountancy firms: new masters of the universe. *Accounting, Auditing & Accountability Journal*, 21(2), 268–95.

Sikka, P. (2010). *Smoke and Mirrors: Corporate Social Responsibility and Tax Avoidance*. Accounting Forum, 21(3–4), 153–68.

Sikka, P. and Hampton, M. (2005). *Tax Avoidance and Global Development: An Introduction*. Accounting Forum, 29(3), 245–48.

Sikka, P. and Willmott, H. (2010). The dark side of transfer pricing: its role in tax avoidance and wealth retentiveness. *Critical Perspectives on Accounting*, 21(4), 342–56.

Spicer, M.W. (1975). New approaches to the problem of tax evasion. *British Tax Review*, 3, 152–54.

Tidewater Inc. (2009). *Code of Business Conduct and Ethics*. New Orleans, LA: Tidewater Inc. Available at: http://www.sec.gov/Archives/edgar/containers/fix071/98222/.../dex141.htm [accessed: 23 November 2013].

Tinker, T. (1985). *Paper Prophets: Fraudulent Accounting and Failed Audits*. Washington DC: Beard Books.

Transocean Inc. (2010). *Annual Report*. Houston, TX: Transocean Inc. Available at: http://www.deepwater.com/fw/main/Financial-Reports-54.html [accessed: 23 November 2013].

Transocean Inc. (2011). *Code of Integrity*. Available at: http://www.deepwater.com/fw/main/Code-of-Integrity-1105.html [accessed: 23 November 2013].

Unerman, J. and O'Dwyer, B. (2007). The business case for regulation of corporate social responsibility and accountability. *Accounting Forum*, 31(4), 332–53.

US District Court Eastern District of Louisiana (2010). Securities and Exchange Commission vs Tidewater Inc. Available at: http://www.sec.gov/litigation/complaints/2010/comp21729.pdf [accessed: 26 December, 2013].

US District Court Southern District of Columbia (2010a). Securities and Exchange Commission vs GlobaSantaFe Corp. Available at: http://www.sec.gov/litigation/complaints/2010/comp21724.pdf [accessed: 15 March 2011].

US District Court Southern District of Columbia (2010b). Securities and Exchange Commission vs Transocean Inc. Available at: http://www.sec.gov/litigation/complaints/2010/comp21725.pdf [accessed: 15 March 2011].

US District Court Southern District of Texas (2010a). Securities and Exchange Commission vs Noble Corporation. Available at: http://www.sec.gov/litigation/complaints/2010/comp21728.pdf [accessed: 15 March 2011].

US District Court Southern District of Texas (2010b). Securities and Exchange Commission vs Panalpina Inc. Available at: http://www.sec.gov/litigation/complaints/2010/comp21727.pdf [accessed: 15 March 2011].

US District Court Southern District of Texas (2010c). Securities and Exchange Commission vs Pride International Inc. Available at: http://www.sec.gov/litigation/complaints/2010/comp21726.pdf [accessed: 15 March 2011].

US SEC (2007). *SEC Charges Baker Hughes With Foreign Bribery* .... Press Release, 26 April. Washington DC: US Securities and Exchange Commission. Available at: http://www.sec.gov/news/press/2007/2007-77.htm [accessed: 23 November 2013].

US SEC (2010). *SEC Charges Seven Oil Services and Freight Forwarding Companies for Widespread Bribery of Customs Officials*. Press Release, 4 November. Washington DC: US Securities and Exchange Commission. Available at: http://www.sec.gov/news/press/2010/2010-214.htm [accessed: 23 November 2013].

US SEC Administrative Proceedings (2007). Accounting and Auditing Enforcement, in a Matter of Bristow Group Inc., September 26, 2007.

US SEC Administrative Proceedings (2010). Royal Dutch Shell plc and Shell International Exploration and Production Inc., 3463243, 4   November. Available at: http://www.sec.gov/litigation/admin/2010/34-6243.pdf [accessed: 23 November 2013].

US Senate Joint Committee on Taxation (2003). Report of the Investigation of Enron Corporation and Related Entities Regarding Federal Tax and Compensation Issue and Policy Recommendations. US Government Printing Office. Washington DC.

US Senate Sub-Committee on Investigations (2005). The Role of Professional Firms in the US Tax Shelter Industry, Committee on Foreign Relations United States Senate, April 13 2005. US Government Printing Office.

Vanasco, R.R. (1999). The Foreign Corrupt Practices Act: an international perspective. *Managerial Auditing Journal*, 14(4–5), 159–262.

Wallace-Bruce, N.L. (2000). Corruption and competitiveness in global business the dawn of a new era. *Melbourne University Law Review*, 13. Available at: http://www.austlii.edu.au/au/journals/MULR/2000/13.html [accessed: 22 November 2006].

World Bank (1997). *Helping Countries Combat Corruption: The Role of the World Bank*. Washington DC: World Bank. Available at: http://www1.worldbank.org/publicsector/anticorruption/coruption/corrptn.pdf [accessed: 31 October 2011].

World Bank (2007). *Stolen Asset Recovery (StAR) Initiative: Challenges, Opportunities, and Action Plan.* Washington, DC: World Bank.

WSWS News, December 11, 2004. [Online – World Socialist Web Site.] Available at: http://www.wsws.org/articles/2004/dec2004/pino-d11.shtml [accessed: 10 October 2011].

3

CSR of Foreign Multinational Corporations in China

MARIA LAI-LING LAM

Abstract

This chapter is based on my seven years of fieldwork in China (2006–2012) researching into the perceptions of 30 Chinese executives from 20 different foreign multinational corporations (MNCs) about their corporate social responsibility (CSR) programmes in China. It examines the CSR practices of foreign MNCs in state-driven CSR with emerging non-governmental organizations (NGOs) in China. The scope of CSR activities is still narrowed to charity, internal economic efficiency and political visibility. The CSR programmes substitute for government services and mirror the institutions in which these companies are embedded. Only four exemplars learned how to provide public services and complements to meet the needs of the Chinese government in their CSR programmes. They learned how to institutionalize their CSR programmes through industry associations, self-regulated industry codes of conduct and collaborations with selected NGOs in China. The four did not follow the institutional norms and the existing efficiency paradigm. They were exemplars due to the moral consciousness of their leaders and the persistence, compassion and humility of their dedicated CSR officers.

Introduction

There is no unique definition of corporate social responsibility (CSR). It can be broadly defined as 'the actions of a company to benefit society beyond the requirements of the law and the direct interests of shareholders' (McWilliams and Siegel, 2001). It is a contested concept and is embedded in a firm's institutional contexts (Brammer, Jackson and Matten, 2012; Campbell, 2007; Matten and Moon, 2008). A firm can develop various strategies to cope with the institutional regulatory, cognitive and normative pressure upon CSR practices (Oliver, 1991). CSR can substitute for institutionalized social solidarity in a liberal economic system (Kinderman, 2012) and mirror the practices of coordinated market economics and extensive welfare states (Campbell, 2007). Will the CSR practices of foreign MNCs in China become substitutes for the Chinese government's services and mirror the characteristics of state capitalism when the Chinese government encourages corporations to approach economic growth, social progress and environmental protection in a 'holistic and integrated manner?' As senior executives' values and behaviour can determine the CSR activities in China (Hambrick and Mason, 1984; Carpenter et al., 2004), will the CSR activities driven by moral consciousness of leaders be more beneficial to the social and environmental development of China?

The effects of the CSR practices of foreign MNCs in China need to be interpreted in broader historical, social, economic and political contexts. CSR in China is mainly driven by the state whose aim is to build a harmonious society, while foreign MNCs' CSR practices have to earn legitimacy from the Chinese government and international organizations (Lam, 2006; 2007; 2009a and b; 2010a, b and c; 2011a, b and c; 2012a, b and c). Certain norms and understanding of CSR practices among Chinese executives working for foreign MNCs in China inform their interpretations of the CSR behaviour of their firms in China. CSR in China is defined mainly in terms of charity, internal economic efficiency and a political tool for better government relations (Lam, 2006; 2007). As the Chinese government changes from a communist system to a market system with socialist characteristics, companies are expected to provide more social and environmental welfare for social stability. Will foreign MNCs' concepts of CSR fulfil the Chinese government's standards of social solidarity? To what extent and in what forms has CSR emerged in China, where the state still has strong administrative control over social and economic activities? Will the state-driven CSR activities give more socially desirable outcomes? Will foreign MNCs' CSR activities become substitutes for government service and strengthen state power? Are foreign MNCs really engaged in social welfare through their CSR programmes in China?

Since 2006, I have interviewed more than 30Chinese executives who are working for foreign MNCs in China and learned their perceptions of their corporations' social responsibility programmes in China (Lam, 2006; 2007). My ongoing research in the area enabled me to understand that the practices of CSR are innovative, complex and political (Lam, 2008a; 2009a; 2011c; 2012a). The development of these companies in China to become better corporate citizens has been deferred and politically whitewashed in the local Chinese media and international media (Lam, 2010a; 2010c). It seems that the impact of these corporations' CSR programmes is disappointing. However, there are four exemplars that do not follow the norms and sincerely practise long-term and corporate-wide CSR programmes in China (Lam, 2012a; 2012b). These exemplars may inspire other companies to make positive differences in China. In this chapter, I will review the literature concerning the CSR movement in China, describe the challenges of practising CSR in China and detail the contributions of the four exemplars in the area of CSR. These ideal examples integrate their CSR programmes into their daily operations, strategies and culture.

Literature Review

The ideal of the modern CSR movement is to promote a decent, peaceful and justified world through corporations' CSR programmes (van Tulder and van der Zwart, 2006). International NGOs demand that MNCs fulfil universally accepted principles in the areas of human rights, labour standards, the environment and anti-corruption practices (UN Global Compact n.d.; OECD, 2000). MNCs need to implement their CSR policies and programmes abroad (Waddock, 2008) and learn how to integrate their CSR practices into the daily operations of their subsidiaries and the global supply chain (Wood and Kaufman, 2007; Zakek, 2004). CSR is based on the voluntary choices of companies. There are different varieties and dynamics of CSR practices in different institutions. There is still no common definition of the concept of CSR (Brammer, Jackson and Matten, 2012). CSR practices in the US are shaped mainly by instrumental motives rather than relational or moral interests (Aguilera et al., 2007). Unfortunately, CSR may be used as a disguise for managerial opportunism and shareholders' enlightened interests. In the institutions with more relationships with stakeholders, CSR practices will be more 'implicit' (Matten and Moon, 2008). The parties involved in the interpretations of required social responsibilities vary in different kinds of capitalism (i.e. corporate, state, and welfare-oriented). MNCs' CSR practices vary in the corporate, state and welfare systems. Their social programmes can become substitutes for and mirror the systems from which they are derived (Koos, 2012). The effects of CSR are related to various governance structures and need to be understood in state regulations, industrial associations, social networks and governance structures of business.

HISTORICAL DEVELOPMENT OF CSR IN CHINA

In the early twentieth century, the concept of CSR was new to the People's Republic of China, since this communist country opened up to the market economy in 1979 (Wilson, 2009). CSR was mainly transferred from foreign MNCs to their Chinese suppliers or subsidiaries in the global supply chain management (Tateisi, 2004; Visser, 2008). Gradually, more and more MNCs were criticized when international NGOs, customers and public citizens found that their Chinese suppliers were not complying with the MNCs' codes of conduct (Murdoch and Gould, 2004). Today, many foreign MNCs, which design products or services, have built up a strong, brand-loyal customer base, or have strong power in the global supply chain, and are required to be responsible for the social and environmental performances of their suppliers in China (International Labour Organization, The Organisation for Economic Co-operation and Development (OECD) guidelines, the United Nations Global Compact). These companies are called upon to put into practice CSR programmes and report their performances to these international organizations. Many foreign MNCs established CSR departments in China from 2004 through 2006. Those MNCs, from developed countries, are expected by the Chinese government and Chinese companies to be good models for Chinese enterprises, as these foreign MNCs are capable of installing 'clean and efficient technologies' and developing the institutional capabilities of their Chinese subsidiaries and suppliers in China by enforcing both international and Chinese environmental regulations (Ho, 2005). They should be very effective vehicles for increasing the awareness of CSR and improving the CSR practices of their affiliated companies and suppliers in China (OECD, 2000; World Business Council for Sustainable Development, 2005; China Finance Economy Company, 2006; China Entrepreneurs Survey System, 2007). However, only four out of twenty foreign MNCs transmitted their CSR practices to local Chinese firms and enabled China to be more receptive to international labour and human rights norms (Lam, 2011b; 2012a; 2012b).

In 2001, China joined the World Trade Organization (WTO), as more and more Chinese companies wanted to fulfil international business standards and learn CSR practices from foreign MNCs. In 2003, the China Business Council for Sustainable Development was set up to facilitate the exchange of information, experiences and best practices in the area of CSR between well-known foreign enterprises, Chinese enterprises, government and communities through the Ministry of Civil Affairs of the People's Republic of China (CBCSD, n.d.: 2–12).

In 2005, the Chinese government initiated a CSR movement for the development of a harmonious society and expected corporations to approach economic growth, social progress and environmental protection in a 'holistic and integrated manner' (China Entrepreneurs Survey System, 2007; National Development and Reform Commission of China, 2009; Syntao, 2010). In 2008, the Chinese government issued numerous CSR guidelines for foreign MNCs, and state-owned enterprises. The Chinese Academy of Social Science, the prominent national centre for comprehensive studies in the People's Republic of China and the key think tank for the State Council, formally established the research centre for CSR in July 2008 and developed deeper understanding of CSR theories, practices and policies (CASS, n.d.). Beginning in 2008, the Chinese government has established increasingly more rigorous environmental and labour laws in China. It has also provided more institutional incentives for CSR activities, such as better financial credit rating of corporations which practise CSR or fulfil home-grown CSR standards. In August 2012 the government introduced public input into decisions over amendments to existing environmental laws. As the Chinese government is interested in establishing a competitive business environment, promoting social cohesion and fostering collective responsibility for the betterment of society, foreign corporations are pushed to engage in social change through their CSR programmes (Aguilera et al., 2007). The Chinese government reduces public expenses and provides financial incentives to those firms providing public service in industrial areas. Thus, CSR programmes can act as a substitute for government services.

The year 2008 became the genesis of CSR among the public in China when the public boycotted some foreign MNCs' donations to Sichuan earthquake disaster relief programmes which conflicted with their presence in the Chinese market (McGinnis et al., 2009). On 12 May, 2008, Sichuan was struck by an earthquake with a magnitude of 7.9 on the Richter scale. At least 87,000 people died or were reported missing and the earthquake left 5 million homeless. Several well-known MNCs, such as Nokia and Coca Cola, responded to the negative critique from the Chinese citizens and tripled their donations from 14 to 17 May, 2008. Companies were ranked in the Chinese social media according to their donations. Thus, the CSR practices of foreign corporations mirrored the institutional demands during this period of crisis. In such circumstances the public learns the facts of the situation and demands of these corporations that they be more transparent and accountable to the local Chinese.

THE ROLE OF NON-GOVERNMENTAL ORGANIZATIONS IN CHINA

The key actors in the CSR movement in China are the Chinese government and foreign MNEs, not Chinese NGOs or local consumers (Lam, 2007; 2008b). Chinese NGOs in China do not command the same degree of organizational autonomy as NGOs in democratic countries (Ma, 2006:9). They must continually negotiate with the Chinese government for political power and resources through *guan-xi*, that is, 'self-censorship', and personal ties. Many Chinese NGOs in China have less financial, informational, and managerial power than do foreign MNCs. The public prefers to rely on the government rather than NGOs in solving environmental problems (Ho, 2005:28). They are very localized and embedded in party–state relationships. They always struggle for financial support, credibility from the public and from enterprises, and government approval. They are limited by the current registration process and cannot exert much pressure on foreign enterprises and the local government (Lam, Lam and Lam, 2010).

MAJOR PROBLEMS OF FOREIGN MULTINATIONAL CORPORATIONS' CSR PRACTICES

Many MNCs do not manage their subsidiaries or supply chain members in China in a socially and environmentally responsible manner even though the management at HQ how to put into practice good CSR programmes. Some are even prone to using their CSR activities to mask their labour and environmental problems in China (Lam, 2011a; Lam, Lam and Lam, 2010; SACOM, 2010a, 2010b). The CSR programmes are not integrated into their organizational structure, system and strategies. There are five major common problems of the CSR programmes of these foreign MNCs:

1. CSR programmes are regarded as a cost rather than an investment. The primary investment objective of foreign MNCs is to lower costs.
2. There are no incentives for an MNC's non-CSR departments to work with CSR programmes for the greater common good within their organization's existing systems.
3. They politicize their CSR programmes in order to enhance their reputation in the media.
4. They use evasive compliance-oriented mechanism to the disadvantage of their Chinese suppliers or partners.
5. They refuse to nurture local NGOs.

Many foreign MNCs just want to foster low cost and production efficiency. They do not want to seek more organizational learning from their CSR officers. Many CSR officers are frustrated because they receive little support from other functional areas. They cannot ask their companies' buyers to implement CSR ideas when these buyers are only rewarded by their economic performance. CSR officers may give some short-term training to Chinese suppliers in the codes of conduct listed in their companies' CSR reports; but they do not work with the buyers on ensuring that the Chinese suppliers understand how to comply with these codes of conduct. When there is neither strong and well-enforced governmental regulation nor strong independent NGOs to monitor the behaviour of foreign MNCs in China, some companies embellish their CSR programmes to disguise the corruption in China and to mislead the international community (Sum and Nagai, 2005; Harney, 2008; Lam, 2007; 2010a). There have been worse situations when foreign MNCs have relied on the local government to bypass some environmental regulations or labour laws (Lam, 2010a; Lam, Lam and Lam, 2010).

Research Method

This chapter is based on my seven years' fieldwork in China, Japan, and the US, an extensive literature review and personal reflections. I used the process model of organizational sense-making, which explains how Chinese managers who were working for foreign

MNCs in China thought, discussed and acted with their key stakeholders and the world (Basu and Palazzo, 2008). During my seven years of fieldwork in China (2006–2012), I interviewed 30 Chinese executives from 20 different foreign MNCs which are classified as global corporate citizens (Logsdon and Wood, 2005). These companies have advocated their universal values and learned how to implement them in their organizations. They are well known for their CSR practices in China and were referred to me by my friends and interviewees. Eighteen (90 per cent) of foreign MNCs have earned corporate citizenship awards in China. Sixteen companies were in the areas of information technology, electronic and plastics industries. One was in the apparel industry and another was in the consumer packaged goods industry. Two were in the pharmaceutical industry.

I conducted my research in various cities with different levels of economic development. These included the most advanced, along the east coast of The People's Republic of China: Beijing (during the years 2006, 2008, 2009, 2010); Dalian (2006); Shanghai (2006, 2010); Hangzhou (2007, 2010); Guangdong (2011); Tianjin (2009); Qingdao (2007); Nanjing (2007). I also visited the western city of Chongqing (2006, 2007, 2009);the city of Wuhan in central China(2012); and my home town, Hong Kong (2006–2012) to experience the increasing political power of the Chinese government in the international business arena. The data for the perception of the CSR practices of foreign MNCs in China by Chinese executives were collected through semi-structured, in-depth personal interviews during 2006–2012. The interpretations of these Chinese executives regarding their CSR programmes needed to be discovered through dialogues, since there are many subtle meanings behind many publicized CSR programmes. These executives might give me socially desirable answers. However, their answers still reflect their perceptions of societal expectations in China. Their perspectives could reveal the theories in use when they implemented CSR practices in their subsidiaries in China. In 2006, I designed a survey in Chinese and English, but failed to ask participants to complete the surveys. Later, I changed my approach to semi-structured, in-depth personal interviews.

Several interviewees were interviewed twice during the seven-year period (2006–2012). Each interview was conducted in the interviewee's native tongue and lasted from one to three hours. The interview comprised four major parts: personal experience; internal organizational practices; the impact of their companies' CSR programmes; and the expectations and recommended changes in their companies' CSR programmes. I also validated the data and my interpretations by evaluating the interviewees' corporate reports, interviews at their American and Japanese headquarters', published Chinese documents, articles, and Chinese students' dissertations about CSR and MNCs (Huberman and Miles, 1984; Glaser and Strauss, 1967). I also used feedback from different professional communities such as the International Center for Corporate Accountability, Corporate Responsibility Officers, and the Academy of Management. In addition, my fieldwork in various cities in China during the last seven years afforded me an opportunity to talk with more than 100 Chinese citizens and employees about their expectations concerning corporations and to learn about their perceptions of the social and economic impact of CSR practices in China.

Challenges of Practising CSR in China

Four of the thirty interviewees viewed corporate social responsibilities as learning and strategic opportunities. These four interviewees perceived their companies as being part of wider communities and their CSR programmes were shaped by the moral consciousness and compassion of their leaders. Twenty-six perceived their companies' CSR as a cost to their companies and perceived that there were poor internal alignments between CSR messages and the practices of other functional areas. They were under pressure to meet many short-term goals and believed that CSR programmes were very time-consuming and expensive. They perceived that the cost of implementing CSR programmes was high and the pressure on institutions to implement CSR guidelines in China was low. Their companies could bypass the local social norms and even local health and safety regulations through the support of the local government. CSR was unfortunately treated as a way to reduce their operating risk rather than as a strategic opportunity in China. When the price competition in the local Chinese market was very high, these 26 interviewees perceived that their companies must have to externalize their costs. These companies donated money for disaster relief when it was recognized as the core element of CSR among Chinese companies (Wang and Chaudhri, 2009). They sought short-term rewards and fulfilled social norms through their CSR programmes. The main objective of the CSR programme was to develop good relationships with their key stakeholder, the local government (Lam, 2010a). CSR programmes are regarded as an investment in the embedded party–state relationships. Several interviewees confessed that their corporate citizenship awards granted by the Chinese government were based on their good relationships with the Chinese government, rather than their CSR performance in China. Several well-known foreign MNCs work closely with governmental non-governmental organizations (GNGOS) in some public forums for promoting China's image as having a good civil society and good global citizenship (Lam, Lam and Lam, 2010). Many embellished CSR activities can be used to enhance the power of the state and the faith in the Chinese Communist party. As a result, political liberation in China can be delayed and democracy and well-being in the US can be endangered (Barley, 2007; Gallagher, 2005; Reich, 2007). The political costs of these companies' CSR programmes are seldom addressed by participants in the CSR forums in China or outside China.

After the recent international financial crises, many foreign companies have found many alternatives to cutting costs in China. CSR activities are becoming more politically oriented as the Chinese government has gained more power over foreign corporations, since China is one of the few countries that has been resilient to the crises. In this study, many foreign companies sought to compartmentalize their activities in China and were not responsible for the conditions of local manufacturing or supply chain management through third-party governance structure. The role of CSR officer was treated as a public relations function and mainly dealt with the local media in China, which is highly controlled by the Chinese Government. Their headquarters dealt with the international media. The chasm between CSR practices in the international media and the local media in China is increasing, the since local CSR news endeavours to maintain the status or face of the local Chinese government. Several interviewees told me their companies wanted to do well in order to increase their share price in the US market. Their companies can fulfil international CSR requirements without describing in detail their work in China. Thus, many CSR practices are used to meet external reporting requirements without much internal organizational learning. There are more 'greenwashing' or window-dressing activities in CSR programmes when these foreign companies can easily bypass many regulations through the support of the local government in an emerging civil society because of the weak system of law enforcement in China. Some foreign corporations even set up more internally controlled mechanisms to protect themselves from criticism or vulnerability resulting from their own 'greenwashing' documents. They want their internal employees to follow many procedures before they can disclose their companies' CSR practices in China. The effect is to generate more CSR reports and cynical attitudes of the public towards these companies' practices. Sadly, more and more Chinese government-owned MNCs adopt these same 'greenwashing' activities. They increasingly publish CSR reports and are seamed to comply with international CSR standards, such as the United Nations Global Compact and ISO 14001. Thus, many CSR reports are still extremely superficial (Syntao, 2008). These Chinese firms are learning how to use the reporting of CSR activities to increase their visibility and credibility in the global market.

Contributions of Four Exemplars' CSR Practices

From my seven years' research work (2006–2012), only four out of twenty companies (8 per cent) practise CSR that has a long-term social and environmental impact in China. Their initiatives of deep commitment to their CSR practices in China were mainly shaped by their leaders' consciousness of the social and environmental consequences of their corporate activities in China. Their CSR officers were willing to learn and experiment with different programmes. They provided a public service to the government through their labour welfare programmes (company A), environmental regulations (company B), and volunteer programmes (companies C and D).

COMPANY A

Company A is a Japanese multinational electronic company and has two subsidiaries in the southern part of China. When the CEO received letters from an international NGO about the horrible working conditions of its factories in China, he decided to set up CSR departments in Japan and China and invested US$2 for each Chinese worker's training per year. Through a series of programmes, 10,000 Chinese factory workers were helped to develop, for the first time in their adult lives, a sense of belonging in the factory, their dormitories, and the city through the education provided by a Chinese NGO. The company was also among the few which did not experience recent rampant labour strikes in China in the summer of 2010. When the company succeeded in solving its labour problems in China, it transferred its experiences to its Chinese suppliers, as they encountered similar problems in China. Through numerous education and training provided to its Chinese suppliers, the company later passed its learning experience to its headquarters and developed shared attainable codes of conduct among its suppliers in the industry.

COMPANY B

Company B already has very high private voluntary environmental standards in Japan and is well known worldwide for its CSR programme. Influenced by the moral stance of the interviewee – the company's global buyer – the company chose to assist its Chinese suppliers to understand and implement its CSR programmes through more person-to-person communication and training.

From his years of experience with the Chinese suppliers, the company's representative being interviewed had learned that poor concepts of environmental stewardship were held by Chinese suppliers and many Chinese employees. The Chinese suppliers tended to create false reports about their environmental performance because of their fear of disclosing their inability to meet the green requirements and losing the contracts from global buyers. He preferred to provide more ongoing education rather than just use a survey to learn whether the Chinese suppliers complied with the green requirements. He persuaded the headquarters to invest more money towards providing numerous training workshops, elaborating the requirements in-depth, developing progressive objectives and managing the performance of its suppliers in China through a three-year comprehensive green certificate programme. As a result, the Chinese suppliers had to continue to learn about the company's CSR practices and to be monitored if they wanted to renew the green certificates issued to them by his company. The process made the company more competitive through the sustainable value chain (Wood and Kaufman, 2007).

During the period 2003–2008, through the association of foreign enterprises, the company also provided comprehensive corporate environmental data and shared its research on environmental issues with the Chinese government to assist the government to draft new regulations for controlling certain polluting substances. In return, the company and selected members from associated countries, who held high private voluntary environmental standards from their home countries, successfully lobbied the Chinese government through environmental data sharing and set up new regulations and industry norms. The collaboration between the association and the Chinese government improved the enforceability and the acceptance of the new regulations. As a result, the company increased its competitiveness through the new environmental regulations in China and the management of the green practices of its selected local suppliers. The company not only managed its CSR programme internally but also ensured that its Chinese partners would learn to practise CSR. The company became the leader, green partner and adviser to China's environmental sustainable programmes through its industrial association.

COMPANIES C AND D

Companies C and D provided public service and added sustainability to the government's abilities to deal with natural disasters. They also improved their corporations' volunteer programmes when the concept of volunteers was new to many Chinese executives. Their initiatives and commitments were derived from their employees' cooperative rescue work in the Sichuan earthquake in May 2008 and their commitment by top-level leaders. Their compassion had been sustained as a 'central building block' for their organizations and their employees' human development (O'Connell, 2009). These leaders transferred their experience from headquarters to the local community in the Sichuan earthquake area quickly.

For example, Company C was an American corporation and used its software systems and expertise to help survivors to be quickly connected with their relatives in China. After many initiatives and dialogues about the earthquake crisis were generated among local stakeholders and its subsidiaries around the world, the company restructured its international organization learning teams and CSR programmes. The company initiated a one-year volunteer and numerous cooperative projects in the Sichuan area. As a result, the company's employees from other countries also learned how to provide public services and add substance to the Chinese government's ability to deal with natural disasters and to manage waste water through collaborative projects.

Company D is a German company in the area of pharmaceuticals. It helped rebuild the community for the earthquake victims for more than four years. It worked with three local Chinese NGOs and three local district governments to reconstruct the Sichuan community systematically. The company transferred its expertise to local government officers in China through teaching and giving local government officers a sense of ownership of the projects. Later, Company C's employees helped Chinese government officials to assess its accomplishments in the community. Company D made its volunteer programmes and a part of its company's culture visible through organizing activities of a compassionate nature in their CSR programmes (Dutton et al., 2006; Lam, 2012b). Activities of this nature have been sustained through continuing volunteer programmes and a long-term commitment to restore the community. After a year of work in the Sichuan area, the company introduced a four-year programme which helped affected communities to access loans to develop small businesses and to learn how to plan and live in more sanitary conditions. Its employees let their compassion towards people who were suffering the effects of the earthquake show, and in return experienced solidarity and personal development within the corporation through a four-year innovative volunteer programme. Company D's corporate volunteer programmes emerged and evolved to be better managed and coordinated through a third party, a local NGO. When its corporate volunteer programmes were seen, through the Chinese and international media, to be more visible, transparent and innovative, more and more employees were motivated to participate in its CSR programmes (Vaill, 1996; 2007). The new volunteer service model, led by the Chinese government, coordinated by NGOs and supported by the company, emerged as a new form of organization dynamics in the process of helping the earthquake-stricken community.

Companies C and D learned how to teach the Chinese officials in the rural areas to learn some new technology and managerial skills. The process of mobilizing their internal staff to reach out to the local community also enabled the companies' employees to internalize their companies' CSR programmes. As there was no established rule of law, democratic political system and transparent process between business and government in China, the disaster relief efforts had to follow the statutes of the Chinese government and be sensitive to the relationships between China and the companies' home governments. The leaders of the CSR programme knew how to act in a manner that would dignify the government officers, and they reached out to help with the tasks that the government officers needed. They also offered training to the government officers and NGOs in the area of corporate cultures, corporate policies and corporate strategies. Their volunteer programmes were recognized by the local government for their efforts to provide a better livelihood for the people in the earthquake-stricken community. In return, all participants in the new volunteer service model were recognized in the public media. Companies C and D received many government contracts. They also learned how to sell and customize their products and service to the Chinese government more effectively.

EFFECTS OF FOUR EXEMPLARS' CSR PROGRAMMES

These four companies enhance their brands through their long-term CSR and corporate-wide CSR programmes. They learn and institutionalize their best CSR practices with their suppliers. They increase the awareness and commitment of CSR programmes in their corporations, supply-chain members, industrial associations and NGOs in China. Thus, the partnership with a local NGO and the transmission of best practices to the company's Chinese suppliers also meant that the local NGO, the Chinese subsidiaries and suppliers, and the companies' senior management all learned how to realize better social programmes and codes of conduct through the supply chain. The company knows how to frame its messages to be more acceptable to the Chinese government and enhance the Chinese government's abilities to develop new institutional requirements and implement new environmental and labour laws effectively. These four ideal examples, regardless of their corporate culture and its inherited capitalist systems, not only provide substitutes for government services but also develop the CSR capabilities of the Chinese government, supply chain members and NGOs.

Implications

In the journey towards attaining better economic, social, democratic and environmental performance through better CSR programmes in China, foreign MNCs are capable of establishing industry norms and regulations through industry associations, self-regulated industry codes of conduct and collaboration with selected NGOs in China. They can incorporate many positive social and environmental issues in their managerial and strategic process when they focus on building up the abilities of their corporate staff, government officers and local NGOs in the process of implementing long-term and wide CSR programmes in China. When there are more communities practicing CSR, local NGOs can learn and become good policy advisers in the future. Through these CSR programmes, China may become more engaged in the international community and more receptive to international norms of human rights and environmental standards. Using CSR as an agent for change in China is possible when foreign MNCs are willing to be transparent and accountable to local stakeholders who seemed not to have power to stop greenwashing or whitewashing activities in the local and international media.

Conclusion

As many foreign MNCs use CSR to develop better relationships with the Chinese government for their own corporate interest, they can easily bypass the voice of the Chinese and get support from the local government for mutual short-term economic interests. The CSR programmes are mainly for short-term outcomes without much development in the abilities of their stakeholders. Many CSR programmes of foreign MNCs are intended to act as substitutes for and mirror government services in a superficial way regardless of whether the MNCs come from corporate or welfare-oriented capitalistic systems. Many embellished CSR activities only reduce companies' investment in productive economic activities and result in more activities to externalize costs with the support of local Chinese government. The state-driven CSR movement can only encourage companies to divert their investment from productive activities to window-dressing activities aimed at getting quick legitimacy from the Chinese government and overcoming the barriers confronting foreigners in China. Many foreign companies are not motivated to invest in strengthening CSR awareness in society as they do not want to be blamed for destroying national sovereignty or internal order.

When the Chinese government's power over foreign MNCs is increasing in a very price-competitive Chinese market, foreign MNCs tend to use their CSR programmes to earn more political legitimacy. CSR programmes are regarded as an investment in the embedded party–state relationships. Many foreign MNCs focus on working with those NGOs which were formally government organizations and foster their relationships with the state. Many foreign MNCs' CSR programmes are becoming more politically oriented or window dressing when they can easily bypass a majority of the regulations through the support of the local government in an emerging civil society because of weak law-enforcement systems and NGOs in China. The state-driven CSR movement in China cannot influence many foreign MNCs to provide more socially desirable outcomes due to the lack of input of civil society. The Chinese state-owned enterprises have learned how to embellish their CSR reports to earn international respect. More embellished CSR activities of foreign MNCs are seemed to substitute public service for political legitimacy and social acceptance. These CSR activities also mirror the power of the state and increase the faith of people in state capitalism.

Although the four exemplars provided a public service for the local government, they also increased the CSR capabilities of local NGOs and established a new institutional framework for better social and environmental outcomes. They did not follow the pervasive institutional norms of using CSR to disguise their political and economic activities in China. Their deep engagement in the welfare of labour, the education of suppliers and the restoration of communities is mainly driven by the moral consciousness of their leaders, in addition to the persistence, compassion and humility of their dedicated CSR officers. When these leaders were committed to providing more training and development for their employees, suppliers, local Chinese government officers and staff of NGOs through their CSR practices in China, they were willing to learn from their experience and improve the implementation of these programmes in their corporations and global supply chains. They gradually institutionalized the practices through industry associations, social networks, and collaboration with the Chinese government and the local NGOs. When they were more open to learning through CSR practices, they also enhanced the productivity of the internal and external partners who participated in their CSR programmes. As China is changing rapidly, more variations of CSR programmes will appear. More socially and environmentally desirable CSR programmes will be put into practice when enlightened public concerns are brought back to business through a greater degree of transparent information and involvement of NGOs. The values and commitment of corporate leaders towards CSR programmes are more important than the institutional pressure upon CSR activities in the process of building a harmonious society in China through private voluntary corporate activities, even though CSR is mainly initiated and driven by a powerful state.

Acknowledgments

This chapter is dedicated to my mentors and friends, Dr Martha Cook, Dr Georgia Eshelman and Dr Peter B. Vaill. I thank all participants and helpers in this ongoing CSR project. I also thank two anonymous reviewers for their very detailed and helpful comments on my earlier draft of this chapter.

References

Aguilera, R., Rupp, D., Williams, C. and Ganapathi, J. (2007). Putting the 'S' back in corporate social responsibility: A multilevel theory of social change in organizations. *Academy of Management Review*, 32(3), 836–63.

Barley, S. (2007). Corporations, democracy, and the public good. *Journal of Management Inquiry*, 16(3), 201–215.

Basu, K. and Palazzo, G. (2008). Corporate social responsibility: A process model of sense-making. *Academy of Management Review*, 33(1), 122–36.

Brammer, S., Jackson, G. and Matten, D. (2012). Corporate social responsibility and institutional theory: new perspectives on private governance. *Socio-economic Review*, 10, 3–28.

Campbell, J.L. (2007). Why would corporations behave in socially responsible ways? An institutional theory of corporate social responsibility. *Academy of Management* Review, 32, 946–67.

Carpenter, M.A., Geletkanycz, M.A. and Sanders, W.G. (2004). Upper echelons research revisited: antecedents, elements, and consequences of top management team composition. *Journal of Management*, 30, 749–78.

CASS (n.d.). Chinese Academy of Social Sciences website. [Online.] Available [in English] at: http:// www.chinacsrmap.org/Org_Show_EN.asp?ID=1115 [accessed: 26 September 2012].

CBCSD (n.d.). China Business Council for Sustainable Development website.[Online.] Available [in English] at: english.cbcsd.org.cn [accessed: 23 November 2013].

China Finance Economic Company (2006). *CSR Report in China* [in Chinese]. The annual report of the Chinese Institute of Business Administration, 2005–2006. Beijing: China Finance Economic Company.

China Entrepreneurs Survey System (2007). *Report on Chinese Entrepreneurs' Growth and Evolution* [in Chinese]. China Machine Press.

Dutton, J., Worline, M., Frost, P. and Lilius, J. (2006). Explaining compassion organizing. *Administrative Science Quarterly*, 51, 59–96.

Gallagher, M.E. (2005). *Contagious Capitalism* Princeton, NJ: Princeton University Press.

Glaser, B.G. and Strauss, A.L. (1967). *The Discovery of Grounded Theory: Strategies for Qualitative Research*. Chicago, IL: Aldine Publications.

Hambrick, D.C. and Mason, P.A. (1984). Upper echelons: the organization as a reflection of its top managers. *Academy of Management Review*, 9, 193–206.

Harney, A. (2008). *The China Price*. New York: The Penguin Press.

Ho, P. (2005). Greening industries in newly industrializing countries: Asian-style leapfrogging? *International Journal of Environmental and Sustainable Development*, 4(3), 209–226.

Huberman, A.M. and Miles, M. (1984). Data management and analysis methods, in Denzin, N.K. and Lincoln, Y.S. (eds) *The SAGE Handbook of Qualitative Research*. Los Angeles and London: Sage Publications.

Kinderman, D. (2012). Free us up so we can be responsible! The co-evolution of corporate social responsibility and neo-liberalism in the UK, 1997–2010. *Socio-economic Review*, 10, 29–57.

Koos, S. (2012). The institutional embeddedness of social responsibility: a multilevel analysis of smaller firms' civic engagement in Western Europe. *Socio-economic Review*, 10, 135–62.

Lam, M., Lam, A. and Lam, L. (2010). The Importance of Non-Government Organizations in the Corporate Social Movement in China. *The International Journal of Humanities*, 7(12), 101–114.

Lam, M.L.L. (2006). *A Study of the Transfer of Corporate Social Responsibility from Multinational Enterprises to Chinese Subsidiaries: Implications for Christian Business Educators. Proceedings of the 22nd Christian Business Faculty Association Annual Conference*, Cedarville University, Dayton, Ohio, U.S.

—— (2007). A study of the transfer of corporate social responsibility from well-established foreign multinational enterprises to Chinese subsidiaries, in Hooker, J., Hulpke, J. and Madsen, P. (eds), *Controversies in International Corporate Responsibility*. International Corporate Responsibility Series, Vol. 3. Pittsburgh, PA: Carnegie Mellon University, 343–63.

—— (2008a). *Being Innovative by Doing Good. Proceedings of Academy of Innovation and Entrepreneurship 2008*, Beijing: Tsinghua University.

—— (2008b). *Non-government Organizations as the Salt and Light in the Corporate Social Responsibility Movement in China. Proceedings of the 2008 Christian Business Faculty Association Annual Conference*. Indianapolis, IN, U.S.

—— (2009a). Beyond credibility of doing business in China: strategies for improving corporate citizenship of foreign multinational enterprises in China, *Journal of Business Ethics*, 86(1).

—— (2009b) Sustainable development and corporate social responsibility of multinational enterprises in China, in McIntyre, J.R., Ivanaj, S. and Ivanaj, V. (eds) *Multinational Enterprises and the Challenge of Sustainable Development*. Cheltenham, UK and Northampton, MA, USA: Edward Elgar, 230–44.

—— (2010a). Political implications of the corporate social responsibility movement in China. *The Journal of International Business Research and Practice (JIBRP)*, 4, 125–34.

—— (2010b). Managing corporate social responsibility as an innovation in China, in Latif, A-H., and Chen, J. (eds), *Innovation in Business and Enterprise: Technologies and Frameworks*. Hershey, PA: IGI Global Publications, 224–38.

—— (2010c). Beyond legal compliance. Toward better corporate citizenship of foreign multinational enterprises in China. *Journal of Biblical Integration in Business*, 13, 100–109.

—— (2011a). Becoming corporate socially responsible foreign multinational enterprises in China. *The Journal of International Business Research and Practice (JIBRP)*, 5, 47–61.

—— (2011b). Successful strategies for sustainability of foreign multinational enterprises in China. *The Journal of International Business Research and Practice*, 5, 89–100.

—— (2011c). Challenges of sustainable environmental programs of foreign multinational enterprises in China. *Management Research Review*, 34(11), 1153–1168.

—— (2011d). Successful strategies for sustainability in China and the global market economy. *International Journal of Sustainable Development*, 3(1), 73–90.

—— (2012a). An alternative paradigm for managing sustainability in the global supply chain. *International Journal of Social Ecology and Sustainable Development* (forthcoming).

—— (2012b). A best practice of corporate social responsibility: Going beyond words on a page and a check, in Jaworski, J. (ed.), *Advances in Sociology Research*, 13, 157–64.

—— (2012c). The Corporate social responsibility movement in China: What can foreign corporations' corporate social responsibility programs in China do to universal values?, in Keping, W. (ed.), *Dialogue Among Cultures: Peace, Justice and Harmony. Proceedings of ISUD 8th World Congress*, Beijing: Foreign Languages Press.

Logsdon, J.M. and Wood, D.J. (2005). Global business citizenship and voluntary codes of ethical conduct. *Journal of Business Ethics*, 59, 55–67.

Ma, Q. (2006). *Non-governmental Organizations in Contemporary China: Paving the Way to Civil Society?* London: Routledge.

Matten, D. and Moon, J. (2008). 'Implicit' and 'explicit' CSR: A conceptual framework for a comparative understanding of corporate social responsibility. *Academy of Management Review*, 33, 404–424.

McGinnis, A., Pellegrin, J., Shum, Y., Teo, J. and Wu, J. (2010). *The Sichuan Earthquake and the Changing Landscape of CSR in China.* Available at: http://knowledge.wharton.upenn.edu [accessed: 6 October 2010].

McWilliams, A. and Siegel, D. (2001). Corporate social responsibility: a theory of firm perspective. *Academy of Management Review*, 26(1): 117–27.

Murdoch, H. and Gould, D. (2004). *Corporate Social Responsibility in China: Mapping the Environment. A Study Commissioned by the Global Alliance for Communities and Workers.* Baltimore, MD: GA Publication Series.

National Development and Reform Commission of China (2009). *Implementation of the Bali Roadmap: China's Position on the Copenhagen Climate Change Conference*, May 20, 2009. Available at: http://www.en.ndrc.gov.cn [accessed: 26 September 2012].

O'Connell, Mauren (2009). *Compassion: Loving Our Neighbor in an Age of Globalization.* New York: Orbis Books.

OECD (2000). *OECD Guidelines for Multinational Enterprises: 2000 Review.* Paris: Organisation for Economic Co-operation and Development. Available at: http://www.oecd.org [accessed: 26 September 2012].

Oliver, C. (1991). Strategic responses to institutional processes. *Academy of Management Review*, 16, 145–79.

Reich, R. (2007). *Supercapitalism: The Transformation of Business, Democracy and Everyday Life.* New York: Alfred A. Knopf.

—— (2010a). *Disney, Walmart and ICTI Together Make Workers Rights' Violations Normal and Sustainable.* Kowloon, Hong Kong: Students and Scholars Against Corporate Misbehaviour. Available at: http://sacom.hk/archivers/748 [accessed: 16 November 2010].

SACOM (2010b). *Dying Young: Suicide and China's Booming Economy.* Kowloon, Hong Kong: Students and Scholars Against Corporate Misbehaviour. Available at: http://sacom.hk/wp-content/uploads/2010/05/dying-young_sucide-chinas-booming-economy.pdf [accessed: 16 November 2010].

Sum, N.L. and Ngai, P. (2005). Globalization and paradoxes of ethical transnational production: Code of conduct in a Chinese workplace. *Competition and Change*, 9(2), 181–200.

Syntao (2008). *A Journey to Discover Values 2008: Study of Sustainability.* Available at: http://syntao.com/Uploads/%7B065554F3-B9D7-4DDC-8BA9-3DFE894119A9%7D_A%20journey%20to%20discover%20values%202008.pdf [accessed: 11 November 2013].

Syntao (2010). *Socially Responsible Investment in China.* [Online – blog [in Chinese].] Available at: http://syntao.blog.sohu.com [accessed: 23 November 2013].

Tateisi, N. (2004). *Corporate Social Responsibility Leads to Sustainable Economic Growth in China – Observations from the Leader of the CBCC Dialogue Mission on CSR in the People's Republic of China.* Available at: http://www.keidanren.or.jp/CBCC/english/report/2004 [accessed: 8 September 2006].

UN Global Compact (n.d.). The Ten Principles. Geneva: United Nations. [Online.] Available at: http://www.unglobalcompact.org/AboutTheGC/TheTenPrinciples/index.html [accessed: 23 October 2011].

Vaill, P. (1996). *Learning as a Way of Being: Strategies for Survival in a World of Permanent White Water.* San Francisco: Jossey-Bass.

—— (2007). Organizational epistemology: Interpersonal relations in organizations and the emergence of wisdom, in Kessler, E. and Bailey, J. (eds.), *The Handbook of Managerial and Organizational Wisdom.* Thousand Oaks, CA: Sage Publications, 327–55

van Tulder, R. and van der Zwart, A. (2006). *International Business–Society Management.* Oxford: Routledge.

Visser, W. (2008). Corporate social responsibility in developing countries, in Crane, A., McWilliams, A., Matten, D. and Siegel D. (eds), *The Oxford Handbook of Corporate Social Responsibility*. Oxford: Oxford University Press, 473–502.

Waddock, S. (2008). Building a new institutional infrastructure for corporate responsibility. *Academy of Management Perspectives,* 16, 312–48.

Wang, J. and Chaudhri, V. (2009). Corporate social responsibility engagement and communication by Chinese companies. *Public Relations Review*, 35, 247–50.

Wilson, S. (2009). *Remade in China: Foreign Investors and Institutional Change in China*. New York: Oxford University Press.

Wood, C.H. and Kaufman, A. (2007). The communication of corporate social responsibility (CSR) through the supply chain: an SME perspective, in Susman Gerald I. (ed.), *Small and Medium-Sized Enterprises and the Global Economy*. Cheltenham, UK and Northampton, MA: Edward Elgar, 140–53

World Business Council for Sustainable Development (2005). *Perspective: Corporate Responsibility and Business Success in China*. Available at: http://www.wbcsd.org [accessed: 14 August 2006].

Zadek, S. (2004) The path to corporate responsibility. *Harvard Business Review*, December, 125–32.

4 The Economic and Social Impact of Multinational Corporations in Romania

MATTHIAS S. FIFKA AND IOANA TEODOREANU

Abstract

This chapter notes that the role that multinational corporations (MNCs) can play in the social and economic development of countries, especially developing and emerging ones, has been controversially discussed since the 1970s. With the advent of corporate social responsibility (CSR) this discussion has received new input. In this context, this paper aims at examining the economic and social impact of the CSR activities of MNCs in Romania as a transition country. To do this, it analyses the specific national political and socio-economic background for CSR and its development as a first step. Afterwards, business operations and CSR activities of MNCs are investigated and three case studies are presented. Our findings show that the understanding of CSR is mostly reduced to philanthropy and does not encompass core business activities. Moreover, governmental and civil society initiatives to promote CSR are very weak. We conclude that the potential of CSR to contribute to economic and social development in Romania is not being used.

Introduction

Corporate social responsibility (CSR) has received increasing attention since the turn of the millennium, also in Eastern Europe, as a number of studies show (Alon et al., 2010; Baskin, 2006; Kuznetsov et al., 2009; Kuzentsova, 2009; Li et al., 2010; Preuss and Barkemeyer, 2011; Soboleva, 2006). Nevertheless, due to their communist past and the dominant function of the government in providing social and economic development, the Eastern European transition economies have a history that is a burden for the establishment of CSR. Moreover, today, their governments are often torn by political strife, legislatures are unstable and legal systems are weak. Thus, political actors are either unwilling or unable to undertake necessary reform initiatives, including in the social and environmental arenas.

In this context, multinational corporations (MNCs) play a special role, as they have entered those countries in search of cheap labour, low environmental standards and promising markets, since consumers had to make up for the deprivation faced during communist times. Due to their economic importance, questions arise as to what degree

MNCs actually contribute to social and economic development, and if they use their potential to bring about progress in these areas (Nicolini and Resmini, 2010). Furthermore, it can be asked whether MNCs can become levers for socio-economic development through their CSR activities?

To address these questions we have selected the example of Romania, which became a member of the European Union (EU) in 2007. Despite this significant achievement, the country is still in a long and difficult process of transition, even more than two decades after the communist regime was overthrown. Together with Bulgaria, the country still has the lowest gross disposable income of all 27 EU members, which only amounts to 41 per cent of the EU average (Eurostat 2012b). On the Corruptions Perception Index published annually by Transparency International (2012), it only ranks 66th and finds itself ranged with countries like Ghana, Lesotho and Saudi Arabia.

In order to examine the social and economic contribution of CSR activities by foreign MNCs in Romania, we will first examine the understanding of CSR in Romania to provide the specific national context. After that, we will analyse specific actions of MNCs and their impact, including interaction with governmental and non-governmental actors, as MNCs certainly do not act in isolation. The investigation of how MNCs respond to the interests and demands of different categories of stakeholders is necessary to understand the relationship between goals on one side and the respective actions and their effectiveness on the other. To better illustrate these relationships and interplays, we will present several small case studies and examples.

CSR and Romania – A Difficult Story

As is pointed out above, the development and understanding of CSR in Romania have been marked by the country's communist history. After the Second World War, the country was within the Soviet sphere of influence. This resulted in strong efforts towards collectivization and the abolition of private property, which were brought to a 'successful' end in the early 1960s. Likewise, isolation from the United States and Western European countries was attempted, because they were regarded as having a negative influence on socialist doctrines and were perceived to encourage an unwanted emancipation at all levels (Dutu et al., 2002). Thus, the country was closed to ideas about CSR, which had begun to develop in the West in the 1950s, until the revolution in Romania started in December 1989.

Its success and the ousting of the communist regime led to widespread euphoria in the country in the early 1990s, based on hopes for a better life through political, social and economic progress. However, the transition from communism to capitalism involved considerable social and economic costs. The lack of solid legislation, a well-connected industrial system and structured socio-economic remedies created significant problems. However, instead of integrating private actors, such as businesses, to address these issues, the government – following old patterns – continued to play an excessive role in the newly emerging social and political life, leading to serious imbalances (Korka, 2004). This reflects the difficulty of achieving a change of attitude and mentality.

Thus, it comes as no surprise that it took Romania's government over 13 years, until 2002, to become aware of CSR and its potential to at least make a small contribution to solving the country's social and economic problems. This development was mainly driven by the new Prime Minister, Adrian Nastase, who admitted the grave necessity for establishing a CSR policy (Stancu and Olteanu, 2008).

Nevertheless, the effort of the government to design a national strategy for CSR still did not represent a priority and the notion of CSR remained rather limited. CSR was primarily seen as philanthropic activity characterized by donations. The idea of a broader engagement that would concern the whole value chain and address wider social and economic problems did not feature prominently, if not to say that it did not feature at all. In order to encourage philanthropic actions, the government changed the sponsorship law in 2006. The new law (No. 394/2006) stated that taxpayers who perform sponsorships can deduct the expenses from their income tax if the total of these expenses meets two conditions:

1. it is within a limit of 3 per cent of total turnover;
2. and does not exceed 20 per cent of the calculated income tax.

Though narrow in scope, there at least was a positive attempt to foster charitable business donations through legal reform. The result, however, was rather unwanted, as the new law became a vehicle for eluding state taxes. On a large scale, companies began to sponsor non-profit organizations, mostly in the form of foundations that they had previously set up. A company's managers often acted as chairmen of those foundations, which guaranteed control over their activities. In 2009, the respectable number of over 23,000 foundations existed in Romania (FDSC, 2011).

Many of the foundations established by companies served two primary purposes. The first was to reduce tax payments, as just pointed out. The second was to serve as political vehicles totransmit business interests. It is not without irony that those foundations could even get additional public funding due to the favourable legal framework.

Membership in the EU had a significant impact on social and economic development, but also on CSR, and created an optimistic atmosphere in that regard (Iamandi, 2011). First of all, it required extensive privatizations demanded by the European Commission as a prerequisite for accession. These privatizations, though being a step towards the economic progress of the country, also raised numerous questions marks, especially with regard to MNCs, which are the subject of this study. A striking example in this context was the speedy privatization process of Petrom. In 2004, 51 per cent of the state-owned oil company were sold to the Austrian group OMV. This sale was explicitly imposed on Romania as a precondition for EU entry approval and was highly lucrative for OMV. It is noteworthy that the elements of the deal were not made public for a long time and the respective contract was only declassified in 2011.

Concerning CSR, the increasing presence of MNCs like OMV – also already before EU membership – helped to promote ideas of social responsibility. Thus, CSR can largely be seen as an 'import' brought by Western companies. Most of the respective actions, however, remained confined to the community level and were of a rather sporadic nature, mainly in the form of donations (Dobrea, 2007). Local small and medium-sized enterprises (SMEs) slowly began to follow that trend (Bibu et al., 2010).It has to be pointed out that the sporadic character of most activities can be attributed not only to the companies' lack of dedication but also to the perpetual legislative volatility and the patchy, constantly modified fiscal code, to which companies, especially MNCs, had to react.

The shortcomings of the governmental framework were also pointed out by a report conducted by the consulting company AccreoTax and (2011), entitled *Review of Tax Incentives in the Context of CSR in Selected European Countries*. The report finds that the Romanian government provides little support for CSR and there are no financial incentives to introduce environmentally friendly technologies. The focus is solely on the social area, where donations and sponsorships by companies are being promoted through tax incentives, as described above. According to the report, stimulation of a sustainable economic development is not attempted by the government, and fundamental problems relating to economic, environmental and social development remain unaddressed.

The inconsistency of governmental CSR policy continued with the publication in 2011 of the 'National Strategy for the Promotion of CSR – 2011–2016'. This strategy had been developed without consulting experts in the field and without organizing a public debate. It consisted solely of assumptions made by the government, which wanted to secure EU funding, and was published in a simple press communication. Unsurprisingly, the document followed the EU understanding of CSR at this point of time, which claimed that CSR was purely of a voluntary nature. For Romania and the MNCs operating there, this has two adverse implications. On the one side, regarding CSR as voluntary initiative falls considerably short of the ideal in Romania, since issues like employee rights or environmental protection are gravely unaddressed by the law, and CSR will not act as a driver to improve legislation in these areas. On the other side, the voluntary notion of CSR gives companies, especially MNCs, which come from countries where social and environmental standards are considerably higher, much room to proactively design CSR and to tailor it to their needs and those of their stakeholders. One could even argue that the absence of effective and far-reaching legal standards places a moral obligation on MNCs to at least attempt to contribute voluntarily to the economic and social development of the country. Thus, it is up to them to prove that CSR can make valuable contributions for both sides.

MNCs and Their Role in the Development of Romania – 'The Modern Veni, Vidi, Vici'

In communist Romania, the concept of MNCs was rather an enigma for ordinary citizens, although there were already about one hundred foreign companies which operated under the Ceausescu regime in the 1980s (Roibu, 2008). Large foreign companies such as Xerox, Dow Chemical, General Electric and even luxury brands like Dior or Chanel, providing products for the elite, survived in an entirely controlled economic market, because Romania could not produce many products itself and was dependent on these MNCs.

After the fall of communism, the MNCs already present in the country were quickly joined by other MNCs following the lure of a fairly large market of 22 million people and low labour costs. Coca Cola (entering the country in 1991), Alcatel (1991), Japan Tobacco International (1993), McDonald's (1995), Unilever (1995), Shell (1996), and Renault (1999)are just a few of the corporations that started operations in Romania in the 1990s. However, due to difficulties of transition and political instability, economic development was weak, as in 1999, Romania had just completed three years of successive contraction of the economy, at about 5 per cent each year and inflation levels were close to 100 per cent (Korka, 2004: 10–11).

This resulted in considerable fluctuation of MNCs, as many of them left the country to relocate production elsewhere, e.g. Shell, Kraft, Palmolive, and Coca Cola. The fluctuation inevitably demonstrated the dependence of Romania on foreign MNCs and their role in economic and social development. Thus, the country's positive development with regard to exports during this time, which was often claimed by Romanian politicians to be the result of successful policies, must by seen ambiguously, as observed by Ilie Serbsnescu, the country's former Minister for Reform, who declared 'Those are not our exports [...] they belong to multinationals', explaining that among the top 100 exporters, there were only three Romanian companies, of which one had already ceased to exist. 'Romania finds itself in the situation of a banana republic', a circumstance that neither the Romanian government nor foreign capital could change because they had no real interest in doing so (quoted in Dumitroiu, 2011).

Despite the created dependence, the operations of MNCs have also had, overall, a positive social and economic impact on Romania. The corporations brought foreign direct investments and employment, the internationalization of exports, facilitated access to technology, a larger variety of quality goods and services, and helped to frame a more competitive and successful business environment. However, as will be discussed now, MNCs in Romania have also acted in ways that have substantially undermined social and economic development, and their CSR activities have been rather superficial.

Extensive Use of Transfer Pricing

The design, if not to say manipulation, of transfer prices is neither new nor unique to Romania. Instead, it has become a common business practice of MNCs to reduce their tax load. However, in the case of Romania, the extensive use of transfer pricing by MNCs has been highly unfavourable for the country because of weak legal structures and its high dependence on MNCs.

In 2011, the ten largest companies in Romania, according to annual turnover, were all affiliates of MNCs (David, 2012). Despite sustained growth of turnover, most of them have increasingly reported financial losses. This practice of minimizing profits and repatriating profits through transfer pricing became so extensive in Romania that it alerted The National Agency for Fiscal Administration (NAFA) to start the investigation of a number of MNCs. Although irregularities were identified, the names of the companies in question were not made public. The problem still exists today; it is estimated that MNCs evaded about €8.6 billion in taxes in 2011 (Buscu, 2011).

MNCs can rely on the support of Romanian clerks for these practices, as is explained by tax lawyer Gheorge Piperea:

> *Consulting companies offer a list with international prices for a certain product to big companies and identify the country with the highest price. The mother company will mandate its subsidiary in Romania to buy the product from the country with the highest price. The product thus is being bought perfectly legally from another subsidiary of the same group and this way the profit stays within the corporation, but escapes taxation in Romania. Aside from the consultancies, even employees of NAFA and politicians are involved in this process and are paid in various ways for their services. For a list of transfer prices, companies pay up to €100.000, but the gains are in the range of tens of millions. (Quoted in Buscu, 2011)*

The Romanian fiscal authority, NAFA, has not taken any far-reaching measures against this practice, aside from some preliminary investigations. Nevertheless, legal procedures have been started against the former director and several employees of NAFA for complicity in tax evasion.

With regard to CSR, this tax evasion is an interesting phenomenon. It usually takes place in a grey legal area and cannot be seen as an outright violation of the law. Nevertheless, the fair payment of taxes represents a sine qua non for a company that seeks to be recognized as a socially responsible member of society and acts accordingly. Only after such basic obligations are met can further commitment to stakeholders be discussed.

Multinationals and Non-governmental Organizations in Romania – A Two-sided Interaction

Owing to the absence of government in the promotion of CSR, non-governmental organizations (NGOs) have played a considerable role in Romania, as observed by the Carpathian Foundation (2007: 22): 'At a national level, CSR practice follows a clear positive trend. Companies and NGOs are the main actors [...] in this field, with little involvement of government and mass media sectors.'

As in other countries, MNCs in Romania sought collaboration with NGOs to identify country-specific stakeholder interests and demands. This marks an integral part of developing a CSR strategy in the first place, independent of the country in question (Crespy and Miller, 2010). In Romania, owing to a lack of local infrastructure and poor social and educational facilities, the majority of MNCs have started community development projects, often in collaboration with NGOs, or have provided financing for projects initiated by NGOs.

This cooperation, however, has two sides. On the one side, it enables MNCs to identify local needs and to address these more effectively through collaboration with NGOs that are familiar with the local situation. For the NGOs, in turn, this collaboration means access to financial resources they would otherwise not enjoy. On the other side, however, the question on the independence of NGOs arises, since they and their projects run the risk of becoming dependent on financial injections from MNCs and, thus, of losing their balancing function. Moreover, in public perception, this might lead to them being perceived as puppets of the MNCs.

Furthermore, providing financial support for development projects, as has primarily been the role of MNCs in Romania, represents a rather narrow notion of CSR, which could most appropriately be described as traditional 'corporate citizenship', consisting exclusively of philanthropy. Aside from its narrow scope, such a monetary approach to CSR also carries the inherent risk that it is highly dependent on the financial success of a company. As a recent study of CSR in Romania has shown, charitable activities of MNCs were reduced in the wake of the financial crisis, which created problems for the NGOs that relied on the contributions (Iamandi et al., 2010).

By most accounts, CSR by MNCs in Romania does not go beyond charitable activities that are made public with a great fanfare. Semida Duriga, a director of a large advertising company, points out the dominance of this understanding among companies in Romania:

For some, CSR just means paying for the sins they have committed. They undertake actions with a social impact attempting to compensate for the negative side effects of their large-scale production activities, such as pollution. For others, it is a matter of pride [...] Charitable actions are accompanied by expensive publicity efforts... It is a kind of possession statement [mandatory for politicians in Romania] that is attached to an aura of generosity. (Duriga, 2012)

Overall, the narrow notion of CSR displayed by MNCs and NGOs alike are problematic for the development of broader and more far-reaching CSR strategies. The perception of MNCs as 'cash cows', displayed by many NGOs, is as cumbersome as is the idea of MNCs that donations are a sufficient contribution to the social and economic development of the country.

The developments, understandings and shortcomings just described will now be illustrated by three case studies involving MNCs.

Case Studies

THE OMV-PETROM CASE – CSR AS DISGUISE

The acquisition of Petrom by the Austrian oil corporation OMV has been one of the most controversial events in the economic history of Romania after the fall of communism. It has been described as a 'robbery' of national heritage and a sale not in the country's interest, as Petrom soon began to generate large profits for OMV. The corporation became subject to fierce criticism for charging customers high prices at gas stations, arguing that this was a result of the high prices for oil on the world market, exceeding $100 per barrel. However, the price for extracting oil from the Romanian oil fields operated by Petrom amounted to only $16 per barrel.

For the year 2011, OMV Group reported a net profit of €1.57 billion, an increase of 30 per cent in comparison with the previous year. More than half of this profit – €866 million – was generated by Petrom. Thus, it is no surprise that Romanians have begun to see OMV as depriving them of the natural resources of their own country and 'robbing' the country of substantial economic benefit, as the profits are mostly transferred to the mother company.

With regard to CSR, Petrom is – without question – one of the most active companies in the country. Its website is one of the few corporate websites in Romania that has a section on CSR and even the annual CSR budget and its allocation are mentioned. What is remarkable is that Petrom began to significantly expand its CSR activities in 2007 and to launch a €5 million CSR campaign, exactly at the time when the mass media began to publish details about the deal for Petrom's sale that had been made in 2004. It became known that the contract contained clauses that clearly were unfavorable for Romania and had most likely been agreed on because of corrupt practices. The Romanian Prime Minister during the time the contract was signed, Adrian Nastase, was sentenced to two years in prison because of 'acts of corruption' in 2012, which were not directly related to the Petrom case, however.

To counter the dissatisfaction and even anger voiced by the media and the public, the CSR campaign that Petrom started aimed at improving education, health, the environment and communities. To illustrate this intention, Mariana Gheorghe, Petrom's CEO, stated:

> *Social responsibility, next to sustainable development, must be integrated in all activities of a company. I am referring to the way in which the business strategy is designed in order to give the company the possibility to be successful in the long run, to business ethics, and to the rigorous evaluation of the social and environmental impact of any project we start. Corporate social responsibility must not be a simple way to improve the company's image and its perception from outside. (Petrom, 2008)*

At the same time, however, Petrom continued to progressively increase the price for fuel, even during the financial crisis. From 2009 until 2011, the price for fuel increased by 50 per cent, according to the National Institute of Statistics for Romania. Like other oil companies, Petrom invoked the world oil price as an explanation, which falls short, however, as the company has the right to extract oil from Romanian oil fields until 2015. Moreover, the price increase came in concert with Petrom's direct competitors, Rompetrol, MOL, ENI and Lukoil, which do not have access to Romania's oil fields and have to import. This made 'price fixing' by Petrom even more evident. More attention was brought to the matter by a decision of the National Council of Competition made in January of 2012, which found Petrom, Rompetrol, ENI, MOL, and Lukoil guilty of an agreement to jointly withdraw the fuel type of Eco Premium from the market.

This case clearly illustrates the disparity between CSR displayed to the outside by philanthropic activities and the obvious absence of responsibility in the core business operations. When such fundamental responsibilities are lacking, CSR activities on the surface are hardly convincing and must be judged as a disguise for improper business activities. This does not necessarily mean that the philanthropic activities cannot contribute to social and economic development, but by neglecting core responsibilities – fair pricing in the case of Petrom – the country is inevitably deprived of a larger economic benefit.

RENAULT-DACIA – A MORE PROFOUND CSR

In July 1999, Romanian car manufacturer Dacia became part of the Renault Group. By injecting large amounts of capital, estimated at a total of €2 billion by the end of 2012, Renault considerably invested in its daughter company. So far, this investment can be judged as beneficial for Renault as well as for Romania. Moreover, Renault carefully went about implementing a profound CSR strategy that took into consideration the needs of its stakeholders.

As a first step, Renault identified all relevant stakeholders and held dialogues to get an idea of the salient issues. Though it did not initiate a broad CSR offensive as a second step, it carefully developed programmes that addressed the crucial issues previously identified. Moreover, in comparison to other MNCs, at Dacia an efficient communications system between management and employees was set up to allow employees to voice concerns. Moreover, Dacia employees earn average monthly wages in the region of €500, while the national average does not exceed €350, and are given a wide variety of professional development opportunities. Thus, CSR did not remain confined to outside philanthropic activities, but also encompassed core business processes. Dacia, like other companies, used its CSR activities for marketing purposes, but in its case these were highly credible due to the policies that had previously been developed in the crucial areas.

The trust in Renault-Dacia developed by stakeholders also became evident when the company announced that it was considering relocating a part of the production to Morocco, as explained by Carol Tavares, the operational director of the Renault Group:

> First I have to say that the world is in continuous change and evolution. Therefore, for every one of us new challenges come along. Romania as a country is no exception to that. The situation of the industry in Romania is one of which we are proud. We have both: quality on the engineering side as well as on the manufacturing side. Yet, things don't stop here. There is always the possibility that operation sites will be moved, either to Morocco or to other countries in Africa [...]. Romania must be careful not to lose its competitiveness. (Quoted in ZF Auto & Transporturi, 2012)

What is remarkable about this event is that the anger of the employees did not turn against Renault-Dacia, as one would expect, but against the Romanian government, since it did not accomplish what had been agreed on in the contract on the Dacia purchase made with Renault. According to Nicolae Pavelescu, the Dacia Union leader, the government of Romania had promised to resolve infrastructure problems, which were regarded as insufficient by Renault, but did not live up to these promises (Enache, 2012).

Thus, the employees clearly saw the neglect on the side of the Romanian authorities and understood Renault's concerns well. In their eyes, Renault had displayed the appropriate responsibility towards them – including fair wages, development opportunities, and the possibility to voice concerns – but could not be held responsible for obligations that were not met by the government. Indeed, CSR in general cannot be regarded as a means of compensating for governmental failure. If treated correctly, stakeholders understand very well that companies are not charitable organizations and need to consider basic conditions for conducting business, such as a working infrastructure.

In this case, the potential economic and social development of the country was endangered by the Romanian government itself and not by Renault as a MNC. The fact that Dacia contributed 2.9 per cent to Romanian GDP in 2011 should have made the government aware of the corporation's significant economic contribution to the entire country. Moreover, there had already been clear signs that foreign MNCs were hesitant to invest in Romania because of bad infrastructure. In 2010, the German Ambassador Andreas von Mettenheim stated explicitly that Daimler had decided in favour of setting up a plant in neighbouring Hungary due to the poor state of infrastructure in Romania. This meant a loss of over €1 billion in foreign direct investment (Just-Auto, 2008), and prevented further economic growth.

Only in rare cases are MNCs willing and able to compensate for the failure of public authorities in market economies, as the following case shows, where an MNC invested substantially in communities vital for its operations (Baleanu et al., 2011).

VODAFONE – IMPROVING HEALTHCARE AND IMAGE IN THE ABSENCE OF GOVERNMENT

An example of a MNC significantly compensating for governmental failure is the cooperation between the British telecommunications company Vodafone and the Romanian emergency rescue service SMURD (Serviciul Mobil de Urgenţă Reanimareşi Descarcerare [Mobile emergency service for resuscitation and extrication]).

The insufficient funding of the Romanian medical system and the resulting lack of facilities and equipment is a grave problem for the country.

Although Vodafone is not a medical equipment provider, an engagement in the area of emergency rescue was a good match, since telecommunications technology is vital for establishing an efficient and quick rescue service. Thus, Vodafone placed it at the centre of its CSR activities. The partnership with SMURD was initiated in 2005 through funding communications services, and Vodafone invested the considerable sum of €1.1 million. In return, Vodafone attempted to profit from the excellent image of SMURD through an image transfer, as pointedly remarked by Dochita Zenoveiov, a well-known branding specialist in Romania: 'SMURD is a clean brand with a solid reputation. Therefore, whoever is found in its presence will have a clean image as well' (quoted in Stefan, 2012).

There is nothing wrong with attempting an image transfer through sponsorship activities, but in the case of Vodafone seeking a 'clean' image seemed to be essential in Romania after the National Council of Competition had started an investigation into the corporation's business practices in 2006. Vodafone was accused of anti-competitive practices and the abuse of its dominant market position, resulting in a fine of €28.3 million. Vodafone appealed against the decision, and the trial is still pending at this point in time.

Although Vodafone had carefully identified a substantial shortcoming in the provision of medical services for the public and reacted to that by cooperating with a renowned and reliable partner, once again this initiative must be seen against a rather doubtful background. By engaging in anti-competitive practices – though no final decision has been made yet – the corporation has violated a core responsibility of any business: fair competition. By committing such a violation of basic business principles, all exceeding responsibility measures hardly seem credible. With regard to social and economic development, the remarkable investment of €1.1 million in the country's medical rescue system is 'eaten up' by the economic damage caused through the anti-competitive practices.

Conclusion

In conclusion, it can be said that the contribution of MNCs towards social and economic development in Romania provides a mixed picture, as is the case with regard to CSR. Though it remains out of question that MNCs have brought foreign direct investment to Romania, as they have to other countries, and created employment, and facilitated access to technology and a wider variety of goods and services, there is also clear evidence – as just described – that they have deprived the country of economic and social benefit through irresponsible or even illegal business practices. It is certainly not possible to calculate the contribution of one or more companies to the social and economic development of a country, since the latter is dependent on many factors. Nevertheless, it can be stated that CSR, as is demonstrated above, can make valuable contributions to a country's development, if it is understood broadly and applied consequently on the different levels of business activity.

However, the understanding of CSR as displayed by MNCs in Romania has mostly been philanthropic and does not encompass core business activities. Inevitably, such a notion falls short of true responsibility and must be perceived as a mere attempt to improve reputation or even to cover up foul behaviour. This perspective is, however, short-sighted. Long-term benefits for the company and for society, as the case of Renault-Dacia shows, can only be created if CSR encompasses the core business activities and includes a firm's stakeholders.

Nevertheless, MNCs as economic actors cannot be solely blamed for not displaying the necessary responsibility in the case of Romania. Governmental authorities that are highly corrupt do not provide an example for ethical business behaviour. Moreover, governmental initiatives to promote CSR through legal obligations and voluntary recommendations have been mostly absent. Thus, MNCs largely operate in terra incognita with regard to CSR in Romania. Although most MNCs have to follow strict social and environmental standards in their home countries and have implemented broad CSR programmes there, the transfer of their activities to host countries with weak legal systems is difficult and standards are often considered to be of lesser importance when the subsidiaries are left without any guidance (Levy and Kaplan, 2008). Overall, government policy in Romania has not created a favorable environment for CSR.

NGOs have partly filled this void, but their function to provide guidance for and a balance to MNCs is partly undermined by the fact that they are dependent on the MNCs for funding. However, a growing public discussion on CSR issues can be observed in Romania (Bibu et al., 2010). The public increasingly demands responsibility from MNCs, and failures and scandals are increasingly covered on the Internet. This development can be expected to lead to more pressure for MNCs to act according to public expectations. Furthermore, the country's continuously poor economic situation on the one side and large corporate profits on the other have led people to question the factual contribution that MNCs make to economic and social development. In 2010, approximately 41 per cent of the population, which equals more than 8.89 million people, was at risk of poverty or social exclusion (Eurostat, 2012a), while the affiliates of MNCs generated substantial profit, as the case of Petrom demonstrates.

Despite increasing public pressure on MNCs, it can be expected that the way to a more profound CSR of MNCs in Romania will still be a long and winding one. The country's ongoing struggle to establish a functioning democracy is reflected in the struggle to come to terms with CSR, especially on the governmental side. In 1990, the well-known political analyst Silviu Brucan (2004) predicted that Romanians would need 20 years to master democracy. Today, more than 20 years after this prediction, Romanians are still struggling to achieve this mastery. Considering that CSR became an issue in the country only after the millennium, one might be inclined to say that it will take until after 2020 for Romania come to terms with CSR, although MNCs could contribute to accelerating this process. At the moment, the disregard of CSR by all actors – government, business and civil society – robs the country of social and economic development potential.

References

AccreoTaxand (2011). *Review of Tax Incentives in the Context of CSR in Selected European Countries*. Warsaw: AccreoTaxand.

Alon, I., Lattemann, C., Fetscherin, M., Li, S. and Schneider, A.M. (2010). Usage of public corporate communications of social responsibility in Brazil, Russia, India and China (BRIC). *International Journal of Emerging Markets*, 5(1), 6–22.

Baleanu, T.E., Chelcea, L. and Stancu, A. (2011). The social responsibility of the top 100 Romanian companies. An analysis of corporate websites. *Amfiteatru Economic*, 13(29), 235–48.

Baskin, J. (2006). Corporate responsibility in emerging markets. *The Journal of Corporate Citizenship*, 24, 29–47.

Bibu, N., Nastase, M. and Gligor, D.C. (2010). The perception over corporate social responsibility in Romania. *Review of International Comparative Management*, 11(5), 764–78.

Brucan, S. (2004). *Profetiidespretrecutsidespreviitor – De ce a ramasRoamania in urmasi cat vamaidura* [Prophecies about past and future – why Romania did not evolve and how much more it will take]. EGO Publicistica. Bucharest: Editura Polirom.

Buscu, S. (2011). Noul El-Dorado pentruangajaţiistatului care se 'reprofilează' înconsultanţă: preţurile de transfer. *Romania Libera*, 13 June. Available at:http://www.romanialibera.ro/bani-afaceri/companii/noul-el-dorado-pentru-angajatii-statului-care-se-reprofileaza-in-consultanta-preturile-de-transfer-228125.html [accessed: 18 October 2012].

Carpathian Foundation (2007). *The Way It Works – Corporate Social Responsibility in the Carpathian Region*. Kosice, Slovakia: Carpathian Foundation.

Crespy, C.T. and Miller, V.V. (2010). Sustainability reporting: a comparative study of NGOs and MNCs. *Corporate Social Responsibility and Environmental Management*, 18(5), 275–84.

David, I. (2012). *Topulcelormaimaricompanii din România*. ZF Companii. Available at: http://www.zf.ro/companii/topul-celor-mai-mari-companii-din-romania-9688890 [accessed: 18 October 2012].

Dobrea, R.C. (2007). Managementul organizatiilorsi Responsabilitatea Sociala Corporativa, [Organizational management and CSR]. *Administratiesi Management Public*, 7, 89–93.

Dumitroiu, O. (2011). Mirajulexporturilorromanesti: multinationalelecastiga, Romania ramane 'bananiera'. *Business24*, 12 April. Available at: http://www.business24.ro/dacia/stiri-dacia/mirajul-exporturilor-romanesti-multinationalele-castiga-romania-ramane-bananiera-1489411 [accessed: 24 September 2012].

Duriga, S. (2012). *Responsabilitatea, intregenerozitatesi business. Responsabilitate Sociala*. Available at: http://www.responsabilitatesociala.ro/editoriale/responsabilitatea-intre-generozitate-si-business.html [accessed: 20 October 2012].

Dutu, A., Negreanu, I.A., Istratescu, E., Popa, V., Ignat, M., Osca, A. and Tunareanu, N. (2002). *România – viaţa politică în documente* [Romania – political life in documents]. Bucharest: The National Archives of Romania.

Enache, S. (2012). *Renault arata pisica autoritatilor de la Bucuresti. Ce ar insemna plecarea francezilor pentru Romania?* Finantistii, 2 October. Available at: http://www.finantistii.ro/companii/renault-arata-pisica-autoritatilor-de-la-bucuresti-ce-ar-insemna-plecarea-francezilor-pentru-romania-75296 [accessed: 25 November 2012].

Eurostat (2012a). *At Risk of Poverty or Social Exclusion in the EU27*. European Commission: Eurostat, 8 February. Available at: http://epp.eurostat.ec.europa.eu/cache/ITY_PUBLIC/3-08022012-AP/EN/3-08022012-AP-EN.PDF [accessed: 25 November 2012].

Eurostat (2012b). *Income Per Capita Varied By 1 to 4 Across EU Countries*. European Commission: Eurostat. Available at: http://epp.eurostat.ec.europa.html [accessed: 25 November 2012].

FDSC (2011). *Atlasul Economiei Sociale* [The atlas of social economy]. Bucharest: Fundaţia pentru dezvoltarea societăţii civile.

Iamandi, I.E. (2011). Application of corporate social responsibility models in Romania in the context of the post-accession to the European Union. *Economic Transdisciplinarity Cognition*, 14(1), 27–35.

Iamandi, I.E., Constantin, L.G. and Joldes, C.S.R. (2010). Corporate social responsibility during the economic crisis. The case of the Romanian companies. *Journal of the Faculty of Economics, University of Oradea*, 1(2), 963–69.

Just-Auto (2008). *Romania – Infrastructure Issues Critical to Daimler Plant Decision*, June 19. [Online auto magazine.] Available at: http://www.just-auto.com/news/infrastructure-issues-critical-to-daimler-plant-decision_id95174.aspx [accessed: 25 October 2012].

Korka, M. (2004). Experiencing corporate social responsibility in Romania. *The Romanian Economic Journal*, 7(14), 529.

Kuznetsov, A., Kuznetsova, O. and Warren, R. (2009). CSR and the legitimacy of business in transition economies: The case of Russia. *Scandinavian Journal of Management*, 25(1), 37–45.

Kuznetsova, O. (2009). CSR in the emerging market of Russia: finding the nexus between business accountability, legitimacy, growth, and societal reconciliation, in Singh, S. (ed.), *Handbook of Business Practices and Growth in Emerging Markets*. London: World Scientific Books, 119–40.

Levy, D. and Kaplan, R. (2008). Corporate social responsibility and theories of global governance: strategic contestation in global issue arenas, in Crane, A., Matten, D., McWilliams, A., Moon, J. and Siegel, D. (eds), *The Oxford Handbook of CSR*. Oxford: Oxford University Press, 432–51.

Li, S., Fetscherin, M., Alon, I., Lattemann, C. and Yeah, K. (2010). Corporate social responsibility in emerging markets. *Management. International Review*, 50, 635–54.

Nicolini, M. and Resmini, L. (2010). FDI spillovers in new EU member states, *Economics of Transition*, 18(3), 487–511.

Petrom (2008). *Despre Petrom. Responsabilitate Sociala*. Bucharest: OMV Petrom S.A. Available at: http://www.responsabilitatesociala.ro/companii/petrom.html [accessed: 24 September 2012].

Preuss, L. and Barkemeyer, R. (2011). CSR priorities of emerging economy firms: is Russia a different shape of BRIC? *Corporate Governance*, 11(4), 371–85.

Roibu, I. (2008). CEO din gardaveche. *Business Magazine*, January 15. Available at: http://www.businessmagazin.ro/analize/industrie/ceo-din-garda-veche-2335702 [accessed: 24 September 2012].

Soboleva, I. (2006). Corporate social responsibility: global context and Russian realities, *Problems of Economic Transition*, 49(8), 82–95.

Stancu, A. and Olteanu, V. (2008). *Corporate Social Responsibility in Romania from a EU Perspective*. Marie Curie Conference. Milan: Fondazione Eni Enrico Mattei.

Stefan, A. (2012). SMURD 'curate' branduri, dar si refuzaceci de donatii. Vezimotivele. *Daily Business*, March 16. Available at: http://www.dailybusiness.ro/stiri-media-marketing/smurd-curata-branduri-dar-si-refuza-zeci-de-donatii-vezi-motivele-74757/ [accessed: 24 October 2012].

Transparency International (2012). Corruptions Perception Index 2012. [Online.] Available at: http://www.transparency.org/cpi2012/results [accessed 23 November 2012].

ZF Auto & Transporturi (2012). *Renault: Oricând putem muta producţia de la Mioveniîn Marocdacă România nu-şi păstrează competitivitatea*. Available at: http://www.zfcorporate.ro/auto-transporturi/renault-oricand-putem-muta-productia-de-la-mioveni-in-maroc-daca-romania-nu-si-pastreaza-competitivitatea-10141520 [accessed: 24 October 2012].

5 A Comparative Study of CSR Practices by Multinational Corporations in their Operations in Developed and Developing Economies

ABUBAKAR SADIQ KASUM AND ASLI YÜKSEL MERMOD

Abstract

This chapter examines the corporate social responsibility (CSR) practices of multinational corporations (MNCs) in their operations in some developed and developing countries. The study specifically compares how CSR is practised by MNCs in the developed countries with that of the developing countries, with the ultimate aim of understanding how influential the CSRs of MNCs are in terms of contributing to socio-economic development of their host countries. The study observes that MNCs, just like every other business unit, are essential to the development stages of every country and some developmental gains have been discovered to accrue from them. It also confirms that MNCs are known to be engaging in CSRs as one of the ways to give back to the communities in which they operate some of the wealth made from them. It observes, however, that there is a wide gap between the CSR practices of MNCs in their operations in developed countries as compared with their operations in the less developed countries. Several factors are responsible for this and those relating to, for example, lower levels of education, lack of awareness of CSR practices and bad leadership in many developing countries are prominent among them. Science, technology, education, research and development, and other sustainable development activities are part of the CSR issues in the developed countries. On the other hand, sport, music, fashion events, leading celebrities' passion for some good causes related to CSR, donations and a handful of infrastructure building projects – roads, electricity, water – which will first serve the needs of MNCs – are their CSR concerns in developing countries. CSR practices therefore contribute further to socio-economic development in developed countries, while close to nothing or further impoverishment is often their result in developing countries. The study aligns with the recommendations that CSR should involve all stakeholders and it should be integrated into education, training and research, with potential funding among other possibilities.

Introduction

It is a popular conclusion that government alone cannot deal with societal issues, including those related to development (Ojo, 2009). 'While governments have traditionally assumed sole responsibility for the improvement of the living conditions of the population, society's needs have exceeded the capabilities of governments to fulfill them' (Jamali and Mirshak, 2007). The business sector provides the economic vehicle for the fundamental human right to development, for all nations as well as individuals. Many governments are thus pinning their hopes of economic growth and technological innovation on strong private sector growth (Fourie, 2009).

Today one of the most popular means by which corporations present and are assessed on their role in society is through the concept of corporate social responsibility (CSR). The World Business Council for Sustainable Development (WBCSD) defines CSR as 'the commitment of business to contribute to sustainable economic development, working with employees, their families and the local communities' (WBCSD, 2001, cited in Jamali and Mirshak, 2007). CSR refers to strategies corporations or firms deploy to conduct their business in a way that is ethical, society-friendly and beneficial to the community in which they operate in terms of development (Ismail, 2009). It is the 'continuing commitment by business to behave ethically and contribute to the economic development while improving the quality of life of the workforce and their families as well as of the local community and society at large' (Holme and Watts, 2000, cited in Lenguyen, 2011). CSR is, therefore, essentially about the relationship between business as an entity and its stakeholders in the community within which the business operates. This perhaps explains why 'Business stakeholders have often been defined as any group or individual who would affect or be affected by the achievement or non-achievement of an organization's objectives' (Freeman, 1984, cited in Lenguyen, 2011). They comprise shareholders and investors, employees, customers, suppliers, governments and other public organizations, trade associations and environmental groups (Clarkson, 1995 and Donaldson and Preston, 1995, cited in Lenguyen, 2011). All these stakeholders are affected by corporate activities and may also have an effect on the corporations.

More than any other business unit, Multinational Corporations (MNCs) are at the centre of CSR discourse. MNCs are spread all over the world and they control a significant percentage of the global economy. Their increased presence in the international political economy has led to the startling reality that companies can be political entities and their influence as political actors can be sizeable, both in positive and negative capacities (Holland, 2010). According to Pimpa (2011), 'it can be argued that the CSR movement would advance if different types of MNCs actively participated in various host country activities' MNCs operate in both developed and underdeveloped countries, which are, of course, characterized by different competencies and needs. Developed countries are characterized by good regulatory and governance systems, and high levels of consumer protection law and customer awareness. On the other hand, 'customers of developing countries are less educated and sometimes don't know their rights or don't care' (Ndzibah and Maxwell, 2008). Their governments have limited capacity to provide good governance and regulatory systems and some governments have institutionalized 'a less regulatory business environment' (Iamandi, 2007).

'While increasing attention has been accorded in recent years to CSR, as a postulate for ethical and responsible behavior in business, very little is known of the practice of CSR in developing countries' (Jamali and Mirshak, 2007). 'Responsibilities assigned to corporations will not be pursued voluntarily' (Kolstad, 2007) in their operations, plus the fact that regulatory framework and consumer education are known to be weak in developing countries. There is therefore a very high probability that CSR delivery may continue to be lopsided in favour of the developed countries. According to Werner (2009), 'there have been many examples in which corporations have taken advantage of developing countries'. Corporations' operations have in addition been criticized for facilitating a situation in developing countries where 'major shops are stocked with inferior products [...] to suit the cheap market, which include electrical and electronic gadgets/appliances, wax prints, [...] second[-hand] goods and discarded gadgets like computers, stereo sets, TVs, industrial machineries, receded tires, etc.' (Ndzibah and Maxwell, 2008); while 'it is evident that the best of technologies, the most innovative products and trends are meant for developed countries as well as the "cream" of every society' (Ndzibah and Maxwell, 2008). By virtue of their wealth, few wealthy citizens of developing countries travel to developed countries to buy these products or import some for consumption by them and their immediate family.

It is against these backgrounds that this study set out to review the CSR practices and the impact of the practices by MNCs on the developed and developing economies of the world. In the remainder of the chapter, the nature and practices of CSR are examined in the section below; the two following sections are devoted to the nature of MNC activities and their CSR practices respectively; there follows a section comparing the CSRs delivered in developed countries with those delivered in developing countries; and then conclusions are drawn.

Corporate Social Responsibility Practices

Fisher (2004) links corporate obligation to all stakeholders, both internal and external. According to him, 'Organizations have a social responsibility to protect and enhance the society in which they operate' (Fisher, 2004). Epstein (1987) sees social responsibility as 'achieving outcomes from organizational decisions concerning specific issues or problems which have beneficial rather than adverse effects upon pertinent corporate stakeholders'. In a similar tone, Strike, Gao and Bansal (2006) define CSR as 'the set of corporate actions that positively affects an identifiable social stakeholder's interests and does not violate the legitimate claims of another identifiable social stakeholder (in the long run)'. Marrewijk (2002) simply defines CSR as a 'more humane, more ethical and a more transparent way of doing business'. Although with different degrees of freedom for corporations, the scholars cited above all believe that an organization is responsible not only to its owners but also to other stakeholders.

In relating social responsibility to ethics, Fisher (2004) states that the 'most widely supported view is that there are four dimensions of corporate social responsibility: economic, legal, ethical and philanthropic'. 'The pyramid places economic responsibilities at the foundation and moving up the pyramid are legal, ethical and philanthropic responsibilities' (Fisher, 2004). Robbins et al. (2000: 183) identify four stages of social responsibility based on stakeholders' categories. They are: shareholders and investors; employees, customers and suppliers; governments and other public organizations; trade associations and environmental groups (Clarkson, 1995 and Donaldson and Preston, 1995, cited in Lenguyen, 2011). Business was originally perceived as being responsible only to shareholders; it was later on extended to include shareholders and employees. At stage three, it was further extended to stakeholders in the specific environment; and at the final stage the society as a whole was included (Robbins et. al., 2000). One way or the other, business is thus responsible to all who would affect or be affected by their activities.

CSR is a concept whereby business organizations consider the interests of society by taking responsibility for the impact of their operations on customers, suppliers, employees, shareholders, communities and other stakeholders, as well as the welfare of the physical environment in the countries where they operate. 'Leaving their stakeholders out of the loop is one of the top mistakes companies make when trying to jump on the green/socially responsible bandwagon. In order for your company to articulate its values, missions, strategy and implementation in the creation of your CSR plan, it is important for everyone to be on the same page' (Lu, 2011). According to Werner (2009), core business activities that can contribute to global development include:

- Producing safe and affordable products and services;
- Generating income and investment;
- Creating jobs;
- Developing human resources;
- Building local businesses;
- Spreading responsible international business standards and practices;
- Supporting technology development and transfer;
- Establishing physical and institutional infrastructure.

According to Kumar and Balakrishnan (2011), CSR activities will involve: measures to sustain the environment; respect for human rights; fair treatment of the workforce, customers and suppliers; being good corporate citizens of the communities in which corporations operate' fair trade conducted on a basis of business ethics; balancing society and community against poverty, illiteracy, ill-health and general low level of awareness; and a pollution-free or safe environment. The concept of CSR put into practice by organizations involves: adopting a highly ethical approach by being transparent and accountable to stakeholders for performance; giving consideration to and actively promoting social responsibility and ecological sustainability; and expressing CSR in an organization's values and integrating its principles within the organization. It also involves open and inclusive stakeholder engagement; seeking out and promoting opportunities to work on mutually beneficial projects with society; and taking care to minimize any adverse impact on the current and future community (EFQM Model 2010, cited in Kumar and Balakrishnan, 2011).'The optimists believe that because businesses are so deeply embedded within the communities they operate, they have great potential to address the social and environmental problems of these communities' (Kamlani, 2011); and 'the question is not whether companies have influence, but whether they use what influence they have responsibly' (Sutherland, cited in Carleton, 2009).

The Nature of MNC Operations

'The increased presence of MNCs in the international political economy has led to the startling reality that companies can be political entities and their influence as political actors can be sizeable, both in positive and negative capacities' (Holland, 2010). This is premised on the extent of operation, level of involvement and the significant value of activities worldwide. 'Although the government plays a leading role in the development of social policy to improve the quality of life of their citizens, international business organizations must play a crucial role in the development of living standards for global citizens' (Pimpa, 2011). However, the turnout of events 'has facilitated a debate in the literature over corporate capacity and responsibility in that role' (Holland, 2010).

An MNC is 'a legal person that owns or controls production, distribution or service, facilities outside the country [where] it is based' (Kamminga, 1999, cited in Amao, 2008). An MNC does not exist as an entity defined or recognized by law, but is made up of complex structures of individual companies (Dine, 2005, cited in Amao, 2008). There are different forms in which MNCs are structured. The head office can be in one country, while production facilities are located in one or more other countries. They can also be organized as a group of companies, where the holding company is located in one country and subsidiaries in one or more other countries; and it can involve the establishment of a headquarters in one country that oversees a diverse conglomeration stretching to many different countries and industries (Ozoigbo and Chukuezi, 2011).

According to Chor, Foley and Manova (2008), MNCs are operated as horizontal, vertical and/or export platform Foreign Direct Investment (FDI). If operated as horizontal FDI, MNCs set up full-edged production facilities in other countries, with the primary intention of selling the output directly to these local markets. If operated as vertical FDI, firms locate production facilities in a foreign country primarily to take advantage of lower factor prices. In this situation, the market of the host country is not, therefore, the primary target of the MNC: products from such facilities are exported to the home and other countries. Export-platform FDI takes place for a hybrid purpose, 'both to tap into lower host country wages, and to provide a base for servicing large third-country markets'.

Most multinationals [...] originate from advanced, developed nations. The theory of the multinational corporation [...] is primarily conceived from the perspective of advanced, developed countries that view the MNCs as a vehicle to relocate labour-intensive activities to affiliates in low-wage countries. They rationalize one-way MNC activity in which MNCs from the capital-abundant North set up affiliates in the labor-abundant South. (Peter, 2004)

Although multinationals predominantly originate from advanced, developed countries, other MNCs from countries that do not belong to this select group are in existence. A significant number of MNCs come from Asian countries (the 'Asian Tiger' economies) (Peter, 2004).

Activities of MNCs have generated a lot of discussion, especially in developing countries. 'Institutions are important for economic development [...] the interaction between multinational corporations and [the] host country's institutions is not well understood' (Wig and Kolstad, 2010, cited in Ozoigbo and Chukuezi, 2011). According to Harila and Petrini (2003), MNC codes are organized in order to cover:

- the MNC and host governments, including economic development policies, laws and regulations, and political involvement;
- the MNC and the public, including technological transfer and environmental protection;
- the MNC and individuals, including consumer protection, employment practices, and human rights.

Unfortunately, the practices are not close to fulfilling these expectations. MNCs' idea of investing in foreign lands is not to better the lot of the host country but to exploit it as much as is possible in order to develop the home country (Ozoigbo and Chukuezi, 2011).Multinational companies might therefore be pursuing profit at the expense of vulnerable workforces while also causing environmental degradation (Edwards et al., 2007). According to Alam, Hoque and Hosen (2010), in the normal course of business, MNCs have little or no concern for social and environmental issues, and even if they do announce strategies to deal with such issues, they may not adhere to them. Most of their plants contribute to pollution and health hazards in their host communities (Ndzibah and Maxwell, 2008). Instead of following procedures, the organizations manoeuvre the host government with tactics, which they call 'lobbying' to seek the government's approval for the questionable processes they employ in conducting their businesses.

CSR of Multinational Corporations

Multinational corporations are at the core of the CSR debate. The need to be responsible in a community is more an issue for a non-citizen than for a citizen. A citizen's ultimate depository of wealth is the home and it is expected that however far that wealth travels around and for whatever length of time, the reservoir of a citizen's wealth will be his home. There are therefore fewer worries about how locals operate in their communities in terms of responsibility to all stakeholders than there are for foreigners, who are very likely to eventually return home with earnings from another land:

> It is unclear whether MNCs are [...] responsible to their home country or to the country in which they operate. Consequently, MNCs have been evaluated and studied [...] with accountability awarded to the companies themselves, the governments of the home country, the governments of the host country, the citizens of the host country, transnational soft law agreements, and the global social community. (Holland, 2010)

In addition, some peculiar CSR practices make their cross-border management difficult, while they are faced with contextually diverse stakeholder expectations and local CSR requirements, MNCs also need to practise differentiated CSR at their local sites, in response to the local context (Alam, Hoque and Hosen, 2010). MNCs' CSRs therefore deserve very careful evaluation.

The practice of CSR by MNCs has attracted varied reactions from observers. Addressing the reasons why MNCs engage in CSR activities, Ismail (2009) stated that CSR for multinationals (MNCs) grows because of global competitions and challenges they have faced. In her words, cultural clashes, due to events such as protests, demonstrations, boycotts, strikes and other negative actions against the employers are also relevant.

'For many MNCs, CSR is an outcome of public pressure arising from their operations in developing countries in relation to human rights, environmental pollution and labour issues' (Alam, Hoque and Hosen, 2010). MNCs' CSR activities in developing countries has generally been reactive to pressure arising from their operations related to issues such as health, education, human rights, pollution and workforce.

Like the pressures driving CSR involvement, the perceived benefits to MNCs, which also determine the nature of their activities, are debatable. According to Pimpa (2011), MNCs identify CSR as a business tool to promote a positive image to business stakeholders. CSR in many corporations is public relations rhetoric. It is about pointing to the benefits these operations bring to poor people in developing countries, who would otherwise be worse off than before, which is nothing more than a communications stunt used by MNCs to appear ethical (Sethi, cited in Holland, 2010). Ndzibah and Maxwell (2008) identify MNCs as therefore most interested in PR activities like sponsorship of soccer and other games, celebrities, entertainments and highly expensive promotions

Multinational Corporations' CSR in Developed and Developing Countries

The business sector is essential to development, and protection of human rights and economic development comes with environmental stewardship and social responsibility (Sutherland, 1997, cited in Carleton, 2009). The origin of the political power of CSR is based on the proposition that business is a social institution and that it must use power responsibly (Davis, 1960 cited in Ismail, 2009). Business units are therefore generally expected to use economic and political powers in a manner that portrays them as partners in progress and not as parasites that are only interested in what they get from society. MNCs are in a critical situation, going on the coverage of their activities over countries with different levels of needs, based on their levels of development. They are therefore faced with contextually diverse stakeholder expectations and local CSR requirements.

'CSR might be most relevant in developing countries where the impacts of business activities on the poor have been mixed' (Werner, 2009). In developed countries, issues like power, water, roads, education and healthcare facilities are significantly provided for and the countries are able to produce both capital and consumer goods. In underdeveloped countries, on the other hand, most of these basic facilities are not available and they produce only primary goods if they produce goods at all. The implication is that developmental CSR will be more required in the developing world than in developed economies. According to Werner (2009), CSR becomes 'an increasingly important tool to maximize the positive development impact of corporations and commercial activity in the developing world'. MNCs can therefore 'have a positive impact in developing countries, especially through corporate social responsibility (CSR) initiatives focusing on sustainable development' (Alam, Hoque and Hosen, 2010).

Contrary to the above, 'the impact of CSR is relatively substantial compared to a situation where MNCs from mostly developed economies execute CSR also in developed economies' (Thinking Made Easy, 2009). The first reason is the fact that 'western-based companies [...] invest in developing countries in the hope of realizing higher potential returns on their investments than would be possible in more stable, developed countries' (Mehmet, 1999, cited in Carleton, 2009). Their initial intention, therefore, is to capitalize on the weaknesses of developing countries to make super-profit. On the other hand, the developed countries are known to enjoy the benefits of CSR. To start with, very little is known of the practice of CSR in developing countries, when most of the CSR studies conducted so far have been in the context of developed countries such as Western Europe, the USA, and Australia (Jamali and Mirshak, 2007).Just as in the area of research, the Western media does not pay the kind of attention to the role of CSR in developing countries as it does to its role in developed countries. Consequently, the negative effects of MNCs' activities in developed countries are taken more seriously than their effects in developing countries. Ultimately, scarcely any information is available about companies that are operating in developing countries taking responsibility for pollution-related problems – such as installing waste management facilities (Ndzibah and Maxwell, 2008).

The general practice of corporations is another issue. 'There have been many examples in which corporations have taken advantage of developing countries' (Werner, 2009). The CSR practices of international business organizations may fail to benefit the poor and marginalized in developing countries (Pimpa, 2011). CSR is a menace in Africa and other developing countries. CSR policies of corporations in these countries are very poor and questionable (Ndzibah and Maxwell, 2008). Rather than behaving partners in progress, MNCs commonly impose corporate practices in developing countries such as sudden the termination of employment contracts and harsh treatment of employees (Ketola, 2006, cited in Ndzibah and Maxwell, 2008). Where the 'best of technologies, the most innovative products and trends are meant for developed countries [...] the laggard state and the rejected innovations [are] dumped on the poor or developing countries'. Most of the plants operated by MNCs in developing countries contribute to local pollution and to health hazards for the local communities (Ndzibah and Maxwell, 2008). The situation is worsened by the fact that government in such countries is weak and compromised. Organizations manoeuvre the government with tactics directed at seeking government favours in support of their questionable activities (Ndzibah and Maxwell, 2008). This exploitative alliance is further enhanced by the intervention of MNCs' home governments in the internal affairs of the less developed countries (Ozoigbo and Chukuezi, 2011). Rather than invest in projects that will lead to socio-economic development, they are interested in projects that will enhance their public profile. In developing countries, MNCs see their interests lying in support of activities such as entertainment and social functions, where they could easily achieve name and fame, instead of projects or programmes that will facilitate development.

Conclusion

Developing countries face so many challenges. A lot of their problems are related to the facts that they are underdeveloped and that whatever is going to bring about their further development is a top priority for these countries. A consequence of their underdevelopment is that they are unable to compare in like for like terms with their counterparts in developed countries.

MNCs operate in both developed and less developed countries. Development is seen as a venture that cannot be accomplished with government effort alone, only with responsible involvement of the private sector. Many governments are thus pinning their hopes of economic growth and technological innovation on strong private sector growth

(Fourie, 2009). MNCs, with their big scale of operations, become vital to development wherever they are operating. The general expectation, therefore, is that they should contribute significantly to the development of a country where they operate.

'Developing' countries are not 'developed'. That is why it is said that they are 'underdeveloped'. The issue of development is therefore more significant for underdeveloped nations. Whereas developed nations may be interested in MNCs for a variety of reasons, the developing nations are definitely most interested in what is going to bring about development. According to Kolstad (2007), multinational corporations are in a powerful position to promote change in developing countries, individually and/or collectively. Whatever MNCs deliver in developing countries, including their CSRs, can only be appreciated in terms of its developmental impact.

Unfortunately, CSRs of MNCs cannot be said to bring about the desired development in developing countries. MNCs really are responsible for some infrastructure projects in underdeveloped nations, in that most of the infrastructure built by them is necessary for their operations in their host countries. The fact is that the 'MNC could take advantage of the less regulated business environment and thus assume little or no other responsibility than profit maximization' (Iamandi, 2007). The Marxists view multinational corporations as a historically progressive aspect of capitalism which is in the process of developing at international level (Gilpin, 1987; Stopford, 1988, cited in Ozoigbo and Chukuezi, 2011). Their interest may therefore be to expand their capitalist empire, which is not in the interest of developing nations. There are also reasons to believe that MNCs in CSR delivery may be biased towards their home country.

'There is a big difference between charity or goodwill and CSR programs rooted in political change and improvement' (Holland, 2010). Whereas developmental issues like education, science and technology, and research and development are some of the CSR issues in developed nations, the kinds of CSR delivered in developing countries include sponsorship of football clubs, games, celebrities, entertainments and highly expensive promotions, which may not necessarily add any developmental value to a country per se. MNCs in developing countries tend to do nothing about the harm that mining activities cause to local communities (Ndzibah and Maxwell, 2008). If they take any action at all, it is likely to be primarily on a short-term basis, in response to nature, and focusing on relief, which is likely to involve only physical reconstruction and recovery that 'may not have a lasting effect on the community or capacity-building to its residents, resulting in short-lived impacts of the activities' (GFDR, 2005). Such capacity-building could take the form of action to prevent future occurrences of harm and insulating the community from its impacts.

Based on the current state of MNCs' CSR delivery, which has been explored in this study, it will not be out of place to agree that MNCs' CSR policies are generally not meeting the need for development in many developing nations but might be argued to be more favourable to MNCs home nations' economic and perhaps social development. It will also be correct to argue that more needs to be done by MNCs operating in several developing nations. The argument cannot be one-sided: citizens of developing nations where self-interest, bribery and corruption and other social ills stand in the way of progressive development need to be CSR-conscious and to behave responsibly. This has resulted in many reactions from scholars and activities, which this study seems to agree with. For a company to articulate its values, missions, strategy and implementation in the creation of a value-adding CSR plan, it is important for all stakeholders to be involved

(Lu, 2011). CSR should be integrated in education, training and research with potential funding possibilities and it should be aligned with and embedded in other international programmes of corporations (Kaufmann and Olaru, 2012). Kasum (2011) argues that as far as is possible, CSR might need to take the legal compulsion route, as is currently the case in India, Indonesia and Mauritius, thereby making corporations do the right things in terms of CSR, for instance, adequately compensating employees, protecting the environment, complying with regulations, paying adequate taxes and acting fairly and responsibly, including in the pricing of products and services. In addition to the above, translating into fair play the sharing of resources from the developed nations, customers evaluate what kinds of businesses corporations are engaged in, how products are produced, and what effect the companies have on society – effects not generated by their products and the features of their offers alone (Harila and Petrini, 2003). Developmental CSR practices will, therefore, also promote a good corporate image.

References

Alam, S.M.S., Hoque, S.S. and Hosen, Z. (2010). Corporate social responsibility (CSR) of MNCs in Bangladesh: a case study on GrameenPhone Ltd. Forthcoming in *Journal of Potuakhali University of Science and Technology*. Available at: SSRN: http://ssrn.com/abstract=1639570 [accessed: 20 September 2012].

Amao, O.O. (2008). Corporate social responsibility, multinational corporations and the law in Nigeria: controlling multinationals in host states. *Journal of African Law*, 52, 89–113.

Chor, D., Foley, F. and Manova, K. (2008). Host Country Financial Development and MNC Activity. Available at: https://editorialexpress.com/cgi-bin/../download.cgi?db.

Carleton (2009). *Corporate Social Responsibility and MNC Decision-Making in Conflict-Prone Countries*. Country Indicators for Foreign Policy (CIFP). Ottawa: Carleton University. Available at: http://www.carleton.ca/cifp/app/serve.php/1049.pdf.

Edwards, T., Marginson, P., Edwards, P., Ferner, A., and Tregaskis, O. (2007). Corporate social responsibility in multinational companies: management initiatives or negotiated agreements. International Labour Organisation (ILO) Discussion Paper Series, Geneva. Available at: http://www.ilo.org/public/english/bureau/inst/publications/discussion/dp18507.pdf [accessed: 16 November 2013].

Epstein, E.M. 1987, 'The Corporate Social Policy Process: Beyond Business Ethics, Corporate Responsibility, and Corporate Social Responsiveness', *California Management Review*, 29(3), 99–114.

Fisher, J. (2004). 'Social Responsibility and Ethics: Clarifying the Concepts', *Journal of Business Ethics*, 52(4), 391–400. Available at: http://www.jstor.org/stable/25123269 [accessed: October 2010].

Fourie, A. (2009). 'Strategic Considerations for the Business Community to Shape a Sustainable Future', *Enviropedia*. Available at: http://www.enviropedia.com.

GFDR (2005). *White Paper on Corporate–Community Interface (CCI), The Corporate Sector*. (Draft Version 1.) Kyoto University: Global Forum for Disaster Reduction (GFDR) And Graduate School of Global Environmental Studies. Available at: http://www.wcdr.gfdr.org/imgs/pdfs/White_Paper_on_the_Corporate_Community_Interface__CCI_.pdf.

Harila, H. and Petrini, K. (2003). Incorporating Corporate Social Responsibility Case Study of Four MNCs. MSc Thesis, Department of Business Administration and Social Sciences, Lulea University of Technology.

Holland, C. (2010). *Multinational Corporations and Global Governance: Is Corporate Social Responsibility Enough? A study of Chevron's Yadana Gas Pipeline Operations in Burma*. Covalence Intern Analyst Paper. Geneva: Covalence SA. Available at: www.ethicalquote.com/docs.

Iamandi, I. (2007). Corporate social responsibility and social responsiveness in a global business environment. A comparative theoretical approach. *Romanian Economic Journal*, 10, 3–18. Available at: http://www.rejournal.eu/portal JE 23 Iamandi.

Ismail, M. (2009). Corporate social responsibility and its role in community development: an international perspective. *The Journal of International Social Research*, 2(9), 199–209.

Jamali D. and Mirshak, R. (2007). Corporate social responsibility (CSR): theory and practice in a developing country context, *Journal of Business Ethics*, 72, 243–62.

Kamlani, F. (2011). *CSR and Development*. Available at: http://www-sbs-ox-ac-uk.

Kasum, A.S. 2014. The responsibilities of corporation: an analytical appraisal, in Mermod, A.Y. and Idowu, S. (eds), *Corporate Social Responsibility in the Global Business World*. Heidelberg: Springer.

Kaufmann, M. and Olaru, M. (2012). *The Impact of Corporate Social Responsibility on Business Performance – Can It Be Measured, And If So, How?* The Berlin International Economics Congress, March 7–10. Available at: www.culturaldiplomacy.org.

Kolstad, I. (2007). Corporate social responsibility of multinational corporations, *CMIBRIEF*, 6(2). Available at: http://www.cmi.noad.

Kumar, D.A. and Balakrishnan, V. (2011). Corporate social responsibility: existing practices vs CSR framework. *Global Journal of Business and Management Research*, 11(9), 50–56.

Lenguyen, T. (2011). Impact of Corporate Social Responsibility Program on a Company's Image and Reputation: A Case Study, *AU-GSB eJournal* 4(2), 22. Available at: http://gsbejournal. au.edu/7V/7V.html.

Lu, C. (2011). Corporate social responsibility's seven best practices: avoid greenwashing through stakeholder engagement. CSR, Green Business Lists. Available at: http://greeneconomypost.com/ Marrewijk, M.V. (2002). Concepts and definitions of CSR and corporate sustainability: between agency and communion, *Journal of Business Ethics*, 44(2/3), 95–105. Available at: http://www. jstor.org/stable/25075020 [accessed: September 2010].

Ndzibah, E. and Maxwell, A. (2008). CSR in Developing Countries? Diversity should not Mean Dumping. Available at: http:// www.crrconference.org/downloads/ndzibah-pdf.

Ojo, O. (2009). CSR as a vehicle for economic development, in Idowu, S.O. and Leal Filho, W. (eds), *Global Practices of Corporate Social Responsibility*. Heidelberg: Springer, 393–434.

Ozoigbo, B.I. and Chukuezi, C.O. (2011). The impact of multinational corporations on the Nigerian economy, *European Journal of Social Sciences*, 19(3), 380.

Peter, D. (2004). *Reversing the Perspective: Expansion Activities of Multinational Corporations From Middle-Income Countries*, CEPR Working Paper 4435, Department of Economics; Centre for Economic Policy Research (CEPR), University of Texas at Austin. Available at: http://ssrn.com/ abstract=564568.

Pimpa, N. (2011).Multinational corporations: corporate social responsibility and poverty alleviation in Thailand, *The International Journal of the Computer, the Internet and Management*, 19 (Special Issue), (SP1).

Robbins, S.P., Bergman, R., Stagg, I. and Coulter, M. (2000). *Management*, 2nd edition. Sydney: Prentice-Hall.

Strike, V.M., Gao, J. and Bansal, P. (2006). Being good while being bad: social responsibility and the international diversification of US firms. *Journal of International Business Studies*, 37(6), 850–62. Available at: http://www.jstor.org/stable/4540388 [accessed: October 2010].

Thinking Made Easy, 2009. The Corporate Social Responsibility (CSR) of MNCs: A Moral or Economic Motivation. Available at: http://ivythesis.typepad.com/term_paper_topics/2009/09/the-corporate-social-responsibility-csr-of-mncs-a-moral-or-economic-motivation.html#ixzz27fCciktT [accessed: November 2012].

Werner, W.J. (2009). Corporate social responsibility initiatives addressing social exclusion in Bangladesh. *Journal of Health Population Nutrition,*27(4): 545–62. Available at: http://www.ncbi.nlm.nih.gov [accessed: September 2012].

6 CSR of Multinational and Indigenous Corporations in Romania

RODICA MILENA ZAHARIA

Abstract

The role of multinational corporations (MNCs) in the development process continues to be a hotly debated issue. On one hand the benefits that MNCs bring to an economy through foreign direct investments (FDIs) are underlined, especially in developing economies: efficiency and modern technologies, job creation, increased exports, higher wages, taxes, and product diversification. On the other hand, the behaviour of MNCs has been under severe criticism: exploitation of a poorer and less educated labour force, disregard for national and local values, unbalanced competition against local companies, environmental abuse and corruption. All these factors have been analysed in relation to different topics, from sovereignty to human rights issues. In the last decades these issues have also been included in the investigation related to the social responsibility of corporations (Utting, 2003).

This chapter proposes an analysis of the corporate social responsibility (CSR) of MNCs and indigenous companies based on literature review and on an analysis of several websites of companies in Romania. The question the chapter aims to answer is whether there are differences in approaching CSR between MNCs and indigenous companies and how such differences are explained in general, and specifically in the case of Romania. Romania, as one of the newest members of the European Union (EU), has a particular history of CSR. Romania's communist heritage, lower level of market development and EU membership transform it into an interesting example.

The conclusions of this analysis reveal differences in CSR approaches of MNCs versus domestic companies. These differences can be explained by the role of MNCs in the development process; the expectations that societies in developed and developing countries have of MNCs compared to domestic corporations – the overwhelming majority of which are small and medium-sized enterprises (SMEs); and by the way CSR is perceived by MNCs and domestic corporations. With regard to Romania, the general understanding of CSR is less favourable to the involvement of local companies in CSR actions; and CSR is still considered a 'luxury' that only large companies – that is, mainly MNCs – can afford. The budgets devoted to CSR actions are unknown and very few companies announce how much money they intend to devote to achieving their CSR aims.

There are important differences in communication policies, MNCs being much more active in communicating CSR actions than indigenous companies.

Introduction

The issue of CSRs of MNCs and indigenous corporations is multifaceted and debatable for several reasons. One is the dispute around the concept of CSR. Although it is not a new concept and it has seen increased development in the last decades, there are still concerns about the vagueness of the term. It is generous and positive by nature, and serves too many causes. As M. van Marrewijk (2003: 96) notes:

> Too often, CSR is regarded as the panacea which will solve the global poverty gap, social exclusion and environmental degradation. Employees' associations emphasize the voluntary commitment to CSR. Local governments and non-governmental organisations (NGOs) believe private–public partnership can, for instance rejuvenate neighbourhoods. Also various management disciplines have recognised that CSR fits their purposes, such as quality management, marketing, communication, finance, human resource management, and reporting. Each of these present views on CSR that align with their specific situation and challenges. The current concepts and definitions are therefore often biased towards specific interests.

Another difficulty arises from the lack of studies carried out on this topic in developing countries. CSR is an issue that developed in Western countries and there are few analyses that have been carried out for developing countries (Jamali, 2007). Even in developed countries researches approaching MNCs' CSR versus indigenous companies' CSR are in their infancy. Furthermore, the studies conducted on developing countries propose different methodological frameworks (Amaeshi et al., 2009) that make it difficult to analyze those studies comparatively.

Also, a reason for the complexity and debatable characteristic of the CSR of MNCs and indigenous corporations lies in the definitions of 'multinational' and 'indigenous' corporation. The understandings thrown up by the definitions influence the expectation that society has of these companies, the way they are perceived by consumers, suppliers and local authorities.

Even if 'multinational corporation' is the term largely used in the literature, its understanding is not a unitary one. As a generic term for those companies that are active in more than one country, 'multinational' companies are similar to 'transnational' companies or 'global' companies. The United Nations defines multinational companies in a generic way, as 'the enterprises which control assets – factories, mines, sales and other offices – in two or more countries' (UNCTC, 1973: 24). In international business or international management, multinational companies can be multi-domestic, global or transnational corporations (Harzing, 1999). These types of companies differentiate themselves through strategies developed in the fields of marketing, financial resources, human resources; or by type of management.

The case of indigenous corporations is even more complex. The term 'indigenous', according to the Oxford English Dictionary, refers to something 'local, regional (belonging to a particular place rather than coming to it from somewhere else)'. The Merriam-Webster online dictionary defines 'indigenous' as something/somebody 'produced, growing, living, or occurring naturally in a particular region or environment'. The vast majority of these kinds of companies are SMEs, both in developed and developing countries, over 90 per cent of the domestic companies falling into this category.

The approach followed by this chapter is to consider CSR:

as an umbrella term for a variety of theories and practices, all of which recognize the following: (a) that companies have a responsibility for their impact on society and the natural environment, sometimes beyond legal compliance and the liability of individuals; (b) that companies have a responsibility for the behaviour of others with whom they do business (e.g. within supply chains); and that (c) business needs to manage its relationship with wider society, whether for reasons of commercial viability, or to add value to society. (Blowfield and Frynas, cited in Prieto-Carrón et al., 2006: 978)

In this chapter, MNCs should be understood under the generic definition provided by the UN, as a company that is active in more than one country; and indigenous companies will be assigned mainly to the category of SMEs.

The chapter starts with a general presentation of the differences between MNCs and domestic companies as the roots of the different approaches towards CSR. An overview of the literature will explain the differences between the CSRs of MNCs and indigenous corporations. The second section of the chapter is devoted to a case study of Romania. A review follows of examples of the literature of CSR practices in Romania, together with a content analysis of the websites of several companies (both MNCs and domestic firms) in order to compare CSRs of MNCs with those of domestic companies in a post-communist country, which is now a member of the EU. Although this analysis is a qualitative one and cannot be extended to all domestic companies or MNCs from Romania, it may be a starting point for further analyses.

The chapter ends with some conclusions from the debate on the CSR of MNCs versus domestic companies and how this debate is illustrated in Romania's situation.

Differences Between Multinational and Indigenous Companies in Approaching CSR

Many studies (Blomstrom and Sjoholm, 1999; Dixon and Boswell, 1996; Liu, 2002; Rothgeb, 1984) associate the achievements in development with the level of FDI that a country may attract, linking in this way development success to the degree of MNCs' involvement and to the number of MNCs involved the country being studied. However, this opinion is largely debated, and recent studies (Herkenrath and Bornschier, 2003; Konings, 2001) focus on the imbalances created by MNCs' strategies developed in different countries, mostly in developing countries or transition economies. The negative influences on developing economies are related to the unequal competition with indigenous companies; and the negative effects on balance of payments when the MNCs do not use the local products as resources and import what they need for production or for exports; and low levels of transfer of technology in the host economies. The evolving MNCs' universe has to interact more closely with national development goals and this poses, according to the United Nations Conference for Trade And Development (UNCTAD, 2010) key challenges for development-geared investment: to bring about a balance between liberalization and regulation, between the rights and obligations of states and investors; to address more explicitly critical issues such as poverty, education and other national development objectives; and to ensure coherence between national and international investment policies, and between investment policies and other public policies. The impact that MNCs have on local firms is evaluated on a scale that goes from positive effects (transfer of technologies, of management and of marketing practices) to negative impact (increasing competition on a level that local companies cannot sustain).

If MNCs are related mostly to the transfer of technology, high productivity, large-scale enterprises, with turnovers larger than the gross domestic product (GDP) of many developing countries, capital influx and increased exports, indigenous companies act mostly domestically and carry out the business process on a small scale. The overwhelming majority of domestic companies are SMEs, which account for over 90 per cent of the companies in developed and developing countries, many of them labour-intensive and developing regional or local scale businesses.

It is difficult to compare domestic companies between different countries–and this is true of both the developed and the developing countries. Data about the number of domestic companies, their size, turnover, employees, suppliers and fields of activity are not easily available. Even for SMEs it is difficult to identify a harmonized pattern. Furthermore, the definitions of SMEs differ from country to country. In the EU, for example, SMEs are those businesses that employ less than 250 people; in the USA, SMEs in the non-agricultural sector are those that employ less than 500 employees. Egypt defines SMEs as having more than 5 and fewer than 50 employees, Vietnam considers SMEs to have between 10 and 300 employees. The World Bank defines SMEs as those enterprises with a maximum of 300 employees, $15 million in annual revenue, and $15 million in assets. The Inter-American Development Bank describes SMEs as having a maximum of 100 employees and less than $3 million in revenue (Dalberg, 2011: 6). SMEs form the backbone of the EU economy – accounting for 99.8 per cent of non-financial enterprises in 2012, which equates to 20.7 million businesses. The overwhelming majority (92.2 per cent) are micro-enterprises, defined as those with fewer than 10 employees. Some 6.5 per cent of SMEs in the EU are classified as small enterprises (employing between 10 and 49 people) and 1.1 per cent are medium-sized (50–249 employees). Large businesses, with more than 250 employees, account for just 0.2 per cent of enterprises in the EU's non-financial sector (Wymenga et al., 2012: 15). Within the US economy, SMEs also account for the vast majority of firms and approximately half the GDP generated by non-agricultural sectors. SMEs accounted for 99.9 per cent of the 27 million employers and non-employer private non-farm businesses in the US in 2006. The vast majority of SMEs are firms with fewer than 20 employees. SMEs employed roughly half of the 120 million non-farm private sector workers in the US in 2006 (USITC, 2010: 2–4).

In developing countries domestic companies included in SMEs count for a similar proportion in the total number of enterprises (over 90 per cent of the total number of businesses). SMEs are a fundamental part of the economic landscape in developing countries, and they play a crucial role in employing the labour force, in addressing local and regional needs for growth and in reducing poverty in specific regions (Dalberg, 2011: 4). They are considered to be labour-intensive businesses, having as main characteristics flexibility and adaptability rather than productivity and technological innovation.

Although domestic companies (categorized as SMEs) are crucial for economic development, the status these companies have in comparison to MNCs in terms of capital inflow, exports, technological progress and synergic effects on the market determine different expectations of these companies. Indigenous companies (especially in developing countries) are seen rather as victims of MNCs' practices. CSR is considered, in a direct relationship with MNCs' behaviour, a claim on large multinational corporations for increasing their commitment to host economies' (mostly developing) national interests.

Also, the demands for special international regulation of MNCs deepens the assumption that CSR is a must for these corporations. Indigenous companies even expect that these codes of responsibilities will introduce some protection for them.

Only in recent years has the debate about CSR extended to domestic companies. CSR is not seen only as an exclusive attribute of MNCs; more and more voices sustain the importance of the CSR approach for SMEs. However, the debate is still in its infancy and the differences between MNCs' and SMEs' involvement in CSR practices are determined by many factors.

One is the preoccupation, discussed above, with the influence of MNCs on the host economies, particularly on fair competition with domestic businesses; and their power to influence the legal framework of host economies to meet the demands of MNCs for labour standards or access to resources. As is mentioned above, indigenous companies are seen as rather oppressed by MNCs' practices and in an unequal position in their ability to be competitive. In considering the ethical component of CSR, SMEs ask for preferential treatment, a requirement that can be identified both in developed and developing countries as fiscal facilities for SMEs, different initiatives to sustain the SME sector, and so on.

The evolution of the CSR concept and the issues in the CSR debate also brought about a different approach to CSR on the part of MNCs as compared to domestic companies. The relationship between CSR and the abuses perpetrated by MNCs in developing countries; and the MNCs' preoccupation with designing international codes of conduct have resulted in the association of CSR with MNCs. Even the term 'corporate social responsibility' encourages the association of responsibility with the large, firms called 'corporations'. Small domestic, companies are considered different in that they do not need to be responsible in a similar way to large firms or corporations.

Another source for a different approach to CSR between MNCs and indigenous companies reveals a dissimilar set of values promoted by MNCs, as compared to domestic companies. Jamali, Zanhour and Keshishian 2009; reproduced in Jenkins, 2004; and see Table 6.1 below) show that MNCs are more organized, planned and formal in approaching CSR; small businesses are more intuitive, personal and informal.

Table 6.1   Cultural differences between corporate and small businesses

	Multinational Corporations	Small Businesses
1	Order	Untidy
2	Formal	Informal
3	Accountability	Trusting
4	Information	Personal observation
5	Clear demarcation	Overlapping
6	Planning	Intuitive
7	Corporate strategy	'Tactically strategic'
8	Control measures	'I do it my way'
9	Formal standards	Personally monitoring
10	Transparency	Ambiguous
11	Functional expertise	Holistic
12	Systems	'Freely'
13	Positional authority	Owner-managed
14	Formal performance	Customer/network exposed

Source: Jenkins (2004), in Jamali, Zanhour and Keshishian (2009: 358).

The manager's personal vision of CSR in a domestic company plays a more important role than in an MNC. The behaviour of an SME expresses the personal values of the owner, which in many cases is the manager, while in MNCs it is harder for an individual to impose a personal vision.

SMEs express greater sensitivity than MNCs in relation to the wellbeing of their employees and their community links. This is explained by the closeness of relationships between managers and their staff and by the fact that SMEs often have very strong links with their immediate locality (Torrès, 2003 cited in Kechiche and Soparnot, 2012: 98).

The CSR of MNCs and domestic companies (the overwhelming majority of which are SMEs) is still a debatable issue. Developments in approaches to CSR cannot be transferred from MNCs to indigenous companies. Indigenous companies have a different position in society; they have less influence on governmental policies, a weaker ability to communicate their CSR practices to both internal and external stakeholders (Murillo and Lozano, 2006), and less mobility on the international stage to exploit the differences between countries in labour standards, environmental regulation, fiscal conditions or financial opportunities. As was stated in the Report of United Nations Industrial Development Organization:

> SMEs already practise some kind of 'silent social responsibility'. SMEs generally have a greater understanding of local cultural and political contexts, more links with local civil society and a greater commitment to operating in a specific area. Family-owned companies in particular often exhibit strong ethical and philanthropic approaches. SMEs need to give a voice to their 'silent' social and environmental responsibility. (UNIDO, 2002: ix)

CSR of Multinational Corporations vs Indigenous Companies in Romania

Romania is a former communist country which became a member of the EU in 2007. The end of communism happened through a bloody revolution; Romania is the only country in Eastern Europe where communism was not peacefully removed.

The communist heritage is still powerful in some respects. The new ideology and market-oriented economy did not bring prosperity to all. Once an egalitarian society, Romania experienced some of the 'negative externalities' of capitalism such as unemployment and the polarization of society. Feelings about Western society became mixed; some of the people embracing the new ideology and new values; others, mostly elderly people, became nostalgic and vulnerable to different types of manipulation.

In Romania before the communist period, philanthropy played an important role in the development of socially responsible behaviour (Zaharia, Stancu and Chelcea, 2010). The Orthodox Church, non-governmental associations and influential industrialists developed projects for social protection (orphans, hospitals and asylums) and benefits for their employees (such as meals, health care or improvements in working conditions).

While Romania was a communist state, CSR, was seen as a capitalist value, the term 'corporate' having negative connotations ('rich "corporation"-owning industrialists exploit poor, helpless employees'). Instead, responsibility was in the nature of socialism, the whole of the people being considered responsible for the entire society. Philanthropy remained at an individual level and companies became enterprises, with extensive social functions (houses for employees, social and health care for employees, etc.) (Zaharia et al., 2010).

After 1989, Romania started to build a private sector from almost nothing. Suffering from a chronic lack of internal private capital, privatization and foreign capital were the solutions for building privately owned companies in Romania after 1989. In the beginning state owned companies dominated the business environment; but, beginning in 1996, the private sector became the dominant contributor to GDP (Comisia Nationala pentru Prognoza, 2007). However, in Romania as in other central and Eastern European countries, most of the largest companies are foreign or state-owned enterprises. In the top 500 companies from Eastern Europe (Deloitte, 2012), Romania was placed in the fifth position, with 37 companies in the top 500 largest companies from the region (after Poland, the Czech Republic, Hungary and Ukraine). The first ten companies listed are foreign-owned, with OMV Petrom being the first (in sixteenth place out of the 500).

An important characteristic of CSR in Romania is the influence of the EU. The EU developed a new strategy towards CSR from 2011 to 2014, emphasizing the importance of business responsibility in meeting EU goals and in promoting European values:

> *The economic crisis and its social consequences have to some extent damaged consumer confidence and levels of trust in business. They have focused public attention on the social and ethical performance of enterprises. By renewing efforts to promote CSR now, the Commission aims to create conditions favourable to sustainable growth, responsible business behaviour and durable employment generation in the medium and long term. (European Commission, 2011)*

CSR in Europe compared to CSR in America is a top-down process, while the voluntary character of CSR is diluted by European polices. For example, the European Commission intends to monitor the commitments made by European enterprises with more than 1000 employees to take account of internationally recognized CSR principles and guidelines (the United Nations Global Compact, the Guidelines for Multinational Enterprises developed by the Organisation for Economic Co-operation and Development (OECD)) and of the ISO 26000 guidance standard on social responsibility in their operation (Frost, 2011). It may be said that CSR in Romania (as in many other East European countries) is the result of the culture of MNCs transferred to the Romanian business environment and of the European legislative system.

Companies involved in CSR are mostly multinational corporations. According to research carried out by Transparency International into the integrity of businesses in Romania, only 11 per cent of the companies sampled publish CSR reports. Only 14 per cent of these businesses are Romanian-owned companies, which means that less than 2 per cent of Romanian companies are concerned about CSR (Fiser, 2012). Companies with a strong CSR policy in Romania are MNCs and they have imported their CSR culture from the country of origin (EcoMagazin, 2012) and have adapted it to the hottest issues for Romanian society. In Romania, large-scale CSR projects, developed by multinational corporations, address well-known problems with a high emotional impact: education (P&G, OMV/Petrom, Zentiva), environment (OMV/Petrom, HP, Vodafone), health (Sanofi-Aventis, Avon Cosmetics, Vodafone) (Zaharia and Grundey, 2011: 201). The largest budgets devoted to CSR are those provided by MNCs, and their CSR communications are the most visible.

Indigenous firms in Romania are less involved in CSR. Among the largest Romanian-owned companies, some are state owned enterprises (Hidroelectrica, CFR) and their involvement in CSR is almost non-existent. The privately owned large companies are modest in developing CSR projects and they address the same topics, those sensitive for Romania or local communities, but on a lower scale. Some of them do not offer CSR information; others are very laconic in describing their CSR projects. It is almost impossible to find out the CSR budget;, most of the companies did not say how much they had spent or intended to spend on CSR. CSR reports are also very rare and those that exist are laconic.

The indigenous Romanian companies which are SMEs are even less involved in CSR. Studies on the CSR of the Romanian SMEs are less developed and most of them are qualitative analyses. However, the conclusions provided by these studies show that for these companies, the understanding of CSR is more closely linked to the vision of Milton Friedman: the mission of a company is to make a profit and respect the laws. SMEs in Romania concentrate their CSRs on employees, clients and local community. Their involvement in CSR activities is sporadic, and most of them do not develop CSR policies on a regular basis. For some of them, CSR is not an investment, but an expense, and is among the first budgets to be cut when the company is in difficulty (Zaharia and Grundey, 2011).

Even if the literature underlines the necessity of responsible behaviour for all companies, large or small, national or multinational; even if the managers and company representatives of small and large, national or multinational companies, recognize the importance of CSR activities, their actions are still far away from discourse.

Difficulties Surrounding the CSR of Indigenous Firms in Romania

One of the most important aspects of CSR in Romania is its development, which is below that of Western European countries. Romania is still on her way to the completion of a market economy, with a developing economic environment, with a market dominated by MNCs, and with a still vulnerable indigenous sector. Economic problems are the most important and indigenous firms (most of them SMEs), face numerous economic constraints. These difficulties, plotted on Carroll's pyramid of CSR (1979), show that Romanian companies, mainly in this period of crisis, are facing obstacles in fulfilling their economic and legal responsibilities, therefore their ethical and philanthropic responsibilities are very hard to achieve.

The voluntary character of CSR is neglected; many activists in the CSR landscape ask for greater involvement of the government is sustaining CSR actions. According to the site CSR Romania (www.csr.ro), the Romanian government offers minimal support for those companies that are active in CSR. Other countries such as Poland, Finland, Spain and France, are more active in offering fiscal incentives to those companies that are active in CSR initiatives. This is a consequence of the European model of CSR. In the USA, the American system of law makes it easy for citizens to approach the courts with complaints that are sometimes unusual and thus allows for increased attention from companies to sensitive social issues (Campbell, 2007). Many American companies have been introducing CSR practices into their activities since the 1970s, in order to improve their image as responsible enterprises. In the EU the preoccupation with responsible corporate behaviour has been subject to institutional regulation from the beginning. In the European model, enterprises have a reactive behaviour, waiting to adapt their CSR strategies to the norms adopted by the European institutions. In Europe, consumers expect the authorities to force companies into responsible activities (Campbell, 2007), and companies expect to be supported and rewarded for their responsible behaviour.

CSR is considered an investment as long as it creates efficiency for the company: a CSR project which cannot be identified with the company that initiated it is a lost investment (Duriga, 2012). The communication campaigns related to CSR initiatives are more important that the initiatives themselves, as long as it is the good image and good name of the company that sell the products, not their quality. Companies invest in CSR mostly due to the benefits for the company's image and reputation. The budgets devoted to CSR actions are small compared with profits and most of the companies sustain those causes with a strong emotional impact on the public (such as the environment, health and education in Romania, domains that are largely advertised as major concerns for Romanian society). For example, the budget devoted to CSR action in 2012 was estimated at €5 million in the case of OMV Petrom, the largest company in Romania and the most important CSR actor on the Romanian market (Nicolici, 2012). The profit of OMV, only in the first quarter of 2012, was €461.7 million, which makes the CSR budget slightly over 1 per cent from the profit of the first quarter (www.mediafax.ro).

CSR is more of a marketing instrument, a PR activity, used in order to increase the awareness of a company. In the Romanian landscape, CSR activities seem to be more cyclical than embedded in strategic vision. Especially during religious holidays many companies, large and small, initiate charitable and philanthropic actions, acting on the high emotions experienced at those times by ordinary people. It is a good moment for publicity; it is a bad moment to miss that show! Furthermore, CSR is used to avoid harder analysis on some controversial aspects of a business. The project 'Tara lui Andrei' [Andrew's country], transformed OMV Petrom into the most visible business actor in sustaining environmental protection and increased public awareness of the company as one of the most environment-respectful enterprises. However, in the CSR reports published by Petrom, the contributions that the company makes towards CO_2 reductions are not analysed, nor is the impact that CSR activities promoted by Petrom have on different stakeholders or on the most polluted areas where Petrom is active (for example, Ploiesti) (Zaharia and Grundey, 2011: 203).

Most of the domestic companies in Romania do not have on their websites information about CSR activities. CSR reports are developed only by MNCs (Baleanu, Chelcea and Stancu, 2011: 240) as part of their group engagement in CSR.

The wide gap between MNCs' involvement in CSR and indigenous companies is another characteristic of CSR in Romania. The main reasons for this gap lie in the financial capacity to sustain CSR activities, which is limited to indigenous companies (SMEs) compared with MNCs, and in the lack of or superficial understanding of the need for CSR. In Romania, as in many other countries, mostly developing countries, CSR is expected of MNCs, not from small firms.

The content analysis of the websites proposed for this chapter considered four MNCs and four domestic companies. Romanian companies have been selected from the top 100 companies ranked by the business magazine *Ziarul Finaciar* published in

November 2012. The selected Romanian companies are large corporations, not, as are most Romanian companies, SMEs, in order to include companies of comparable size. However, the difference between MNCs and Romanian-owned companies is still important. The first five Romanian companies have, together, half of the value of Petrom, the first company on the Romanian market. The analysis considered: (1) whether CSR is explicitly mentioned on the website; (2) which are the fields around which CSR is concentrated; (3) what type of CSR activities are developed by these companies. This analysis has the value of an example and its results cannot be considered the rule for companies from Romania. However, the conclusions of other studies on the Romanian CSR landscape (Baleanu et al., 2011; Bibu, Nastase and Gligor, 2010) are not different from these results.

Table 6.2   CSR of multinational vs indigenous companies in Romania

Company	Company type	CSR on websites	CSR interests	Types of CSR
Dacia Renault/ www. daciagroup. com	MNC	explicit	Sustainable development, environment, education, community	Philanthropy, partnerships with public bodies (universities), in-house projects
Orange/ www.orange.ro	MNC	explicit	Education, environment	Philanthropy, partnerships with public bodies (universities), in-house projects
Petrom/ www.petrom.ro	MNC	explicit	Environment, education, health, community, voluntary actions	Philanthropy, partnerships with public bodies (universities), in-house projects
BCR/ www.bcr.ro	MNC	explicit	Education, entrepreneurship, social solidarity	Philanthropy, partnerships with public bodies (universities), in-house projects
Dedeman/ www.dedeman. ro	Indigenous	Non-explicit	Education, community	Philanthropy
BGS/ www.bgs.ro	Indigenous	Non-explicit	Education, environment, health, community	Philanthropy, partnerships with public bodies universities), in-house projects
RCS-RDS/ www.rcs-rds.ro	Indigenous	Non-explicit	No information	No information
Dante International/ www.emag.ro	Indigenous	Non-explicit	Education	Philanthropy

The analysis of the websites of these companies (Table 6.2) reflects the extent of their preoccupation with CSR, particularly MNCs. Romanian companies do not offer too much information about their CSR policy and they do not have a special place on their websites for CSR. Some of them mention their CSR actions in the 'News' or 'Projects' sections.

CSR activities are oriented towards environment, education, health and community. Both MNCs and domestic companies identify these fields as sensitive and suitable focuses for their CSR actions. These areas are also considered the most sensitive for Romanian society. The fact that both types of companies orient their CSR policies towards them may be considered a mimetic behaviour (in the case of domestic companies, which imitate MNCs) or a sort of automatism (for both types of companies), for those companies wanting to increase the visibility of their actions by addressing those issues considered to be the most important for the public.

As CSR types, philanthropic actions are the most common. MNCs develop a larger set of CSR actions and on a larger scale than domestic companies.

Conclusion

MNCs and indigenous companies (small and large) show a definite difference in their approach to CSR in developed and developing countries. These differences are determined by many elements, starting with the complexity and often vagueness of the CSR concept and ending with society's requirements of MNCs compared to domestic companies. CSR was from the beginning related to MNCs and the Western philosophy of doing business. The demands of society for business responsibility were considered in a direct relationship with the size of companies and their power to influence political decisions, legislation or competition. Society considers domestic firms, the vast majority of which are small companies, to be in a weaker position compared to MNCs and having a different kind of responsibility towards society.

In the last decade, however, CSR has started to be understood as a competitive advantage, even for small companies. Also, theoretical developments of the CSR concept have enlarged the understanding responsibility. As the UNIDO report (2002) mentions, companies should not be analysed through a fix set of indicators. A more flexible framework has to be used for considering when and how a company is or is not socially responsible, especially when considering small companies.

In the case of Romania, two elements may be considered essential for appreciating the CSR involvement of companies. One is determined by the communist heritage and the infancy of CSR behaviour. The awareness of CSR is limited and the involvement of large MNCs in CSR actions is still considered a duty.

The second element is determined by the level of development of the market, competition among firms and the public demand for responsible business. The Romanian market and its consumers are not too demanding of companies and their responsible behaviour is more formal. Communication policy definitely favours MNCs. They invest a lot in promoting their CSR initiatives and use CSR actions for enhancing the public profile of the company.

The example presented, even if it is not relevant for the companies in the Romanian market, reveals the difference in addressing CSR actions by MNCs and by domestic companies. MNCs have a more articulate CSR policy, communicate it better, and involve more types of CSR actions. Domestic companies are almost indifferent to the need to present CSR actions, orient more towards philanthropy and do not use CSR as a strategic advantage.

References

Amaeshi, K.M., Adi, A.B.C., Ogbechie, C. and Amao, O.O. (2006). *Corporate Social Responsibility in Nigeria: Western Mimicry or Indigenous Influences?* Available at: http://ssrn.com/abstract=896500 or http://dx.doi.org/10.2139/ssrn.896500

Baleanu, T.E., Chelcea, L. and Stancu, A. (2011). The social responsibility of the top 100 Romanian companies. An analysis of corporate websites. *Amfiteatru Economic*, 13(29), 235–48.

Bibu, N., Nastase, M. and Gligor, D.C. (2010). The perception over corporate social responsibility in Romania. *Review of International Comparative Management*, 11(5), 764–78.

Blomstrom, M. and Sjoholm, F. (1999). Technology transfer and spillovers: Does local participation with multinationals matter? *European Economic Review*, 43(4/6), 915–23.

Campbell, J.L. (2007). Why would corporations behave in socially responsible ways? An institutional theory of corporate social responsibility. *Academy of Management* Review, 32(3), 946–67.

Carroll, A.B. (1979). A Three-Dimensional Model of Corporate Performance. *Academy of Management Review*, 4(4),497–505.

Comisia Nationala pentru Prognoza (2007). *Evoluția sectorului privat în România*. Available at: http://www.cnp.ro/user/repository/13d8770e862eb522b62f.pdf.

Dalberg (2011). *Report on Support to SMEs in Developing Countries Through Financial Intermediaries*. Available at: http://www.eib.org/attachments/dalberg_sme-briefing-paper.pdf.

Deloitte(2012).DeloitteCentralEuropeTop500.NewYork:DeloitteToucheTohmatsuLtd.[Online.]Available at: https://www.deloitte.com/en_GX/global/insights/deloitte-research/strategy-cross-industry-research/af9c388a90ffd110VgnVCM100000ba42f00aRCRD.htm [accessed: 21 November 2013].

Dixon, W.J. and Boswell, T. (1996). Dependency, disarticulation, and denominator effects: another look at foreign capital penetration. *American Journal of Sociology*, 102(2), 543–62.

Duriga, S. (2012). *Inovatie si CSR*, 12 November. Available at: http://www.csr-romania.ro/articole-si-analize/inovatie-si-csr/1201-inovatie-si-csr-.html.

EcoMagazin (2012). *Firmele autohtone se adapteaza politicilor europene de CSR*. 15 June. Available at: http://www.ecomagazin.ro/firmele-autohtone-se-adapteaza-politicilor-europene-de-csr/.

European Commission (2011). *A Renewed EU Strategy 2011–14 for Corporate Social Responsibility*. COM (2011) 681 final. Brussels: Commission of the European Communities, 25 October. Available at: http://eurlex.europa.eu/LexUriServ/LexUriServ.do?uri=COM:2011:0681:FIN:EN:PDF.

Fiser, R. (2012). *Ce inseamna cu adevarat raportarea de mediu si de ce este esentiala pentru o economie sustenabila*. 19 June 2012. Available at: http://www.responsabilitatesociala.ro/editoriale/ce-inseamna-cu-adevarat-raportarea-de-mediu-si-de-ce-este-esentiala-pentru-o-economie-sustenabila.html.

Frost, R. (2011). *European Commission backs ISO 26000*. 29 November. Available at: http://www.iso.org/iso/home/news_index/news_archive/news.htm?refid=Ref1490.

Harzing, A.W. (1999). An empirical test and extension of the Bartlett and Gohshal Typology of Multinational Companies. *International Business Studies*, 31(1), 101–120.

Herkenrath, M. and Bornschier, V. (2003). Transnational corporations in world development – still the same harmful effects in an increasingly globalized world economy? *Journal of World-Systems Research*, ix(1), 105–139.

ISO (2012). *ISO 26000 – Social responsibility.* [Online.] Available at: http://www.iso.org/iso/home/standards/iso26000.htm.

Jamali, D. (2007). The case for strategic corporate social responsibility in developing countries. *Business and Society Review*, 112(1), 1–27.

Jamali, D., Zanhour, M. and Keshishian, T. (2009). Peculiar strengths and relational attributes of SMEs in the context of CSR. *Journal of Business Ethics*, 87, 355–77.

Kechiche, A. and Soparnot, R. (2012). CSR within SMEs: literature review. *International Business Research*, 5(7), 97–104.

Konings J. (2001). The effects of foreign direct investment on domestic firms: Evidence from firm-level panel data in emerging economies. *Economics of Transition*, 9, 619–33.

Liu, Z. (2002). Foreign direct investment and technology spillovers: evidence from China. *Journal of Comparative Economics*, 30(3), 579–602.

Marrewijk, M. van (2003). Concepts and definitions of CSR and corporate sustainability: between agency and communion. *Journal of Business Ethics,* 44(2/3),95–105.

Murillo, D. and Lozano, J.M. (2006). SMEs and CSR: an approach to CSR in their own words. *Journal of Business Ethics*, 67(3), 227–40.

Nicolici, M. (2012). *PETROM investeste anual 5 milioane de euro in proiecte de Responsabilitate Sociala, 3 July.* Available at: http://www.csrmedia.ro/petrom-investeste-anual-5-milioane-de-euro-in-proiecte-de-responsabilitate-sociala/.

Prieto-Carrón, M., Lund-Thomsen, P., Chan, A., Muro, A. and Bhushan, C. (2006). Critical perspectives on CSR and development: what we know, what we don't know, and what we need to know. *International Affairs* 82(5), 977–87.

Rothgeb, J.M. (1984). The effects of foreign investment on overall and sectoral growth in Third World States. *Journal of Peace Research*, 21(1), 5–15.

UNCTC (1973). *Multinational Corporations in World Development.* United Nations Department of Economic and Social Affairs, Doc. ST/ECA/190. New York: United Nations Center for Transnational Corporations. Available at: unctc.unctad.org/data/e73iia11a.pdf [accessed: 21 November 2013].

UNCTAD (2010). *World Investment Report 2010.* Geneva: United Nations Conference on Trade and Development. Available at: http://www.unctad.org/en/docs/wir2010_en.pdf [accessed: 21 November 2013].

UNIDO (2002). *Corporate Social Responsibility Implications for Small and Medium Enterprises in Developing Countries.* Vienna: United Nations Industrial Development Organization. Available at: http://www.unido.org/fileadmin/user_media/Publications/Pub_free/Corporate_social_responsibility.pdf [accessed: 21 November 2013].

USITC (2010). Small and Medium Sized Enterprises: U.S. and EU Export Activities, and Barriers and Opportunities Experienced by U.S. Firms. USITC Publication 41269, July. Washington: International Trade Commission. Available at: http://www.usitc.gov/publications/332/pub4125.pdf.

Utting, P. (2003). Promoting development through corporate social responsibility – does it work? *Global Future*, Third Quarter. Available at: http://www.unrisd.org/UNRISD/website/newsview.nsf/0/b163470112831808c1256da90041ecc5?OpenDocument&Click=.

Wymenga, P., Spanikova, V., Barker, A., Konings, J. and Canton, E. (2012). *EU SMEs in 2012: At the Crossroads.* Annual Report on Small and Medium-sized Enterprises in the EU, 2011/12. Rotterdam, The Netherlands: ECORYS. Available at: //ec.europa.eu/enterprise/policies/sme/facts-figures-analysis/performance-review/files/supporting-documents/2012/annual-report_en.pdf.

Zaharia, R.M. and Grundey, D. (2011). Corporate social responsibility in the context of financial crisis: a comparison between Romania and Lithuania. *Amfiteatru Economic*, XIII(29), 195–206.

Zaharia, R.M., Stancu, A. and Chelcea, L. (2010). Romania, in Visser, W. and Tolhurst, N. (eds). *The World Guide to CSR: A Country by Country Analysis of Corporate Sustainability and Responsibility.* Sheffield, UK: Greenleaf Publishing, 325–30.

CSR and Socio-economic Progress

7 *The Diamond-shaped Socio-economic Development of Botswana*

ZORORO MURANDA

Abstract

This chapter addresses corporate social responsibility (CSR) in Botswana's largest diamond-mining company, Debswana. The paper adopts a historical analysis to the case by first introducing the country's historical and economic background in order to give context to the study. The objective of the chapter is to show how CSR in Debswana is not just a result of philanthropy, but is influenced by the structure of shareholding in the mining company. Botswana's socio-economic development has largely been financed through diamond-mining. Debswana's participation in CSR and the country's socio-economic development are intertwined in the country's development trajectory. This chapter adopts a case study method. Information for the case study is from record analysis and interviews with Debswana executives. The approach was adopted to allow for multiple perspectives to shape the case study. An intricate state–corporate symbiotic relationship exists between Botswana and Debswana. Discharge of CSRs, especially in communities where its mines are located, has given Debswana a social licence to operate. The case analysis shows that the higher the levels of community appreciation of CSR activities the more likely the community will be to welcome the company's presence. Such appreciation only comes through an improvement in quality of infrastructure, amenities and welfare as adjudged by the community itself. Communities are likely to abhor hosting irresponsible companies that do not contribute to their socio-economic development.

Introduction

Corporate social responsibility (CSR) is now a concept deeply ingrained in business and society and occupies a significant space in the nexus of corporate and community relations. Due to its wide use, the concept has attracted various definitions each emphasizing stakeholder interests. According to the United Nations Economic Commission for Africa and the African Union (UNECA and AU, 2010), CSR is a framework for formulating and implementing the expanded roles and responsibilities of the corporate sector to include incorporation of the expectations and needs of a wider community in the business model.

Central to the issues around which CSR initiatives have been articulated in the mining and other extractive industry sectors are: (a) the environment; (b) social and community development; (c) employment and labour; and (d) human rights. Socio-economic development within the context of CSR has remained inadequately explained, especially in the African context. This is mainly a result of inadequate information coming from companies. Campbell (2011) noted that CSR provides firms with a strategic response to the risks that systematic dynamics present, by addressing governance gaps that can, in turn, increase the potential for obtaining a 'social licence to operate'. CSR Europe, an association of large companies in Europe, has proposed that CSR should address the following components in fulfilling any such responsibility: workplace; marketplace; environment; community; ethics; and human rights. Several theories have been developed to analyse and explain corporate social responsibilities. Garriga and Mele (2004) classified CSR theories into four categories: instrumental theories, political theories, integrative theories and ethical theories. The aggregation of these theories converges on how corporate entities bring forth power to influence the moral, ethical and developmental space in stakeholder societies. The instrumental theories posit achievement of economic objectives, with emphasis on wealth creation alongside social activities. Friedman's conception epitomizes this group of theories. Citing the corporate–community interface, Friedman (1970: 126) noted that

> *it will be in the long-run interest of a corporation that is a major employer in a small community to devote resources to providing amenities to that community or to improving its government. That makes it easier to attract desirable employees, it may reduce the wage bill or lessen losses from pilferage and sabotage or have other worthwhile effects.*

It is now widely accepted in theory and practice that shareholder maximization coexists with social objectives. Such social objectives should, in practice, relate to the company's contribution to socio-economic development of host communities. This can be observed in competitive advantages a company realizes through active participation in social and cause-related investments.

The second group of theories, political theories, revolve around the responsibilities of business in exercising power in its interactions with the body politic. Two theories anchor political theories: corporate constitutionalism and corporate citizenship. According to Davis (1960), 'Whoever does not use his social power responsibly will lose it.' As a social institution the business is bound to exercise its social power in order to maintain its social position lest it loses that position. Social power is legitimized by corporate citizenship. The expectation is that corporate entities build community belongingness, especially in situations where the entity commands pervasive influence in its various interactions with the community.

The third group of theories, the integrative theories, recognize the significance of social demands as the course for the legitimacy and social acceptance of businesses. The recognition of social demands requires business to demonstrate social responsiveness to and public responsibility for social issues of the time. There exists a social contract between the business and its society. Donaldson and Dunfee (1999), in their integrated social contracts theory, propose macro social contracts and micro social contracts as the basis for fulfilling the societal expectations by businesses. Fulfilment of such expectations gives legitimacy to businesses in the eyes of communities. Integrative theories have long advocated the practice of stakeholder management, i.e. the achievement of cooperation between stakeholder groups and the corporate objectives. In seeking such cooperation, the business has to formulate and implement strategies that galvanize multiple stakeholders. Within the integrative theories resides the stakeholder theory. It is the theory propounded in analysing stakeholders, primary and secondary. It posits the basis and context on which to analyse the various groups to which the business should pay attention and exercise responsibility.

The last group of theories, the ethical theories, emphasize focus on the requirement for an ethical bond between businesses and communities. The theories relate issues of human rights and sustainable development to corporate responsibility. CSR practices have come unstuck sometimes due to conflicting perceptions between companies and stakeholders. CSR initiatives are legitimized by stakeholder input. It should be seen as more of a process than an outcome (Walton, 1967; Jones, 1980).

In Botswana, Debswana, the case study, has established itself as a partner in social development through its role in economic activity and CSRs. This chapter adopts case study method with the primary goal of providing a discursive evaluation of Debswana's CSR activities. In addition, the case provides a background to Botswana's economic and political development in order to put the role of CSR in socio-economic development in the proper context.

Botswana: A Brief Background

Botswana is located in Southern Africa and shares borders with South Africa, Zimbabwe, Namibia and Zambia. It is landlocked and occupies a surface area of 582,000 square kilometres. The country has a population of 2,038,228 as at the 2011 Census. It is largely semi-arid with approximately 84 per cent of the land being unsuitable for cropping. The main form of agriculture is commercial and open pasture ranching, the latter being practised by small-scale farmers. Human settlement and infrastructure development is mainly concentrated on the east side of the country. The development corridor – sometimes called the 'eastern' corridor – runs from the deep south right up to the north of the country. The corridor is home to 80 per cent of the population. The soils on the eastern corridor are suitable for agriculture although the challenge is with the rain and water flow patterns in the area. The west of the country, because of the Kalahari (Kgalagadi) Desert, is sparsely populated. The country has rapidly urbanized and in 2001, 55 per cent of the population lived in urban areas.

Botswana attained self-governance in 1965 and independence in 1966. Before then the country had been a British Protectorate for 80 years. At independence the country had a population of 600,000 people. It was also one of the least developed nations with a per capita income estimated at US$70. There was very little infrastructure apart from the railway line built in 1897 which belonged to the Rhodesia Railways. At that time only 29,000 people were formally employed in the country. Approximately 30,500 Batswana people were migrant workers mainly from South Africa and to a lesser extent from Rhodesia (now Zimbabwe). The ethnic composition of Botswana as reflected through language shows that 79 per cent speak Setswana, 11 per cent Kalanga, 3 per cent Sekgalagadi, 3 per cent Sesarwa; and other languages are mostly spoken by people settled in the far west and up north in the border regions.

Botswana poses a unique development scenario. Its development is mainly founded on one commodity, diamonds, and the successful exploitation of the mineral. As a result of the unique structure of the country's socio-economic situation, the economy has sometimes suffered serious disruption when global demand for diamonds is disrupted. Starting from the last quarter of 2008, weak global demand and falling prices of minerals has led to lower exports receipts and lower revenues for Botswana. While in a normal year Botswana's diamond sales are in the range of US$200–300 million per month, 2008 was a difficult year. To contain costs, Debswana (the 50–50 joint venture between Botswana and De Beers) closed the Orapa 2 and Damtshaa mines for the rest of 2009, and suspended operations at the Letlhakane and Orapa No. 1 mines until April 2009. Other smaller diamond exploration companies, as well as nickel and copper mines, followed suit. The linkages of mining with other sectors imply that the whole economy was affected directly or indirectly. Nearly 2,000 employees, mostly in mining and quarrying, lost their jobs. The government expected diamond prices in 2009 to be 15 per cent lower than the 2008 book price, hence the overall Debswana revenue was expected to fall by 50 per cent due to reduced diamond production, and exports, which would have a substantial impact on government revenues, since the revenue from this source depends on Debswana's tax and after-tax profits (ADB, 2009: 4).

ECONOMY

Botswana's economic growth has been phenomenal. The growth has been attributed to prudent economic policies and thorough planning based on a consultative framework. The planning phases have been based on planning timelines of four to six years since attainment of independence. The current development plan is the National Development Plan (NDP) 10. It covers the period 1 April 2009 to 31 March 2015. Underpinning the thorough planning has been a very simple but overly difficult principle to implement: that all income collected by government will be directed to development and the sovereign fund, not to consumption. Botswana has consistently maintained a fiscal surplus in recent years, which reached a high of nearly 12 per cent of gross domestic product (GDP) in 2006/07. By 2008 the country had import cover of 27 months, one of the highest in sub-Saharan Africa. These surpluses were influenced mainly by high revenues from minerals (ADB, 2009). The principle has seen Botswana accumulating sovereign net reserves of US$8.3 billion as at February 2012 (equivalent to 18 months' cover). The reserves have only gone down during years of serious droughts and recession when the government has had to refinance some of its obligations. Over the 33-year period between 1966 and 1999 the country maintained an average growth rate of 9.2 per cent. During the same period, the GDP per capita grew at an average of 7 per cent. As at 2005 the GDP per capita was estimated at US$3,500. Over the same period the national budget grew from US$3 million to US$3 billion as at 2004. In the comparable period exports grew from US$2 million to US$2.5 billion, while imports grew from US$3 million to US$ 2 billion. Employment in the formal sector grew from 29,000 people in 1966 to 296,387 by 2005. As the economy grew so did its structure. In 1966 agriculture contributed 40 per cent of GDP, as at 2005 it contributed a mere 3 per cent. At independence beef was the main export product. Diamonds have since become the main export product. Due to the recent global financial crisis there has been sluggish demand for and consequent decline in the prices of diamonds, the mainstay of the economy. As a result, real GDP growth declined from 5.3 per cent in 2007 to 3.3 cent in 2008 (ADB, 2009). Recovery in global markets has also seen recovery in the fortunes of Debswana and consequently Botswana.

Sector-specific growth has been positive with particular reference to services. Trade in services increased as a proportion of total trade, from 12 per cent in 1990/91 to over 15 per cent in 2000/01. A significant contribution through tourism has also occurred. The sector grew at an average of 9.3 per cent between 1999 and 2004. As an indicator to the growth of the sector, the number of licensed tourism enterprises grew from 331 in 2000 to 543 in 2005. Growth has also been recorded in the textiles sector as a result of the Africa Growth and Opportunity Act (AGOA). Between 2004 and 2005 the sector grew by 86.9 per cent.

MINING

Botswana's mining sector has grown for decades on the back of firming commodity prices. Although there have been deep periods of recession hitting mineral prices, these have had limited impact on the growth pattern of Botswana based on the track record of mineral revenue deployed to development. As at 2007–2008, mining contributed 39 per cent to the country's GDP and the contribution is through diamonds. The mining sector is governed by the Mines and Minerals Act of 1999, which is considered investor-friendly compared to other countries in the region. Although the government can participate in new mining projects up to a shareholding of 15 per cent, it has not been following up these rights given that most mining outside the diamond industry comprises small mines. The country's mining policy attempts to encourage prospecting and new mine development. The policy also emphasizes the importance of linkages with the whole economy and the training of the Batswana in the process. Although the new economic thrust is to diversify away from diamond-mining as the fulcrum of economic growth, the growth of mining in base metals such as gold, silver, nickel, copper, zinc, and others indicates that mining will be sustaining economic growth for the foreseeable future.

SOCIAL DEVELOPMENT

Botswana's social development is intertwined with diamond mining and thus Debswana. The country's social development indicators have been positive for most indices, but with declines in a few. Social development has tracked economic development, although at a varying rate. At independence in 1966 life expectancy at birth was 48 years. By 1991 it had risen to 65.3 years before taking a knock down to 55.7 years due to HIV/AIDS. Botswana's health systems have largely grown on government efforts. Development partners such as Debswana through its hospitals and clinics have been constrained by the sheer size of the country and resource requirements. Social progress has also shown in a decline in infant mortality rate from 100 per 1,000 live births in 1971 to 55 per 1,000 births in 2001 (Mogae, 2005).

HIV/AIDS has been associated with a slowdown in economic development experienced later in the 2000s. At 17 per cent the prevalence rate is considered quite high. To counter the effects of HIV/AIDS the government has been heavily involved in provision of anti-retroviral treatment. The roll-out programmes, through government programmes and non-state actors, have been increasingly accessible to patients. To tackle the pandemic head-on, the government, through the health and the local administrative systems, has been heavily involved in campaigns to raise awareness and change behaviour.

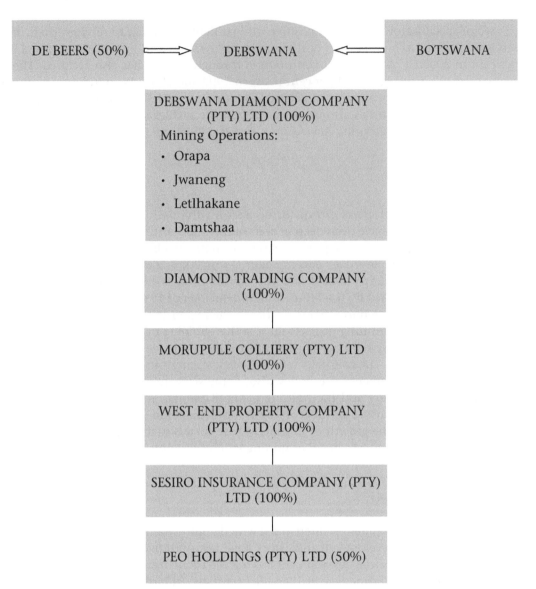

Figure 7.1 Debswana organizational

Source: Adapted from van Wyk et al. / The Bench Marks Foundation, 2009.

Indictors for education as a basis for social development have been positive for most of the post-independence period. The country's literacy rate is 83 per cent, which is admirably high. From 1997 to 2004 primary school enrolment increased by 98.5 per cent, although enrolments have declined and entered levels of stability in recent years. Progression has improved especially at secondary level, where the rate is now consistently above 40 per cent. There is a higher progression rate for female students compared to male students although enrolment is 52.9 per cent for boys compared to 47.1 per cent for girls. At the University of Botswana the ratio of female to male students is 65 per cent to 35 per cent, so that unlike most sub-Saharan Africa countries, in Botswana female students' enrolment in higher education and progression is higher than males.

Resulting from the consistently positive economic and social development, Botswana's poverty levels have consistently gone down, although at a slow rate for a middle-income country. In a 2002–2003 analysis, poverty levels were recorded at 30 per cent. The prevalence of poverty is higher in rural areas, as high as 40 per cent in some areas, thus requiring higher focus on CSR than the urban areas. Botswana's income inequality is high, as reflected through a Gini coefficient as high as 0.61. Botswana's poverty spread is complex due to the semi-arid state of agricultural land, which leaves the rural areas exposed to limited opportunities.

Debswana: Case Background and Role in CSR

Debswana, Botswana's largest company by capitalization and contribution to the economy, has a long history. It is the world's largest diamond producer by volume and value. It contributes 30 per cent of the world's diamonds and gems on the market. Botswana has a very high ratio of gem-quality to industrial-quality diamonds, which places Debswana among the market leaders. The company contributes approximately 30 per cent of Botswana's GDP and 50 per cent of government revenue. It is also the country's main foreign exchange generator. It is Botswana's largest private employer: it employs 6,300 people, 93 per cent of the staff being Botswana citizens. The company contributes 80 per cent of the country's foreign exchange earnings. Although Debswana is associated with diamond mining, it has other investments in several wholly owned companies. See Figure 7.1.

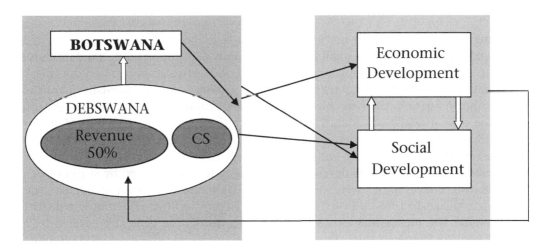

Figure 7.2   The Botswana/Debswana symbiotic relationship in development

The De Beers and Botswana Public/Private Partnership

The foundation of the De Beers/Botswana Public Private Partnership was laid in 1969 when De Beers came to prospect for diamonds in Botswana. To date the partnership has been in operation for 44 years. The partnership is based on a 50/50 shareholding in Debswana, the company that binds the two in commerce and in development. To further their relationship the Government of Botswana has a 15 per cent shareholding in De Beers. The core of this partnership is the Debswana Sales Agreement, which is renewable every five years. The latest agreement was negotiated and signed in 2011. The contract will commence on 1 January 2011 and will run for 10 years. It is the longest sales agreement between the partners to date. The latest agreement goes beyond just marketing diamonds on behalf of Botswana. The Diamond Trading Company (DTC), previously located in London, has now moved to Botswana. The Botswana operations were launched in September 2013 and the first auction of rough diamonds was held on 11 November 2013 Trading will now take place through a new company, Okavango Trading Corporation. The company is a result of the new sales agreement. From its new Headquarters in Gaborone, the DTC will aggregate production from De Beers' mines and its joint venture operations worldwide. The DTC will continue to sort and value Debswana production before selling it on to the DTC. The DTC will support the local cutting and polishing industry in Botswana, and increase its commitment by making more diamonds available for manufacturing businesses operating in Botswana. As a result of its ownership structure, Debswana has a strong symbiotic relationship not only with the Government of Botswana but also with the Batswana society. Its contributions to CSR and government revenue surpass that of any other business in Botswana, giving the company major explicit and implicit influence in socio-economic development. See Figure 7.2.

DIAMOND EXPLORATION AND MINE ESTABLISHMENT

Searching for diamonds began in 1955 in the Tuli Block, an area now heavily invested in commercial farming. Three small alluvial diamonds were found along the Motloutse River. In 1967, after extensive exploration over a period of two years between the village of Letlhakane and Mopipi Pan, a team of De Beers geologists found abundant quantities of elmenite and garnet, the two chief indicators of diamondiferous kimberlite. In April 1967, the pipe at Orapa was found. This was to be the largest (117 hectares) of all the kimberlite pipes which were eventually located in this area. Due to the size of the pipe and the variable grade, sampling and evaluation took two years. The Orapa pipe showed considerable potential and the development of the mine was affirmed by shareholders. In 1968 two smaller pipes were discovered 40 kilometres southeast of Orapa near Letlhakane village. In 1969 De Beers' geologists began prospecting in the southern district of Botswana. The rock formations in the southern district are generally covered by a layer of sand 20–50 metres thick. Prospecting operations using systematic solid sampling techniques covered the area. The pipe that was to become Jwaneng Mine was eventually found in 1972 beneath a 40–metre layer of sand and calcrete in the Naledi River valley. The town of Jwaneng is located on the perimeter of the Kgalagadi (Kalahari) Desert, 125 kilometres west of Lobatse and 160 kilometres south west of Gaborone, Botswana's capital, Jwaneng is the most valuable diamond mine in the world. Before the construction of the Jwaneng-Kanye road by Debswana, the area was only accessible by four-wheel drive and high-clearance vehicles. In 1971 Orapa Mine was commissioned. Four years later, in 1975, Letlhakane Mine was commissioned.

In May 1978 De Beers Consolidated Mines Limited and the Government of Botswana signed an agreement to establish Jwaneng Mine. Debswana was also formed in 1978. It is a company in which the Botswana Government and the De Beers Consolidated Mines Ltd. each hold a 50 per cent share. The company has four mines:

1. Jwaneng: the world's second richest diamond mine by value after Argile Mine in Australia. The mine is located in south central Botswana about 160 kilometres southwest of Gaborone. It was discovered in 1973. It contributes between 60 per cent and 70 per cent of Debswana's revenue.
2. Orapa: the oldest operating diamond mine and the largest open pit diamond mine in the world. It is second to Jwaneng in volume of production. Although it is the oldest of the four mines, the Orapa has reserves to last another three decades.
3. Letlhakane: within the Orapa kimberlite area and discovered when Orapa was being sampled and evaluated, this was the second mine opened by Debswana. It is the deepest of the Debswana mines.
4. Damtshaa: opened in 2003, is the youngest of the Debswana mines. It is located about 20 kilometres east of the Orapa kimberlite pipe in Central Botswana. It cost P [Botswana pula] 225 million to develop the mine.

Construction of the Iwaneng Mine and township commenced rapidly, with the mine coming into full production in July 1982. The opening of the Jwaneng Mine placed Botswana among the world's top diamond producers. In August 1996, the Botswana Government, De Beers Centenary AG and the Debswana Diamond Company signed an agreement to double production. The expansion increased Orapa Mine's annual production of 6 million carats to 12 million carats from the No. 1 and No. 2 production plants to about 26 million carats per year. Besides the Orapa 2000 project, the Aquarium Project, undertaken at Jwaneng Mine, has established the world's first completely automated recovery plant (CARP) and fully integrated sort house (FISH) (see Debswana.com, n.d.).

Debswana's CSR

Debswana's CSR initiatives started in 1971 soon after the first diamond mine was opened. A decision was taken then by the shareholders, De Beers and the Government of Botswana, to include surrounding communities in mining areas in mine development plans. The priority objective of Debswana was to create a legacy of the empowerment of communities and the lives of the people of Botswana. Owing to low development in communities surrounding mining settlements, Debswana's relationship with the communities has been defined in terms of uplifting and bringing change to them. To date, one of Debswana's core CSR objectives is 'to ultimately ensure that Debswana does not leave the mining communities worse off than when the company began operating in these areas'. To do so will 'enhance Debswana's reputation and the well-being of the communities in which it operates, as well as the country in general' (Debwana CSI, n.d.). In line with its CSR, where livelihoods of communities are affected they receive fair compensation for their losses. The objective of engaging in CSR in communities in mining areas has been the development of social infrastructure such as roads, educational institutions and hospitals. In addition there is support that goes to the non-governmental organizations and community-based organizations such as community development trusts. In its Corporate Social Investment Policy (CSI) guideline, Debswana notes that in order to improve the consultative processes with communities in mining areas the company has to establish a consultative structure that includes a senior director and representatives of stakeholders identified by local communities, and its own workforce. The committee meets on a regular basis to discuss the company's business goals in relation to community needs, including social and environmental needs. The company has had to commit itself publicly to contribute to long-term environmental, social, cultural and economic sustainability of communities in which it operates. To furtherance the policy, the company has had to develop indicators for measuring its contribution to community sustainability. The areas of CSR focus are: education (primary and secondary); environment, with particular emphasis on education; small business skills training; arts and culture development; health, including HIV/AIDS support to communities; and sports development (Debswana CSI, n. d.: 6).

The original Debswana CSR programme was called the 'Donations Fund'. It was launched with a budget of R [South African rands] 50,000. The first disbursement from the programme was given to Our Lady of the Desert, a school in Botswana's second largest city, Francistown. In 2006 the programme was renamed the 'Corporate Social Investment Programme'. The overall budget for CSI has since increased over the years. During the tenure of the Donations Fund the programme would give grants to various institutions. Beneficiaries of the Donations Fund included the Kalahari Conservation Society, the Botswana Council for the Disabled, and the Botswana Chess Federation. Debswana then realized that giving grants was not sustainable because the recipients knew funding would be coming and therefore their spending was not focused on project sustainability. At the time of the review in 2006 it was decided that from then onward beneficiaries would have to submit proposals in order to be given funding. In line with the Debswana Corporate Social Investment guidelines, proposals considered would have to meet the following new criteria:[1]

1. Programmes and organizations that will have a wide impact, rather than meet the needs of a few;
2. Programmes and organizations with the mission of improving the educational and economic opportunities of disadvantaged and/or low income groups of people, families and communities;
3. Organizations that deliver effective programmes with measurable outcomes in response to identified community needs;
4. End beneficiaries should be involved in project planning;
5. Beneficiary organizations should be registered nonprofit organizations or exclusively public institutions, or comparable organizations; or alternatively:
6. Organizations can be groups of concerned people operating at grassroots level with demonstrable developmental aim to benefit their local community or a disadvantaged group;

---

1   The source of this list of criteria for proposals submitted for funding in a flyer sent to the author by the Debswana Diamond Mining Company in response to his enquiry (Debswana CSI, n.d.).

7. The organization should be able to demonstrate that progress will result from a social investment by Debswana;
8. The organization should be financially stable and/or have credible financial records;
9. Receive and provide strong leadership;
10. Be willing to collaborate with other similar organizations to maximize delivery effectiveness to the intended beneficiaries; and
11. Present opportunities for staff involvement;
12. Provide essential infrastructure and services to local communities;
13. Work to strengthen the local civil society by building capacity in the NGO sector;
14. Respond to disasters;
15. Support Debswana's local licence to operate, including local and regional membership organizations such as chambers of commerce and United Way/ Community chests;
16. Request for ad hoc minimal support for local charitable cause; and charitable causes brought to our attention by staff (Debswana CSI, n.d.: 8–9).

In line with the requirement for submitting proposals, evaluation guidelines were also developed to ensure fairness in the process. The evaluation framework advocated:

a) Submission of progress reports on a quarterly basis;
b) Site visits by the Debswana CSI Project manager at least once a year;
c) Interim evaluation conducted by an external consultant; and
d) Post-completion evaluation to measure impact of the project.

Following the adoption of the CSI Programme Debswana also decided to increase the budget to P9 million. In 2011 the company further increased its CSI Programme budget from P9 million to P15 million in 2012.

IMPACT OF DEBSWANA CSR: SELECTED PROJECTS

Debswana as a mining company has largely shown its commitment to social responsibilities starting with local communities and has now expanded to national causes. The impact of CSR on socio-economic development has been in the following areas:

Health care

The company's health care provision through introduction of antiretroviral therapy to miners and their families had a major impact on the mining industry, the nation and in the Southern Africa region. The programme immediately became the benchmark worldwide. It is an important reference point to date for ways in which HIV/AIDS can be tackled in the workplace. The nature of the HIV/AIDS crisis galvanized CSR response in developing countries (Dunfee, 2006). Debswana's will to replicate its CSR agenda to also cover communities outside but within reach of the mines, while clearly a public relations manoeuvre, catered for vulnerable communities of people who would otherwise have perished without much notice during the early days of the disease. The impact of the health care provision has also been felt in mobile dental care in primary schools. Originally meant to cater for mining and adjacent communities, the dental care provision is now catering widely for many communities in the country.

Hospitals

Debswana runs two hospitals and a clinic in Jwaneng and Orapa. The health facilities serve employees and communities around the Debswana mines. Annually, over 70,000 patients are consulted at Orapa hospital and over 40,000 patients visit Jwaneng Hospital. Non-employees of Debswana who are hospitalized pay a nominal fee. The hospital sometimes provides free health care to members of the community in cases of emergency.

Debswana anti-retroviral programme

Debswana was the first company in the world in 2001 to proactively roll out free anti-retroviral drugs (ARVs) to its employees and their spouses who are infected. Children and young people below 21 years were included in 2006. Management of HIV/AIDS is integral to Debswana's CSR programmes. The company aims at minimizing the socio-economic and developmental consequences of HIV/AIDS in the workplace. An HIV/AIDS Committee oversees the implementation of its programmes at its operations in Botswana. The company has a public–private partnership with the government, through which it has leveraged its existing company infrastructure and human resources to increase access to Highly Active Anti-Retroviral Therapy to over 100,000 HIV/AIDS positive Batswana living in communities around its mines. HIV/AIDS is highly prevalent in communities around mines due to income disparities between the mine employees and the rural communities adjacent to the mines.

Mobile dental clinic in primary schools

In 2009 Debswana partnered with one of its major suppliers, Caterpillar, to start a health care initiative whose aim is to take dental care to local schools as a way of contributing to dental health care in Botswana. The two companies commissioned a mobile dental clinic which visited schools in its mining communities and the capital. Through the 2011 initiative the dental clinic received general dental care and education from a dentist.

INFRASTRUCTURE

A major socio-economic development priority for Debswana's CSR has been infrastructure development. In communities where Debswana has mining operations, its first mandate has been to build infrastructure for the displaced communities, thus bringing social development to the concerned stakeholder. Over and above this immediate compensatory responsibility to displaced communities, the company has prioritized provision of electricity and roads in communities distant from its operations but in great need of such infrastructure.

Electrification of communities adjacent to the mines

Debswana has been involved in the electrification of villages in sub-districts where it operates. In the Boteti sub-district it electrified the Madikola Village to improve the lives of people in the village.

Social Amenities and support for sport

Debswana has over the years also given priority to development of social amenities such as construction and rehabilitation of sports facilities. The amenities have become associated with success in sport in the country. Over and above providing amenities, the company has been associated with Botswana's Olympic team, earning a reputation for corporate citizenry. CSR by Debswana is now widely associated with success in sport at the highest level.

Construction and rehabilitation of sports facilities

Debswana has constructed some of the best sports facilities in the country at its mine locations. In addition to their use for recreation by mine employees, the surrounding communities are given access to these world-class facilities. The facilities are also available to top athletes preparing for sports competitions in and outside the country. As part of its commitment to sports development the company has contributed financially to funding the rehabilitation of the National Sports Stadium.

Rebabonaga grassroots sports development programme

One of Debswana's social commitments in sports has been in grassroots sports development. 'Rebabonaka' is a Setwana word which translates literally as 'we see them here'. The programme is for sports development targets children and teenagers aged 5–15. It covers all sports and is spread throughout the country. The approach in the project is to train youngsters in the 5–15 age range in all sports as a way of identifying talent in early age. The Botswana National Sports Council oversees the project, which was introduced in 2008 with funding of P1.7 million. The initial phase ran up to 2010; a new phase began in 2011 and will run until 2013. The budget for this phase will be P2 million.

Support to Olympic participants

Debswana has supported the Olympic teams sent by Botswana to compete. In the 2012 London Olympics the company funded the Olympians with P500,000. On the team's return the company gave prizes to the four participants amounting to P165,000.

SOCIAL WELFARE

CSR has also been used as a source for welfare support by needy groups in the country. Support by Debswana of rehabilitation centres and children's homes demonstrate to communities a caring attitude by the company. The impact of such philanthropy is greater in times of crisis.

Mahalapye Rehabilitation Centre

The Mahalapye Rehabilitation Community Centre in Mahalapye Town was built as a rehabilitation centre for the physically challenged members of the community. Debswana built the centre and provided equipment worth P1,128,000.

SOS Children's Village

Debswana then built an SOS Children's Village in Sorowe, a large rural village in the Central District in Botswana. SOS villages for children caught in vulnerable circumstances are common worldwide. At the SOS Village the company built an accommodation hall worth P500,000 in response to an appeal to improve accommodation facilities at the village.

Botswana Society for the Deaf

In Francistown Debswana built a Vocational Training Unit block at the Francistown Centre for the Deaf. The block has three classrooms. The project cost P488,000. The block caters for training in leatherwork, home economics and woodwork. The Francistown Centre for the Deaf is an institution of the Botswana Society for the Deaf, which was formed in 1978 as the Ramotswa Society for the Deaf. It provides services for 200 deaf children from all parts of the country at two centres, Francistown and Ramotswa.

Cultural Sites

TSODILO HILLS WORLD HERITAGE SITE

The Tsodilo Hills have been a UNESCO World Heritage Site since 2001. The hills have some of the oldest rock paintings sites in Southern Africa. In supporting the project, Debswana wanted to bring focus to cultural tourism. In order to bring in the community into the project, the company built a campsite where locals could develop and sharpen their skills in arts and crafts. The funding also brought a water network to the village. The Tsodilo project is being funded up to P10 million over a period of five years starting in 2009.

SME Supply Chain Support

SMALL BUSINESS SUPPORT THROUGH PROCUREMENT

Debswana set up a holding company, Peo Holdings (Pty) Ltd., to assist citizen enterprises through its supply chain. This is a citizen empowerment programme. The investment was worth P32.6 million. Peo Holdings' intervention is through providing preferential procurement opportunities for SMEs that could do business with Debswana focused on one of the activity areas in its supply chain. Although the nature of the relationship creates dependence, especially at the start, the small business is expected to wean itself away from Debswana over time and grow out of this dependence. By end of 2008 Debswana had funded 58 businesses through the programme, creating 1,167 jobs.

Conclusion

Debswana, the Government of Botswana's diamond mining joint venture with De Beers, has been involved in CSR since its establishment. Its involvement is inevitable. Debswana is the largest company in Botswana by value and employment. Due to its size it has acquired social power in communities where it operates and hence is bound morally and ethically to exercise social responsibility. CSR contributions have been one of the major ways to justify its co-existence with the communities. As a result of the trust between communities and Debswana and knowing the socio-economic benefits from the company's social development agenda, communities have given Debswana the social licence to operate. The resulting trust has been a perception of shared value between the communities and the company. The company's contribution to CSR is also in the context of its special relationship with the Government of Botswana. It is the only company in the world which is a 'joint trustee' to the country's most valuable asset, the diamonds. In practice, the relationship is symbiotic and in a major way imposes responsibility on the company. The company has been involved in tackling 'hard problems' (Drucker, 1984) such as community infrastructure (e.g. providing electricity, housing for the disabled in existing institutions, and other projects). Its involvement in CSR has asserted its legitimacy and respect in communities from which it extracts natural resources. That the company's operations have the hallmark of influencing development in the country is not in doubt. It is the impact of CSR contribution to socio-economic development which has to remain visible to the communities. The contribution to CSR has accelerated development to recipient communities, thus enhancing social understanding with them. In one of its projects, the creation of a supply chain linked to Debswana mining operations has created a new dimension in CSR by spawning SMEs, with a far-reaching trickle effect.

Owing to its involvement in socio-economic development Debswana has the attention of government. It therefore has the power to influence policy. The company has been a trendsetter in some of its social responsibility programmes. It was the first company in the world to provide anti-retroviral therapy to its employees, setting a worldwide trend and in the process earned the respect of its employees and their communities. The position of trust comes with a public responsibility. The company's expansive influence bestows on it the responsibility of not only focusing on communities adjacent to its mining operations but also spreading its influence far and wide, so that its

CSR is appreciated nationwide. The influence of its CSR policies is still more visible when it chooses to address macrosocial issues in communities distant from its operations. Although the company has formalized procedures and processes through which to select and allocate resources, the communities' perceptions of its initiatives are paramount. Criticism has arisen over how Debswana, due to its close relationship with the society it serves, has the potential to abuse such trust. Although in theory it has an implicit social contract with Botswana society, its commercial interests may not always coincide with those of development.

Acknowledgements

The author acknowledges support from Debswana's Corporate Social Investment executives who provided information on past and present CSR activities of the company.

References

ADB (2009). *Botswana 2009–2013 Country Strategy Paper. Regional Development – South Region A.* Tunis: African Development Bank.

Campbell, B. (2011). Corporate social responsibility and development in Africa: redefining the roles and responsibilities of public and private actors in the mining sector. *Resources Policy* [doi: 10.1016/j.resourpol.2011.05.002].

Davis, K. (1960). Can business afford to ignore social responsibilities? *California Management Review, 2*, 70–76.

Debswana.com (n.d.). Debswana Diamond Mining Co. website. [Online.] Available at: http://www.debswana.com [accessed: 26 November 2013].

Debswana CSI (n.d.). Debswana Corporate Investment Programme. Gaborone, Botswana: Debswana Diamond Mining Co. Available at: http://www.debswana.com/People/Pages/CSI.aspx [accessed: 26 November 2013].

Donaldson, T. and Dunfee, T.W. (1999). *Ties that Bind: A Social Contracts Approach to Business Ethics.* Cambridge, MA: Harvard Business School Press.

Drucker, P.F. (1984). The new meaning of corporate social responsibility. *California Management Review, 26*, 53–63.

Dunfee, T.W. (2006). Do firms with unique competencies for rescuing victims of human catastrophes have special obligations? Corporate responsibility and the Aids catastrophe in Sub-Saharan Africa. *Business Ethics Quarterly, 16*(2), 185–210.

Friedman, M. (1970). The social responsibility of business is to increase its profits. *New York Times Magazine, 33*, 122–26.

Garriga, E. and Mele, D. (2004). Corporate social responsibility theories: mapping the territory. *Journal of Business Ethics, 53*, 51–57.

Jones, T.M. (1980). Corporate social responsibility revisited, redefined. *California Management Review, 22*(3), 59–67.

Mogae, F. (2005). *Botswana's Development Experience.* Lecture at the Institute of Development Studies, University of Sussex, Brighton, UK.

UNECA and AU (2010). *Minerals and Africa's Development: A Report of the International Study Group on Africa's Mining Regimes, Second Draft. August.* Addis Ababa: United Nations Economic Commission for Africa and African Union. Available at: http://www.eisourcebook.org/cms/files/attachments/other/Minerals%20and%20Africas%20Development.pdf [accessed: 26 November 2013].

Van Wyk, D., Conjé, F. and Van Wyk, J. (2009). *Corporate Social Responsibility in the Diamond Mining Industry in Botswana*. SADC Research Report. Johannesburg, South Africa: The Bench Marks Foundation. Available at: http://www.bench-marks.org.za/research/West%20Coast%20final%2085%20pages.pdf [accessed: 26 November 2013].

Walton, C.C. (1967). *Corporate Social Responsibility*. Belmont, CA: Wadsworth Publishing.

8

Towards a Political Economy Perspective on CSR in a Developing Country Context: A Case Study of Tanzania

SARAH LAUWO AND OLATUNDE JULIUS OTUSANYA

Abstract

The role of multinational corporations (MNCs) in fostering socio-economic development in developing countries has been the subject of considerable debate by civil society organizations, academics and practitioners. It has been argued that, by working closely with host governments, MNCs have a role to play in alleviating poverty and stimulating economic development particularly in poverty stricken developing countries. This requires a strong commitment on the part of both corporations and host governments. However, in the context of the contemporary global economy, the ability of governments in developing countries to demand accountability, responsibility and transparency from modern corporations has remained questionable. This is in part due to the fact that governments in developing countries are desperate to attract foreign investment in order to deal with the various socio-economic problems including and in particular, poverty. Thus, a tension exists between encouraging foreign investment and issues associated with promoting socio-economic order. This chapter adopts a political economy perspective to considering how neo-liberal ideologies adopted in the global capitalist economy have been manifested within institutional structures as well as in CSR practices and to show how this has serious implications for the socio-economic development of many developing countries, such as is the case in Tanzania. It is argued here that any attempt to change CSR practices and their potential to promote socio-economic development in Tanzania need to be accompanied by changes in the governance structures at both domestic and global levels.

Introduction

In the last decade there has been a considerable increase in the variety and volume of the literature on corporate social responsibility (CSR) (see, for example, Banerjee, 2010; Belal and Owen, 2007; Cooper and Owen 2007; Detomasi, 2008; Solomon and Darby, 2005; Unerman and O'Dwyer, 2007). As the literature shows, the interest in CSR practices has been in part due to the increasing public pressure, coming from bodies such as non-governmental organizations (NGOs),[1] trade unions and the media, and from academics, for corporations to act in socially and environmentally responsible ways (see, for example, Unerman and O'Dwyer, 2007; Moon and Vogel, 2008; Christian Aid, 2005, 2008, 2009; Action Aid, 2008). The literature on CSR has emerged from a variety of disciplines, which include sociology, philosophy, accounting, management, finance, law, and politics (see Banerjee, 2007, 2008; Porter and Kramer, 2006; Vogel, 2005; Jones, 2008). Using various theoretical frameworks, such as agency, stakeholder, legitimacy and political economy theories, these studies provide useful insights into the development of key social responsibility issues and contribute to the understanding of CSR discourse (see, for example, Jensen and Meckling, 1976; Jones, 1995; Balkaoui and Karpik, 1989; Guthrie and Mathews, 1985; Ullmann, 1985; Guthrie and Parker, 1990; Islam and Deegan, 2010). However, despite the increasing literature on CSR as a postulate for accountability, ethical and responsible business practices, most studies have been primarily Western-centric (see, for example, Adams, Coutts and Harte, 1995; Adams and Harte, 1998; Campbell, 2004; Gray et al., 1987, 1995a and 1995b; Guthrie and Parker, 1990; Hackston and Milne, 1996; Matten and Moon, 2004). As a result, comparatively, little attention has been paid to CSR issues in developing countries (Andrew et al., 1989; Belal, 2001, 2008; Belal and Owen, 2007; Kuasirikun, 2005; Tsang, 1998; Ite, 2004; Jamali, 2007), which includes Tanzania (see Egels and Kallifatides, 2006; Lange, 2006). However, as studies on developing countries have tended to replicate Western studies and adopt Western theoretical frameworks, their relevance for addressing the issues peculiar to developing countries has been regarded as questionable (see Tsang, 1998; Idemudia, 2007; Belal, 2001). Tsang (1998), for example, argued that it is inappropriate to apply conclusions reached from studies on developed countries to what happens in developing countries, as the different socio-political and economic environments of developed and developing countries shape CSR practices differently. Jones (1999) drew attention to the significance of the national socio-cultural environment and the level of national economic development as important variables influencing our understanding of CSR. With these points in mind, this chapter aims to add to the current literature on CSR by considering the contradictions and dilemmas relating to CSR practices in Tanzania, a developing country in East Africa. It argues that CSR practices have the potential for stimulating socio-economic development and addressing the problem of poverty, which is endemic in Tanzania. As a socially constructed practice, CSR is shaped by the history, institutional and power structures of a particular society, as well as the influence of countervailing structures, such as the influence of NGOs and other pressure groups. The following paragraphs consider these matters.

---

1   For example, in the early twentieth century an increasing number of active and sophisticated civil society organizations in the UK and the US began campaigning against increasing corporate power, as well as disseminating information about the increasing impact of corporate-related activities as a way creating new forms of awareness, scrutiny and public accountability (Davis, 1960; Hirschland, 2006).

A number of laws and regulations, including international conventions (such as the United Nations Global Compact (UNGC) and the Organisation for Economic Co-operation and Development (OECD) Guidelines for Multinational Enterprises) have been passed, mainly in Western countries, to regulate the conduct of businesses and requirements for the adoption of responsible business practices.[2] In addition, NGOs and other pressure groups[3] have continued to put pressure on organizations to behave more responsibly (see Vogel, 2005). In order to be seen to be responding to public opinion and public pressure, some companies have begun to change their CSR policies and to develop their social obligations to include other issues such as taxation and human rights (Kobrin, 2009; Sikka, 2011). However, despite the introduction of laws and regulations at both the domestic and international levels, their capacity to regulate corporate activities in developing countries such as Tanzania has remained questionable.

Furthermore, although the CSR literature has used theories such as agency, legitimacy and stakeholder as frameworks for explaining and understanding the business–society relationship, the appropriateness of such theories to 'capture' the complexities of CSR in a developing country such as Tanzania has also remained questionable. In fact, researchers have criticized these theoretical frameworks for attaching little explicit weight to the broader socio-political, economic and historical structures which shape CSR practices (see Andriof and McIntosh, 2001; Banerjee, 2007; Cooper and Scherer, 1984; Puxty, 1991; Tinker et al., 1991). In particular, these frameworks have been criticized for paying insufficient attention to the impact on CSR practices of factors such as institutional structures, power relations, social conflict and also the role of the state (Andriof and McIntosh, 2001; Puxty, 1986; Tinker et al., 1991). In order to understand CSR practices in a developing country, such as Tanzania, it is necessary to consider the historical, political and economic structures and the power relations which shape and influence it. There is also a need to consider such practices not only from a domestic perspective but also in the context of the contemporary global economy (see Cooper and Scherer, 1984; Puxty, 1986, 1991; Tinker et al., 1991; Banerjee, 2007). In particular, there is a need to appreciate and understand the contradictions and complexities faced by a developing country in promoting CSR as a social practice. One of the difficulties, however, for developing countries is that they need to secure foreign investment in order to create employment and to deal with the various socio-economic issues which need to be addressed (see, for example, Hoogvelt, 2001). For example, developing countries had attracted at least U$380 billion by way of foreign direct investment (FDI) as at the end of 2006 (see UNCTAD, 2007).[4] Such investment has had, and continues to have, important implications for the protection and well-being of society, in particular with regard to advancing and promoting responsible corporate practices. Furthermore, as corporations, particularly transnational

---

2   For example, in the 1950s and 1960s, many laws were enacted in the USA to regulate business conduct and to protect employees and consumers (for example, the Textile Fiber Products Identification Act 1958; Fair Packaging and Labeling Act 1966; Equal Pay Act 1963; National Traffic and Motor Safety Act 1966; National Environmental Policy Act 1969; Truth in Lending Act 1969; and Clean Air Act 1970). In order to promote corporate disclosure and transparency, a number of regulatory agencies were also established in the USA, such as the Occupational Safety and Health Administration; the Equal Opportunities Commission; the Consumer Product Safety Commission; and the Environmental Protection Agency (Roper, 2007).

3   For example, in 2005, a coalition of 50 organizations, which included labour unions, and environmental and community organizations, joined together to launch a public a campaign against a retailer (Roner, 2005: 16–17).

4   Tanzania is one of the top recipients of FDI in Africa (UNCTAD, 2009). For example, in Tanzania, MNCs account for over two-thirds of gross domestic product (GDP) and employ nearly 90 per cent of paid employees (AFRODAD, 1999).

ones, are increasingly responsible for FDI in developing countries, this has given them considerably more power than many developing countries themselves (UNCTAD, 2007). For example, it has been shown that 500 corporations control 80–90 per cent of global FDI and 70 per cent of world trade (see Korten, 2001; Trade Union Congress, 2005). As a result, some developing countries, including Tanzania, seem poor when compared with the wealth possessed by multinational corporations (MNCs). Because of their reliance on foreign aid and foreign investment, it is difficult for governments in developing countries to question and challenge corporate activities and to demand that MNCs engage in responsible business practices (see Bakan, 2004; Korten, 2001; Picciotto, 1991). Thus, in particular, the capacity of such governments to pass and enforce laws to protect the welfare of citizens is often constrained by economic imperatives. In other words, the need for governments to ensure responsible business practices is superseded, and often obliterated, by the government's primary objective, which is the desire to attract and maintain foreign investment.

This chapter considers CSR practices in Tanzania. It does so by adopting a political economy approach to explore the socio-political economic and historical context of these practices. It examines the extent to which both local and global institutional structures have shaped and influenced such practices. The chapter is structured as follows. The next section considers the various theoretical perspectives adopted in the literature. The following section considers the broader institutional structures of globalization, corporate power, and the contradictory role of the state with regard to the development of CSR practices in developing countries. There follows a section that examines the socio-political and economic environment of Tanzania and considers in particular the economic imperatives which have shaped its institutional structures, its governance system and CSR. It also considers the various legal and regulatory frameworks which govern CSR practices in Tanzania, and the role played by bodies such as NGOs and the media in advancing or marginalizing the various aspects of such practices. The final section provides a discussion and a conclusion.

Theoretical Frameworks for Studying CSR

Corporate social responsibility (CSR), despite having a long history,[5] has in recent years become a much-debated topic in the context of the contemporary global economy (see Spence, 2007, 2009; Puxty, 1986; Tinker et al., 1991). In order to understand the complexities associated with CSR, scholars have adopted various theoretical frameworks which have provided insights into some of the social, environmental and other problems relating to corporate activities (see, for example, Balkaoui and Karpik, 1989; Deegan and Gordon, 1996; Guthrie and Parker, 1989; Guthrie and Mathews, 1985; Ullman, 1985). This section examines these theoretical frameworks in order to assess their appropriateness for understanding the complexities of CSR in developing countries, including, in particular, Tanzania. Figure 8.1 below shows in diagrammatic form the theories commonly used in CSR studies.

---

5   Avi-Yonah (2006) has stated that the history of CSR can be traced back to the emergence of the modern corporation in the seventeenth and eighteenth centuries, with the introduction of legislation in the form of acts of incorporation in Europe and America, which led to the formation of limited liability companies.

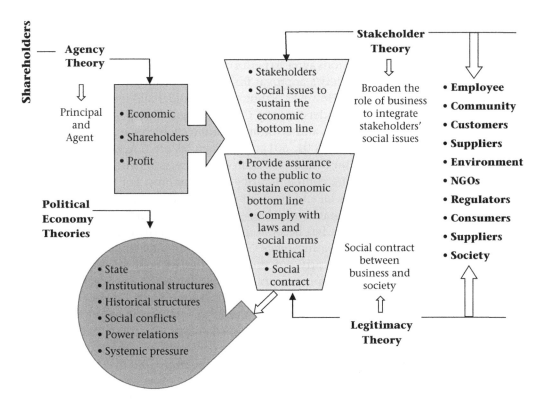

Figure 8.1   Theories used in CSR studies

An increasing body of CSR scholarship has adopted a functionalist perspective and has used agency theory, a theory which views corporations as an instrument of wealth creation and which have as their sole responsibility the need to advance economic benefits for their owners (Friedman, 1970; Jensen and Meckling, 1976; Jones, 1995).[6] However, although agency theory provides a useful framework for studying CSR, it has been criticized for focusing purely on the economic function of businesses and for failing to consider the complexities they face in dealing with related inefficiencies, information asymmetries and multiple incentive problems (Banerjee, 2007). McDonald and Puxty (1979), for instance, have argued that companies are not the instruments of shareholders alone but, as they exist within society, they also have responsibilities to society as a whole.

To integrate social needs and the needs of the various stakeholders into the CSR discourse, some studies have chosen to adopt a framework based on stakeholder and legitimacy theories (see, for example, Freeman, 1984; Carroll, 1999; Donaldson and Preston, 1995). From the perspective of stakeholder theory, CSR disclosure is seen as

---

6   Agency theory describes the relationship between principal and agent. which is based on a 'nexus-of-contract' (see Jensen and Meckling, 1976). From an agency theory perspective, the social activities that companies can engage in are acceptable if they are prescribed by law or if they contribute to the maximization of shareholder wealth. Applying agency theory, researchers have argued that a corporation's sole social responsibility is merely to maximize shareholder wealth, as there is no enforceable legal requirement to serve non-shareholder interests (see Jensen and Meckling, 1976; Friedman, 1970). From the perspective of agency theory, CSR is regarded as a misuse of corporate resources that could be better spent on valued-added internal projects or be returned to the shareholders (McWilliams, Siegel and Wright, 2006).

part of the dialogue between a company and its stakeholders (Roberts, 1992). Legitimacy theory, on the other hand, explicitly recognizes that organizations are bound by the social contract in which corporations agree to perform various socially and environmental desired actions in return for society's approval for their continuing existence (Deegan, 2002; Guthrie and Parker, 1989). However, although stakeholder and legitimacy theories provide useful frameworks for understanding CSR, Banerjee (2007: 28) has criticized them for ignoring the many social and economic conflicts which can exist in society. Furthermore, according to Lantos (2001: 601), these theories often neglect the tensions and contradictions faced by businesses in addressing the competing needs of the various stakeholder groups in the contemporary global economy. For example, from a legitimacy theory perspective, social and environmental disclosure is perceived as one of the strategies employed by corporate entities to seek society's acceptance and approval of their operations. However, this has become questionable, particularly in developing countries where, despite the increasing social and environmental impact of corporate activities, companies continue to carry out their activities without any challenge (see Banerjee, 2007). In essence, developing countries have neither the economic nor the political resources to discipline giant corporations. This is often quite different from what happens in developing countries. For example, the BP oil spills in the Gulf of Mexico, in April 2010, showed how governments of developed countries can use their power to demand public accountability and responsibility from corporations. After the BP oil spill, Baraka Obama, the US President, made a public speech requesting BP to compensate the victims. Requiring and enforcing the public accountability of corporations in developing countries may, on the other hand, be very difficult as the governments of such countries often depend on giant corporations for tax revenues, employment and the provision of publics services, such as roads, water supply and utilities, hospitals, schools and security (Banerjee 2008).

Therefore, as agency, stakeholder and legitimacy theories, as frameworks for studying CSR, have been criticized for attaching insufficient weight to the various social and institutional structures which shape CSR practices, in recent years, political economy theories have been increasingly adopted in the CSR literature (see Adam and Whelan, 2009; Banerjee, 2007; Kuasirikun and Scherer, 2004; Scherer and Palazzo, 2007; Tinker, 1980; Tinker et al., 1991). This is because of the importance of taking into account the social, political and economic contexts in which business organizations conduct their activities. In essence, political economy theories draw on interdisciplinary perspectives to explain the influence of the socio-political context on social practices in the capitalist global economy. The emerging interest in political economic theory is associated with the emergence of a rapidly integrated and interconnected global world and an increased awareness of the socio-economic and environmental impact of corporate activities on the wellbeing of employees, communities and individuals. Political economy theories focus on analyzing: power, social conflicts, exploitation and the unequal relationships between actors; the historical and institutional structures; and the role of the state in the integrated global world. Political economy theorists have explored CSR within a social, political and economic framework and examined the distribution of power in society and the socio-political and institutional structures that mirror the distribution of power. For political economy theorists, contemporary CSR has been driven by globalization and the deregulation and technological advances that escalated in the 1980s and 1990s. A number of critical scholars have urged CSR researchers to investigate the power relations and structural inequalities in society and the underlying social antagonism inherent in the capitalist system (see Puxty, 1986, Spence, 2007; Tinker et al., 1991). Guthrie and Parker have explained how political economy theory can help contribute to an understanding of corporate social disclosure practices:

> [A] political economy theory of social disclosure is both viable and may contribute toward our understanding of observed developments in national reporting practices. Corporate social disclosures have appeared to reflect public social priorities, respond to government pressure, accommodate environmental pressures and sectional interests, and protect corporate prerogatives and projected corporate images. (1990: 172–73)

The next section examines the politics of CSR in order to understand, inter alia, the role played by corporate actors in producing or modifying the existing institutional structures within which their CSR practices are embedded.

The Politics of CSR

CSR practices have a powerful potential to make positive economic contributions, which can in turn make a significant contribution to the needs to disadvantaged communities especially those in developing countries (Vogel, 2005; Frederick, 2007). However, as companies are under continuous pressure to increase shareholder profit; their commitment to socio-economic development in their host country may be seriously constrained. To understand CSR in the context of a developing country, it is important to understand the nature of the contradictory role played by the state and to identify the systemic pressures, conflicts and challenges faced by corporations in the context of contemporary globalization and which act as constraints on CSR practices. It has been argued that economic globalization has produced substantial changes in the structure of societies which have created significant challenges with regard to the nature and form of CSR practices (see, for example, Held and McGrew, 2002) particularly in developing countries (Hoogvelt, 2001).

Globalization has increased the economic interconnectedness of the global economy, expanded the global network of MNCs, and also substantially enhanced their size and power (see Bakan, 2004; Korten, 2001). Thus, MNCs have become dominant governance institutions, with the largest among them reaching into virtually every country of the world and sometimes exceeding governments in size and power (Korten, 2001). For example, with a global annual FDI flow of US$1.7 trillion in 2008, developing countries received 43 per cent of this sum (UNCTAD, 2009), giving corporations enormous influence as to the terms and nature of trade in such countries. Furthermore, the economic size of the largest MNCs exceeds that of many countries (Korten, 2001). In fact 95 of the world's largest 150 economic entities are corporations (63.3 per cent), not countries. It has been argued that, through trade, mergers and acquisition, corporations have acquired vast monopoly powers to shift jobs, investment and taxes, as well as to discipline states (Sikka, 2011: 3). However, within the dynamics of capitalism, the most important corporate concern is to generate economic surpluses for shareholders (Friedman, 1970). Since corporations are primarily motivated by profit, the pursuit of higher profits often brings corporations into conflict with social policies, such as those devoted to the provision of housing, transport, healthcare, and education, and also the protection of human rights (see Rayman-Bacchus, 2004; Sikka, 2010). It is in this context that the economic imperative driving globalization has been challenged by many researchers. Thus, for example, it has been considered responsible for weakening governance mechanisms for promoting social and environmental responsibility in developing countries (Bakan, 2004; Korten, 2001).

It has been argued that MNCs have become adept at exploiting the governance gap that exists between weak states and fledging international regulatory frameworks (Detomasi, 2008). Bakan (2004), for example, states that corporations are no longer tethered to their home jurisdiction, but produce goods and services at substantially lower costs by buying cheap labour from poor developing countries, where social and environmental regulations are weak, and by selling their products in wealthy countries where people have disposable income and are willing and able to pay for them. It has also been argued that, whereas managers enjoy considerable autonomy to appropriate economic surpluses for their shareholders, their discretion to pursue social and environmental objectives may often be severely constrained by economic rationality (Sikka, 2010; Banerjee, 2007). Such corporate practices raise questions about the morality of neo-liberal ideology and its associated policies of privatization, free trade and deregulation which have been implemented in the contemporary globalizing era.

As neo-liberal ideologies continue to prioritize market-driven competition, market forces are expected to coordinate the interaction amongst the socio-economic actors while admitting a subsidiary role for the state in protecting the welfare of its citizens (Harvey, 2005). Proponents of the global market (such as the World Bank) stipulate, however, that the first requirement of the state is to ensure that the property rights, free exchanges, and profit opportunities of the market remain secured and protected. Privatization, liberalization, the removal of exchange controls, the lowering of trade barriers and deregulation to increase the mobility of capital, and thereby to finance the continuing supply of social order and basic public goods, have become the core economic agendas of the neo-liberal state (Picciotto, 1991; Offe, 1984). Nevertheless, as the state's revenue and survival is dependent on the long-term development of the corporate sector (Offe, 1984), its economic policies and institutional frameworks are often devised in such as way as to facilitate the expansion of capital (Cox, 1996; Sklair, 1995). This has entailed using a variety of contradictory measures, such as tax concessions, subsidies, investment protections, guarantees and stabilization clauses (Sikka and Willmott, 2010; Cotula, 2008). However, these mechanisms have serious implication for a state's capacity to control giant corporations and promote responsible business practices.

As a result, states have become enmeshed within the capitalist social-economic crisis (see Harvey, 2005; Klimecki and Willmott, 2009; Holloway and Picciotto, 1978). The complexities of the neo-liberal state in developed countries also inform the operation of states in developing countries. Therefore, with respect to developing countries, there is a need to consider the dynamics of colonial histories, the power relations and the extreme poverty levels which exist in many of these countries, and which includes Tanzania. Faced with the need to stimulate their economies and reduce poverty, governments in developing countries have increasingly turned to MNCs to provide investment, create employment, increase government revenues and promote economic development. This has entailed offering less stringent regulations, and offering investment incentives, subsidies, investment protection, guarantees and stabilization clauses (Cox, 1996; Lobel,

2006).[7] However, ensuring that developing countries adopt global standards, which promote transparency, public accountability and responsibility, while at the same time attracting foreign investment, poses compelling moral challenges and dilemmas in the globalizing era (Korten, 2001; Bakan, 2004).

In the contemporary global economy, investment incentives, concessions and stabilization clauses have increased the inflow of FDI and the growth of MNC operations in developing countries. However, whereas investment concessions and stabilization clauses increase investor protection, little attention has been paid to the state's duties to protect employees, the environment and local communities (Banerjee, 2008; Sikka, 2010), and to promote human rights (Frankental et al., 2011). Thus, being captured by corporate interests, the ability of developing countries to develop and enforce laws and regulations which protect employees, communities, and the environment may be seriously constrained (Ratner, 2001; Korten, 2001; Bakan, 2004). In essence, the strings attached to FDI pose serious question about the boundary between the state and corporations particularly in respect of the governance of business operations (see Ratner, 2001: 458). In sum, the governments of developing countries find it difficult to strengthen domestic, social and environmental laws due to fears of losing foreign investment (Hoogvelt, 2001; Korten, 2001).

Although strong governments may be able to challenge corporate conduct and deal with externalities and business consequences, the ability of governments in developing countries to address the adverse socio-economic and environmental impact of contemporary capitalism has remained constrained (Harvey, 2006; Sikka, 2010). As Klimecki and Willmott (2009) have argued, interventions to protect citizens tend to be counterbalanced by the pressure to stimulate private sector expansion, with a preparedness to weaken the interventions that protect the vulnerable if they are likely to impede or penalize profitable private sector growth.

Government strategies and policies which prioritize the promotion of investment at the expense of public welfare in developing countries have received strong criticism from NGOs and other pressure groups. In response to such criticism, some governments in developing countries, including Tanzania, have adopted a number of institutional and regulatory reforms with the hope of promoting good governance and public accountability (Lauwo, 2011). However, corporations can sometimes weaken the efficacy and impact of such reforms by adopting various strategies which include, for instance, lobbying and sponsoring prominent politicians, lobbying trade associations, the media and think tanks in order to prevent the implementation of such reforms (see Sikka, 2008b: 400). Furthermore, even though governments in developing countries may be willing to introduce new laws to promote public accountability, transparency and corporate governance, stabilization clauses and investment guarantees often constrain a government's ability to implement laws to protect its citizens (Cotula, 2008).

As has been shown above, in the context of the contemporary global economy, developing countries including Tanzania have become subject to various social, political and economic tensions and conflicting interests. In other words, the ability of governments in developing countries to enact and enforce regulations to promote CSR and to protect the welfare of their citizens by encouraging responsible business practices

---

7   These are contractual clauses in foreign investment agreements with developing countries which guarantee foreign investors that the terms agreed will remain unchanged over the life of the project, including its fiscal and regulatory regime.

has been constrained by political and economic pressures including, in particular, the desire to attract international capital and investment.

The next section examines the socio-political and economic context of Tanzania to show how the desire to attract capital has shaped, and continues to shape, local structures and how there has been a failure to promote CSR practices on the part of MNCs conducting their business in the country.

The Socio-political and Economic Environments of Tanzania

To understand the potential of CSR practices to promote the social welfare of Tanzanian citizens it is necessary to appreciate the socio-political and economic background of the country, which has shaped and continues to shape such practices. The socio-political and economic environment of Tanzania, like that of many other developing countries in Africa, has been shaped to a large extent by its colonial past,[8] and by its recent integration into the global capitalist economic system.[9] During the colonial period, an effort was made to integrate Tanzania into the capitalist industrialized countries in order to supply raw materials (such as minerals and agricultural commodities) and cheap labour to European countries (Richardson, 2000). As a result, corporate public accountability and responsibility became less of a priority (see Lauwo, 2011; Shivji, 1975).

Tanzania has continued to experience considerable economic challenges, which have acted as a thrust for major policy and institutional changes (Lauwo, 2011). It has been for many years one of the poorest countries in the world, with many of its people living below the world poverty level (UNDP, 2009). In order to address its endemic poverty, Tanzania has over the years introduced a number of institutional reforms. For instance, in 1967 the government attempted to bring the economic sector and the political sphere under the control of the state through nationalization policies (Tsikata, 2001).[10] However, a lack of public accountability and monopoly control, plus too much discretion, skewed the benefit in favour of the political elite instead of the intended societal beneficiaries (Bagwacha, Mbele and Van-Arkadie, 1992). In fact, the Tanzanian government failed to create policies and institutional structures which were capable of promoting public accountability, responsibility and transparency in the state-owned enterprises (SOEs) (Bagwacha, Mbele and Van-Arkadie, 1992; Melyoki, 2005). As a result, various antisocial practices (such as corruption, embezzlement and nepotism) became endemic in Tanzania, and also severe and widespread poverty (Heilman and Ndumbaro, 2002).

---

8   Tanzania, like many other developing countries, has been subjected to colonialism and subordinated to the dominant poles of the world capitalist economy (Leftwich, 2000). Tanzania was initially colonized by Germany (1884–1917) and later by the British (1918–1961). Colonialism had the effect of laying the foundations for continued economic control and domination over colonial resources, even in the absence of direct colonial political administration (Hoogvelt, 2001). In fact, colonialism had prepared and firmed up those institutions necessary for the 'historical structure' of global capitalism in the globalizing era (Hoogvelt, 2001).

9   Despite the formal recognition of political independence in 1961, Tanzania continued to depend on its established relationship with its former colonial master through loans, aid and grants.

10   This reform was contained in the Ujamaa policy which called for economic and political policies oriented towards self-reliance to replace the capitalist private sector market economy inherited from the colonial government with the state-owned centrally planned and controlled economy (Ngowi, 2007).

In 1985, in order to address governance problems and the problem of poverty, the Tanzanian government adopted the structural adjustment programmes (SAPs) and liberalization policies of the World Bank and the International Monetary Fund (IMF). SAPs required the Tanzanian government to introduce political and legislative reforms,[11] remove state controls and implement free trade and liberalization policies in order to attract the inflow of foreign investment and MNC operations. Furthermore, to address governance problems, Tanzania introduced a number of political and institutional reforms with the aim of promoting good governance, public accountability and transparency. For example, the third President of Tanzania, Benjamin Mkapa, established the Public Leadership Code of Ethics in 1995 in order to curb impropriety at the higher levels of public service; the Presidential Commission on Corruption (the Warioba Commission) in 1996; and the Commission for Human Rights and Good Governance in 2001 (Heilman and Ndumbaro, 2002). It has been argued, for example by Heilman and Ndumbaro (2002: 7), that Mkapa's government took a pragmatic approach to addressing corruption through public campaigns and by strengthening the powers of the anti-corruption institutions. However, despite Mkapa's efforts to create institutional structures to promote democracy, public accountability, responsibility and transparency, Tanzania continued to perform poorly in Transparency International's Corruption Perceptions Index (CPI). Thus, in 2003 Tanzania was ranked 92 out of 133 corrupt countries (with a CPI score of 2.5) (Transparency International, 2003).

Although successive Tanzanian governments have professed a willingness to introduce policies and institutions to promote good governance, public accountability, transparency and responsibility, the government's desire to attract capital to address the country's pressing economic needs has impacted on political developments and on CSR practices in the country. In fact Tanzania has continued to experience considerable economic challenges, and, despite the inflow of foreign investment, has remained economically poor with stagnant economic growth and deteriorating social services (World Bank, 2010). With a population of approximately 41.3 million (in 2008), it is one of the poorest countries in the world, with many of its people living below the world poverty level (UNDP, 2009). About 45 per cent of the population has no access to clean water (UNDP, 2009), and only 31 per cent of the urban population has access to proper sanitation facilities (UNDP, 2006). According to the *United Nations Development Report* (2009), average life expectancy in Tanzania is 55 years, and 96.6 per cent of the population live on less than US$2 per day. As a result, the Human Development Index (HDI) (of 0.53) has remained very low with Tanzania ranked at number 151 in the list of the 184 poorest countries in the world in 2007 (UNDP, 2009). Tanzania's gross national product (GNP) of US$400 per capita has also remained very low and far less than that of other countries in sub-Saharan Africa, which have averages of US$952 (World Bank, 2007). Although total gross domestic product (GDP) in Tanzania increased from US$10.2 billion in 2000 to US$20.7 billion in 2008 (UNDP, 2009), this has not been enough to improve the lives of most Tanzanians. In fact, the economy has remained overwhelmingly dependent on donors[12] and foreign investors, especially for

---

11   One of the political reforms implemented was the creation of a multiparty democratic system aimed at removing the monopoly in the political sphere in order to improve democracy, public accountability, responsibility and transparency (Mmuya, 2000).

12   By the end of December 2008, Tanzania had an external debt of US$5.311 billion (IMF, 2007). This huge external debt has had a negative impact on the economy (due to various attached conditions) and has continued to restrict the

the provision of social services such as education, healthcare and other infrastructures (IMF, 2007).

Tanzania has also experienced an HIV/AIDS pandemic, which has also constrained its economic development. In 2007, 1.4 million people in Tanzania had HIV/AIDS. of whom 70.5 per cent were aged 25–49 and 15 per cent aged 15–24 (UNDP, 2007/2008). The impact of this pandemic has been felt in all the social and economic sectors of Tanzanian society. It has contributed to increasing health costs, increased infant and child mortality, greater poverty and growing numbers of orphans (estimated at 2.6 million) (UNDP, 2007/2008).

Tanzania has also witnessed growing levels of unemployment in recent years, particularly among the younger population in urban areas, partly as a result of privatization and other economic reforms which have led to the closure of many state-owned enterprises (ILO, 2009). The Integrated Labour Survey (ILFS) conducted in Tanzania in 2005/2006 reported a general unemployment rate of 11.7 per cent, and an unemployment rate of 13.4 per cent for those aged 15–35 (ILO, 2008).

In order to address these social and economic issues, the Tanzanian government implemented a number of economic recovery programmes. These included embracing the World Bank and IMF structural adjustment programmes (SAPs) and free trade and liberalization policies in order to open up its economy to foreign investors. Foreign investment, particularly by MNCs, was sought in order to create employment, promote socio-economic development and increase government revenues. As a result, the liberalization of the domestic economy and the increasing integration of the Tanzanian economy into the global market led to an increase in the total investment to GDP ratio, which rose from 16.5 per cent in 1996 to 21 per cent in 2004 (World Bank, 2009). Tanzania's efforts to create an attractive business environment for the private sector led to an increased inflow of FDI (from US$12 million in 1992 to US$744 million in 2008), due to the massive privatization of the state-owned enterprises (World Bank, 2010). However, in the integrated global economy, Tanzania, like many other developing countries, has had to compete with other countries for private investment (UNCTAD, 2009). In order to attract FDI, the Tanzanian government has chosen to adopt a favourable investment environment, which has included, for instance, tax holidays, subsidies, substantial investment incentives, low taxes and with there being only minimal obligations to the workforce and to the environment (Ngowi, 2007; Oxfam, 2008). These incentives have inevitably increased investment by MNCs in Tanzania. However, contracts signed with MNCs often 'cherry pick' the most profitable sector of the economy (such as minerals, oil, and manufacturing), and contain terms providing investment protection, guarantees and stabilization clauses (Oxfam, 2008). The concentrated nature and size of foreign investment has given MNCs corporate 'clout' which can be used to demand further favourable investment conditions, but which constrains the performance of their corporate social responsibilities (see Lauwo, 2011; Oxfam, 2008). There is also evidence to show that some MNCs have even lobbied Tanzanian government officials in order to safeguard their investment interests and reduce their social obligations (Oxfam, 2008; Fischer, 2006). For example, in February 2008, the Tanzanian Prime Minister, Edward Lowassa, was alleged to have been involved

---

Tanzanian government's efforts to alleviate poverty and lay down frameworks to promote responsible business practices. Domestic debt increased to US$1.67 billion from US$1.43 billion during December 2006 to December 2007.

in a radar equipment scam costing £28 million (Said, 2008). Thus, the radar equipment was overpriced, sold to the Tanzanian government by the UK military manufacturer, BAE, and kickbacks were purported to have been paid to a Swiss bank account in the name of a businessman who was expected to transfer some or all of the kickbacks to officials in the government of former President Mkapa (Said, 2008). Such antisocial practices involving corporations and officials deprive the Tanzanian government of revenues which could be used to improve the social welfare of its citizens (see Lauwo, 2011). Corporate Watch (2003) has observed that business between BAE and the governments of impoverished countries like Tanzania would not be possible without the sanction of the British government, as Britain is responsible for issuing export licences in order to allow such sales.

The Tanzanian government's reliance on MNC activities to stimulate socio-economic development has therefore posed, and continues to pose, serious questions about the boundary between the state and corporations, and about how to make MNCs accountable, responsible and transparent. As Tanzania has become deeply enmeshed in, and integrated into, the world economy, the global processes of capital accumulation have continued to shape government regulations and socio-economic development. Although CSR practices can be encouraged, promoted and enforced by an appropriate regulatory framework, the Tanzanian government has found it difficult to control corporate conduct as it is constantly under pressure to attract and retain foreign capital. The legal and regulatory framework of Tanzania with respect to CSR practices is considered next.

THE LEGAL AND REGULATORY FRAMEWORK

Since independence in 1961, there has been a strong local desire to encourage and maintain ethical business practices, public accountability, transparency and good governance in Tanzania (Oxfam, 2008; Mmuya, 2000; Killian, 2006). Thus, successive Tanzanian governments have attempted to pass new laws and regulations to promote public accountability and good governance and to foster 'good' CSR practices (Mmuya, 2000). However, as post-independence codes of conduct have retained most of the features of the former colonial regime,[13] Tanzania's ability to address the demands of CSR and to protect the public interest and promote social and environmental issues has been restricted (see Shivji, 1976). For example, the Companies Act 1932–CAP 212, which was enacted in 1929 during the British colonial period in order to lay down requirements for addressing governance issues in the colonial government, remained in force for many years post-independence and was not amended until 2002 (see further below). Although the Act required directors to act in good faith to promote the best interests of the company (see Section 185), stakeholder interests have remained (and continue to remain) subordinate to the financial interests of shareholders.

To address trade union demands for enhanced rights for workers, the Tanzanian government passed minimum wage legislation, the Security of Employment Act 1964, and established the National Provident Fund. However, despite these developments,

---

13   While colonial codes of conduct were created to deepen the colonial interest of wealth accumulation, their pertinence in addressing post-independence socio-political and economic issues in Tanzania, and CSR practices in particular, has been questionable (Shivji, 1975).

the evidence shows that little success has been achieved in improving working conditions (see Killian, 2006). In other words, working conditions have remained comparatively poor (Shivji, 1976). In 1967, President Nyerere's government enacted new codes of conduct, enshrined in the 1967 Arusha Declaration, with the aim of promoting socio-economic development, public accountability, responsibility, good governance and corporate responsibility. However, despite the rhetoric of the Declaration, the reality left much to be desired (Bierrman and Wagao, 1986; Killian, 2006). Thus, laws and regulations have continued to promote rent-seeking practices among the elite at the expense of the needs of wider society (Bierrman and Wagao, 1986; Killian, 2006). This has constrained the possibility of promoting good governance, public accountability and responsible business practices. In other words, the legal and regulatory reforms have largely failed to achieve their intended socio-economic aims (Fischer, 2006).

In the 1990s, major legislative reforms (privatization and neo-liberalization) were implemented by the Tanzanian government in order to integrate its economy into the global market. This led to a proliferation of new laws and regulations which contained inter alia provisions requiring public accountability, responsibility, transparency, and the improvement of corporate disclosures and employee working conditions. These laws and regulations also sought to address the issues of environmental degradation and social unrest. For example, in 1997, in line with Agenda 21 of the Rio Declaration (which required a cross-sectoral integration of policies, plans and programmes for the effective management of the environment), the National Environment Policy (NEP) 1997 was introduced in Tanzania. The NEP 1997 required companies to ensure the sustainable and equitable use of resources without degrading the environment or risking health and safety. However, although the NEP required companies to prevent and control environmental degradation, it failed to lay down specific provisions requiring companies to create structures that would combat pollution and environmental degradation, and promote sustainable environmental management (Lauwo, 2011). As a result, the provisions of the NEP 1997 on pollution and environmental degradation in Tanzania have continued to attract media and NGO criticism (Lissu, 1999; Bitala, 2008; Kitula, 2006; *This Day*, 2009, 27 June and 2009, 14 July). For example, despite the NEP 1997 provisions on the environment, total carbon dioxide emissions increased from 2.3 metric carbon tonnes in 1999 to 4.3 metric carbon tonnes in 2004 (UNDP, 2010).

The government of Tanzania has had to respond to the activism of local NGOs and the global environmental concerns of the UN Conference on the Environment and Development (UNCED) at the Earth Summit in Rio Janeiro in 1992 and reaffirmed in Johannesburg in 2002. As a result, in 2002 the Tanzanian government enacted the Environmental Management (EM) Act No. 20 of 2004 to replace the National Environment Management Council (NEMC) Act of 1983. The 2004 Act requires a company to submit an environmental impact assessment (EIA) before commencing operations in Tanzania, together with an environmental management plan (EMP). The Act requires companies to control and prevent pollution, manage waste products, and provide restoration plans. The penalties for failing to comply with the provisions of the Act are set out in Table 8.1.

However, it has been argued that, as the penalties imposed for breach of the Act have remained relatively low, companies may find it cheaper to pay a penalty than to internalize the environmental costs (see, for example, Lissu, 1999; Lauwo, 2011).

Table 8.1 Offences and penalties for breaching the Environmental Management Act 2004

Section of the Act	Infringement	Penalty
s.186	Failure to submit a project brief, EIA or making a false statement in an EIA.	TZS 0.5–10 million and/or imprisonment for 2–7 years.
s.187	Causing pollution contrary to the provisions of the Act.	TZS 3–5 million and/or imprisonment for up to 12 years, *and* the full cost of cleanup of the polluted environment.
s.191	General penalty for non-compliance with any provision in the Act for which no specific penalty is prescribed.	TZS 50,000–50 million and/or imprisonment for 3 months to 7 years.

Source: United Republic of Tanzania: Environmental Management Act, 2004

EIA: environmental impact assessment; TZS: Tanzanian shillings. In 2004, TZS2000 was approximately equivalent to £1.

In 2002, in an attempt to respond to local and global pressures and to improve corporate governance, the Tanzanian government enacted the Companies Act 2002 (CA 2002), which amended the Companies Act 1932. The 2002 Act made significant reforms to Tanzanian company law in order to take into account global developments with regard to corporate governance and directors' duties. For example, Section 183(1) provides that: 'the matters to which the directors of the company are to have regard in the performance of their functions include, in addition to the interests of the members, the interests of the company's employees.' However, although the Act requires directors to consider the interests of other stakeholders, not just shareholders, stakeholder interests are often subordinated to the pursuit of shareholder interests. Furthermore, although Section 206 requires audited financial reports to disclose details of the remuneration of directors and other officers, there is no obligation on companies to disclose information about, for instance, employee discrimination, employee health and safety, tax planning schemes, pollution and the environmental degradation caused by corporate activities and also the social difficulties caused by corporate acts and omissions in local communities (see, for example, Curtis and Lissu, 2008; Lauwo, 2011).

In response to the requirements of the International Labour Organization (ILO) and the Universal Declaration of Human Rights (UDHR) with regard to employee working conditions and human rights, the Tanzanian government enacted the Employment and Labour Relations Act 2004 and the Labour Institutions Act 2004 (which came into force in 2007 and 2006 respectively). Furthermore, in response to ILO requirements about improving health and safety in the workplace and reducing workplace injuries and accidents, the government enacted the Occupation Health and Safety Act 2003 and the Workers' Compensation Act 2008. These enactments contain provisions requiring companies to improve workplace conditions and to protect employees against hazards to health and safety arising out of, or in connection with, activities at work. However, despite these provisions, CSR reports have remained silent about occupational injuries, the numbers of which increased from 90 in 1999 to 309 in 2008 (ILO, 2010). In fact, more than 2,000 accidents are reported annually for compensation purposes.[14]

As has been shown above, the legal and regulatory framework in Tanzania has been shaped by global pressures and the desire to attract capital. The role of regulatory controls on public accountability, transparency and corporate responsibility in Tanzania has attracted both local and international NGO attentions. NGOs and other pressure groups (including academia and the media) have expressed concern about the activities of corporations, as their pursuit of profit and the maximization of shareholder returns are often in conflict with the social welfare interests of ordinary citizens (Detomasi, 2008, Oxfam, 2000; Christian Aid, 2005, 2008; Action Aid, 2008). The role of NGOs with respect to CSR practices in Tanzania is considered next.

THE ROLE OF NON-GOVERNMENTAL ORGANIZATIONS

The work of NGOs and other independent pressure groups is crucial in promoting corporate disclosure, transparency and public accountability. NGOs have sought to step into the regulatory gap created by the inadequacy of both national governments and international institutions in demanding social and environmental accounting and improved public accountability (Moon and Vogel, 2008). NGOs have played an increasingly significant role globally in challenging government policies and the activities of corporations with regard to abuses of human rights, environmental degradation and social unrest (see Mercer, 1999; Lauwo, 2011; Curtis and Lissu, 2008).

In Tanzania, the rise of NGO activism dates back to the colonial period when a number of organizations mobilized campaigns against colonial exploitative practices and demanded respect for human rights and public accountability (Levin, 2001). However, colonial government policies and regulations (such as the Societies Ordinance of 1954) constrained NGO activism and NGO involvement in scrutinizing government policies (Shivji, 1980). In the post-independence period, successive governments embraced the colonial legal regime, which undermined the freedom of association and freedom of expression of NGOs (Shivji, 1976). The Arusha Declaration of 1967, in particular, restricted the independence of NGOs and their role in promoting public and corporate accountability, enhanced corporate disclosure and good governance. As a result, the activities of the few registered NGOs remained under strict government control, with their ability to campaign against government policies and to address democratic governance, enhanced disclosures, humanitarian and ecological problems being severely constrained.

In the 1980s and 1990s, local and global pressures to liberalize the political and economic spheres, in order to reduce the role of the state and improve democratic governance, led to an increasing numbers of NGOs being established in Tanzania (Lange et al., 2000). NGO activism in this context expanded to include local, national and international development organizations, such as Oxfam, the Norwegian Church and Christian Aid (Lange et al., 2000). According to Kelsall (2001: 140), there were approximately 8,000 local and international NGOs in Tanzania dealing with a range of activities, such as gender issues, human rights, the environment, advocacy and participatory development. In fact NGOs have emerged as important actors working closely with other civil society organizations to promote democratic governance,

---

14   See https://www.ilo.org/public/english/region/afpro/daressalaam/download/oshabymusindo_2010.pdf.

responsible corporate practice, the protection of human rights, and to support the government in providing social services (Lange et al., 2000). NGOs have often urged the Tanzanian government to introduce reforms to address issues such as abuses of human rights, community unrest, pollution and environmental degradation (Lissu, 1999; Curtis and Lissu, 2008). However, due to the level and scale of poverty in Tanzania, a number of NGOs have chosen to focus more on social service delivery and poverty reduction (Shivji, 2004). Shivji has argued that Tanzanian NGOs are mainly represented by donors who claim to have an interest in poverty eradication and in promoting good governance (2004), but he has also argued that NGO activities 'let the government off the hook':

> Using the name 'promoting good governance', they facilitate in the legitimation of the neo-liberal policies of hegemonic Western powers and the international financial institutions (IFIs) applied in developing countries. Thus, by pretending to be partners in policy making, these NGOs let the government off the hook as it abdicates its own primary interest. (Shivji, 2004: 690–91)

Although increasing numbers of international NGOs (such as Christian Aid, Amnesty International, Corporate Watch, Mining Watch and Friends of the Earth) have played an important role in promoting social disclosure and CSR practices at the global level, relatively few local NGOs in Tanzania have been actively involved in advocating such practices (Shivji, 2004; Lissu, 1999).[15] Indeed, Tanzanian NGOs have not been sufficiently strong and active to be able to mobilize pressure with respect to such issues as enhanced corporate disclosure, public accountability and transparency in Tanzania. The role of trade unions is examined next.

THE ROLE OF TRADE UNIONS

Recent years have witnessed an increasing role being played by trade unions with regard to CSR. They play an important role in advancing employee welfare by inter alia demanding better working conditions and respect for human rights. They also play a major role in promoting workers' rights and articulating demands for health and safety, decent wages, pensions and employee benefits. The extent of their success or failure, however, depends on trade union density,[16] and on the legal and political environment. As in many other developing countries, however, trade unions in Tanzania have remained comparatively weak and poorly organized which has made it difficult to launch CSR initiatives (see Debrah, 2004). Trade union activism has a long history in Tanzania. However, lack of stability in the workplace for employees during colonial times and in the post-independence period weakened union membership and union activities

---

15   One of the active local NGOs in Tanzania is the Lawyers' Environmental Action Team (LEAT), established in 1994 with the mission to ensure sound natural resource management and environmental protection. LEAT carries out policy research, advocacy and selected public interest litigation with its members, who largely include lawyers concerned with environmental management and democratic governance in Tanzania. Other organizations have been campaigning for reform in Tanzania. Thus, Norwegian Church Aid (an international organization formed in 2005 by the Norwegian Church to fight global poverty, and social and environmental injustices) has been actively involved in addressing environmental pollution and degradation in Tanzania, facilitating access to improved, affordable and sustainable energy services to the public in both urban and rural areas. It has published several reports on the destructive social and environmental actions of MNCs in the mining sector.

16   The trade union density rate is calculated as: (trade union members/paid employees) × 100% (see ILO, 2010: 44).

(Shivji, 1976; Debrah, 2004). After independence, trade unions began to become more influential (Shivji, 1976). With a small working population, due to a narrow industrial base, trade union membership remained relatively low (Shivji, 1976). For example, with only 182,000 trade union members in the newly independent Tanzania, it was difficult for trade unions to fight against the inherited colonial regulations which appeared to favour the colonial government and the small number of elite in power (Shivji, 1976). As neo-colonial government policies and legislation constrained trade union activities and provided limited support, this undermined the ability of trade unions to campaign for workers' rights and for public and corporate accountability and good governance (Shivji, 2004). For example, in 1967, the National Assembly passed legislation to restrict the role of the National Union of Tanzania (Shivji, 1976).[17] According to Shivji, strikes were considered illegal and no agreement between a trade union and its employees was considered to be binding unless it was registered by the Labour Tribunal.

It has been argued that post-independence government policies and legislative frameworks in the political and economic spheres actively constrained trade union efforts to campaign against poor working conditions and other unethical corporate practices (see Shivji, 2004; Debrah, 2004). Along with the introduction of the multiparty political system in Tanzania in 1992, the Organisation of Tanzania Trade Unions (OTTU) was established. It consisted of 11 trade unions and allowed for the creation of sectoral unions as independent entities from the ruling party (LO/FTF Council, 2003). In 1995, the 11 trade unions decided to dissolve the OTTU and form the Tanzania Federation of Free Trade Unions (TFTU), which had approximately 348,000 members out of an estimated workforce of 17 million workers (LO/FTF Council, 2003). Trade union membership, however, declined with the retrenchment of workers from government institutions (LO/FTF Council, 2003). With an estimated workforce of only 17 million, trade union membership decreased to 300,000 in 2001, representing a unionization rate of less than 2 per cent (LO/TFT Council, 2003), but increased to 403,838 in 2008 (ILO, 2010). According to the International Confederation of Free Trade Unions (ICFTU, 2006: 2), only 27 per cent of the employed workforce was affiliated to a trade union, representing only 8 per cent of the workforce from the agriculture sector. It has been argued that the lack of a voice and the lack of collective bargaining for most workers in Tanzania has posed a serious challenge to the chances of promoting decent workplaces in the country (Casale and Pursey (2002). Although the Trade Unions Act 1998 was enacted[18] to accommodate the demand for independent trade unions, it nevertheless contained several restrictions on trade union rights, with excessive powers being vested in the Registrar of Trade Unions (see Shivji, 2004; Debrah, 2004). Debrah (2004) has argued that privatization and liberalization of the Tanzanian economy constrained trade union capacity as it relaxed the enforcement of the country's labour laws so as to create a favourable environment for FDI. According to Debrah:

> *The adoption of market-oriented reforms also resulted in the retrenchment and decline in trade union membership which reduced trade union density and weakened the ability of trade unions to fight against practices which were detrimental to the interests of workers. (2004: 82)*

---

17 The Labour Tribunal Act was enacted in 1967 to regulate collective disputes between employees and employers (Shivji, 1976).

18 The Act came into force on 1 July 2000. It dissolved the Federation of Free Trade Unions (TFTU) and required the re-registration of the existing industrial workers' unions, which led to the formation of the Trade Union Congress of Tanzania (TUCTA) (LO/FTF Council, 2003).

Thus, the trade union density rate declined from 26.6 per cent in 2001 to 20.2 per cent in 2008, so that approximately only one in five employees was a member of a trade union (ILO, 2010: 45). Also the percentage of female members of trade unions has remained low, representing only 33.6 per cent and 36.9 per cent of the working population in 2007 and 2008 respectively (ILO, 2010: 44).

Therefore, although a series of Acts of Parliament was enacted in the 1990s with the aim of democratizing the workers' movement and enhancing collective bargaining, instead they seemed to further weaken trade union collective bargaining power and to undermine the possibility of trade unions articulating demands for human rights, improved working conditions and responsible business practices (Shivji, 2004). For example, the Employment and Labour Relations Act 2004 not only made it more difficult for workers to strike but it also prohibited workers from striking at all in certain sectors (such as those relating to water and sanitation, electricity, health services and associated laboratory services, fire fighting, air traffic control, civil aviation and telecommunications).

As a result of corporate pressures and the bargaining power and influence of MNCs in Tanzania, trade unions have remained relatively weak with regard to articulating CSR demands and improving workers' rights and workplace standards. This is evidenced by the grievances and disputes prevalent between workers and employers concerning terms and conditions of employment, particularly in the private sector (ILO, 2010). While government policies have restricted trade union activism, employees in MNCs have found it difficult to unionize because of fears of threats of dismissal if employees are members of, or wish to join, a trade union (LO/FTF Council, 2003).[19] The next section of this chapter examines the role of the mass media in articulating demands for responsible business practices in Tanzania.

THE ROLE OF THE MEDIA

The media, in particular the news media, can play a key role in articulating demands for the promotion of responsible business practices (such as accountability, transparency and social responsibility) by giving visibility to competing discourses (Reverte, 2008; Islam and Deegan, 2010). In order to do this, the media needs to be mature and relatively unrestricted so as to raise public awareness about government and business practices and shortcomings. In Tanzania, however, due to its historical development, the media has remained relatively weak with regard to making a significant contribution to scrutinizing corporate practices and articulating demands for public accountability, responsibility and transparency (see Lauwo, 2011).

The history of the media, like other civil society organizations in Tanzania, can be traced back to the colonial period when the press was used to mobilize the social movement for the independence struggle (Kamuhanda, 1989). In the post-independence

---

19   For example, the Tanzania Mines and Construction Workers Union (TAMICO) has been fighting for mining workers' rights, demanding, for example, more pay, better healthcare and increased risk allowances (Lauwo, 2011). In November 2007, TAMICO organized a workers' strike at Barrick Gold Corporation's Bulyanhulu gold mine, in order to dispute the disparity in wages between foreigners and local workers. The Chairperson of TAMICO claimed that a foreign worker earned TZS [Tanzanian shillings] 24 million (US$20,820) a month, whereas local workers earned TZS200,000 (US$180) a month. A Tanzanian professional worker received US$4,000 a month, while foreign workers received, in addition, a bonus of 20 per cent of their salary, which was denied to local workers. Local workers were not paid any risk allowances for exposure to hazards while working in the mine (see Lauwo, 2011).

period, the media continued to be a crucial resource for scrutinizing state power and mobilizing national awareness (Lawson and Rakner, 2005). However, during the single party period, under the various authoritarian governments, the media came under state ownership and was expected to support the ruling party and the government (Mpangala, 2004). This constrained the media's freedom of expression and association and its ability to scrutinize and raise public awareness about the practices of the elite and corporate entities (Mpangala, 2004). As a result, the number of media institutions (i.e. radio stations, television stations and newspapers) has remained relatively small (Lauwo, 2011).[20]

The liberalization of the Tanzanian broadcasting industry in the late 1990s was sought in order to increase the media's freedom of expression and association and its ability to articulate demands for public accountability, corporate responsibility and good governance (Mpangala, 2004). Although the adoption of a multiparty system and the liberalization of the broadcasting industry in 1992 increased the number of privately owned media bodies,[21] the potential role of the media to uphold public accountability and responsibility on the part of the political elite and private organizations has remained constrained. This has been evidenced by the increasing tension between the media and the government of Tanzania in recent years. For example, the report on human rights in Tanzania by the US Department of State (2009) has drawn attention to the ongoing conflict between journalists and government officials in Tanzania. The report indicates that the Tanzanian government had alleged that a Swahili newspaper, the *Mwana-Halisi*, had published seditious material involving key government officials, which led to a three-month suspension of the newspaper in October 2008.[22] Incidents like this raise serious questions about freedom of expression and the media in Tanzania and its ability to articulate demands for public accountability and good governance.

Although Article 18 of the Constitution of Tanzania stipulates the right to freedom of expression of the broadcasting industry, laws have been passed to constrain the freedom of the press and its ability to investigate corporate practices. For example, the law on immunities, protection and privileges for members of the House of Representatives (passed in April 2007) further restricted the media's freedom of expression. This law removed the right of the media to attend House sessions and laid down a prison sentence of up to three years and a fine of not less than US$250 (TZS [Tanzanian shillings] 300,000) for publishing articles on scandals involving members of the House of Representatives.

Therefore, despite liberalization, Tanzania's mass media, like other civil society organizations, has remained relatively weak with respect to being able to act as a catalyst for promoting democratic governance, public accountability, governmental responsibility and also the corporate responsibility of business organizations.

---

20   For example, in 1967 there were only four newspapers (*Standard, Nationalist, Ngurumo,* and *Uhuru,* and only one radio station (Radio Tanzania Dar es Salaam, RTD). The first TV station was established in 1974 on the Tanzanian island of Zanzibar. This situation continued up to the 1980s, with only two government-owned newspapers (*Daily News* and *Sunday News*), two party-owned newspapers (*Uhuru* and *Mzalendo*), and one government-owned radio station (RTD).

21   Media ownership has become more diverse. Thus, by 2003, the number of radio stations had increased to 30, and a TV station was established in mainland Tanzania (see Lauwo, 2011).

22   The suspension followed the *Mwana Halisi*'s publication of an article on an alleged plot involving the President's son (US Department of State, 2009).

Conclusion

This chapter has argued that, in investigating the potential of CSR to address the socio-economic needs within and from a developing country context, it is important to consider the historical, political, economic and institutional structures and power relations which shape CSR practices. The review of the literature showed that various theoretical perspectives have been adopted for studying CSR (i.e. agency, stakeholder and legitimacy theories). However, it has argued that, although such theories can provide a useful framework for studying CSR, they fail to pay sufficient attention to the institutional structures, the power structures and the systemic pressures inherent in capitalist societies, and also the conflicting and contradictory role of the state with regard to impacting on, and shaping, CSR practices. The chapter has argued that a political economy approach is a 'useful' approach for examining CSR practices, as it considers the peculiar structures shaping CSR practices in developing countries such as Tanzania.

The chapter has examined the socio-political and economic environment of Tanzania by considering the institutional structures which may affect the nature and scale of CSR practices. It has showed that Tanzania's socio-political and economic environment has been shaped by both global and local institutional structures. In particular, CSR practices in Tanzania have been significantly influenced by global structures, such as the mobility of capital and by globalization and liberalization policies. It has shown how the Tanzanian government is dependent on corporate activities, particularly foreign investment, in order to stimulate economic growth, create employment, and increase foreign exchange and government revenues. As a result, MNC activities have become dominant in the economy, which in turn has had a significant influence on the institutional structures and the laws of Tanzania and, consequently, on CSR practices. However, the desire of the Tanzanian government to attract MNCs and FDI has posed, and continues to pose, serious challenges for the country's governance system. Thus, despite the enactment of various laws and regulations to promote corporate governance and public accountability, the Tanzanian government lacks the necessary political, financial, legal and administrative resources to discipline giant corporations. Thus, the enforcement of laws and regulations with respect to CSR, or the lack of it, remains problematic in Tanzania.

The chapter has shown that NGOs and civil society organizations have the capacity to play an important role in fostering the development of CSR, but that, in Tanzania, they have been insufficiently strong enough to be able to mobilize pressure against human rights abuses, environmental degradation and social unrest. This is because, since colonial times, successive governments have attempted to restrict the movement and powers of civil society organizations and their capacity to fight for the implementation of 'good' CSR practices.

Although the adoption of neo-liberal policies in Tanzania has increased the potential of NGOs, the media and trade unions to act as countervailing power structures, their capacity to promote public accountability and responsible business practices has been weakened by the policies of successive governments. For example, tight government control, censorship and intimidation of the media and trade unions have constrained the ability of these bodies to promote CSR and good business practices in Tanzania. As the neo-liberal agenda has focused on privatization, deregulation and rolling back the state as necessary conditions for economic growth, it has become difficult for laws and regulations and the activities of civil society organizations and the media to promote the socio-economic welfare of Tanzanian citizens. As a result, socio-economic and environmental problems have remained prevalent in Tanzania and have threatened the lives of many citizens (Bitala, 2008; Kitula, 2006; Almas, Kweyunga and Manoko, 2009). The reality is that poverty is endemic in Tanzania with 96.6 per cent of the population living in poverty. Unemployment has also been increasing in recent years, due in part to the privatization of state-owned enterprises. The quality of social services (such as healthcare and education) has also been deteriorating. These developments pose serious questions about who is actually benefiting from neo-liberalization, privatization and deregulation in Tanzania.

Lack of transparency and corruption involving corporate bodies are also issues of particular concern in Tanzania. As Curtis and Lissu (2008) have observed, foreign investment agreements in Tanzania have remained shrouded in secrecy. Tanzania is considered to be one of the most corrupt countries in the world. According to Transparency International's Corruption Perceptions Index (CPI), in 2009 Tanzania had slipped 24 places in the global corruption ranking, dropping from 102 in 2008 to 126 in 2009 in the list of 180 countries (Mosoba, 2009).

It is therefore argued that any attempt to change CSR and its potential to promote socio-economic development, particularly in developing countries, should be accompanied by changes in governance structures at both the local and global levels. Any attempt to change governance structures at the local level may require the Tanzanian government to be more proactive (for example, by introducing new laws and regulations or amending existing ones) in order to put more pressure on MNCs, such as mining companies, to discharge their obligations to local citizens. As part of such a process, the government of Tanzanian would need to amend the Company Act 2002 to impose a duty on companies to be accountable to the various constituencies. However, within the contemporary neo-liberal order, Tanzania, like other developing countries, has to compete to attract capital and in that process is forced to offer investment protection guarantees, tax holidays and concessions, and stabilization clauses, which in turn poses serious questions about the government's ability to implement and enforce regulatory changes. In particular, stabilization clauses (and other investment terms offered to attract FDI) guarantee fiscal stability over the long-term life of investment agreements, thereby preventing the Tanzanian government from reviewing the terms in such agreements (see SID, 2009).

In addition to civil society organizations and the media, academics can also play an important role in shaping and reconstructing the way in which CSR is currently being practised whether in Tanzania or elsewhere. They can play a pivotal role by criticizing and challenging governance structures and by producing counter accounts, in order to give visibility to governance dilemmas. Through rigorous critical analysis and intellectual intervention to mobilize public opinion on CSR practices, academics may be able to bring about change and improve the standard of living in Tanzania. Working closely with civil society organizations, academics can challenge the impact of increasing corporate power on the lives of Tanzanians, many of whom live in poverty, and the impact of such power on their socio-economic and environmental welfare. However, one of the difficulties is that the Tanzanian government is on the 'horns of dilemmas' in that it needs to reduce poverty by attracting foreign investment in order to stimulate the economy. It does so by offering various guarantees and protections as incentives to MNCs to invest in Tanzania, but, in doing so, fails to control such organizations sufficiently with regard to their corporate social responsibilities (for example, with regard to the environment, health and safety at work and the protection of human rights). Thus, the need to attract foreign investment makes it difficult for the government to promote the welfare of its citizens with regard to controlling and eradicating unethical corporate social practices. If the Tanzanian government places too many stringent requirements on companies to ensure that they conduct their business in a socially responsible way (such as by giving greater consideration to environmental and human rights concerns), this may have a negative effect in that they may decide not to invest in Tanzania which will, in turn, have a detrimental impact on the socio-economic development of the country. These problems and contradictions for the Tanzanian government have existed for many years and continue to exist. It is to be hoped that the difficulties can be resolved in the future by the Tanzanian government and MNCs adopting positions which respect not only the rights of employees, the rights and the environment of local communities living, for instance, in the mining areas, but which also do something to help those Tanzanian citizens (of which there are many) living in abject poverty.

Acknowledgements

I am grateful to Professor Prem Sikka of the University of Essex for his encouragement, intellectual support and constructive remarks, which have been useful in the development of this chapter. The author is also grateful to Professor Warwick Funnell and Dr Robert Jupe of the University of Kent for their helpful feedback and invaluable and illuminating comments. The helpful support of Kate Standley, proofreader, is also acknowledged.

References

Action Aid. (2008). *Taxing Solutions: How Tighter Tax Rules for Big Business Could Help End Poverty*. London: Action Aid. Available at: http://www.actionaid.org.uk/doc_lib/taxing_solutions_report.pdf.

Adams, C.A. and Harte, G. (1998). The changing portrayal of the employment of women in British banks' and retail companies' corporate annual reports. *Accounting, Organizations and Society*, 23(8), 781–812.

Adams, C.A. and Whelan, G. (2009). Conceptualising future change in corporate sustainability reporting. *Accounting, Auditing and Accountability Journal*, 22(1), 118–43.

AFRODAD. (2002). *Reality of Aid: Does Africa Need Aid?* Available at: http://mobile.opendocs.ids. ac.uk/opendocs/bitstream/handle/123456789/1676/AFRODAD-%20230765.pdf?sequence=1

Adams, C.A., Coutts, A. and Harte, G. (1995). Corporate equal opportunities (non-disclosure). *British Accounting Review*, 27(2), 87–108.

Almas, A.R., Kweyunga, R.C. and Manoko, M.L.K. (2009). *Investigation of Trace Metal Concentrations in Soil, Sediments and Waters in the Vicinity of 'Geita Gold Mine' and 'North Mara Gold Mine' in North West Tanzania*. IPM-report 2009. Ås, Norway: Norwegian University of Life Sciences. Available at: http://www.protestbarrick.net/downloads/FinalTanzania-2.pdf [accessed: 29 November 2013].

Andrew, B.H., Gul, F.A., Guthrie, J.E. and Teoh, H.Y. (1989). A note on corporate social disclosure practices in developing countries: The case of Malaysia and Singapore. *The British Accounting Review*, 21(4), 371–76.

Andriof, J. and McIntosh, M. (2001). *Perspectives on Corporate Citizenship*. Sheffield, UK: Greenleaf Publishing.

Avi-Yonah, R.S. (2006). *Corporate Social Responsibility and Strategic Tax Behaviour*. Public Law and Legal Theory Working Paper Series No. 69. [Online – Social Science Research Network]. Available at: http://papers.ssrn.com/sol3/papers.cfm?abstract_id=944793.

Bagwacha, M.S.D., Mbele, A.V.Y. and Van-Arkadie, B. (1992). *Market Reforms and Parastatal Restructuring in Tanzania*. Dar es Salaam: Economics Research Bureau.

Bakan, J. (2004). *The Corporation: The Pathological Pursuit of Profit and Power*. London: Constable and Robinson.

Banerjee, S. (2007). *Corporate Social Responsibility: The Good, the Bad and the Ugly*. Cheltenham, UK: Edward Elgar.

Banerjee, S. (2008). Necrocapitalism. *Organization Studies*, 29(12), 1–25.

—— (2010). Governing the global corporation: A critical perspective. *Business Ethics Quarterly*, 20(2), 1–11.

Belal, A.R. (2001). A study of corporate disclosure in Bangladesh. *Managerial Accountability Journal*, 16(5), 274–89.

—— (2008). *Corporate Social Reporting in Developing Countries: The Case of Bangladesh*. Aldershot, UK: Ashgate.

Belal, A.R. and Owen, D.L. (2007). The views of corporate managers on the current state of, and future prospects for, social reporting in Bangladesh: An engagement-based study. *Accounting, Auditing and Accountability Journal*, 20(3), 472–94.

Belkaoui, A. and Karpik, P.G. (1989). Determinants of the corporate decision to disclose social information. *Accounting, Auditing and Accountability Journal*, 2(1), 36–51.

Biermann, W. and Wagao, J. (1986). The quest for adjustments: Tanzania and the IMF 1980–1986. *African Studies Review*, 29(4), 89–103.

Bitala, M.F. (2008). *Evaluation of Heavy Metals Pollution in soil and Plants Accrued from Gold Mining Activities in Geita, Tanzania*. Unpublished dissertation on Integrated Environmental Management. Dar es Salaam: University of Dar es Salaam.

Campbell, D. (2004). A longitudinal and cross-sectional analysis of environmental disclosure in UK companies – a research note. *The British Accounting Review*, 36, 107–117.

Carroll, A.B. (1999). Corporate social responsibility: Evolution of a definitional construct. *Business and Society*, 38, 268–95.

Casale, G. and Pursey, S. (2002). Tanzania: Towards a decent work strategy for poverty reduction in Tanzania. Working Paper No. 8, in *Focus Programme on Strengthening Social Dialogue*. Geneva: International Labour Organization.

Christian Aid (2005). *Behind the Mask: The Real Face of Corporate Social Responsibility*. London: Christian Aid. Available at: http://www.christian-aid.org.uk.

—— (2008). *Undermining the Poor: Mineral Taxation Reforms in Latin America*. London: Christian Aid. Available at: http://www.christianaid.org.uk.

—— (2009). *False Profits: Robbing the Poor to Keep the Rich Tax-Free*. London: Christian Aid.

Cooper, D.J. and Sherer, M.J. (1984). The value of corporate accounting reports: Arguments for a political economy of accounting. *Accounting, Organizations and Society*, 9(2/3), 207–32.

Cooper, S.M. and Owen, D.L. (2007). Corporate social reporting and stakeholder accountability: The missing link. *Accounting Organizations and Society*, 32, 649–67.

Corporate Watch (2003). *BAE System's Dirty Dealings*. Corporate Watch Report. London: Corporate Watch. [Online.] Available at: http://www.corpwatch.org/article.php?id=9008.

Cotula, L. (2008). *Regulatory Takings, Stabilisation Clauses and Sustainable Development*. OECD Global Forum on International Investment. Paris: Organisation for Economic Co-operation and Development. Available at: http://www.oecd.org/dataoecd/45/8/40311122.pdf.

Cox, R.W. (1996). A Perspective on Globalization, in Mittelman, J.H. (ed.), *Globalization: Critical Reflections*. Boulder, CO: Lynne Rienner, 21–30.

Curtis, M. and Lissu, T. (2008). *A Golden Opportunity: How Tanzania is Failing to Benefit from Gold Mining*. Dar es Salaam: Christian Council of Tanzania (CCT), National Council of Muslims in Tanzania (BAKWATA) and Tanzania Episcopal Conference (TEC). Available at: http://www.leat.or.tz [accessed: 30 August 2010].

Dasgupta, S. (2002). Attitudes towards trade unions in Bangladesh, Brazil, Hungary and Tanzania. *International Labour Review*, 141(4), 413–40.

Davis, K. (1960). Can business afford to ignore social responsibilities? *California Management Review*, 2(3), 70–76.

Debrah, Y. (2004). HRM in Tanzania, in Kamoche, K., Debrah, Y., Horwitz, F. and Muuka, G.N. (eds), *Managing Human Resources in Africa*. London: Routledge, 103–120.

Deegan, C. (2002). Introduction: The legitimising effect of social and environmental disclosures: A theoretical foundation. *Accounting, Auditing and Accountability Journal*, 15(3), 288–311.

Deegan, C. and Gordon, B. (1996). A study of the environmental disclosure policies of Australian corporations. *Accounting and Business Research*, 26(3), 187–99.

Detomasi, D.A. (2008). The political roots of corporate social responsibility. *Journal of Business Ethics*, 82, 807–819.

Donaldson T. and Preston, L.E. (1995). The stakeholder theory of the corporations: Concepts, evidence and implications. *Academic of Management Review*, 20(1), 65–91.

Egels, N. and Kallifatides, M. (2006). The corporate social performance dilemma: Organizing for goal duality in low-income African markets, in Visser, W., McIntosh M. and Middleton, C. (eds), *Corporate Citizenship in Africa: Lessons from the Past, Paths to the Future*. Sheffield, UK: Greenleaf Publishing.

Fischer, P.V. (2006). *Rent-Seeking Institutions and Reforms in Africa: Theory and Empirical Evidence from Tanzania*. New York: Springer.

Freeman, R.E. (1984). *Strategic Management: A Stakeholder Approach*. Boston, MA: Pitman.

Friedman, M. (1970). The social responsibility of businesses is to increase its profits. *New York Times Magazine*, 13 September, 32–33.

Gray, R., Kouhy R. and Lavers, S. (1995a). Constructing research database of social environmental reporting by UK companies. *Accounting, Auditing and Accountability Journal*, 8(2), 78–101.

Gray, R., Kouhy, R. and Lavers, S. (1995b). Corporate social and Environmental Reporting, A review of the literature and a longitudinal study of UK disclosures. *Accounting Auditing and Accountability Journal*, 8(2), 47–77.

Gray, R., Owen, D.L. and Maunders, K.T. (1987). *Corporate Social Reporting: Accounting and Accountability*. Hemel Hempstead, UK: Prentice-Hall.

Guthrie, J. and Mathews, M.R. (1985). Corporate social accounting in Australasia. *Research in Corporate Social Performance and Policy*, 7, 251–77.

Guthrie J. and Parker, L.D. (1989). Corporate social reporting: A rebuttal of legitimacy theory. *Accounting and Business Research*, 19(76), 343–52.

—— (1990). Corporate social disclosure practice: A comparative international analysis. *Advances in Public Interest Accounting*, 3, 159–75.

Hackston, D. and Milne, M.J. (1996). Some determinants of social and environmental disclosures in New Zealand companies. *Accounting, Auditing and Accountability*, 9(1), 77–108.

Harvey, D. (2005). *A Brief History of Neoliberalism*, Oxford: Oxford University Press.

Heilman, B. and Ndumbaro, L. (2002). Corruption, politics and societal values in Tanzania: An evaluation of the Mkapa administration's anti-corruption efforts. *African Journal of Political Science*, 7(1), 1–20.

Held, D. and McGrew, A. (2002). *Globalisation/Anti-Globalisation*. London: Blackwell.

Hirschland, M.J. (2006). *Corporate Social Responsibility and the Shaping of Global Public Policy*. London: Palgrave Macmillan.

Holloway J. and Picciotto, S. (1978). Introduction: Towards a materialist theory of the state, in Holloway J. and Picciotto, S. (eds), *State and Capital: A Marxist Debate*. London: Edward Arnold, 1–31.

Hoogvelt, A. (2001). *Globalisation and the Postcolonial World: New Political Economy of Development*. 2nd edition. London: Palgrave.

ICFTU (2006). *International Recognised Core Labour Standards in Tanzania*. Report to the WTO General Council Review of the Trade Policies of Tanzania, Geneva, 25 and 27 October. Brussels: International Confederation of Free Trade Unions. Available at: http://www.icftu.org/www/pdf/corelabourstandards2006tanzania.pdf.

Idemudia, U. (2007). Community perceptions and expectations: reinventing the wheels of corporate social responsibility practices in the Nigerian oil industry. *Business and Society Review*, 112(3), 369–405.

ILO (2008). *Technical Memorandum United Republic of Tanzania Labour Administration and Inspection Audit, Labour Administration and Inspection Programme, Social Dialogue Sector*. Geneva: International Labour Office. Available at: http://www.ilo.org/wcmsp5/groups/public/---ed_dialogue/---lab_admin/documents/publication/wcms_144184.pdf [accessed: 29 November 2013].

—— (2009). Glob*al Employment Trends January 2009*. Geneva: International Labour Organization. Available at: http://www.ilo.org/wcmsp5/groups/public/---dgreports/---dcomm/documents/publication/wcms_101461.pdf [accessed: 29 November 2013].

—— (2010). *Decent Work Country Profile: Tanzania (mainland)*. Geneva: International Labour Organization. Available at: http://www.ilo.org/public/english/region/afpro/daressalaam/download/decent_work_tz.pdf [accessed: 29 November 2013].

IMF (2007). U*nited Republic of Tanzania: Poverty Reduction Strategy Paper – Annual Implementation Report 2006/07*. IMF Country Report No. 08/22. Washington DC: International Monetary Fund. Available at: http://www.imf.org.

Islam, M.A. and Deegan, C. (2010). Media pressures and corporate disclosure of social responsibility performance information: A study of two global clothing and sports retail companies. *Accounting and Business Research*, 40(2), 131–48.

Ite, U.E. (2004). Multinational companies and corporate social responsibility in developing countries: A case of Nigeria. *Corporate Social Responsibility and Management*, 11(1), 1–11.

Jamali, D. (2007). The case for strategic corporate social responsibility in developing countries. *Business and Society Review*, 112(1), 1–27.

Jensen, M.C. and Meckling, W.H. (1976). Theory of the firm: Managerial behaviour, agency costs and ownership structure. *Journal of Financial Economics*, 3(4), 305–360.

Jones, M. (1995). Instrumental stakeholder theory: A synthesis of ethics and economics. *Academy of Management Review*, 20, 404–37.

—— (1999). Structuration Theory, in Currie, W. and Galliers, B. (eds), *Rethinking Management Information Systems: An Interdisciplinary Perspective*, Oxford: Oxford University Press.

—— (2008). Disr*obing the Emperor: Mainstream CSR Research and Corporate Hegemony*. Hertfordshire, UK: Ashridge Business School and Maastricht School of Management.

Kamuhanda, S. (1989). The role of the mass media in the implementation of Tanzania's foreign policy: Reality and prospects. *Africa Media Review*, 3(3), 25–28.

Kelsall, T. (2001). Donors, NGOs and the state: Governance and civil society in Tanzania, in Barrow, O. and Jennings, M. (eds), *The Charitable Impulse: NGOs and Development in East and North-East Africa*. Oxford, James Currey, 133–48.

Killian, B.M. (2006). Globalisation demands and the governance of Tanzania's response: A myth of national policy ownership, in Msambichaka, L.A, Mwamba, N.E. and Mashindano, O.J. (eds), *Globalisation and Challenges for Development in Tanzania*, Dar es Salaam: Dar es Salaam University Press, 557–85.

Kitula, A.G.N. (2006). The environmental and socio economic impacts of mining on local livelihoods in Tanzania: A case study of Geita District. *Journal of Cleaner Production*, 14(2/3), 405–414.

Klimecki, R. and Willmott, H.C. (2009). From demutualization to meltdown: A tale of two wannabe banks. *Critical Perspective in International Business*, 5(1/2), 120–40.

Kobrin, S.J. (2009). Private political authority and public responsibility: Transnational politics, transnational firms, and human rights. *Business Ethics Quarterly*, 19(3), 349–74.

Korten D.C. (2001). *When Corporations Rule the World*. San Francisco, CA: Berrett-Koehler.

Kuasirikun, N. (2005). Attitudes to the development and implementation of social and environmental accounting in Thailand. *Critical Perspectives on Accounting*, 16(8), 1035–1057.

Kuasirikun, N. and Sherer, M. (2004). Corporate social disclosure in Thailand. *Accounting, Auditing and Accountability Journal*, 17(4), 629–60.

Lange, S. (2006). *Benefit Streams from Mining in Tanzania: Case Studies from Geita and Mererani*. CMI Report 2006: II. Bergen, Norway: Chr. Michelsen Institute.

Lange, S., Wallevik, H. and Kiondo, A. (2000). *Civil Society in Tanzania*. Bergen, Norway: Chr. Michelsen Institute.

Lantos, G.P. (2001). The boundaries of strategic corporate social responsibility. *Journal of Consumer Marketing*, 18(7), 595–630.

Lauwo, S. (2011). *Analysis of Corporate Social Responsibility (CSR) and Accountability Practices in a Developing Country Context: A Study of the Mining Industry in Tanzania*. Unpublished thesis, University of Essex, UK.

Lawson, A. and Rakner, L. (2005). *Understanding Patterns of Accountability in Tanzania*. Final Synthesis Report. Oxford: Oxford Policy Management; Bergen, Norway: Chr. Michelsen Institute; Dar es Salaam: REPOA.

Leftwich, A. (2000). *States of Development: On the Primacy of Politics in Development*. Cambridge: Polity Press.

Levin, J. (2001). *Taxation in Tanzania*. Discussion Paper No. 20001/80. Helsinki: United Nations University World Institute for Development Economic Research.

Lissu, T.A. (1999). *Plunder Unlimited: The Social Economic and Environmental Implications of Foreign Investments in Africa with Reference to Tanzania. Paper presented at CSAE Conference at St Anne's College*, Oxford, 15–16 April.

Lobel, O. (2006). Sustainable capitalism or ethical transnationalism: offshore production and economic development. *Journal of Asian Economics*, 17, 56–62.

LO/FTF Council (2003). *Profile of the Labour Market and Trade Unions in Tanzania*. Copenhagen: LO/FTF Council. Available at: http://www.loftf.dk.

Matten, D. and Moon, J. (2004). *'Implicit' and 'Explicit' CSR: A Conceptual Framework for Understanding CSR in Europe*. ICCSR Working Papers No. 29. Nottingham, UK: University of Nottingham, International Centre for Corporate Social Responsibility.

McDonald, D. and Puxty, A.G. (1979). An inducement contribution approach to corporate financial reporting. *Accounting, Organizations and Society*, 4(1/2), 53–65.

McWilliams, A. Siegel, D. and Wright, P. (2006). Corporate social responsibility: Strategic implications. *Journal of Management Studies*, 43(1), 1–18.

Melyoki, L. (2005). *Determinants of Effective Corporate Governance in Tanzania*. PhD Thesis, University of Twente, The Netherlands. Available at: http://doc.utwente.nl/50856/.

Mercer, C. (1999). Reconceptualising state–society relations in Tanzania: Are NGOs 'making a difference'? *Area*, 31, 247–58.

Mmuya, M. (2000). Constitutional Debate, the Status of then Union and Decentralisation, in Engel, U., Erdmann, G. and Mehler, A. (eds), *Tanzania Revisited Political Stability, Aid Dependence and Development Constraints*. Hamburg: Institute of African Affairs.

Moon, J. and Vogel, D. (2008). Corporate social responsibility, government, and civil society, in Crane, A., Matten, D., McWilliams, W., Moon, J. and Siegel, D. (eds), *The Oxford Handbook of CSR*. Oxford: Oxford University Press, 303–323.

Mosoba, T. (2009). Tanzania: Country drops 24 places in global corruption ranking. *The Citizen*, 18 November. [Online – allAfrica.] Available at: http://allafrica.com/stories/200911180948.html [accessed: 29 November 2013].

Mpangala, G.P. (2004). *Origins of Political Conflicts and Peace Building in the Great Lakes Region. Paper to be presented at a Symposium Organized by the Command and Staff College, Arusha, held on 23rd February 2004 on the theme 'Ramifications of Instability in the Great Lakes Zones'*. Dar es Salaam: University Institute of Development Studies.

Ngowi, H.P. (2007). *Economic Development and Change in Tanzania Since Independence: The Political Leadership Factor. Paper presented at the African Association for Public Administration and Management, 29th AAPAM Annual Roundtable Conference*, Mbabane, Swaziland, 3–7 September 2007.

Oxfam (2008). *From Poverty to Power: How Active Citizens and Effective States can Change the World*. London: Oxfam.

Picciotto, S. (1991). Internationalisation of the State. *Capital and Class*, 43, 43–63.

Porter, M.E. and Kramer, M.R. (2006). Strategy and society: The link between corporate social responsibility and competitive advantage. *Harvard Business Review*, 84(12), 78–92.

Puxty, A.G. (1986). Social accounting as immanent legitimation: A critique of a technicit ideology. *Advances in Public Interest Accounting*, 1, 95–111.

—— (1991). Social accounting and universal pragmatics. *Advances in Public Interest Accounting*, 4, 35–47.

Rayman-Bacchus, L. (2004). Assessing trust in, and legitimacy of the corporate, in Crowther, D., and Rayman-Bacchus, L. (eds), *Perspectives on Corporate Social Responsibility*. Farnham: Ashgate, 109–139.

Reverte, C. (2008). Determinants of corporate social responsibility disclosure ratings by Spanish listed firms. *Journal of Business Ethics*, 88, 351–66.

Rice, X. (2008). *Water: Campaigners Cheer Defeat of Biwater's £10m Tanzanian Claim*. The *Guardian*, 29 July. Available at: http://www.guardian.co.uk/environment/2008/jul/29/water.tanzania [accessed: 29 November 2013].

Richardson, J. (2000). Environmental law in postcolonial societies: Straddling the local–global institutional spectrum. *Colorado Journal of International Law and Policy*, 1, 1–82.

Roberts, R. (1992). Determinants of corporate social disclosure: An application of stakeholder theory. *Accountancy, Organizations and Society*, 17(6), 595–612.

Roner, L. (2005). *Corporate Responsibility and Public Relations. Ethical Corporation Special Report*. Available at: http://www.ethicalcorp.com/content.asp.

Roper, J. (2007), *The Debate over Corporate Social Responsibility*. London: Oxford University Press.

Said, D. (2008). Tanzania: Fourth prime minister on way out over radar scandal. Kampala: *East African Business Week*, 14 April. Available at: http://allafrica.com/stories/200804141278.html [accessed: 29 November 2013].

Scherer, A.G. and Palazzo, A.G. (2007). Towards a political conception of corporate responsibility – business and society seen from a Habermasian perspective. *Academy of Management Review*, 32(4), 1096–1120.

Shivji, I.G. (1975). Peasants and class alliance. *Review of African Political Economy*, 3 (May–August), 10–18.

——— (1976). Class *Struggles in Tanzania*. New York: Monthly Review Press.

——— (1980). The state in the dominated social formation of Africa: Some theoretical issues. *International Social Science Journal*, XXXII.

——— (2004). Reflection on NGOs in Tanzania: What we are, what we are not, and what we ought to be. *Development in Practice*, 14(5), 689–95.

SID (2009). *The Extractive Resource Industry in Tanzania: Status and Challenges of the Mining Sector*. Nairobi: Society for International Development. Available at: http://www.sidint.org/PUBLICATIONS/571.pdf.

Sikka, P. (2008a). Enterprise culture and accountancy firms: New Masters of the Universe. *Accounting, Auditing and Accountability Journal*, 21(2), 268–95.

——— (2008b). Globalisation and its discontents: Accounting firms buy limited liability partnership legislation in Jersey. *Accounting, Auditing and Accountability Journal*, 21(3), 398–426.

——— (2010). Smoke and mirrors: Corporate social responsibility and tax avoidance. *Accounting Forum*, 34(3–4), 153–68.

——— (2011). Accounting for human rights: The challenges of globalisation and foreign direct investment. *Critical Perspectives on Accounting*, 22(8), 811–827. [Online: doi:10.1016/j.cpa].

Solomon, J.F. and Darby, L. (2005). Is private social, ethical and environmental reporting mythicizing or demythologizing reality? *Accounting Forum*, 29, 27–47.

Spence, C. (2007). Social and environmental reporting and hegemonic discourse, *Accounting, Auditing and Accountability Journal*, 20(6), 855–82.

——— (2009). Social accounting's emancipatory potential: A Gramscian critique. *Critical Perspectives on Accounting*, 205–227.

This Day (2009, 27 June). The human cost of gold in Tanzania: and a deadly price to pay. [Online journal.] Available at: http://protestbarrick.net/article.php?id=500 [accessed: 29 November 2013].

——— (2009, 14 July). Independent researchers detect high levels of pollution around North Mara gold mine. [Online journal.] Available at: http://protestbarrick.net/article.php?id=500.

Tinker, A.M. (1980). Towards a political economy of accounting: an empirical illustration of the Cambridge controversies. *Accounting, Organizations and Society*, 5(1), 147–60.

Tinker, T., Lehman C., and Neimark, M. (1991). Falling down the hole in the middle of the road: Political quietism in corporate social reporting. *Accounting, Auditing and Accountability Journal*, 4(2), 278–54.

Transparency International (2003). Corruption Perception Index 2003. Berlin: Transparency International. [Online.] Available at: http://www.transparency.org/research/cpi/overview [accessed: 29 November 2013].

Tsang, E.W.K. (1998). A longitudinal study of corporate social reporting in Singapore: The case of banking, food, beverages and hotel industries. *Accounting, Auditing and Accountability Journal*, 11(5), 624–35.

Tsikata, Y.M. (2001). Owning Economic Reforms. A comparative Study of Ghana and Tanzania, in Kayizzi-Mugerwa, S. (ed.), *Reforming Africa's Institutions: Ownerships, Incentives, and Capabilities*. Helsinki: United Nations University World Institute for Development Economic Research, 30–53.

TUC (2005). *Trade and Trade Unions: A TUC Fact File and Activities Pack for Trade Union Tutors*. London: Trades Union Congress. Available at: http://www.tuc.org.uk/extras/tdfactfile.pdf.

Ullmann, A.A. (1985). Data in search of a theory: A critical examination of the relationships among social performance, social disclosure, and economic performance of US firms. *Academy of Management Review*, 10(3), 540–57.

UNDATA (2013). *United Republic of Tanzania*. New York: United Nations Statistics Division. Available at: http://data.un.org/CountryProfile.aspx?crName=United%20Republic%20of%20 Tanzania [accessed: 27 November 2013].

UNCTAD (2007). *World Investment Report: Transnational Corporations, Extractive Industries and Development*. Geneva: United Nations Conference on Trade and Development.

—— (2009). *World Investment Report: Transnational Corporations, Agricultural Production and Development*. Geneva: United Nations Conference on Trade and Development.

UNDP 2006. *Human Development Report 2006. Beyond Scarcity: Power, Poverty and the Global Water Crisis*. New York: United Nations Development Programmes Office. Available at: http://hdr.undp. org/en/media/HDR06-complete.pdf.

—— (2007/2008). *Human Development Report (2007/2008). Fighting Climate Change: Human Solidarity in a Divided World*. New York: United Nations Development Programmes Office. Available at: http://hdr.undp.org/en/media/HDR_20072008_EN_Complete.pdf.

—— (2009). *Human Development Report 2009. Overcoming Barriers: Human Mobility and Development*. New York: United Nations Development Programmes Office. Available at: http://hdr.undp.org/ en/media/HDR_2009_EN_Complete.pdf.

—— (2010). *Human Development Report 2010. The Real Wealth of Nations: Pathways to Human Development*. New York: United Nations Development Programmes Office. Available at: http:// hdr.undp.org/en/reports/global/hdr2010/ [accessed: 27 November 2013].

Unerman J., and O'Dwyer, B. (2007). The Business Case for Regulation of Corporate Social Responsibility and Accountability. *Accounting Forum*, 31, 332–53.

US Department of State (2009). *2008 Human Rights Report*. Bureau of Democracy, Human Rights and Labor, 2008 Country Reports on Human Rights Practices. Washington DC: US Department of State. Available at: http://www.state.gov/g/drl/rls/hrrpt/2008/af/119028.htm [accessed: 27 November 2013].

Vogel, D. (2005). *The Market for Virtue: The Potential and Limits of Corporate Social Responsibility*. Washington DC: The Brookings Institution.

Wanzala, P.N. (2007). *Whose Development Counts? Political Ecology of Displacement of Bulyanhulu Mining Community in Tanzania*. Unpublished M.Phil thesis Norwegian University of Science and Technology (NTNU).

World Bank (2007). *Tanzania: Sustaining and Sharing Economic Growth, Country Economic Memorandum and Poverty Assessment*. Dar es Salaam: World Bank.

—— (2010). 2010 *World Development Indicators*. Washington DC: World Bank. Available at: http:// data.worldbank.org/sites/default/files/wdi-final.pdf.

9 CSR and Energy Investments in Turkey

SIBEL YILMAZ TÜRKMEN AND GÜLCAN ÇAĞIL

Abstract

In a globalized world, the importance of Corporate Social Responsibility (CSR) has further increased and become a significant part of sustainable development (SD). CSR enhances the benefits of firms, yet does not have a high cost. According to most financial literature, the main objective is to maximize the value of the business. In addition to this principle, firms should embrace SD, especially in developing countries. Corporate responsibility practices affect society and other related parties in the long and short run. Many financial organizations support efforts for CSR, so that socially responsible investment has started to attract investors' attention. Green investments and investments in renewable energy are tools of these efforts. The perception of CSR is improving in areas such as education, healthcare, environment, technology use, etc. In this study we argue that the practice of CSR continues to extend to different sectors of the economy in Turkey and we examine the extent of socially responsible investment (SRI) and green investments in the energy sector in Turkey in comparison with their global extent in this sector.

Introduction

The term 'corporate social responsibility' (CSR) refers to corporate social and environmental issues. The ability to protect the environment and meet social needs are issues of considerable importance to the achievement of SD.

CSR is about managing the economic, social and environmental impacts of business activities, with the aim of diverting risks and creating new business opportunities responding to the legitimate demands and expectations of stakeholders including employees, suppliers, customers, governments, non-governmental organizations (NGOs), investors, etc. (CSR Consulting, 2010).

The involvement of institutions in socially responsible projects within the scope of CSR provides multiple benefits for them. The degree of an entity's social prestige and reputation increases the value of its standing in the eyes of its stakeholders when it demonstrates a socially responsible ethos in its strategy. The advertising and PR activities of institutions, as well as their contributions to the solution of social problems, enhance their reputations as perceived by society. At the same time, activities relating to CSR give employees of those institutions involved in them a reason to feel that they are a factor in creating value in the social arena (Özgen, 2007).

The link between SD and socially responsible investing (SRI) is simple and straightforward. With SRI the investor tries to account – in some way or another – for SD. In practice, this usually boils down to taking into account environmental, social and governance issues of firms in their investment decisions (Cerin and Scholtents, 2011).

Review of the Literature

A literature review of CSR Investment, SD and the Energy Sector can be summarized as follows:

- **Bossche et al. (2010)** investigate the robustness of companies' CSR rankings with respect to several modelling assumptions and built on Gini's transvariation concept to select/reject specific companies in the SRI-eligible universe of assets.

- **Buskirk (2006)** aims to discuss energy efficiency and renewable energy investments in Eritrea from the strategic long-term economic perspective of meeting Eritrea's SD goals and reducing greenhouse gas emissions. The results of the model which express the contributions that efficiency and renewable energy projects can make in terms of reduced energy sector operating expenses and carbon emissions.

- **Duarte (2012)** examines the relationships between the parameters characterizing Spanish households and their behaviour with regard to consumption and the demand for goods and services. The main result is that analysed factors determine the volume of emissions for each household in terms of their correlation with income, which is the primary determinant of consumption patterns.

- **Hussain (2012)** explores the relationship between oil and gas industry investments in alternative energy and CSR. The paper's results have promoted positive social change by increasing public awareness regarding the degree to which oil and gas companies invest in developing alternative energy sources, which might, in turn, inspire public pressure on companies in the oil and gas industry to pursue the use of alternative energy.

- **Jun et al. (2010)** have estimated the social value of nuclear energy consumers' willingness to pay for nuclear energy using the Contingent Valuation Method and they suggest that the social value of nuclear energy increases approximately 68.5 per cent with the provision of adequate information about nuclear energy to the public.

- **Lambooy (2011)** explores the role of today's companies in relation to fresh water. The paper demonstrates that companies are expected to bear responsibility for their impact on water resources, in particular when it influences the public access to water in areas with fresh water scarcity and/or weak government.

- **Maruyama et al. (2007)** examine how Japanese citizens initiatives can affect the social acceptance of renewable energy as well as social change and analyse the interests of the various actors involved in community wind power projects in a framework of 'actor network theory', which enables the readers to understand the detail of each actor's position.

- **McManus et al. (2010)** explain environmental concern in the light of how anthropogenic climate change will impact the housing sector as one of the major energy-consuming and carbon dioxide-producing sectors. The paper demonstrates that policy changes are needed to deliver sustainable energy for this sector and to ensure that the delivery of crucial new housing needs is not hampered while also failing to meet energy goals.

- **Pop et al. (2011)** analyse the role of social capital and the promotion of active ageing in order to assure the establishment of CSR at national and international level. CSR is an efficient tool for combating the acute state of the economy and bringing about a shift to a new green economy by capitalizing on the knowledge, competences and abilities of senior citizens.

- **Salmela (2006)** investigates the barriers identified by consumers to purchasing green electricity and contrast these with the interpretation that actors in the energy sector give to consumer passivity. The paper reveals that consumers need more information on the environmental impact of different electricity products and, in particular, about the electricity supply and electricity contracts in a liberalized electricity market if they are to become active in the market.

- **Streimikienea et al. (2009)** examine CSR development in the energy sector of the Baltic States and provided positive impact of CSR on sustainable energy development.

- **Vertigans (2011)** studied the impact of oil and gas companies in Nigeria under the concept of CSR. The paper recognizes increased emphasis on socially responsible policies.

The following research studies summarize CSR, SRI and the energy sector in Turkey. As can be seen from the studies, literature on these topics is not available in Turkey.

- **Ertuna and Tükel (2009)** found that CSR disclosures consist mostly of activities that involve traditional motivations and stakeholders. However, CSR disclosures include a considerable amount of profit-oriented activities, together with traditional philanthropic activities.

- **Gunay (2010)** wanted to depict the determinants of CSR based on the perceptions of top managers and directors of large-scale industrial firms in Turkey and notes that top managers and directors believe that as the hierarchy in their firms increases CSR activities will also increase.

- **Özgüç (2009)** aimed to determine the level of CSR policies and practices of companies listed on the Istanbul Stock Exchange 30 Index. The results show that environmental disclosures should be detailed to cover the use of natural resources and the effect of activities on ecological balance, emission of greenhouse gases, waste management, recycling ratios, and noise levels.

- **Poroy et al. (2012)** investigated the relationship between CSR and financial performance on the Istanbul Stock Exchange Corporate Governance Index of 28 listed companies which are ranked according to their corporate governance rating scores as having high social responsibility scores. The findings note those firms with better financial indicator performances.

- **Selvi et al. (2010)** examined the benefits of implementing CSR and CSR activities in Turkey from 2005 to 2009; and they investigated the relationship between CSR and companies' reputations in Turkey before and after the recent financial crisis. They regard 2007 as a transition period from a non-crisis to a crisis environment.

- **Yanık, İçke and Aytürk (2010)** examined the performance of socially responsible mutual funds compared to other mutual funds – which are constituted based on conventional financial criteria in Turkey. Their paper looks at the concepts of socially responsible investing and socially responsible mutual funds, which are mostly applied with regard to the special approach of socially responsible investing.

The remainder of this chapter is organized as follows: the next section introduces the topics of socially responsible investment and sustainability. The following section deals with energy use and energy investments, explains renewable energy and green investments in terms of the global perspective. The section that follows presents CSR and green investment applications in Turkey and the chapter is summarized in the Conclusion.

Socially Responsible Investment and Sustainability

SRI, also known as 'green' or 'ethical', 'sustainable' or 'responsible' investing, is the practice of incorporating social goals into the investment decision-making process. These social goals are based on environmental issues, human rights, community involvement and labour relations (Ooi and Lajbcgier, 2012).

SRI is an investment strategy that integrates social, environmental and corporate governance criteria into investment decisions. SRI investors and funds generally avoid companies that they believe are engaged in 'undesirable' businesses such as arms, alcohol, tobacco, gambling, animal testing and nuclear power – the so-called 'sin' sectors; instead they invest in companies that they are sure are engaged in 'desirable' areas such as environmental management, alternative energy, green technology, green construction, sustainable living, equal treatment of minorities and fair trade, or a combination of the above (Leahy, 2008).

During the last few decades the idea of sustainable investment has hit the global market. Investors – both private and institutional – have started to supplement financial considerations with social and ecological ones (Koellner et al., 2005). While it would appear that SRI is a modern phenomenon, its history dates back several hundred years. During its early development stage, religious beliefs and values (such as Jewish Law, Catholic edicts, and Quaker and Methodist determinations and activism) drove SRI (Kinder and Domini, 1997; Vyvyan et al., 2007).

'Socially responsible' investors favour certain companies over others according to criteria such as the production of weapons or use of alternative energy sources (Hamilton et al., 1993). Accordingly, there has been a growing interest in SRI products from the media, regulators, fund managers, institutional investors and other stakeholders (Vyvyan et al., 2007).

The principle of sustainability, by which is meant the pursuit of positive environmental and social goals in addition to economic return, is of growing importance (Sayce et al., 2009). Business plays a vital role through corporate sustainability – defined as a company's delivery of long-term value in financial, social, environmental and ethical terms (Rio+20, 2012).

Investors with sustainability goals need to compare and assess a variety of funds based on financial and non-financial criteria. While approaches to and methods for assessing financial performance exist, the assessment of non-financial performance (i.e. ecological and social performance) is rather underdeveloped. Consequently, fund managers are not able to set up standards for non-financial performance, and thus they are unable to account for this aspect to investors and their stakeholders. For example the investment banking sector plays a serious role in SD; however, accountability is imperative, otherwise, sustainable investment will remain a buzzword (Koellner et al., 2005).

Energy Use and Investments

Global energy use has grown by a factor of 25 over the past 200 years (Figure 9.1). This increase, far in excess of the roughly sevenfold increase in population over the same period, constitutes the first major energy transition, a transition from penury to abundance (Wilson and Grubler, 2011).

The way the world produces and uses energy today is not sustainable. The main fossil fuel sources – oil, coal and gas – are finite natural resources and we are depleting them at a rapid rate. Furthermore they are the main contributors to climate change, and the race to the last 'cheap' fossil resources evokes disasters for the natural environment. A fully sustainable renewable power supply is the only way to secure energy for all and avoid environmental catastrophe (WWF, 2011).

RENEWABLE ENERGY

Renewable energy is energy which comes from natural resources such as sunlight, wind, rain, tides and geothermal heat, which are renewable (naturally replenished). In 2008, about 19 per cent of global final energy consumption came from renewables.

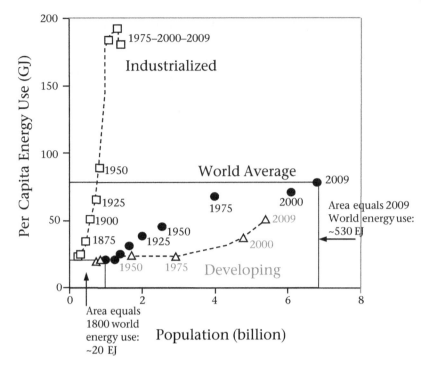

Figure 9.1   Capital energy use (GJ*)

Source: Wilson and Grubler, 2011: 166.

GJ: gigajoule (109 joules); EJ: exajoule (1018 joules).

New renewables (small hydro, modern biomass, wind, solar, geothermal and biofuels) are growing very rapidly as well (Anwar and Mulyadi, 2011).

The United Nations Secretary General Ban Ki-moon has repeatedly stressed the critical importance of sustainable energy and is mobilizing key constituencies from all sectors of society in a major global initiative intended to shape the fundamental policy and investment decisions needed to put countries on a more sustainable energy pathway over the next two decades. This new global initiative, 'Sustainable Energy for All', will engage governments, the private sector and civil society partners to achieve three major targets by 2030 (UNGC, 2011):

- Achieving universal access to modern energy services;
- Improving energy efficiency;
- Increasing the share of energy generated from renewable resources.

With surging demand for renewable energy across Europe, Japan and many developing countries, not to mention new consumer incentives in the US, clean technology has emerged as one of the hottest new investment sectors (Scheer, 2004). Shrinking reserves of fossil fuels and growing anxiety over future energy security have boosted investments in renewable energy worldwide. Alarming climate change scenarios have also increased the focus on creating sustainable energy economies. It is common knowledge that a sustainable future for both the world economy and the planet are inconceivable without renewable energy sources (The Broker, 2009).

The risks associated with dependence on fossil and nuclear fuels have never been greater. Soaring prices of oil and natural gas threaten to bankrupt many developing countries and raise havoc with the world economy. Supplies of these fuels, on which the world's economy depends, are dangerously insecure. While coal is plentiful, the emissions of carbon dioxide from the burning of fossil fuels (especially) threaten to exacerbate climate change, and associated sulphuric and nitrous oxide emissions are an increasing health hazard for populations of many of the world's cities. Last but not least, the advent of terrorism requires re-evaluation of all nuclear plants, oil and natural gas pipelines, liquid petroleum gas (LPG)/liquid natural gas (LNG) ports, central electricity transmission systems and large dams, with relation to their vulnerability to sabotage. Modern civilization and the world economy literally are sitting on the edge of an energy precipice. It will take many years and an estimate of trillions of invested dollars for the world to convert from fossil and nuclear fuels to an economy driven primarily by the truly safe, environmentally sound renewable energy resources – solar, wind, geothermal, small hydro, oceans and biomass – even though these are the fastest-growing energy media and should be expanded urgently (Ottinger, 2006).

A growing concern about climate change and its risk for portfolios is intensifying the interest in SRI. In fact, climate change is now widely recognized as the most significant environmental issue facing the global economy. Therefore, investor demand is growing for portfolio opportunities in clean and green technology, alternative and renewable energy, green building and responsible property development, and other environmentally driven businesses (SIF, 2007; on SRI generally see, for example, Sparkes, 2003; Pivo and McNamara, 2005).

The way we produce energy requires a major systemic overhaul on a global scale. We will need to shift progressively towards renewable energy sources. We will need to capture and sequester the carbon dioxide emitted from continued fossil-fuel use. We will need to decide on the future of nuclear power, and find ways to expand its use while reducing dramatically the threats of proliferation and nuclear terror. Markets alone will not find the way forward. Currently, it costs nothing to put carbon dioxide into the atmosphere. At a minimum, such emissions should be capped by regulation, or taxed, or both. But more than that, technological changes on a large scale will require major social decisions about public safety, land use, intellectual property and many other considerations (Sachs, 2010).

Increasing ecological scarcity is a sign that current global economic development is unsustainable. An important source of natural capital that should be kept intact is being irreversibly degraded, which is putting the current and future generations at risk (Barbier, 2011).

GREEN INVESTMENTS

Resources such as air, water, food, wood, fibre, minerals and energy sources are the foundation of the economy. The economy also draws on the Earth as a sink for its wastes, such as carbon dioxide, toxic chemicals and chlorofluorocarbons (May, 2010).

Soaring energy needs, volatile oil prices and an increased focus on curbing global warming have spurred investments in clean energy, or 'green financing', in the last few years. Governments, financial institutions, investors and businesses started pouring money into technologies that would help the world address its energy requirements with a minimal impact on the environment (Browne, 2011).

The concept of a 'green economy' is now an instrumental part of the agenda for promoting environmental sustainability and equitable social development. This green economy agenda increasingly refers to political ecology, which sheds light on the 'deliberative engagement of stakeholders in environmental valuation and management, rather than simply presenting trade-offs among alternative courses of action in terms of discounted monetary benefits and costs' (May, 2010).

Rio+20, the United Nations Conference on Sustainable Development held in Rio de Janeiro, Brazil, in 2012 was 'the biggest-ever United Nations Conference and a major step forward in achieving a sustainable future' – the press release of June 2012 (UNCSD, 2012a) summarizes the main points of the final agreement, entitled 'The Future We Want', adopted by the United Nations General Assembly on 27 July 2012 (UNCSD 2012b).

There is not enough academic research on green investments. Most of the existing studies focus on analysing environmental investing from a corporate finance perspective (Climent and Soriano, 2011). For example, the results of the review by Chang et al. (2012) demonstrate that green mutual funds have generated lower returns and similar risks compared to traditional mutual funds. A study by an asset management firm found that socially responsible investment will account for 15 to 20 per cent of worldwide equity assets – reaching an enormous figure of $27 trillion by 2015 (Schwartz, 2009).

There is the need to innovate among energy options, recycle materials and make better use of environmental services. A few of the policy options that are supported by members of the Ecological Economy Community include (May, 2010):

- Decouple energy and material use from economic growth.
- Replace fossil fuels with renewable solar and wind power and second-generation biofuels, whether or not they are 'cheaper'.
- Tax the 'bads' (e.g. resource exhaustion and pollution) rather than the 'goods' (employment and investment).
- Freely share common-pool knowledge and information to stimulate and spread innovation.
- Reform national accounts to measure whether people are happier, not whether they are consuming more.

Environmental protection and sustainable ecological balance have emerged as significant themes of the twenty-first century as increasing numbers of 'green' technologies are finding their way into the various functional areas, including banking. In an economy characterized by increasing globalization, industries and firms are bound to be affected by stringent environmental policies. Since banks provide funds to the industries and firms, they can come across severe credit and liability risks under such environmental policies. Further, the quality of their assets and rate of return in the long run may also be affected by environmental and ecological factors as part of their lending principle, which would force industries and other categories of borrowers to direct themselves towards environmental management, use of appropriate technologies and appropriate management systems. The new generation banks and financial institutions are increasingly embracing environment protection, as part of their CSR and as a drive towards socially and ethically responsible banking (Bihari, 2011).

Social venture capital is a type of venture capital, typically debt or equity investing. Capital is invested in companies whose commercial enterprises produce social and environmental benefits, or support non-profit-making social enterprises. Renewable energy, clean technology, sustainable farming and forestry, affordable housing and health care delivery are among the areas where social venture capital has seen the most concentrated activity (SIF, 2009).

Green incentives, subsidies and tax breaks are instruments designed to provide economic incentives to correct market failure in pollution control. They thereby foster enterprises to reduce loads on the environment, while tax revenues can be spent on promoting more environmentally friendly practices or used to create double dividends. Green incentives encourage producers and consumers to shift to more environmentally friendly behaviour (Paras, 1999; Anbumozhi and Bauer, 2011). Finding financing solutions to bring energy efficiency projects to scale (i.e. to measure the size of the renewable energy market) will deliver a host of important financial, social and environmental benefits to stakeholders, including lower costs, reduced environmental impact and greater opportunities for economic development (Business Wire, 2011).

SOCIALLY RESPONSIBLE INVESTMENT AND GREEN INVESTMENTS IN THE WORLD

The Group of 20 (G20) Leaders' Declaration at the Seoul Summit indicates that the international policymakers view 'green growth' – SD and the promotion of energy efficiency and clean energy technologies as complementary goals. The implication is that the development of energy efficiency and clean energy technologies is the means by which 'sustainable green growth' and, ultimately, SD, will be attained. The G20, which comprises the world's 20 largest and richest countries, has already made some progress in this area. A unique feature of the global policy response to the 2008–2009 recession is that, as part of their efforts to boost aggregate demand and growth, some governments adopted expansionary policies that also incorporated a sizeable 'green fiscal' component. Such measures were wide-ranging, including support for: renewable energy; carbon capture and sequestration; energy efficiency; public transport and rail; and improving electrical grid transmission; as well as other public investments and incentives aimed at environmental protection. Of the US$3.3 trillion allocated worldwide to fiscal stimulus over 2008–2009, US$522 billion (around 16 per cent) was devoted to such green expenditures or tax breaks (Barbier, 2011).

Table 9.1   Socially responsible investing in the United States

	1995	1997	1999	2001	2003	2005	2007	2010
Total ($ billion)	$639	$1,185	$2,159	$2,323	$2,164	$2,290	$2,711	$3,069

Source: SIF, 2010 (http://www.ussif.org/).

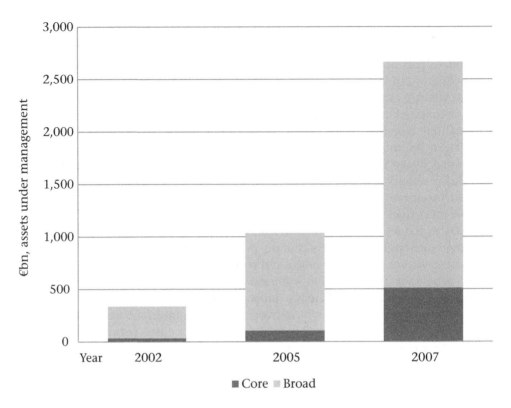

Figure 9.2   Responsible investments in Europe

Source: Deutsche Bank, 2010: 3.

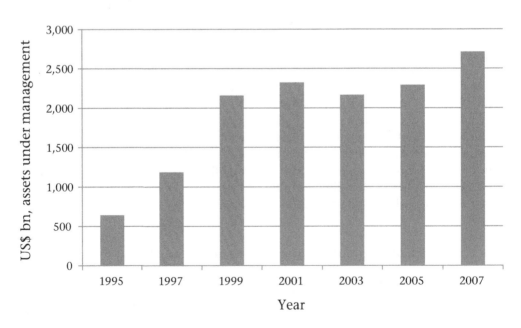

Figure 9.3   Responsible investments in the US

Source: Deutsche Bank, 2010: 3.

There has been a growth in demand for responsible investments over past years. According to estimates published by the European Sustainable Investment Forum (Erosif), global assets under management in SRI amounted to €6.8 trillion in 2008. The European market (Figure 9.2) developed relatively late compared to the US market (Figure 9.3). Not only in comparison with the US but also within Europe, the market share of responsible investments appears to differ widely (Deutsche Bank Research, 2010).

As is shown in Table 9.1, sustainable and socially responsible investment in the US has continued to grow at a faster pace than the broader universe of conventional investment assets under professional management. At the start of 2010, professionally managed assets following SRI strategies stood at $3.07 trillion, a rise of more than 380 per cent from $639 billion in 1995 (SIF, 2010).

SRI funds are largely invested in the 'clean energy' sector. Wind power, solar and geothermal energy offer new possibilities for generating electricity and have also benefited from the ambitious renewable energy programmes launched by governments across Europe in the past few years (Eurosif, 2010).

Although they have experienced more than a 200 per cent increase in growth since 2005, investments in clean energy received a setback in late 2008–2009, owing to the global financial crisis. However, 2010 broke all records – at $243 billion, investments were double the figure for 2006 and nearly five times that of 2004. Marking a complete turnaround from the low of 2009, the main drivers of the rapid growth were: China, with an investment jump of 30 per cent – the single largest for any country; European offshore wind and solar projects; and an increased focus on research and development (Browne, 2011).

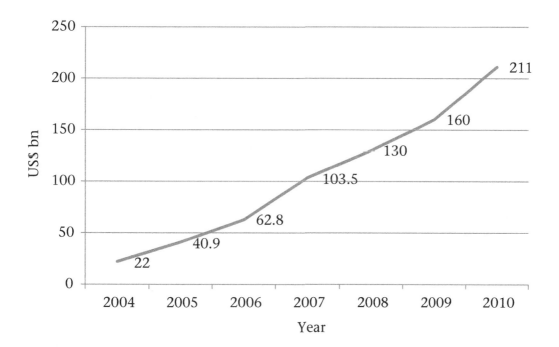

Figure 9.4   Total investment in renewable energy 2004–2010

Source: REN21, 2011: 35 (http://germanwatch.org/klima/gsr2011.pdf).

In 2009, renewable energies comprised 20 per cent of total electricity supply worldwide (REN21, 2010) and an overall investment of $160 billion. As shown in Figure 9.4, in 2010 total investment in renewable energy reached $211 billion, including reported asset finance, venture capital, private equity investment, public markets (stock purchases), and corporate and government research and development (REN21, 2011).

In Germany the Green Funds Scheme has facilitated more than 6,000 projects with almost €12 billion ($17 billion). With the Green Funds Scheme, the government's goal is for society to develop a clearer focus regarding environmental and energy issues when investment and consumption decisions are made (Scholtents, 2011).

The recovery policies adopted by China and South Korea reflect the belief that investments in clean energy technologies can have a major impact on growth, expand exports and create employment. One reason that China has adopted green fiscal measures is that its renewable energy sector already has a value of nearly $17 billion and employs close to one million workers. Overall, China views the promotion of green sectors as a sound industrial policy. It aims to be the world's market leader in solar panels, wind turbines, fuel-efficient cars and other clean energy industries. South Korea also sees its industrial strategy tied to green growth. In addition to the Green New Deal, the South Korean government plans to establish a $72.2 million renewable energy fund to attract private investment in solar, wind and hydroelectric power projects. Developing economies currently account for 40 per cent of existing global renewable resource capacity, 70 per cent of solar water-heating capacity and 45 per cent of biofuel production. Expanding these sectors may also be critical for increasing the availability of affordable and sustainable energy services for the poorest households in these economies (Barbier, 2010).

The growing energy challenge – particularly in Asia – will lead and sustain future growth in clean energy investments (Browne, 2011). In asset finance of new utility-scale renewable projects (wind farms, solar parks, biofuel and solar thermal plants), the largest investment asset class reached a record $128 billion in 2010, or almost 60 per cent of the total. Other types of investment activities in 2010 are notable as well. Venture capital and private equity investment in renewable energy companies increased 19 per cent over 2009 to $5.5 billion. Renewable energy investment in public markets increased 23 per cent in 2010 to $15.4 billion. Research and development (R&D) on renewable energy rose to $9 billion in 2010, with most R&D worldwide going into solar energy ($3.6 billion) followed by biofuels ($2.3 billion). In 2010, $60 billion was invested in small-scale distributed generation projects, accounting for more than 25 per cent of total investment in renewable energy (REN21, 2011).

This trend is only expected to continue, with China leading the way in attracting clean energy investments in the near future. Along with China, India, Japan and South Korea will account for the lion's share of investments in 2020, with the Americas and Europe trailing. While the US will lose its leadership position, it does maintain the potential to attract $342 billion in private clean energy investments over the next decade. Similarly, given its early leadership in clean energy development, the European marketplace is expected to mature, with growth opportunities strongest in southern Europe and offshore wind (Browne, 2011).

The on-ground situation already seems to reflect a certain enthusiasm for clean energy investments – i.e. investors in countries such as China, India and South Korea, and the European and North American regions seem to have enthusiasm for clean energy. Mercer, a global consulting firm, states in a report entitled 'Top Investment Trends of 2011' that across markets, environmental, social and governance factors are increasingly being integrated into investment decision-making today (Browne, 2011).

Most of the regulatory frameworks that exist in developing countries were created in the last quarter of the twentieth century and are characterized by prioritizing and subsidizing conventional energies and fossil fuel technologies. To move towards a sustainable energy supply requires a fundamental change in regulation – away from the conventional systems (characterized by having few agents and large infrastructure projects) towards a dispersed multi-agent focus (characterized by a higher dispersion of installations and a greater number of participants). These changes will face financial, legal and institutional barriers which need to be overcome to improve efficiency, especially in addressing rural poverty and disseminating renewable energy technologies. The equitable redistribution of subsidies and incentives to address the needs of the poorest segments of the population and their energy and resource demand would require the realignment of financing models. Financing mechanisms coupled with a revision of fiscal and regulatory policies should enable the elimination of some of the barriers that affect the dispersion of renewable technologies and the intermediaries and instruments for financing these projects, and overcome the dependence on fossil fuels (Anbumozhi and Bauer, 2011).

CSR and Green Investment Applications in Turkey

The experience of the philanthropic stage of CSR in Turkey goes back to Ottoman times. In the Ottoman era, the *waqf* (foundation) was the premier institutional mechanism for philanthropic provision of public services such as education, health and social security. Today, most family- owned conglomerates in Turkey have an associated *waqf*. In this sense, the public demand from the companies is shaped within the historical *waqf* philosophy and social responsibility becomes identical to the donations and philanthropic actions by companies. The assessment of the total amount of donations, however, is not easy to identify (Bikmen, 2003).

Multinational Corporations (MNCs) positively affect CSR practices in Turkey. The MNCs put positive pressure on their local branches and their suppliers, and this process sets the trend for Turkish wholly owned companies. Nonetheless, the activities of local branches lag behind their headquarters and they are usually project-based. CSR is widely known as a business case and considered especially on the basis of marketing and reputation. By projects through sponsorships, many companies and stakeholder groups are actively trying to be involved and to shape this process. On the other hand, CSR discussions in Turkey suffer from the lack of institutional leadership that would create better understanding, tools and systems (UNDP, 2008).

On the other hand, Turkish SMEs' owner–managers are observed to be applying CSR practices inadequately – for financial reasons and also because they consider them more suited to larger, more 'institutionalized' organizations. In fact they are not still not fully aware of the relevance of socially responsible practices. Furthermore, they are convinced that sustainability and CSR will become relevant in the long term, in a healthier financial situation. Although in general they believe that philanthropy is not a part of business practice, they tend to regard CSR as more modern, broader and so more business-related CSR (Kalaz, 2012).

Increasing competition in Turkey since the 1980s has created price pressure on companies and forced them to postpone their CSR activities in order to protect their profitability. Despite the fact that the role of the state in the economy has been diminishing during the last 30 years, it is still very strong in Turkey when compared to the other EU countries. However, stable inflation and growth rates monitored in recent years have created an atmosphere conducive to companies being involved in social issues (UNDP, 2008).

International issues and the economic and social crises in Turkey have together created an environment for the discussion of CSR where business has the major role to play and the role of civil society is to monitor and benefit. According to CSR Monitor, an international survey, corporate citizenship is highly recognized in Turkey; however, companies are not expected to have operational presence in fields such as labour rights and environmental issues. The time schedule is also supported by the findings of this research, as the research indicates that CSR as a component of corporate reputation in Turkey has been increasing since 1999 (UNDP, 2008).

Currently, there is no specific governmental department responsible for CSR as a whole. There is no CSR-specific legislation either. However, Turkish companies are subject to the relevant national laws and regulations on, for example, labour practices, human rights and the environment. While most of these laws and regulations are developed taking into account international conventions and EU regulations, their enforcement is still weak, often resulting in non-compliance (CSR Consulting, 2010).

Companies in Turkey in the twenty-first century face competition domestically and internationally for customers and capital. Internationally and in Turkey there is increasing awareness of the threats to business as usual from diminishing resources and changing investor, regulator and public attitudes that demand accountability for the role of companies as corporate citizens and the size of their environmental, social and governance footprints. On 10 August 2010 in Istanbul, the Istanbul Stock Exchange (ISE) and the Turkey Business Council for Sustainable Development (TBCSD) launched the Istanbul Stock Exchange Sustainability Index (ISESI) Project. The Project's aim is to review listed companies on the ISE based on their management of sustainability issues and to create an index that will demonstrate the leadership of listed Turkish companies. ISESI will assess how businesses are addressing urgent sustainability issues important for Turkey such as climate change, the depletion of natural resources and ecosystems, diminishing water supplies, health and safety, community relations, employee relations and their resulting impact on Turkey's economic development (ISESI, 2012).

As of September 2010, nearly 150 Turkish enterprises have signed up to the Ten Principles of the United Nations Global Compact (UNGC, 2011), while 10 firms have published sustainability reports based on the GRI (Global Reporting Initiative) Guidelines. With regard to environmental challenges; companies are becoming more familiar with efficient production methods as they consume less energy, water and other natural resources. The main drivers for these efficiency improvements are high-energy prices, concerns for 'climate change/carbon legislation' and pressing water scarcity in certain regions. The government's efforts to tighten environmental quality standards in line with European regulations, which have recently gained momentum, are also stimulating responsible behaviour among enterprises (CSR Consulting, 2010).

The energy sector is another sector which has shown high growth rates over recent years. Actually, Turkey is one of the world's fastest growing energy markets. According to figures from the Ministry of Energy and Natural Resources, between 1995 and 2004 the annual electricity demand growth rate was 6.6 per cent and for the decade 2005–2015, it is projected to be 8.5 per cent. The level of electricity consumption, 150 billion kilowatt-hours in 2004, is expected to increase to around 500 billion kilowatt-hours by 2020. The Turkish energy sector, which has a current size of US$30 billion and a projected size of US$55 billion by 2015, attracts local and foreign investors. There is need of an investment amount of approximately US$130 billion in the sector by 2020 (UNDP, 2008).

Turkey is an energy-importing country. Turkey currently has considerable renewable energy sources, the most important being hydropower, wind, solar, geothermal and biomass. Turkey has about 1 per cent of the total world hydroelectric potential and its significant potential for geothermal power production is ranked seventh in the world (Istwise, n.d.). The passing of Renewable Energy Law No. 5346 on 10 May 2005 marked an important step in the direction of reducing Turkey's energy dependence on foreign countries, in reducing greenhouse gas emissions, and meeting other international energy requirements. It is expected that this law will improve employment opportunities, contribute to socio-economic integration, and protect source supplies by providing resource diversification and increase (UNDP, 2008). By giving price and purchase guarantees, this law has attracted investment into the sector (Beşkök, 2010).

Energy investments in Turkey are increasing, but the country needs US$100 billion more in investments by 2020, according to the chairman of the Istanbul Chamber of Industry. The trend towards renewable energy is increasing, fossil fuel resources have a short lifespan, and price increases in oil and natural gas have forced investors towards environmentally friendly and renewable energy resources (*Hurriyet Daily News*, 2012).

Over the next several years Turkey plans to invest over US$20 billion in renewable energy production, including 10,000 megawatts of wind energy and 300 megawatts of geothermal capacity over the next five years; and to develop 5,000 megawatts of hydroelectric capacity over the next five years (export.gov Turkey, 2012).

Solar hot water technologies are becoming widespread and contribute significantly to hot water production in several countries. According to the existing capacity as of the end of 2010, Turkey is second (5 per cent) after China (70.5 per cent) in production of solar hot water/heat (REN21, 2011). There is some evidence that the Turkish solar heating market is shrinking due to lack of government support, a value added tax on solar thermal systems and the introduction of new natural gas pipelines. At the same time, use of solar thermal in remote villages in Turkey is increasing rapidly thanks to zero-interest government loans (REN21, 2010).

Geothermal power plants now exist in nineteen countries, and new plants continue to be commissioned annually in some other countries, including Turkey. Geothermal resources provide energy in the form of direct heat and electricity. Since 2004, significant additions of electric capacity have occurred in Indonesia, Iceland, New Zealand, the US and Turkey, with Turkey and Iceland each experiencing growth of more than 200 per cent (REN21, 2010).

The new Renewable Energy Law No. 5346 will provide feed-in tariffs for electricity from renewable energy sources and support mainly wind power by setting up a purchase guarantee of the average wholesale electricity price (some 5 US cents per kilowatt hour) for a period of seven years for electricity generated from renewable energies (RenewableEnergyWorld.com, 2012). Geothermal energy is separately regulated by Act No. 5686, passed in 2007, governing geothermal and mineral resources (Şeref, 2010).

An Energy Efficiency Law, aimed at increasing efficiency in the use of energy sources and energy, avoiding waste, easing the burden of energy costs on the economy and protecting the environment was also approved in 2007 (*Official Gazette*, 2007).

On 29 December 2010, the Turkish Parliament finally passed law amending Renewable Energy Law No. 5346, upgrading and differentiating the feed-in tariff structure with regard to sources. The Amendment Law guarantees prices of 7.3 US cents per kilowatt-hour for hydroelectric and wind power, 10.5 US cents for geothermal energy, 13.3 US cents for solar energy, as well as waste products from, for example, plants and wood (Saygın and Çetin, 2011). Turkey has legislation in place guaranteeing the purchase of electricity generated from renewable sources at set feed-in tariffs, along with construction incentives, to advance the ambitious target of 20 gigawatts of wind power by 2020 (IEA, 2010).

Turkey has a huge renewable energy potential, although the recent high costs of renewable energy investments have been limiting the exploitation of this potential. As a result of the recent changes in the legislation governing renewable energy, it is anticipated that the market will grow measurably in the near future (Gedik et al., 2011). In Turkey, renewable energy promotion policies are made in terms of feed-in tariffs and capital subsidies, grants and rebates (REN21, 2010). Feed-in tariffs are a key means of creating a more favourable climate for renewable energy. Under these schemes, payments are guaranteed to households, businesses, communities and other organizations that generate their own electricity from renewable sources (WWF, 2011).

Project financing mechanisms for renewable energy projects in Turkey vary depending on the financial strength and reputation of a project management and consultancy company and its controlling shareholders, and on the status and location of the generation facility – the renewable energy power plant. Deals financed by international banks or financial institutions are often – at least for the operational phase – on a non-recourse basis, whereas Turkish banks tend to provide loans to a project management company only subject to receiving a corporate guarantee from its controlling shareholder. In order to ring-fence a company for security purposes, the financing for a project in the Turkish market would include a combination of pledges of shares, bank accounts, commercial enterprises, mortgages, assignment of receivables, etc. (Gedik et al., 2011).

Developing countries expand rapidly and are growth markets for banks, while banks play a key role in their financial and economic development (Beck et al., 2010; Hu and Scholtents, 2012). Turkish banks competed from 2005 to finance commercial renewable energy and energy efficiency projects. Although Turkey is not a member country of the European Union, European and Turkish banks are prepared to consider proposals from Turkish companies for environmental financing purposes. Hence, those banks that use European renewable energy credits extended the credit period to 15 years; others offered monthly interest rates beginning at 1 per cent. Banks offering renewable energy credits at lower interest rates than other commercial credits are: The European Investment Bank, The Council of Europe Development Bank, The European Bank for Reconstruction and Development (EBRD), Proparco a financial development institution, JBIC, KfW (a Dutch industrialization fund) and many other foreign banks and funds offer green funds with long credit periods and low interest rates through Turkish banks. Turkey Sustainable Energy Financing (TURSEFF) is one of the financial institutions that provide the highest amounts of foreign funds. For instance,

TURSEFF offers credits with a 1 per cent interest rate over up to 60 months. Other financing sources that offer suitable renewable energy credits in Turkey are Vakıfbank, TSKB (Türkiye Sınai Kalkınma Bankası), TEB (Türk Ekonomi Bankası), Denizbank and İş Bankası (Para, 2012).

Consumers in Turkey generally do not choose environmentally friendly products over other products primarily based on price comparisons. In most cases, they seem unwilling to pay more for green products. Furthermore, there is also a tendency not to prefer products with recycled content due to socio-cultural or health-related considerations. More radical changes in life preferences such as housing choice, car-buying choice and the level of consumption take place not because of environmental concerns but because of financial constraints (Izci and Sezgin, 2012).

Turkey aims to utilize its energy potential, including from renewable sources, in a cost-effective manner. Large investments in energy infrastructure, especially in energy and natural gas, are needed to avoid bottlenecks in supply and to sustain rapid economic growth. To attract that investment, the country needs to continue reforming its energy market (IEA, 2010).

Conclusion

CSR is the key factor that will enable Turkey to implement SD and clean energy sources – in terms of renewable energy – that has the potential to increase the quality of life and sustainability. The energy that the world produces and uses is not sustainable and renewable energy supply is a way to reduce environmental impact and bring energy efficiency.

Fostering increased investments in clean energy and energy efficiency is an important step to achieving more sustainable economic development, but it is unlikely to be sufficient. Unless a concerted global policy effort is devoted to overcoming the sustainability and funding challenges of rising ecological scarcity worldwide, the welfare of current and future generations is at risk (Barbier, 2011).

The Turkish energy market is currently the scene of important changes. The country has established a new national energy plan based on diversification of supplies, and has started on the development of renewable energy end energy efficiency. It seems to be moving towards a low-carbon energy sector. In this context, it has three strategies: increasing energy efficiency; increasing renewable energy use; and increasing natural gas use. This implies that Turkey is stepping up its engagement on climate change internationally and nationally (Saygın and Çetin, 2011).

Green investment aims to protect the environment. In the light of social responsibility, all related parties should place importance on clean and sustainable energy investments for the safety of future generations.

References

Anbumozhi, V. and Bauer, A. (2011). *Flexible Financial Incentives for Inclusive and Green Growth. Presentation at The Environments of the Poor in the Context of Climate Change and the Green Economy.*

Making Sustainable Development Inclusive, Conference held 24–26 November 2010, New Delhi. *Asian Development Bank* (ADB) Poverty Reduction, 1–44.

Anwar, Y. and Mulyadi, M.S. (2011). Income tax incentives on renewable energy industry: case of geothermal industry in USA and Indonesia. *African Journal of Business Management*, 5(31), December, 12264–12270.

Barbier, E. (2010). Dealing in green. *The Broker*, 20/21, July, 6–9.

—— (2011). The policy challenges for green economy and sustainable economic development. *A United Nations Sustainable Development Journal: Natural Resources Forum*, 35(3), 233–45.

Beck, T., Demirgüç-Kunt, A. and Levine, R. (2010). Financial institutions and markets across countries and over time: the updated financial development and structure database. *The World Bank Economic Review*, 24(1), 77–92.

Beşkök, O. (2010). *Financing Renewable Energy Investments*. ADFIMI Development Forum, 5–6 October.

Bihari, S.C. (2011). Green banking – towards socially responsible banking in India. *International Journal of Business Insights and Transformation*, 4(1), 82–87.

Bikmen, F. (2003). Corporate philanthropy in Turkey: building on tradition, adapting to change. *SEAL (Social Economy and Law Project Journal)*, Autumn.

Bossche, F.V., Rogge, N., Devooght, K. and Puyenbroeck T.V. (2010). Robust corporate social responsibility investment screening. *Ecological Economics*, 69, 1159–1169.

The Broker (2009). *The Rise of Solar Energy*. Amsterdam: IDP. [Online.] Available at: http://www.thebrokeronline.eu/Special-Reports/Special-report-The-rise-of-solar-energy [accessed: 27 November 2013].

Browne, R.W.C. (2011). Green financing: more than a trend. *Environmental Leader*. [Online.] Available at: http://www.environmentalleader.com, 20 July [accessed: 27 November 2013].

Business Wire (2011). Citi Collaborates with Environmental Defense Fund to Co-Host Innovations in Energy Efficiency Financing Conference, 20 September. New York: Business Wire. [Online.] Available at: http://www.businesswire.com/news/home/20110920005775/en/Citi-Collaborates-Environmental-Defense-Fund-Co-Host-Innovations [accessed: 27 November 2013].

Buskirk, R.V. (2006). Analysis of long-range clean energy investment scenarios for Eritrea: East Africa. *Energy Policy*, 34(14), September, 1807–1817.

Cerin, P. and Scholtents, B. (2011). Linking responsible investments to societal influence: motives, assessments and risks. *Sustainable Development*, 19, 71–76.

Çetinel, E. (2012). Bankalar yeşil finans yarışı başlattı! *Para*, 388, 46–9.

Chang, C.E., Nelson, W.A. and Witte, H.D. (2012). Do green mutual funds perform well? *Management Research Review*, 35(8), 693–708.

Climent, F. and Soriano, P. (2011). Green and good? The investment performance of US environmental mutual funds. *Journal of Business Ethics*, 103(2), 275–87.

CSR Consulting (2010). *CSR Principles in International Business*. Istanbul: CSR association of Turkey and Utrecht: CSR Netherlands. Available at: http://www.agentschapnl.nl/sites/default/files/CSR%20Principles%20in%20International%20Business.pdf [accessed: 27 November 2013].

Deutsche Bank (2010). Deutsche Bank Research. [Online.] Available at: http://www.dbresearch.com/PROD/DBR_INTERNET_EN-PROD/PROD0000000000259180/Responsible+Investments%3A+A+new+investment+trend+here+to+stay.PDF.

Duarte, R., Mainar, A. and Sánchez-Chóliz, J. (2012). Social groups and CO2 emissions in Spanish households. *Energy Policy*, 44, 441–50. Available at: http://www.sciencedirect.com/science/article/pii/S0301421512001371 – aff1#aff1 [accessed: 27 November 2013].

Ertuna, B. and Tükel, A. (2009). Türkiye'de KSS uygulamaları: geleneksel ve küresel arasında. *Yönetim Araştırmaları Dergisi*, 9(2), 145–72.

Eurosif (2010). European SRI study 2010. Brussels: European Sustainable Investment Forum. [Online.] Available at: http://www.eurosif.org/research/eurosif-sri-study/2010 [accessed: 27 November 2013].

export.gov Turkey (2012). *Re-energize with Turkey: Investment Opportunities in the Turkish Energy Sector*, 14 September. [Online – US Commercial Service website.] Available at: http://www.usea.org/event/turkish-energy-sector-investment-roadshow. USEA – United States Energy Association (2011). Available at: http://www.usea.org/event/turkish-energy-sector-investment-roadshow [accessed: 22 December 2013].

Gedik, H., Özeke, H.B. and Boz, U.S. (2011). Renewable energy in Turkey: recent regulatory developments. *EBRD: Law in Transition*, October, 1–8.

Gunay, S.G. (2010). The determinants of corporate social responsibility in Turkey. *European Journal of Social Sciences*, 17(3), 404–413.

Hamilton, S., Jo, H. and Statman, M. (1993). Doing well while doing good? The investment performance of socially responsible mutual funds. *Financial Analysts Journal*, 49(6), 62–66.

Hu, V. and Scholtens, B. (2012). Corporate social responsibility policies of commercial banks in developing countries. *Sustainable Development*. [Online – Wiley Online Library: doi: 10.1002/ss.1551].

Hurriyet Daily News (2012). Turkey's energy dependency to be solved with renewable energy. Istanbul. Available at: http://www.hurriyetdailynews.com/energy-dependence-to-grow-in-turkey.aspx?pageID=238&nid=40585 [accessed: 3 February 2012].

Hussain, K. (2012). The relationship between oil and gas industry investment in alternative energy and corporate social responsibility. Unpublished PhD Dissertation, *Walden University*, Minneapolis, MN, 1–115.

IEA (2010). Energy Policies of IEA Countries. Turkey 2009 review. Paris: International Energy Agency. [Online.] Available at: http://www.iea.org/publications/freepublications/publication/turkey2009.pdf [accessed: 29 November 2013].

ISESI (2012). Istanbul Stock Exchange Sustainability Index. Available at: http://www.isesi.org/ISESI_ENG/About_ISESI.html [accessed: 11 September 2012].

Istwise (n.d.). *Investment in Turkey*. Istanbul: Istanbul Property Wise. Available at: http://investment-in-turkey.com/page11.html [accessed: 27 November 2013].

Izci, R. and Sezgin, Z. (2012). *Consumption, Futurity and Sustainability: Sustainable Consumption in Turkey? 18th Annual International Sustainable Development Research Conference*, University of Hull, 24–26 June.

Jun, E., Kim, W.J., Jeong, Y.H. and Chang, S.H. (2010). Measuring the social value of nuclear energy using contingent valuation methodology. *Energy Policy*, 38(3), 1470–1476.

Kalaz, T. (2012). Corporate social responsibility in Turkey. *Universiteit Gent, Faculteit Economie En Bedrijfskunde, Academiejaar*, 2011–2012, 1–110.

Kinder, P.D. and Domini, A.L. (1997). Social screening: paradigms old and new. *Journal of Investing*, 6(4), 12–21.

Koellner, T., Weber, O., Fenchel, M. and Scholz, R. (2005). Principles for sustainability rating of investment funds. *Business Strategy and the Environment*, 14, 54–70.

Lambooy, T. (2011). Corporate social responsibility: sustainable water use. *Journal of Cleaner Production*, 19, 852–66.

Leahy, J. (2008). Socially responsible investing: the quest for financial return and social good. *Accountancy Ireland*, 40(6), 47–49.

Maruyama, Y., Nishikido, M. and Lida, T. (2007). The rise of community wind power in Japan: enhanced acceptance through social innovation. *Energy Policy*, 35(5), 2761–2769.

May, P. (2010). Revaluing the environment. *The Broker*, 18, 17–20. [Online.] Available at: http://www.thebrokeronline.eu/en/Special-Reports/Special-report-Greening-the-global-economy/Revaluing-the-environment [accessed: 27 November 2013].

McManus, A., Gaterell, M.R. and Coates, L.E. (2010). The potential of the code for sustainable homes to deliver genuine 'sustainable energy' in the UK social housing sector. *Energy Policy*, 38(4), 2013–2019.

Official Gazette (2007). Energy efficiency law. 26510, Turkey, 2 May 2007.

Ooi, E. and Lajbcgier, P. (2012). Virtue remains after removing sin: finding skill amongst socially responsible investment managers. *Journal of Business Ethics*, 7 April, 1–26. [Online.] Available at: http://link.springer.com/article/10.1007%2Fs10551-012-1290-x#page-1.

Ottinger, R.L. (2006). Energy efficiency: the best immediate option for a secure, clean, healthy future. *A United Nations Sustainable Development Journal: Natural Resources Forum*, 30, 318–27.

Özgen, E. (2007). Kurumsal sosyal sorumluluk kavramı ve çalışan memnuniyetine etkisi. *D.Ü. Ziya Gökalp Eğitim Fakültesi Dergisi*, 8, 1–6.

Özgüç, E. (2009). Kurumsal sosyal sorumluluk uygulamaları kapsamında IMKB – 30 endeksi şirketleri. *Sermaye Piyasası Kurulu Araştırma Raporu*, 30.03.2009 EO–1.

Paras, S. (1999). A global and multicriteria environmental taxation model for industrial pollution prevention and control. *Sustainable Development*, 7, 1–12.

Pivo, G. and McNamara, P. (2005). Responsible property investing. *International Real Estate Review*, 8(1), 128–43.

Pop, O., Dina, G.C. and Martin, C. (2011). Promoting the corporate social responsibility for a green economy and innovative jobs. *Procedia – Social and Behavioral Sciences*, 15, 1020–1023.

Poroy-Arsoy, A., Arabacı, Ö. and Çiftçioğlu, A. (2012). Corporate social responsibility and financial performance relationship: the case of Turkey. *The Journal of Accounting and Finance*, 53, 159–76.

REN21 (2010). Renewables 2010: Global Status Report. Paris: REN21 Secretariat. Available at: http://www.ren21.net/REN21Activities/GlobalStatusReport.aspx [accessed: 27 November 2013].

REN21 (2011). Renewables 2011: Global Status Report. Paris: REN21 Secretariat. Available at: http://www.ren21.net/REN21Activities/GlobalStatusReport.aspx [accessed: 27 November 2013].

Renewable Energy World (2005). Turkey adopts national feed-in law for renewables, 16 May 2005, Available at: http://www.renewableenergyworld.com [accessed: 20 September 2012].

RIO+20 (2012). Rio+20 Corporate Sustainability Forum: Innovation and Collaboration for the Future We Want. 14–18 June 2012, Windsor Barra Hotel, Rio de Janeiro. Rio de Janeiro, 21 June 2012. New York: UNCSD. [Online – overview and outcomes.] Available at: http://www.uncsd2012.org/index.php?page=view&nr=534&type=13&menu=23 [accessed: 27 November 2013].

Sachs, J. (2010). *Rethinking Macroeconomics. The Broker*, 18, 14–16.

Salmela, S. and Varho, V. (2006). Consumers in the green electricity market in Finland. *Energy Policy*, 34(18), 3669–3683.

Sayce, S., Sundberg, A., Parnell, P. and Cowling, E. (2009). Greening leases: do tenants in the United Kingdom want green leases? *Journal of Retail and Leisure Property*, 8(4), 273–84.

Saygın, H. and Çetin, F. (2011). Recent developments in renewable energy policies of Turkey, in Nayeripour, M. and Khesti, M., *Renewable Energy – Trends and Applications*. Croatia: InTech Open Access Publisher, 25–40.

Scheer, R. (2004). Greening venture capital: are clean technologies the next new thing? *E Magazine*, November/December, 46–47.

Schmidt, S. and Weisterofer, C. (2010). *Responsible investments*. Frankfurt am Main, Germany: Deutsche Bank Research, June 24. Available at: http://www.dbresearch.com/PROD/DBR_

INTERNET_EN-PROD/PROD0000000000259180/Responsible+Investments%3A+A+new+invest ment+trend+here+to+stay.PDF [accessed: 27 November 2013].

Scholtents, B. (2011). The sustainability of green funds. *A United Nations Sustainable Development Journal: Natural Resources Forum*, 35(3), 223–32.

Schwartz, R. (2009). Social investment is not an asset class, nor should it be. *Third Sector*, 17 November.

Selvi, Y., Wagner, E. and Türel, A. (2010). Corporate social responsibility in the time of financial crisis: evidence from Turkey. *Annales Universitatis Apulensis Series Oeconomica*, 12(1), 281–90.

Şeref, O. (2010). Geothermal energy regulations and incentives under Turkish Law. Istanbul: GSI Meridian. Available at: http://www.gsimeridian.com/files/17.pdf [accessed: 22 December 2013].

SIF (2007). 2007 Report on the Socially Responsible Investing Trends in the United States. Washington DC: Social Investment Forum Foundation. Available at: http://www.ussif.org/files/ Publications/07_Trends_%20Report.pdf [accessed: 27 November 2013].

—— (2009). *The Mission in the Marketplace*. Washington DC: Social Investment Forum Foundation. Available at: http://www.ussif.org/files/Publications/MissioninMarketplace2009.pdf [accessed: 27 November 2013].

—— (2010). 2010 Report on the Socially Responsible Investing Trends in the United States. Washington DC: Social Investment Forum Foundation. Available at: http://community-wealth. org/content/report-socially-responsible-investing-trends-united-states [accessed: 27 November 2013].

Sparkes, Russell (2003). *Socially Responsible Investments A Global Revolution*. Chichester, UK: John Wiley.

Streimikiene, D., Simanaviciene, Z. and Kovaliov, R. (2009). Corporate social responsibility for implementation of sustainable energy development in Baltic States. *Renewable and Sustainable Energy Reviews*, 13(4), 813–24.

UNCSD (2012a). Rio+20 concludes with big package of commitments for action and agreement by world leaders on path for a sustainable future. Press release, 20–22 June. Rio de Janeiro: United Nations Conference on Sustainable Development. Available at: http://www.un.org/en/ sustainablefuture/pdf/rio20%20concludes_press%20release.pdf [accessed: 29 November 2013].

UNCSD (2012b). *The Future We Want*. Resolution Adopted by the General Assembly on 27 July 2012. (A.Res.66/288). New York: United Nations. Available at: www.un.org/en/sustainablefuture/ [accessed: 27 November 2013].

UNDP (2008). *Turkey Corporate Social Responsibility Baseline Report*. New York: United Nations Development Programme. Available at: http://www.undp.org.tr/publicationsDocuments/CSR_ Report_en.pdf [accessed: 27 November 2013].

UNGC (2011). The United Nations Global Compact. Geneva: United Nations. [Online.] Available at: http://www.unglobalcompact.org/ [accessed: 23 October 2011].

Vertigans, S. (2011). CSR as corporate social responsibility or colonial structures return? A Nigerian case study. *International Journal of Sociology and Anthropology*, 3(6), 159–62.

Vyvyan, V., Ng, C. and Brimble, M. (2007). Socially responsible investing: The green attitudes and grey choices of Australian investors. *Corporate Governance*, 15(2), 370–81.

Wilson, C. and Grubler, A. (2011). Lessons from the history of technological change for clean energy scenarios and policies. *A United Nations Sustainable Development Journal: Natural Resources Forum*, 35(3), 165–84. Available at: http://web.ebscohost.com/ehost/pdfviewer/ pdfviewer?vid=3&sid=3987eb66-9794-48fc-8126-c4904ccf026d%40sessionmgr15&hid=26.

WWF (2011). *The Energy Report: 100% Renewable Energy by 2050*. World Wildlife Fund. [Online.] Available at: http://www.panda.org/energyreport [accessed: 27 November 2013].

Yanık, S., Turan-İçke, B. and Aytürk, Y. (2010). Sosyal sorumlu yatırım fonları ve performans özellikleri. İ.Ü. *Siyasal Bilgiler Fakültesi Dergisi*, 43, 109–134.

CSR in the General Environment

10 Corporate Social Responsibility to Small and Medium-sized Enterprises: Extending Sustainable Development in Society

MIA MAHMUDUR RAHIM

Abstract

Sustainable development (SD) and corporate social responsibility (CSR) could be perceived as a meta-fix whose ideas and philosophies have evolved from an objective perspective to one of process. While SD aims to sustain economic growth with the required maintenance and protection of the environment, CSR is a long-term business strategy that balances corporate rights with economic, environmental and social obligations towards its stakeholders. The semantics of these two terms have changed over time to a point where these concepts have become interrelated processes for ensuring a long-reaching development. This chapter posits the notion that SD can contribute to realizing the objective of integrating development throughout society if small and medium-sized enterprises (SMEs) could be sensitized to the core dimensions of CSR.

Introduction

Sustainable Development (SD) and Corporate Social Responsibility (CSR) unequivocally affirm that economic and environmental approaches should support the development of society in the long run. Both concepts have received considerable attention in market, social, governmental and globalization policies of late.

Besides environmental development focus, SD has a wide and varied focus on human and economic development. It links economic development and environmental standards in the context of human social standards. It can also be viewed in light of the positive contribution business enterprises can make to the economic and environmental growth of society. CSR could be a potential strategy for business enterprises to realize such growth in society. For example, while SD emphasizes the necessity of using natural resources cautiously, CSR urges business enterprises to take reasonable steps to fulfil their environmental liabilities to society. CSR is concerned with corporate philosophies. It denotes that a business enterprise may make substantial profit while ignoring the social and environmental concerns of its activities. Such actions have the potential to negatively affect society and the environment and, ultimately, business strategy and long-term profitability.

CSR presupposes the formulation of different strategies to link business enterprises with the environments in which they operate to secure a better business case. Strategies formulated in response to, for example, major environmental damage by business enterprises, help them not only to get a 'licence to operate' but also to minimize the costs arising from civil liability suits and public criticism; and to shield consumer markets from media exposure, which might discourage consumer purchase and brand loyalty. The environmental dimension of CSR reflects and addresses environmental imperatives for business success. Since the cumulative social and environmental impact of small and medium-sized enterprises (SMEs) is highly significant in most economies, they could offer the potential for significant progress towards SD if their managements could adopt broader ethical consideration to reduce those externalities that affect the environment.

Given this premise, it is posited in this chapter that integrating the core values of the environmental dimension of CSR into the corporate governance of SMEs could help to implement the basic notion of SD in a wide spectrum of society. The chapter first briefly explicates the concepts of SD and CSR; then, it synthesizes these concepts with particular reference to their economic and environmental dimensions. Finally, it discusses the scope of introducing the core notions of these dimensions into SMEs' corporate management.

The Concept of Sustainable Development

The concept of SD formally originated[1] in the Brundtland Report *Our Common Future* by the United Nations World Commission on Environment and Development 1987 (Bebbington, 2001; Dixon and Fallon, 1989; Mebratu 1998). The Commission defined SD as 'development which meets the needs of the present without compromising the ability of future generations to meet their own needs' (UNWCED, 1987b). Gradually this definition has been adopted both domestically and internationally in an incredibly broad area of social and economic policy. Of particular relevance to this chapter is the fact that the concept of SD aligns with the notion of CSR in all its economic, environmental and social dimensions (Shawkat, 2008).

Although it has often been noted that there appears to be no common understanding of the definition of SD or of the possible measures needed to be taken in order to achieve it, the notion has become pre-eminent in discussions on the relationship between humankind and nature (Callens and Tyteca, 1999; Gladwin, Kennelly and Krause, 1995; Hajer, 1997; Livesey and Kearins, 2002; Robinson, 2004). It has been used to mean different things to different people in different contexts but gradually it has gained widespread support as an appropriate policy goal for humankind (Bebbington and Gray, 2001;

---

1   From the date of its formal orientation this concept could seem comparatively new, but actually it has older roots. For details, see Bebbington, 2001; Dixon and Fallon, 1989; UNWCED, 1987a.

Meadowcroft, 2000) and has gathered a consensus that the present way of living is not sustainable (Ekins, Folke and Groot, 2003). While this document supports the need for development in a sustainable way, the dissemination of the concept has inaugurated a debate about current social practices and the kinds of measures that should be taken in order to achieve it (Hajer, 1997).

SD focuses on economic, environmental and social approaches and/or a combination thereof. Among these approaches, some economic approaches focus narrowly on the physical aspects of SD and stress the maintenance of stocks of renewable and non-renewable natural resources (Hanson, 1992). Some economic focuses are on optimal resource management to maximize 'the net benefits of economic development, subject to maintaining the services and quality of natural resources' (Hanson, 1992), or on the broader idea that 'economic systems should be managed so that we live off the dividend of our resources, maintaining and improving the asset base' (Hanson, 1992). Besides these focuses, SD has a wide and varied focus on human and environmental development, as SD is also being defined in human terms. An important component of such development is the right of people to participate in decisions that affect their lives (UNDP, 1991). Though this concept masks some inherent contradictions, it approaches some common themes and characteristics that hold a particular linkage between economic development and environmental standards in the context of human social conditions.

The nexus between economic development and environmental standards through this concept is also amplified in the meaning and structure of the term 'sustainable development'. Lélé (1991) interprets it as 'sustaining development' or as 'a form of societal change that, in addition to traditional development objectives, has the objective or constraint of ecological sustainability'(Lélé, 1991). The author presents a framework which gives the meaning of the word 'sustainability' a literal, an ecological, and a social sense. The literal meaning refers to the continuation of anything. The ecological meaning relates to maintaining the 'ecological basis of human life' within a time-based structure, indicating concern for both the future and the present. In describing the social meaning of SD, Lélé (1991) draws on Barbier's concept of social meaning, which focuses on maintaining desired 'social values, institutions, cultures, or other social characteristics' (Barbier, 1987). The author gives the term 'development' two meanings. When referring to a process it means growth and change; and when referring to an objective, it means satisfying basic needs (Lélé, 1991). Hence, the foundational meaning of SD establishes, according to Lélé, two different interpretations (1) sustaining growth; and (2) achieving traditional objectives by meaningfully following a process[2] for such development that sustains values, reflect progress in intra-social relationships and consequently develops the meaning of 'human' in the natural environment (Fergus and Rowney, 2005).

The process for achieving this concept denotes an instrumental rationality that could be exercised through the neoclassical economic framework for sustaining growth. However, SD is not just about economic development, but about the development of society as a whole. Agenda 21 (UN, 1993), proposes that social, economic and environmental concerns be fully and effectively integrated in decision-making in the policies and practices of each country in international institutional arrangements and in

---

2   Lélé, 1991. In recognizing the second interpretation as mainstream, Lélé reflects the historical context of the argument. At that time, the term 'sustainable development' received widespread media and public attention, partly as a result of the 1987 World Commission on Environment and Development (the Brundtland Commission) and the anticipated Earth Summit in Rio de Janeiro in 1992.

international legal instruments. Here, integration in practice implies, 'on the one hand, all environmental, social and economic factors (including, for example, impacts of the various economic and social sectors on the environment and natural resources); and, on the other, all environmental and resource components together (i.e., air, water, biota, land, geological and natural resources)' (UN, 1993).

The United Nations Conference on Environment and Development (UNCED) in 1992 in Rio de Janeiro, Brazil, repeated the inevitability of the nexus of economic and environmental aspects for the SD of any society. The Rio Declaration on Environment and Development recommends that 'states should promote a supportive and open international economic system' which would contribute to economic growth and SD (UN, 1992). This international declaration unequivocally affirms that economic and environmental approaches should support long-reaching development. Thus, the need for a process of integration between trade and the protection of the natural environment becomes a salient feature of SD (Shawkat, 2008). The urge towards this process was affirmed in the Johannesburg Declaration on Sustainable Development,[3] which declares that 'globalization has added a new dimension to these challenges. The rapid integration of markets, mobility of capital and significant increases in investment flows around the world has opened new challenges and opportunities for the pursuit of sustainable development'.[4]

From the discussion it emerged that it is conceivable that social justice, human rights and environmental, economic and cultural factors are integrally considered in the SD concept, and that these considerations are not readily separable. However, by analogy, it would be reasonable to assume that the concept of SD is a meta-fix, whose ideas and philosophies move from an objective perspective to one of process. Therefore, the semantics of the term 'sustainable development' have changed over time to a point where the concept becomes a supplement to the dominant paradigm of economic growth. The scientific–economic paradigm, manifested through the cognitive structure of the economic framework, moves the meaning of SD from an inclusive exploration of objectives to a process. This process is an integrated effort with far-sighted aims and its success is measured through a concerted outcome that integrates every corner of society (Lawson, 1997).

The Concept of CSR

In its broader sense, CSR is about the impact business makes on society and also the role of business in SD. It is a wide-ranging concept, the definition and perception of which varies depending on the particular context – for instance: types of industry sectors; types and sizes of business enterprises; and ownership structure. In its narrower sense, it is a complex and multidimensional organizational phenomenon which could be defined as the extent to which and the way in which an organization is consciously responsible for and accountable for its actions and non-actions and the impact of these on its stakeholders (Rahim, 2013).

---

3   This declaration was passed in 2002 at the World Summit on Sustainable Development.

4   Johannesburg Declaration on Sustainable Development (2002), adopted at the 17th plenary meeting of the World Summit on Sustainable Development, 4 September 2002, Para.14 UN Doc.A/Conf.199/L.6/Rev.2(2002).

CSR is a fluid concept, the definition and perception of which varies depending on the particular context and hence its interchangeable and overlapping character is dominant in its definitional cohort. For some it is looked at as the source of competitive advantage; for others it is an important response to the increasing demands of key stakeholders such as employees, investors, consumers and environmentalists. Given this character and circumstances, this concept can be described using a number of terms: 'corporate citizenship', 'ethical corporation', 'corporate governance', 'corporate sustainability', 'socially responsible investment', 'corporate accountability', etc. (Bowfield and Frynas, 2005; Matten and Moon, 2008; Commonwealth of Australia, 2006) and there is no overall agreement on its definition.

Although there is no universally agreed definition of CSR, there is indeed a proliferation of in-use definitions. Carroll gives a long account of the evolution of the definition of the concept of CSR from the 1950s to the 1990s, with a specific feature of each decade in terms of its development (Carroll, 1999). In the 1980s some alternative theoretical issues were added to the concept itself, including corporate social performance, stakeholder theory, and business ethics theory (Carroll, 1999: 280). In a definitional development that occurred in the 1990s these alternative themes took centre stage in the manifestation of CSR (Carroll, 1999: 288) and subsequently all subsequent definitions of CSR were dominated by a stakeholder and societal approach with the recognition of social, economic, and environmental issues as the basic components of responsibility. The best illustration of this is available in the definitions and views developed in the late 1990s and thereafter by the different intergovernmental, governmental and development organizations and some postmodern academics (Dahlsrud, 2006a).

The World Business Council for Sustainable Development defines CSR as 'the continuing commitment by business to behave ethically and contribute to economic development while improving the quality of life of the workforce and their families as well as of the local community and society at large' (Watts and Holmes, 1999). According to this definition, business societies have a responsibility to contribute, working with employees, their families, the local community and society at large to improve their quality of life and thereby try to ensure sustainable economic development. The phrase 'continuing commitment' used in this definition indicates that CSR is not a temporary or a momentary issue that the company considers under certain conditions, rather it is a permanent issue that should be placed strategically in the company's policies and programmes. Business for Social Responsibility (BSR) defines CSR in a more holistic way. This organization defines CSR as a tool for 'achieving commercial success in ways that honour ethical values and respect people, communities, and the natural environment' (White, 2006). Thus, BSR relates CSR to the idea of recognizing and responding to a broader spectrum of stakeholder interests. The International Business Leaders Forum extends this idea and accepts it as a responsible business practice which could benefit business and society by maximizing the positive impact business has on society and minimizing the negative.

In a similar fashion the Commission of the European Communities defines CSR as a concept whereby companies integrate social and environmental concerns in their business operations and in their interactions with their stakeholders on a voluntary basis (European Commission, 2001). In another definition by the Commission it is said that CSR is essentially a concept whereby a company decides voluntarily to contribute to a better society and a cleaner environment (Dahlsrud, 2006b). Given these definitions, CSR appears to be a managing element that starts at company level by its performance in a socially responsible manner, where the trade-offs between the requirements and the needs of the various stakeholders are in balance, which is acceptable to all parties.

In a recent publication, rather than give any conclusive definition of CSR the Australian Parliamentary Joint Committee on Corporations and Financial Services, looks into the concept of CSR from the following standpoints: (a) considering, managing and balancing the economic, social and environmental impacts of companies' activities; (b) assessing and managing risks, pursuing opportunities and creating corporate value beyond the traditional core business; and (c) taking an 'enlightened self-interest' approach to considering the legitimate interests of the stakeholders into corporate governance.

Over the last decade some academics have – like different business and development organizations – contributed to the broad-based definitions of CSR, focusing on its basic features and dimensions. Among them Michael Hopkins, Chris Marsden and Archie B. Carroll are prominent. Michael Hopkins relates CSR to treating the stakeholders of the firm ethically or in a responsible manner. By the words 'ethically' and 'responsible', he emphasizes that the treatment of stakeholders in a manner deemed acceptable in civilized society is an economic responsibility of business enterprises (Hopkins, 2004). Marsden (2000) observes CSR as a core behavioural issue for the business enterprises, he states that 'CSR is not an optional add-on nor is it an act of philanthropy. A socially responsible corporation is one that runs a profitable business that takes account of all the positive and negative environmental, social and economic effect it has on society' (Dahlsrud, 2006b). Andersen defines CSR following a broader societal approach; he says, 'we define corporate social responsibility broadly to be about extending the immediate interest from oneself to include one's fellow citizens and the society one is living in and is a part of today, acting with respect for the future generation and nature'.

All these definitions reveal that there is no conclusive definition of CSR. CSR is an ever-growing, multifaceted concept and it can have different meanings for different people and organizations. Nevertheless, it may be said that these meanings are inwardly consistent and converge on some common characters and similar elements. More precisely, if CSR is looked into from a practical and operational point of view, two points emerge: that CSR requires a company: (a) to consider the social, environmental and economic impacts of its business operations; and (b) to be responsive to the needs and expectations of its customers, employees, investors, shareholders, and the community or communities (otherwise known as stakeholders) in which it operates in the context of those impacts (Rahim, 2013). These two points are also embedded in the meaning of the three words that make up the term 'corporate social responsibility'. 'Corporate' generally means 'business operations'; 'social' covers all the stakeholders of business operations; and 'responsibility' generally means the relationship between corporations and the societies with which they interact. The term also embraces the responsibilities that are inherent on both sides of this relationship. Accordingly, CSR is an integral element of business strategy: the way the business enterprise goes about delivering its products or services to the market; it is also a way of maintaining the legitimacy of its actions in larger society by bringing stakeholder concerns to the foreground.

CSR in Sustainable Development: A Strategy for Developing a Process

CSR is related to economic as well as environmental and human development. Its approaches are multidimensional, as CSR involves the interests of different types of stakeholders, where the range of these stakeholders' interests, either internal or external, expands with time in the face of increased expectations from the corporations. The dimensions of CSR have been separated into internal and external dimensions. The internal dimension of CSR includes human resource management, health and safety at work, management of environmental impacts, and natural resources.[5] The external dimensions involve local communities, business partners, suppliers, consumers, human rights and global environment (European Commission, 2001). At this point, like SD, CSR could be termed a meta-fix since it is also a multidimensional concept with different kinds of liabilities and abilities for business enterprises to maintain, build and use their social capital.

Dahlsrud (2006a) identifies five dimensions of CSR, on the basis of the analysis of thirty-seven definitions of CSR developed mostly within the last twelve years. These five dimensions are: voluntary, stakeholder, economic, social and environmental (Dahlsrud, 2006b). However, these dimensions, from theoretical and operational perspectives, could be classified into two: nature-based dimensions and content and/or issue-based dimensions, of which voluntariness and stakeholder dimensions are nature-based, and economic, social and environment are issue- based dimensions. Here, the nature-based dimensions refer to be factors that focus on the inherent character and actionable value. Content or issue-based dimensions refer to the main concerns and areas of a CSR and also demarcate the purview of action.

These dimensions of CSR not only serve different aspects of corporations but also relate corporations to different social responsibilities. Carroll holds that CSR consist of four responsibilities: economic, legal, ethical and philanthropic (Caroll, 1991). Ethical responsibility refers to doing what is right and just, fair and non-harmful; legal responsibility means to obey the law; economic responsibility means to make the company's business profitable; and philanthropic responsibility means that company should be a good citizen in society (Carroll, 1991). This division of social responsibility covers the mainstream CSR agenda and hence relates to the core of the SD process.

Economic, social, and environmental issues are fully recognized and distinguished as fundamentals of the CSR agenda. Simon Zadek (2001) marked these issues as the core of 'corporate citizenship', which is about business taking greater account of its social, environmental and financial footprint. Triple Bottom Line – one of the operational approaches of CSR – focuses on three issues, namely, social responsibility (people), environmental responsibility (planet), and economic responsibility (profit).[6] Therefore, a business organization following CSR guidelines could be considered an economic institution, a social actor and an environmental protector. The River Buriganga, for an example, an important watercourse that flows through the capital city of Bangladesh,

---

5   The European Commission Green Paper of 2001 identifies two types of dimension of CSR: internal and external (European Commission, 2001)

6   The Concept of Triple Bottom Line was developed by the business consultant John Elkington in his book *Cannibals with Forks: Triple Bottom Line of 21st Century Business* (1997).

would not be a 'toxic dump' if the tanneries beside it were barred by CSR-related standardization norms from discharging their waste into it (Sharif and Mainuddin, 2003).

Both SD and CSR have strong economic dimensions. Rising from almost the same generic form, dimensions of these concepts are reciprocal to each other. The principle of social dimension of CSR agenda is that corporations should work towards building a better society and, therefore, integrating environmental concerns in their business operations and considering the full scope of their impacts on communities (Dahlsrud, 2006b). The United Nations Global Compact – which sets out some of the guiding principles of CSR – acknowledges this principle and urges business enterprises to support and respect the internationally proclaimed environmental rights within 'their sphere of influence'.[7] Among the ten principles of the Global Compact three environment-oriented principles are primary responsibilities of the business organizations.

Environmental dimension of CSR create scope for business enterprises to link with the major international environmental developmental frameworks nationally or even trans-nationally. All major international instruments providing normative standards of CSR have introduced corporate responsibilities for environmental protection. This implies that business organizations should adopt a precautionary approach to environmental challenges (UNGC, n.d.), to undertake initiatives to promote greater environmental responsibility (UNGC, n.d.) and to encourage the development and diffusion of environment-friendly technology (UNGC, n.d.). Accordingly, for example, the International Chamber of Commerce Business Charter for Sustainable Development introduced 16 principles for environmental management covering, inter alia, the establishment of environmental management on the basis of priority, integrating management systems, the efficient use of energy and materials, the sustainable use of renewable resources, the minimalization of adverse environmental impact and waste generation, and the safe and responsible disposal of residual waste, adopting a precautionary approach, developing emergency preparedness plans, etc. (ICC, 1991). Organization for Economic Co-operation and Development Guidelines for Multinational Enterprises supports these principles and in association with other corporate responsibilities provides some other principles for environmental protection (OECD, 2006).

International normative standards of CSR developed so far heavily emphasize environmental issues, as these issues have become a strong driver of ever-growing sensitive consumerism. Consumers' willingness to punish companies that are not fulfilling their social responsibilities has dramatically increased. In their 2008 study, Nilsson and Rahmani found that 70 per cent of respondents in Europe said that CSR commitment from companies was important for them when deciding whether or not to buy a product or service. Along with the key buying criteria such as price, quality, availability, safety and convenience, business has to satisfy other values-based criteria, such as factories free from child labour, lower environmental impact of products, the absence of genetically modified materials in products, etc.[8] In a recent poll, when consumers were asked whether they would buy a car that does 25 miles to the gallon or one that does 35 miles to the gallon

---

7   The phrase (as quoted from the preamble of The Universal Declaration of Human Rights) 'within their sphere of influence' indicates the inclusion of a wide range of people who are either in or outside the corporations and linked to or influenced by their business operations. It also proclaims that companies must ensure that they are not complicit in human rights abuse. For details, see the United Nations Global Compact (UNGC, n.d.), which was launched in 2000 and revised in 2004.

8   For details, see OECD, 2006; Nilsson and Rahmani, 2008.

but costs $2,000 more, 78 per cent said that they would be willing to pay an extra $2,000 or more for lower fuel consumption (Richard, 2009). Big business enterprises have started embracing this ethos. They are incorporating appropriate measures into their corporate governance to relate to consumers environmental demands. They are moving to slash use of fossil fuels, water and packaging (Richard, 2009). Wal-Mart's recent initiatives to green its stores and its 100,000 suppliers show that it wants to ensure that its suppliers are efficient in energy and labour use. From 2003 to 2008, Gap Inc. cut greenhouse-gas emission by 20 per cent and cleaned up child labour from its suppliers' floors (Richard, 2009). The Allanblackia Oil Supply Chain in Tanzania is worthy of mention among global companies' initiatives for environment-friendly business planning. Unilever initiated this public–private partnership. It has engaged the farmers of four mountainous regions of Tanzania to collect, dry, transport and crush allanblackia nuts to produce crude oil. Previously allanblackia seeds had a very limited use in local markets and did not have any market price in sub-Saharan or international markets. Unilever chose these seeds to produce oil as a replacement for palm oil and a potential base for soap. Through this initiative, this company engages local farmers to carry out a profitable business and relieves them from the pressure to transform indigenous forests into arable lands (Tamara, 2006).

While CSR is an important component in developing a business case, societal concerns and the stakeholder integration and business ethics dimensions of CSR have been criticized on the point that 'the domain of CSR cannot be assessed by primarily economic criteria, and neither can an environmental ethic be developed through an "ethically pragmatic managerial" mortality that primarily serves organisational interests' (Fineman, 2006). The critics of CSR question the construct and concepts of discourses, for example, on corporate greening based on 'deep ecology', 'ecocentric' or 'sustaincentric' management. The models of strategies for incorporating CSR notions into corporate management are not beyond criticism as these models are not conclusive in attaining their purpose. Nonetheless, CSR dimensions in business strategies have received considerable acknowledgement. They are creeping towards making an effective impact on the relationship between the need for SD of natural resources and business strategies for sustainable profit (Rahim, 2012). Beyond fulfilling laws and other regulatory requirements, business enterprises can make good business sense by developing the right strategies for cutting pollution and waste out of their business operations. A 3M programme called Pollution Prevention Pay discovered a huge savings that it had overlooked. STMicroelectronics, for example, saved $173 million by their planning to reduce their energy consumption by using larger ducts in the air conditioners, which allows the air-circulating fans to run more slowly. By investing $40 million, they reduced the energy consumptions of the fans by 85 per cent. Here, the main driver of this success was the corporate intention to reduce energy consumption. It was in fact not legislation but the company's urge to take on CSR principles supported by a sound business case that lay behind this management strategy.

CSR thinking is used as a vital tool for controlling eco-risk for global enterprises/retailers. A business enterprise's responsibility is not to harm the environment; should it do so, the enterprise is likely to face legal action and, in most cases, lose market share. With the rise of transparency, ethical consumerism and the impact of branding on market share, unethical business practices or irresponsibility usually cause a huge negative impact on business. Accordingly, for instance, McDonalds pushes back on its supply chain to lower antibiotic use in chickens, or asks for documentation that ensures that cattle farmed by its suppliers do not have mad cow disease. Intel spends millions to ship its hazardous waste from developing countries to the United States, so that it can be disposed of properly. Thus, these companies try to be more socially responsible as well as save their brand from contamination: combining the two results in better market share.

Environmental concern in business operations can generate profit. Helping customers to reduce their environmental problem can generate customers' loyalty and attract new sales; reducing the energy use or toxicity of a product can also add to customer value. Hence, strategies for minimizing the burden on customers can also be the strategies for maximizing profits. John Deere's recent foray into renewable energy is a good example at this point. This tractor manufacturer started up a business unit to help farmers harvest wind energy, offering financial support and consultation services. This may seem to have been an odd fit, but it became a source of value innovation: an enterprise known for providing farmers with the tools they need is offering to help them survive and create new revenue streams.

Proliferation of environmental standardization agencies is another example that shows business companies' growing interests in environmental dimensions of CSR. Aligning with their interests in environment friendly business operations, numerous external standards, measurements and guidelines for environmental management issues have been developed. The ICC Business Charter for Sustainable Development, the International Organization for Standardization 14000, the European Community's Eco-management and Audit Scheme, the Global Reporting Initiative, are some of the environmental schemes that are well recognized in business society. Global buyers are using these schemes to incorporate CSR agendas into their corporate governance and to monitor their suppliers' environmental and ethical business practices.

Though CSR thinking is voluntary on the part of business enterprises, transnational mechanisms for implementing SD principles help to implement most of this thinking in a national context. CSR ideas and principles could become binding on corporate bodies through national policies or regulation of the environment, as most of the countries in the world have incorporated most of the principles of SD into their environmental laws. Moreover, in some countries where there is no adequate framework for implementing these principles, the judiciary has begun to contribute by explaining them. Furthermore, the wide acceptance of transnational environmental instruments such as the Rio Declaration on Environment and Development; Agenda 21, the Convention on Biological Diversity, the Framework Convention on Climate Change, and the Statement of Forest Principles, and the implementing mechanisms set out in these instruments, put pressure on transnational corporations to fulfil their environmental responsibilities. Accordingly, in most of the codes of conduct of transnational corporations, SD principles are essentially embedded as corporate responsibilities to the societies in which they operate.

Nonetheless, CSR tries to inject environmental issues of societies into business operations. In this way, CSR helps business enterprises to make an impact on the living and non-living natural resources of a society. Business enterprises have gradually acknowledged that integration of environmental management tools into business plans, including life-cycle assessment and costing, environmental management standards, eco-labelling and so on can ensure a better business case. They are being encouraged to accept s environmental dimension of CSR into their core business strategies. Strategies for ensuring greater material recyclability, better product durability and greater use of renewable resources in business production are ensuring a stable return for the business and helping environmental sustainability.

Indeed the semantic meaning of SD is also closely related to economic arguments, along with social and environmental issues (Habermas, 1987), and CSR relates business enterprises with their environmental rights and liabilities in societies where SMEs are a major component of development. This strategic relationship, together with the principles of CSR and SD, and the influence of SMEs in a society, make it possible that a link between SMEs and CSR can help in implementing SD principles in a wide spectrum of society. SMEs and SD can be brought together through two holistic aspects. First, SMEs can contribute more to SD; and second, SMEs – as one of the largest employers of labour, business innovators and distributors of wealth – have wide scope to contribute to sustainable social and environmental development (Stewart et al., 2003). The next section of this chapter elaborates on this issue.

Sensitizing Small and Medium-sized Enterprises to CSR for Sustainable Development

There is no unanimity or universality to an acceptable definition of SMEs, as it depends upon the practice of different institutions to establish their own perspectives and strategies. In general, SMEs encompass a very broad range of firms, from established traditional family businesses employing over 100 people to 'survivalist' self-employed people working in informal micro-enterprises. While the upper end of the range is comparable across developed and developing countries, SMEs in the latter category are concentrated at the lowest end (Fox, 2005). For instance, in Bangladesh, variations in definitions arise in terms of numbers employed and volume of invested capital. According to the SME Policy Strategies 2005 of this country, manufacturing enterprises having capital of $0.21 million excluding land and buildings would be treated as small enterprises and those having capital up to $1.43 million would be called medium enterprises. For the non-manufacturing enterprises, however, this policy takes the number of employees as the basis of defining enterprises. The Bangladesh Bureau of Statistics (BBS) definition is based on employment status only. At this juncture, the Bangladesh Bank (BB) defines SMEs according to both the volume of investment and the number of workers. To define SMEs, this bank has based its definition on the recommendation of the Better Business Forum and arrived at the definition after consulting the government ministry concerned. According to this bank, a small manufacturing enterprise has an investment of between $690.50 and $207,111, excluding land and buildings, and/or employs up to 50 workers. For a medium-sized manufacturing enterprise, the investment is set at between $207,111 and $2,761,480, excluding land and buildings. For this enterprise, the number of workers is no more than 150.

The picture is blurred further by the distinction between the formal and informal sectors. The term 'small and medium-sized enterprises' usually refers only to firms operating within the formal (legally registered) economy, and attempts to relate the CSR agenda to SMEs are likely to be restricted to these enterprises. Micro enterprises may be in the formal or the informal sectors. However, it is not unusual for statistics to group these enterprises together, where data is available (Fox, 2005). The informal sector is particularly significant in many developing countries.

In the kaleidoscope of globalization, economic development of societies depends on the development of a vibrant private sector, in which SMEs play a central role. They are a seedbed for entrepreneurial development, innovation and risk-taking behaviour and provide the foundation for long-term growth dynamics. They support the building up of systemic productive capacities. They help to absorb productive resources at all levels of the economy and contribute to the creation of resilient economic systems. For societies depending upon agriculture, SMEs are the key to the transition of an agriculture-led economy to an industrial economy. Likewise, for societies in which labour is abundant, they tend to employ more labour-intensive production processes and contribute significantly to generating sustainable livelihoods. In Bangladesh, for example, SMEs account for about 45 per cent of manufacturing value, 80 per cent of industrial employment, 90 per cent of total industrial units and 25 per cent of the total labour force. Therefore, the potential benefit of developing socially and environmentally responsible SMEs is widely emphasized for creating employment, furthering economic growth and ensuring the foundation of a robust and competitive industrial sector. Evidence from elsewhere on the relationship between the relative size of the SME sector, economic growth and poverty is more equivocal. Using a sample of 76 countries, Becht et al. (2003) find a strong association between the importance of SMEs and gross domestic product (GDP) per capita growth. Indeed, the cumulative impact of SMEs on society and environment is significant. This is not due only to the large number of enterprises of this type, but also to their role in the distribution of income and consumption of natural resources. There is, therefore, the potential for significant progress towards SD if they can raise their social and environmental performance (Fox, 2005).

CSR thinking incorporated into SMEs should have a positive impact on social and environmental development. A link between CSR and SMEs would ensure that SD could be achieved better in issues of pollution control, development of alternative non-fossil-fuel energy sources, and awareness in the wider business community regarding the benefits of working together with non-governmental organizations (NGOs), interest groups and non-value chain stakeholders (Fergus and Rowney, 2005). SMEs have a great understanding of local culture and politics, more links with local civil society and a greater commitment to operate in a specific geographical area. These abilities of SMEs could be used for SD. Peters and Turner (2004) found in their environmental attitude survey among 62 SMEs in East Anglia that SMEs have organizational management capability and willingness to embrace the issues of environmental performance improvement, and they suggested that SMEs have the potential to do better in this area if they could combine more opportunity with a more tailored approach.

The environmental dimension of CSR could be turned into an effective strategy for ensuring SD in a society if the corporate consciences of SMEs could be sensitized to it; this could contribute to creating an environmentally responsible corporate culture. How this sensitization could be effected within their corporate governance structures and management practices is a crucial question that sparks many ideas as well as many controversies. Indeed, this sensitization depends upon the unique nature of CSR and SMEs. Though there are controversies regarding the basic nature of CSR, 'voluntariness' is well conceived in CSR literature and practices as a predominant aspect of this concept. Again, despite the heterogeneity of the business group encompassed by the term 'SME', this type of business group has certain characteristics in regard to business ethics and socially responsible practices. Control and ownership usually coincide in SMEs and this causes a concentration of assumed functions and responsibilities (Lahdesmaki, 2005; Spence, 1999). Management in SMEs is often oriented towards short-term survival, rather than being carried out within the framework of strategic planning. However, in SMEs the personal relationships between the owner–manager and employees are often fluid and this enables control activities to be performed more informally (Rivera-Lirio and Muñoz-Torres, 2010). This informal relationship is vital for incorporating CSR thinking into SMEs because the personal values of the owner or the manager involved in it provide scope for emphasizing ethical factors or customer loyalty and community relations in the interests of earning economic and intangible benefits.

An important factor that might cause resistance from SMEs to environmental development is that many of them consider it a peripheral issue (Peters and Turner, 2004). They usually do not want to consider it. Also, in most cases, they are not able to function following the theoretical construct for implementing CSR principles into their internal regulation. Hence, they leave room for adopting strategies that include cost saving and improvements in product quality and process design. Without incentive-based regulatory sanctions, voluntary initiative and the partnership approach may not, therefore, be a potential addition to the package of policy instruments to be deployed by SMEs to protect the environment. Given these circumstances, any strategy seeking resonance between environmental aspects of CSR and SMEs may preferably consider encouraging quasi-legal strategies based on cultural and economic factors of SMEs' business operations.

The underlying principles of the environmental dimensions of CSR could be linked with SME-related laws, regulations and guidelines, which have what might be termed 'meta'-regulatory effects on corporate governance and on the role of business in the society. The term 'meta-regulation' applied to corporate governance is intended to convey an emphasis on collaboration, partnership and networks linking state, business, non-governmental organizations and people operating outside these three sectors (Braithwaite and Drahos, 2000; Morgan, 2003; Parker, 2007). Governmental organizations and command-and-control regulation may be included in this concept (but it would not be the dominant actor and certainly not the only important mechanism of regulation). These approaches could lay the basis of initiating suitable procedures to regulate 'self-regulation' and non-legal methods of regulating internal management.

The stakeholder dimension of CSR could be an appropriate meta-regulatory approach for incorporating environmental CSR practices into the corporate governance of SMEs. Simply put, this dimension denotes that the person who affects or is affected by an enterprise's operations has a stake in the enterprise's operations (Freeman, 1984). It reflects the idea that the conduct of enterprises can affect a broader range of people than mere shareholders. This dimension could be incorporated into the core of SMEs' corporate governance management with appropriate meta-regulatory sanctions. For instance, there could be directives from the government that business enterprises have to obtain clearance from local communities for formal registration. Since obtaining formal registration carries various incentives, entrepreneurs would rather not avoid local boards/councils/committees (which generally comprise peoples' representatives) to obtain clearance to proceed with business operations within particular areas. Thus, local people (who are the stakeholders of any local business operations) would have a chance to consider the environmental impact of the business operations of the enterprises applying for their consent.

It would be worth mentioning that the purpose of this chapter is not to critically analyse the concepts of CSR and SD or the different strategies for incorporating CSR thinking in SMEs. Its aim is to highlight the potential nexus among environmental dimensions of CSR, the goal of SD and the potential of SMEs for extending the benefits of the nexus of CSR and SD in society. It argues that promoting environmental thinking of CSR through SMEs has a strong potential to accomplish the objective of transmitting SD to the core of a society. Since SMEs are the niche of a society's economic and social activities, and make up the largest sector of business activities, their attachment to CSR practices could benefit society's human and environmental development. This attachment would help businesses to internalize environmental costs to a large extent. If SMEs can internalize, for example, the idea that manufacturers have a responsibility for their products' full life-cycle uses, the cost of cleaning up waste would be less for business. At the same time the negative impact of business on the environment would be reduced. For real progress towards SD, there is a need to view SMEs as CSR actors themselves, with their own social and environmental impacts. The argument that CSR is exorbitant or extraneous for SMEs should not be used as a reason behind which to hide or ignore poor social and environmental practices. Rather, there should be reforms in SME regulations to strengthen the overall enabling environment for CSR among SMEs (Fox, 2005). SME-oriented regulatory and voluntary institutions should help to create the drivers for SMEs' engagement in economic and environmental development in society.

Conclusion

CSR is an increasingly important part of the business environment (Moon and Vogel, 2008; Vogel, 2005). It is a complex and multidimensional organizational phenomenon which could be defined to the extent to which and the way in which an organization is consciously responsible for and accountable for its actions and non-actions and the impact of these on its stakeholders. Hence, CSR is increasingly understood as a means by which business tries to reach a balance between its drive for profit and the environment in which it makes an impact along the way (Luetkenhorst, 2004). It offers SMEs opportunities for greater market access, cost savings, productivity and innovation, as well as spreading broader environmental benefits such as rational use of natural resources, restoring ecology, etc. It might safely be argued that CSR could easily be perceived as a strategy within the concept of SD. While SD aims to sustain required maintenance and protection of the environment with the economic growth of society, CSR is a long-term business strategy balancing corporate rights with economic, environmental and social obligations towards its stakeholders. CSR is not only a strategy for businesses to secure legitimacy in society; its different dimensions if properly included in SMEs' corporate governance can contribute to the full realization of SD.

References

Barbier, E.B. (1987). The concept of sustainable economic development. *Environmental Conservation*, 14(2), 101–110.

Bebbington, J. (2001). Sustainable development: a review of the international development, business and accounting literature. *Accounting Forum*, 25(2), 128–57.

Bebbington, J. and Gray, R. (2001). An account of sustainability: failure, success and a reconceptualization. *Critical Perspectives on Accounting*, 12, 557–87.

Becht, M., Bolton, P. and Röell, A. (2003). Corporate governance and control, in *Handbook of the Economics of Finance*, 1, 1–109.

Bowfield, M. and Frynas, J.G. (2005). Setting new agendas: critical perspectives on corporate social responsibility in the developing world. *International Affairs*, 81(3).

Braithwaite, J. and Drahos, P. (2000). *Global Business Regulation*. New York: Cambridge University Press.

Callens, I. and Tyteca, D. (1999). Towards indicators of sustainable development for firms. A productive efficiency perspective. *Ecological Economics*, 28, 41–53.

Caroll, A.B. (1991). The pyramid of corporate social responsibility: towards the moral management of organizational stakeholders. *Business Horizons*, 34(4), 39–41.

—— (1999). Corporate social responsibility: evolution of a definitional construct. *Business and Society*, 38(3), 268.

Commonwealth of Australia (2006). *Corporate responsibility: managing risk and creating value*. Canberra: Parliament of Australia.

Dahlsrud, A. (2006a). How corporate social responsibility is defined: an analysis of 37 definitions. *Corporate Social Responsibility and Environmental Management*.

—— (2006b). *How Corporate Social Responsibility is Defined: An Analysis of 37 Definitions*. Wiley Online Library. Available at: http://www.interscience.wiley.com [accessed: 16 November 2013].

Dixon, J.A. and Fallon, L.A. (1989). The concept of sustainability: origins, extensions and usefulness for policy. *Society and Natural Resources*, 2, 73–84.

Ekins, P., Folke, C. and Groot, R.D. (2003). Identifying critical natural capital. *Ecological Economics*, 44, 159–63.

Elkington, J. (1997). *Cannibals with Forks: Triple Bottom Line of 21st Century Business*. Oxford: Capstone).

European Commission (2001). *Green Paper: Promoting a European Framework for Corporate Social Responsibility*. Brussels: Commission of the European Communities. Available at: http://www. europa.eu.int [accessed: 7 August 2010].

Fergus, A. and Rowney, J. (2005). Sustainable development: lost meaning and opportunity? *Journal of Business Ethics*, 60, 17–27.

Fineman, S. (2006). The natural environment, organisation and ethics, in Parker, M. (ed.), *Ethics and Organisations*. London: Sage, 238–52.

Fox, T. (2005). Corporate social responsibility and development: in quest of an agenda. *Development*, 47(3), 29–36.

Freeman, R.E. (1984). *Strategic Management: A Stakeholder Approach*. Boston, MA: Pitman Publishing.

Gladwin, T.N., Kennelly, J.J. and Krause, T.S. (1995). Shifting paradigms for sustainable development: implications for management theory and research. *Academy of Management Review*, 20(4), 874–907.

Habermas, J. (1987). *The Theory of Communicative Action*. Vol.1. Boston, MA: Beacon Press.

Hajer, M.A. (1997). *The Politics of Environmental Discourse. Ecological Modernization and the Policy Process*. Oxford: The Clarendon Press.

Hanson, D.M. (1992). *World Resources 1992–93: Guide to Global Environment*. Washington DC: World Resources Institute.

Hopkins, M. (2004). *Corporate Social Responsibility: An Issues Paper* (Working Paper No 27), ILO Policy Integration Department. Geneva: International Labour Organization.

ICC (1991). *Business Charter for Sustainable Development*. Available at: http://www. bsdglobal.com/tools/principles_icc.asp [accessed: 20 June 2010].

Johannesburg Declaration on Sustainable Development (2002). [Online.] Available at: http://www. unescap.org/esd/environment/rio20/pages/Download/johannesburgdeclaration.pdf [accessed: 16 November 2013].

Lahdesmaki, M. (2005). When ethics matters – interpreting the ethical discourse of small nature-based entrepreneurs. *Journal of Business Ethics*, 61(1), 55–68.

Lawson, T. (1997). *Economics and Reality*. London: Routledge.

Lélé, S.M. (1991). Sustainable development: a critical review. *World Development*, 16(6), 608.

Livesey, S. and Kearins, K. (2002). Transparent and caring corporations? A study of sustainability reports by The Body Shop and Royal Dutch/Shell. *Organisation and Environment*, 15(3), 233–58.

Luetkenhorst, W. (2004). Corporate social responsibility and the development agenda: the case for actively involving small and medium enterprises. *Intereconomics*, 166.

Marsden, C. (2000). The new corporate citizenship of big business: part of the solution to sustainability? *Business and Society Review*, 105(1), 8–25.

Matten, D. and Moon, J. (2008). 'Implicit' and 'explicit' CSR: a conceptual framework for understanding CSR in Europe. *The Academy of Management Review*, 33(2), 404.

Meadowcroft, J. (2000). Sustainable development: a new(ish) idea for a new century? *Political Studies*, 48, 370–87.

Mebratu, D. (1998). Sustainability and sustainable development: historical and conceptual review. *Environmental Impact Assessment Review*, 18, 493–520.

Moon, J. and Vogel, D. (2008). Corporate social responsibility, government, and civil society, in Crane, A. (ed.), *The Oxford Handbook of Corporate Social Responsibility*. Oxford: Oxford University Press.

Morgan, B. (2003). The economization of politics: meta-regulation as a form of nonjudicial legality. *Social and Legal Studies*, 12, 489–523.

Nilsson, C., and Shadi, R. (2008). *Global Considerations in Corporate Social Responsibility*. Unpublished Masters thesis, Lulea University of Technology, Lulea, Sweden.

OECD (2006). *Guidelines for Multinational Enterprises*. Available at: http://www. oecd.org/department/0,3355,en_2649_34889_1_1_1_1_1,00.html [accessed: 13 June 2010].

Parker, C. (2007). Meta-regulation: legal accountability to corporate social responsibility, in McBarnet, D., Voiculescu, A. and Campbell, T. (eds), *The New Corporate Accountability: Corporate Social Responsibility and the Law*, 9–237). Oxford: University of Oxford.

Peters, M. and Turner, K. (2004). SME environmental attitude and participation in local-scale voluntary initiatives: some practical applications. *Journal of Environmental Planning and Management*, 47(3), 449–73.

Rahim, M.M. (2013). *Legal Regulation of Corporate Social Responsibility: A Meta-regulation Approach*. New York and London: Springer.

Rahim, M.M. (2013). The impact of 'social responsibility' on business: the rise of standardization of CSR principles, in Mermod, A.Y. and Idowu, S.O. (eds) (2014). *Corporate Social Responsibility in the Business World*. New York and London: Springer, 93–115.

Rahim, M.M. (2012). Corporate governance as social responsibility: a meta-regulation approach to incorporate CSR in corporate governance, in Boubaker, S. and Nguyen, D.K. (eds), *Board of Directors and Corporate Social Responsibility*. London: Palgrave Macmillan, 145–67.

Richard, S. (2009). The responsibility revolution. *The Times*, 21 September.

Rivera-Lirio, J.M. and Muñoz-Torres, M.J. (2010). Sustainable development in the Spanish region of Valencia and the social responsibility of SMEs. A multi-stakeholder vision on the role of public administrations. *Journal of Environmental Planning and Management*, 53(3), 573–90.

Robinson, J. (2004). Squaring the circle? Some thought on the idea of sustainable development. *Ecological Economics*, 48, 369–84.

Sharif, M.I. and Mainuddin, K. (2003). *Country Case Study on Environmental Requirements for Leather and Footwear Export from Bangladesh*. Dhaka: Bangladesh Centre for Advanced Studies.

Shawkat, A. (2008). *Sustainable Development and Free Trade: Institutional Approaches*. London: Routledge.

Spence, L.J. (1999). Does size matter? The state of the art in small business ethics. *Business Ethics: A European Review*, 8(3), 163–74.

Stewart, R.A., Miller, C., Mohamed, S. and Packham, G. (2003). Sustainable development of construction small and medium enterprises (SMEs): IT impediments focus, in Amor, R. (ed.), *Proceedings of CIB w78-2003: Construction IT Bridging the Distance April, 2003, Waiheke Island, New Zealand*. Available at: http://itc.scix.net/paperw78-2003-361.content.

Tamara, B. (2006). *Tanzania: Lessons in Building Linkages for Competitive and Responsible Entrepreneurship*. UNDP: Human Development Report 1991. Available at: http://www.unido.org/fileadmin/import/69451_CSRI_09.pdf [accessed: 18 December 2013]

UN (1992). Rio Declaration on Environment and Development (Rio Declaration), 14 June 1992, Principle 12, UN doc.A/ CONF. 151/5/Rev.1(1992) (Vol. UN doc.A/ CONF. 151/5/Rev.1(1992)).

UN (1993). *Agenda 21: Earth Summit – The United Nations Programme of Action from Rio*. New York: United Nations Organization. Available at: https://unp.un.org/details.aspx?entry=E93020.

UNDP (1991). *Human Development Report 1991*. New York: United Nations Development Programme. Available at: http://www.undp.org [accessed: 16 November 2013].

UNGC (n.d.). UN Global Compact. The Ten Principles. [Online.] Available at: http://www.unglobalcompact.org/AboutTheGC/TheTenPrinciples/index.html [accessed: 20 June 2010].

UNWCED (1987a). World Commission on Environment and Development, *Our Common Future*. Oxford: Oxford University Press.

UNWCED (1987b). *Report of the World Commission on Environment and Development*. (Annex to United Nations document A/42/427 Development and International Co-operation: Environment), NGO Committee on Education of the Conference of NGOs [Online: UN Documents.] Available at: http://www.un-documents.net/our-common-future.pdf [accessed: 13 October 2013].

Vogel, D. (2005). *The Market for Virtue: The Potential and Limits of Corporate Social Responsibility*. Washington DC: Brookings Institution.

Watts, P. and Holmes, L. (1999). *CSR: Meeting Changing Expectations*. Geneva: World Business Council for Sustainable Development.

White, A.L. (2006). *Business Brief: Intangibles and CSR Business for Social Responsibility*. New York: Business for Social Responsibility. [Online.] Available at: http://www.bsr.org/reports/BSR_AW_Intangibles-CSR.pdf [accessed: 16 November 2013].

Zadek, S. (2001). *The Civil Corporation: The New Economy of Corporate Citizenship*. 1st edn. Oxford: Earthscan.

11 *The Effectiveness of CSR Initiatives and their Impact upon Stakeholders*

MARIA ALUCHNA

Abstract

Corporate social responsibility (CSR) is a concept that describes the practice whereby companies integrate social and environmental concerns into their business operations. The interaction of businesses with stakeholders on a voluntary basis is to achieve long-term sustainable growth and development. Thus the concept of CSR derives from the social model of a corporation and emphasizes social performance as the additional dimension for the evaluation of company operation. The group of stakeholders includes shareholders, employees, suppliers, customers, local communities and management. On the operational level, CSR refers to a set of different initiatives undertaken in various spheres of social and economic lives (environmental protection, national heritage, social programmes, sports, education, etc.) to solve social problems, provide for stakeholder management and social dialogue and minimize the negative impact upon environment.

The paper discusses the practical dimensions of CSR, analysing the effectiveness of the activities of three of the largest companies, listed on the Warsaw Stock Exchange. The article presents detailed CSR initiatives undertaken by these companies and evaluates the efficiency of CSR in addressing two questions: What impact do CSR programmes have upon stakeholders? and How do stakeholders benefit from these programmes?

Introduction

Economic, social and environmental challenges contribute to the growing demand in both theoretical and empirical studies for the inclusion of corporate social responsibility (CSR). The concept of CSR constitutes an important section of management studies and it is incorporated into business practice with the use of different operational and strategic schemes such as action on environmental protection, education, information initiatives and social dialogue programmes. The growing interest in CSR reflects a shift in the role and responsibilities of companies in society and the economy. It also represents significant changes in the perception of companies' dedication to their social performance, stakeholder policy and social dialogue. The clearly formulated expectations of well-structured and powered stakeholders which are able to exert an impact on companies remain the main driver for change, supported by reporting and disclosure procedures and frameworks.

Despite the growing popularity of CSR programmes among companies, empirical evidence of CSR effectiveness and actual fulfilment of stakeholders' expectations remains scarce. In addition, little is known about the place and role of CSR in company management systems, the scope and direction of CSR programmes, or implications for the development of the social performance of companies. This paper attempts to fill the gap in research on the delivery of results and the effectiveness of CSR policies with respect to the realization of stakeholder expectations. The paper provides a case study of three Polish public listed companies and their CSR activities related to formulated social and environmental goals. In addition the paper presents the CSR programmes adopted by the three Polish companies and to refer these practices to the post-transition reality of Poland. By focusing on the general characteristics of the three selected companies, the paper aims to identify the potential for fulfilling stakeholders' expectations and the degree of effectiveness of their CSR policies. Therefore, the paper contributes to the state of knowledge of CSR in several dimensions. Firstly, it delivers an analysis of the CSR policies of the largest Polish public listed companies, which operate in sensitive industries such as petroleum, coal mining and gas extraction and distribution. Secondly, it addresses the question of how the overall social performance of the companies analysed corresponds with the expectations of their stakeholders. And thirdly, the paper provides some insights on CSR in the post-socialist and post-transition reality.

This chapter is organized as follows: the next section presents a theoretical framework of CSR, discussing its role and place in contemporary management literature and corporate practice. The review of studies of and research into CSR effectiveness with reference to fulfilling stakeholders' expectations is delivered in the third section. The fourth section presents a short overview of the characteristics of Polish society and CSR practices and this is followed by the presentation of the case study and the discussion of the collected empirical evidence. The concluding section summarizes the analysis.

Theoretical Framework of Corporate Social Responsibility

THE DEVELOPMENT OF THE CSR CONCEPT

CSR remains one of the most influential and highly researched themes in management studies. Its concept and findings are very often related to the issues of corporate citizenship, sustainable development and business ethics, while activities informed by CSR encompass a wide range of company operations, from the production system and finance to marketing and human resources (Warhurst, 2011). The concept of CSR is embedded in a set of theories, which include social contract theory, legitimacy theory and stakeholder theory (Moir, 2001). The growing interest in CSR is heavily rooted in an understanding of the need to change the role of business in society, its reaction to stakeholder expectations and the way it addresses social, economic and environmental challenges. CSR is defined as a concept 'whereby companies integrate social and environmental concerns in their business operations and in their interaction with their stakeholders on a voluntary basis' (European Commission, 2001; Neal, 2008; Crowther and Jatana, 2005a; Prieto-Carron et al., 2006) to achieve long-term sustainable growth and development. Its principles are often perceived as an enlightenment of business (Clement-Jones, 2004) and as a declaration of understanding of the expectations and interests of a wide group of stakeholders. The World Business Council for Sustainable Development proposes a definition stating that 'CSR is the commitment of business to contribute to the sustainable economic development, working with employees, their families, the local community and society at large to improve the quality of their lives' (quoted in Sternberg, 2011). CSR is the response to social expectations and current business environment challenges related to the globalization process, climate change, the risk of corruption and abuse of workers, and the need for reporting. The main tasks of CSR include providing accountability and transparency, as well as assuring responsibility and sustainability (Hollender and Fenichell, 2004; Crowther and Jatana, 2005b).

As noticed by Moir (2001) and Kemper and Martin (2011), the emergence of the CSR concept is viewed as a crucial element of the ongoing debate on the role and responsibilities of business in society and the economy. Its development has been reinforced by criticism and concern over the focus on shareholders and prevalence of the creation of shareholder value as a company's main goal, which had been dominant. The concept of CSR has been developing based on the definition formulated by Ackerman (1973), theoretical frameworks elaborated by Sethi (1975) and the triple bottom line formulated by Carroll (1979), who stated that companies should balance the economic, social and ethical dimensions of their activities. The dominance of the profits maximization approach was criticized and the need for emphasis on the responsibilities of companies towards society were pointed out by Thomas Donaldson in his seminal book, *Corporations and Morality* (1982). The formulation of the stakeholder theory by R. Edward Freeman suggested widening the group to which companies are accountable for their activities to the other stakeholders to include employees, customers, suppliers, media, local communities and non-governmental organizations (NGOs) (Freeman and Reed, 1983; Freeman, 1984). The stakeholder theory was viewed as a response to the principal agent theory, narrowly perceiving shareholders as the only group of stakeholders to whom the company should be responsible. Further development of the concept proved the strategy based on shareholder value to be outdated and primitive and called for the incorporation of CSR into strategic management (Charan and Freeman, 1980). This was supported by the contribution of S. Prakash Sethi and his elaboration of the measure of social performance tied to financial indicators (Sethi, 1975). The studies conducted after the year 2000, which treated CSR as the strategic direction for companies, are viewed as the third wave of the debate on the role of business in society (Martin, 2002; Porter and Kramer, 2002). CSR is perceived as a crucial component of corporate strategy and the potential source of competitive advantage. Stakeholders are given the crucial role in the process of corporate decision-making, which identifies them as owners of fiduciary rights; this enriches the previous approach, which emphasized the stakes and rights controlled by shareholders (Martin, 2002). In order to provide for the efficient implementation of sustainable development and CSR in business, the political, social and economic aspects of CSR should be integrated. Therefore the role of the regulators, business leaders and NGOs proves to be crucial for the successful adoption of sustainable development (Matten and Crane, 2005; Palazzo and Scherer, 2008). The development of the CSR concept is driven by three main factors: theoretical developments (regulations and reports prepared within the international debate); growing social awareness and activism (Kendall et al., 2007); and business self-regulation (Mele and Garriga, 2004).

CSR AND STAKEHOLDER MANAGEMENT

CSR is heavily rooted in the notion of the importance for the company operations of the role of different stakeholders. The fundamental principles of CSR assume the need to incorporate the suppositions and interests of a wide range of stakeholders into corporate strategies (Hawkins, 2006). CSR is a participatory process based on the identification of the stakeholders' expectations and the building up of a complex system of measuring and reporting (MacIagan, 1999). The group of stakeholders includes all entities and individuals who are influenced by or may have an impact on the company, and these comprise shareholders, employees, suppliers, customers, local communities and managers (Freeman, 2005). The currently supported approach emphasizes that CSR should be incorporated into company strategy as the result of the idea that business has to respond to changing societal expectations (Idemudia, 2011). The researchers observe a synthesis of various dimensions of company operations, pointing at the importance of both economic and social performance and the requirement of increased transparency. The key issues that are usually monitored by stakeholders from the perspective of CSR include:

- Climate change and reduction of CO_2 emissions;
- Access to drugs for HIV/ AIDS;
- Food labelling;
- Food and drink marketing, practices linked to obesity;
- Alcohol use by minors, and marketing practices;
- Labour standards in supply chains;
- Biodiversity;
- Child labour in the consumer goods and commodities industries;
- Bribery and corruption – particularly for companies operating in high-risk, politically unstable developing countries;
- Lending practices for the retail sector and for infrastructure projects;
- Corporate governance practices – particularly compensation-related;
- Health and safety in high-risk industries;
- Environmental impact of, for example, energy consumption, waste emissions and toxic release and management;
- Tobacco advertising practices and smuggling;
- Use of renewable resources. (Oulton and Hancock, 2004)

The integration of CSR, strategic management and corporate governance has contributed to the formulation of principles of responsible companies and allowed for the development of measuring and disclosure regimes. The adoption of either of the reporting standards or participation in CSR/sustainability indexes strengthen the efforts for integration of these concepts and increase the coherence of company operation while improving the methodology of the concept. In addition, the setting of measuring and reporting standards has helped develop the practical dimensions of CSR such as social dialogue, employee volunteering and company involvement in CSR initiatives. Initiatives of CSR emphasize the accountability towards society to be borne by business, as well as the importance of the investment of social capital (Habisch and Moon, 2006). The development of CSR characterized by deeper integration of company operational dimensions (Birch and Jonker, 2006) and the adoption of standards, and the structuring of the organization around general guidance principles assure the shift of the concept from a negative or passive orientation towards an active and proactive approach and strategic engagement (Maclean and Crouch, 2011; Warhurst, 2011); or, as presented in the Dehrendorf model of applied CSR, from the 'essential' (must) to the 'nice to have' (can) approach (Leisinger, 2011). In the context of significant changes 'the traditional decision making of the powerful bureaucracy and corporations of the industrial era is no longer either appropriate or acceptable' (Benn and Dunphy, 2007). Thus, more power and influence remain in the hands of various well-organized stakeholder groups whose expectations determine the direction of companies' activities. An important lesson is also drawn from the recent financial crisis, which indicates the role of CSR in corporate strategy and performance in the long term (Kemper and Martin, 2011). Companies engaging in CSR activities are less affected by the negative results of the crisis as compared to their peers who did not adopt CSR policy (Arevalo and Aravind, 2010; Charitoudi et al., 2011).

Efficiency of CSR Policy

CSR perceived as enlightened business practice (Jamali and Mirshak, 2007) is based on contributing to corporate social performance (CSP), which remains the other dimension – as opposed to financial performance – of company operation. As emphasized by Hillman and Keim (2001) CSP incorporates the interaction between the principles of social responsibility, the process of social responsiveness and the policies and programmes designed by corporations to address social issues. Despite the lack of recognition of the shared definition, CSP is viewed as a construct which includes stakeholder management and social issue management (Wood, 1991; Hillman and Keim, 2001). According to another proposed approach, social programmes and social impact are outcomes of corporate behaviour that result from three areas: environmental assessment; stakeholder management; and issues management in the four main domains: economic; legal; ethical; and discretionary (Jamali and Mirshak, 2007). CSR rests on five key principles: fair treatment of employees; ethical operation and integrity; respect for human rights; the sustainable treatment of the environment; and care for neighbouring communities (Moir, 2001). Integrating key CSR principles with CSP allows a set of measures undertaken by companies to be identified, as presented in the proposed framework in Table 11.1.

As shown in Table 11.1 combining CSR principles and CSP dimensions leads to the specification of initiatives and actions which a company may undertake with reference to both identified areas – stakeholder management and social issues management. Despite the growing popularity of CSR programmes among companies, empirical evidence of their effectiveness and factual fulfilment of stakeholders' expectations remains insufficient. CSR activities are mostly focused on lowering risks related to stakeholder mismanagement and weakening negative consequences of corporate operations, with little interest in the factual fulfilment of stakeholders' expectations. In many cases CSR initiatives are treated instrumentally and more focused on improving public relations or mitigating a bad reputation than on solving social problems or addressing stakeholders' needs. The absence of powerful and well-structured stakeholder groups and the lack of reporting and disclosure standards and auditing affects the efficiency of CSR activities. Table 11.2 elaborates on the dimensions and criteria for evaluating the fulfilment of stakeholders' expectations and suggests measures for the implementation of key CSR principles to be adopted by companies.

Table 11.1   Proposed framework combining CSR principles and corporate social performance (CSP) dimensions

Key principle/ CSP dimension	Stakeholder management	Social issue management
Fair treatment of employees	Setting standards of working conditions for employees and contractors Engagement of employees in management – e.g. employee volunteering	Promotion of employee rights Providing a platform for employee participation in management
Ethical operation and integrity	Standards and procedures for operation Setting a whistle-blowing system	Education and promotion in public sphere and among business partners
Respect for human rights	Code of conduct Anti-discrimination policy	Involvement in selected social campaigns
Sustainable treatment of environment	Formulation of sustainability strategy	Promotion and information on environmental protection
Care for neighbouring communities	Social dialogue	Promotion and information on social topics

Source: Author's compilation.

Table 11.2   Suggested measures for implementing key CSR principles to be adopted by companies

Key principle and prime stakeholder	Suggested measures undertaken by companies	Possible evaluation criteria
Fair treatment of employees (employees)	Good working conditions	Absenteeism indicators Fluctuation indicators
Ethical operation and integrity (employees, customers, suppliers, investors, general public)	Standards and procedures for operation, HR, marketing, supplies, etc. Code of conduct	Presence of complaints, scandals, frauds Effectiveness of whistle-blowing system
Respect of human rights (employees, customers, suppliers, general public)	Anti-discrimination policy Code of conduct	Social perception
Sustainable treatment of environment (general public)	Efficient use of materials, energy, water, waste management Lowering impact on climate change	Use of water/ energy, etc. per employee/ unit of product, €1, etc., and its dynamics
Care for local communities (local communities)	Social consultation, social dialogue	Social perception of members of local community Number of projects with local communities

Source: Author's compilation.

As shown in Table 11.2, companies dispose of a wide range of measures to be adopted in order to monitor the efficiency of their CSR policies. The integrated approach to stakeholder management and efficient CSR activities is offered by several models and frameworks such as the AA 1000 Stakeholder Engagement Standards, the Stakeholder Research Associates model and the model offered by the United Nations Environmental Programme.

The Effectiveness of CSR – the Polish Evidence

THE POST-TRANSITION POLISH REALITY

The analyses of CSR in Poland requires a reference to its political, economic and social specificity which incorporates transition reforms outcomes and emerging market characteristics, as well as the harmonization process within the accession to the European Union. The transition reforms, while bringing a market economy and providing for macroeconomic stability, resulted in the relative passiveness of society. The transition process was associated with a high social cost, leading to the rise of social inequalities, the rise of unemployment and a growing number of people living in poverty, as well as the problem of weak institutions (e.g. an inefficient legal system) and state withdrawal from many spheres of public life. The reality of the emerging economy brought aggressive capitalism, liberal economic policies and the dominance of consumerism patterns as indicators of the individual's success. The harmonization process within EU laws and institutions provided frameworks for CSR and environmental protection and encouraged companies to transfer know-how from Western Europe. For the purpose of further analysis of CSR the following characteristics of Polish society should be taken into account (Aluchna, 2010):

- The underdevelopment of civil society is demonstrated by social passivity in parliamentary or presidential elections, placing the percentage of Polish citizens who voted at the level of 30 per cent to 40 per cent.
- The underdevelopment of social capital is seen in the diminishing need for volunteering or social contribution. Research shows that Poles appear not to engage in the volunteer programmes of NGOs (Sułek, 2009). The current rate of participation in social initiatives is estimated at 13 per cent, which is significantly below the rates identified for Germany (40 per cent) or Scandinavian countries (80 per cent).
- A deficit of trust and cooperation is observed by sociologists with respect to the low and decreasing level of trust of institutions among members of society (Gasparski, 2006; Czapiński, 2009). Poland also lags behind the EU average in trust of other member of society (Czapiński, 2009).
- The erosion of moral standards – sociologists note the negative aspects of the erosion of moral standards. Other symptoms include the marginalization of moral categories, hidden mental structures of a 'moral system', a low level of moral reflection, moral autonomy, moderation in the moral assessment of others, situational ethics dominating over principalism and acceptance of people with different ethical choices (Gasparski, 2005, discussing works by Kiciński).

- The passiveness of stakeholders and the decreasing importance of social performance. Studies show that despite the growing interest in the CSR activity at the company level, the awareness of the CSR concept remains relatively low among members of society. CSR-related criteria referring to products or services do not play a crucial role in purchasing decision-making by customers and their importance is taken over by the criteria of price.

These characteristics of Polish society definitely are subject to change. However, the identified patterns outlined above have been relatively stable over the time period. Such features result in low trust in the government and state institutions and give rise to corruption and illegal behaviour (e.g. development of a shadow economy, avoiding taxes, breaking laws and corruption). This may, in the longer run, affect the development of social capital and prove to be detrimental to further economic growth (Boni, 2009).

In line with these characteristics of Polish society, the development of CSR appears to be a significant challenge. Despite the problems mentioned above, the social responsibility concept has experienced growing interest and popularity as the NGOs and companies have taken over the implementation of CSR from the weak state (Aluchna, 2010). First, NGOs, professional or sectoral associations actively promote the idea of social responsibility and develop volunteer programmes. Second, the increased transparency accompanied by a special law allowing the taxpayer to allocate 1 per cent of paid taxes to a selected NGO contributes to the development of CSR initiatives. Third, social campaigns provide information highlighting certain social problems and increase the awareness of society. Fourth, many activities originating in small communities or implemented by small- and medium-sized companies may not be regarded as CSR initiatives, as the awareness of the concept remains relative low (Gasparski, 2005). Therefore, engaging in solving social problems, helping poor people or donating money are more associated with social obligations rooted in the entrepreneurial contribution to society or the Roman Catholic religion. Fifth, companies interested in CSR decided to team up and jointly form the Forum of Responsible Business (Forum Odpowiedzialnego Biznesu, FOB), which promotes the concept and encourages transparency and reporting (http://www.fob.org. pl/). And finally, in 2009 the Warsaw Stock Exchange created a new index, RESPECT, which evaluates and includes corporations that are assessed by independent auditors and are viewed as socially responsible firms (http://www.respectindex.pl/). It is the first such initiative in Central and Eastern Europe covering currently 20 out of 450 listed companies. All these aspects are driving forces increasing social interest in CSR.

THE EFFECTIVENESS OF CSR – THE CASE OF POLISH COMPANIES

The analysis of the effectiveness of CSR policies and its impact on stakeholders is based on case studies of three Polish companies listed on the Warsaw Stock Exchange: PKN Orlen; PGNiG SA; and KGHM SA. Characteristics of these companies are summarized in the following.

Polski Koncern Naftowy Orlen SA (PKN Orlen SA)

This company is one of Central Europe's largest refiners of crude oil specializing in processing crude oil into unleaded petrol, diesel, heating oil and aviation fuel, as well as plastics and other petroleum-related products. After its privatization and initial public offering (IPO) the State Treasury held a stake of 28 per cent and remains the largest institutional investor. PKN ORLEN operates via seven refineries, of which three are located in Poland), three in the Czech Republic and one in Lithuania. The total processing capacity of the refineries reaches 31.7 million tons per annum. In 2011 all the ORLEN Group refineries processed 27.8 million tons of crude oil. The company's retail network consists of approximately 2,700 outlets offering services in Poland, Germany, the Czech Republic and Lithuania. The 2011 profits accounted for 3.2 billion PLN (€0.8 billion). As at the end of 2011 the ORLEN Group employed 22,380 people, of which 4,445 worked for PKN ORLEN (the parent company); 4,275 for the Unipetrol Group in the Czech Republic; 2,552 for ORLEN Lietuva in Lithuania; and 138 for ORLEN Deutschland in Germany.

Polskie Górnictwo Naftowe i Gazownictwo SA (PGNiG SA)

This company is the largest Polish oil and gas exploration and Production Company, as well as the only vertically integrated Gas Company in Poland. The company is a leader in the natural gas segments in Poland, which include trade, distribution, oil and gas exploration and production, as well as gas storage and processing. The company is also the largest importer of natural gas to Poland. Operating in a corporate group allows for the coordination of the upstream and downstream operations – from exploration and production to storage, trade and distribution of gaseous fuels. In 1996 the state owned company PGNiG was privatized into a joint stock company, having its IPO in 2003. The State Treasury holds the stake of 72 per cent of shares. The 2011 profit accounted for 1.6 billion zł (€0.4 billion); the group employed approximately 30,000 workers.

KGHM Polska Miedź SA (KGHM SA)

This company is the ninth largest producer of mined copper and the largest producer of silver in the world. The electrolytic copper of KGHM is registered by the London Metal Exchange (LME) as Grade Λ, while its silver – in the form of bars – is registered under the KGHM HG brand and holds a Good Delivery certificate issued by the London Bullion Market Association (1995) and by the Dubai Multi Commodities Centre (2006). Other products of KGHM include gold, lead, sulphuric acid and rock salt. The KGHM Group comprises the parent company and 83 subsidiaries. Some of them operate within the corporate groups (e.g. the largest of these is KGHM International Ltd. consisting of 34 entities). KGHM SA is viewed as a company of strategic importance for Poland. In 2011 refined copper production reached its all-time peak at 571,000 tonnes, and silver production reached 1,260 tonnes. The 2011 profit hit its historical level of 11.3 billion PLN (€3 billion). KGHM SA employed 18,500 workers, while the Group employed over 28,000 people. Like the other two companies, KGHM SA used to be a state-owned company and was privatized via its IPO in 1997, the stake of the State Treasury remaining at nearly 32 per cent.

Tables 11.3a, 11.3b and 11.3c present insights into the effectiveness of CSR policies of the analysed companies, relating their activities to the impact upon their stakeholders.

Table 11.3a Effectiveness of CSR policy – PKN Orlen SA

Key principle and prime stakeholder	Measures undertaken by the analyzed company	Evaluation (selected criteria)
Fair treatment of employees (employees)	Work safety policy (reporting and auditing)	Reporting on accident rate (dropping accident per one million man hours) Monitoring employee satisfaction Plan to launch stress management
	Personnel management	Reporting on personnel by gender, age etc. and fluctuations Recruitment procedures Implemented professional development programme Support for employees (benefits co-financing, loans, assistance, etc.) Dialogue and empowerment – Collective Labour Agreement, employee volunteering
Ethical operation and integrity (employees, customers, suppliers, investors, general public)	Corporate governance compliance and disclosure	Compliance with corporate governance code of best practice (board committees, board reporting, independent directors, disclosure), no information on e-voting, no data on quotas for females on board
	Integrated Management System policy in place	System control for supplies, environment, quality management, data safety, product safety, food safety
	Purchase policy	Equal treatment of suppliers
	Responsible marketing policy	VITAY loyalty system contribution to corporate foundations and charity Member of ProMarka Association to promote the highest standards of customer protection No cases of non-compliance in marketing, advertising, promotion and sponsoring recorded
	Policy of service system improvement	Awarded Golden Trusted Brands Logo and Most Valuable Polish Brand Centralized complaints and claim management system in the retail sales (1,080 complaints reported, with 332 accepted and 748 dismissed) Plan to launch online application system
	Risk management	Risk evaluation procedures
	Health, Safety and Environmental (HSE) policy for external contractors and transportation	Plan to launch scenarios of possible crisis situations

Key principle and prime stakeholder	Measures undertaken by the analyzed company	Evaluation (selected criteria)
Respect for human rights (employees, customers, suppliers, general public)	Set of values in code of ethics	Monitoring and report on the compliance with the code of ethics
Sustainable treatment of environment (general public)	Environmental protection policy	Policy in place, reporting and auditing by plant, investments in environmental protection
	Measurement and reporting of water consumption, sewage discharge, air pollutants (sulphur dioxide, nitrogen monoxide, carbon monoxide and dioxide, hazardous waste)	Lower water consumption Increased sewage discharge Increasing emission of air pollutants Increasing hazardous waste Positive verification of CO_2 emissions reports
	Calculation of the environmental impact and environmental fees charged on the production plant Detailed reporting on oil production	Increasing fees charged (€6 million annually) Restoration of peregrine falcon population in Poland Projects adopting waste segregation
Care for local communities (local communities)	Support for national heritage	Involvement in several national heritage projects Support for Polish athletic team Charity via Dar Serca ('A gift of a heart') Foundation Support for fire brigades Project 'Safe roads'

Source: Author's compilation based on PKN Orlen SA CSR and Environmental Reports.

The analysis of PKN Orlen's CSR policy reveals the company's dedication to social and environmental performance. The company has been participating in the Global Compact for eight years, has been involved in the Responsible Care Programme focused on implementation of CSR-related projects for fourteen years and is included in the RESPECT Index, the CSR and sustainability index of the Warsaw Stock Exchange. Regarding reporting practice, the case study of PKN Orlen shows that the company has been issuing a Corporate Responsibility Report for seven years, while developing its reporting in accordance with B-level Global Reporting Initiative G 3.1 Guidelines for three years now. It has attained the level of incorporation of Global Reporting Initiative (GRI) 3.1 Guidelines and GRI Reporting Framework.

Table 11.3b Effectiveness of CSR policy – KGHM SA

Key principle and prime stakeholder	Measures undertaken by the analyzed company	Evaluation (selected criteria)
Fair treatment of employees (employees)	Dialogue with employees – 18,000 workers organized in 15 trade unions Financing health care centre for employees	Reports on no. of employees, no. of employees participating in trainings] Dialogue (on wage increases, the Collective Bargaining Agreement, the Employee Pension Plan, the economic and social position of the company, occupational health and safety conditions, health protection and illness prevention) Support for employees (benefits co-financing, loans, assistance, etc.) Coverage of the company's pension liabilities under defined-benefit plans
	Work safety policy (reporting and auditing)	Reporting on accident rate (dropping) Monitoring employee satisfaction
Ethical operation and integrity (employees, customers, suppliers, investors, general public)	Corporate governance compliance and disclosure	Compliance with corporate governance code of best practice (board committees, board reporting, independent directors, disclosure), no information on e-voting, no data on quotas for females on board
	Implementation of ISO 26000 Guidance on CSR Integrated Management System policy in place Product quality certificates	System control for supplies, environment, quality management, data safety, product safety, food safety Suppliers registered in the SAP system
	Risk management	Risk evaluation procedures
Respect for human rights (employees, customers, suppliers, general public)	Code of ethics – training on compliance with human rights Internal control regulations	Monetary value of penalties and total number of non-financial sanctions in respect of non-compliance

Key principle and prime stakeholder	Measures undertaken by the analyzed company	Evaluation (selected criteria)
Sustainable treatment of environment (general public)	Programme to minimize the negative impact on the natural environment ISO 14000	Emissions meet standards of Polish and European Union law Decreasing fees charged Decreasing pollution emissions (sulphur dioxide, lead and carbon monoxide, dust) Decreasing GHGs emission Slight increase in water uptake Waste management Falling energy consumption
	R&D centre for environmental friendly technologies and solutions	Value of investment
Care for local communities (local communities)	Involvement in selected social project Building a platform for social dialogue Financing health care centre for local community	Significant involvement in community development Support for local community project Monitoring the opinion of local community Repairing mining damage Restoring falcon population in Poland Programme realized within the Foundation (education, sport, health care initiatives, charities, national and regional heritage) – funds devoted

Source: Author's compilation based on KGHM SA CSR Report.
GHG: greenhouse gases.

The analysis of KGHM CSR policy reveals the company's dedication to social and environmental performance. The company is included in the RESPECT Index – the CSR and sustainability index of Warsaw Stock Exchange. The analysed report of KGHM is consistent with the GRI 3.1 Guidelines and GRI Reporting Framework. KGHM SA remains Leader of Polish Ecology, holds an Environmentally Friendly Company award and has been honoured as an Ecological Laureate of the Polish Chamber of Ecology. For the employee safety policy the company was awarded a Gold Card.

Table 11.3c Effectiveness of CSR policy – PGNiG SA

Key principle and prime stakeholder	Measures undertaken by the analyzed company	Evaluation (selected criteria)
Fair treatment of employees (employees)	Public consultations, Employee Council, the system of communicators Collective Bargaining Agreement	No. of employees participating in training Employee volunteering programme
	Work safety policy (reporting and auditing) Strategy of the Employee of Choice	Reporting on accident rate (dropping) Monitoring employee satisfaction No. of interns/ newly employed Employee development programme Support for employees (benefits co-financing, loans, assistance, etc.) also those affected by natural disasters Long-term strategy with four operational objectives
Ethical operation and integrity (employees, customers, suppliers, investors, general public)	Corporate governance compliance and disclosure	Compliance with corporate governance code of best practice (board committees, board reporting, independent directors, disclosure), no information on e-voting, no data on quotas for females on board
	Supplier and customer satisfaction policy Extended communication with customers and suppliers Adoption of the Interior Design Guidelines for Customer Service Offices and the Interior Design Implementation Concept for PGNiG's Customer Service Offices	2,912 phone calls received by the Contact Centre 25,000 customers registered to the Electronic Customer Service Office Long-term strategy with four operational objectives
Respect for human rights (employees, customers, suppliers, general public)	Uniform Internal Communications Standards, Development of a Shared Corporate Culture Code of ethics – training on compliance with human rights	

Key principle and prime stakeholder	Measures undertaken by the analyzed company	Evaluation (selected criteria)
Sustainable treatment of environment (general public)	Implementing, Maintaining and Enhancing Environment Management Systems	Limiting impact on the environment: monitoring the level of emissions of pollutants into the air, energy consumption, amount of waste produced, water consumption, impact on flora and fauna, surface area of land covered by company operations, by limiting areas occupied by equipment and installation. Estimating adverse effect on the quality of soil and water by using seals on land surface where waste, hazardous substances and chemicals are stored, effect on vegetation cover and animals through limited tree clearance, protecting root systems during earthworks and reducing noise emissions, vibrations and contamination during breeding and mating seasons Environmental projects – funds devoted
Caring for local communities (local communities)	Public consultations, activities of the PGNiG Foundation and donations fund, direct interaction with local authorities and organizations Involvement in selected social project Building a platform for social dialogue	Significant involvement in community development Support for local community project Monitoring the opinion of local community Programme realized within the Foundation (sponsorship, education, sport, health care initiatives, charities, national and regional heritage) – funds devoted Long-term strategy with three operational objectives

Source: Author's compilation based on PGNiG SA CSR Report (see PGNiG, 2011).

The analysis of the PGNiG CSR policy reveals the company's dedication to social and environmental performance. The company has been participating in the United Nations Global Compact since 2008 and is included in the RESPECT Index – the CSR and sustainability index of Warsaw Stock Exchange. Its 216-page report follows the GRI guidelines and IPIECA indicators. It is based on the guidelines and indicators following from the Global Compact and ISO 26000 'which were also incorporated into the Code of Responsible Business signed by PGNiG and drawn up under the Coalition for Responsible Business' (PGNiG, 2011).

For the purpose of the study the selected companies belong to the largest Polish companies operating in 'sensitive' sectors such as oil processing, gas extraction and copper mining and they have a significant potential for negative impact on the natural environment and the stakeholders. Hence, these three companies are required to get involved in stakeholder management and their operations need to be carefully observed and audited.

The presented case studies indicate the main components of CSR policy of three Polish companies relating to their efficiency and potential impact on stakeholders. The analysis of the websites and CSR reports reveals that all three companies integrate CSR into their strategies, perceiving stakeholder management as a core of their businesses. The evidence collected in tables 3a, 3b and 3c shows that companies do identify their stakeholders and address their expectations and postulates. They adopt a wide range of programmes and undertake many initiatives in all CSR dimensions, formulating criteria for the measurement of CSR effectiveness. Many of the reported activities concentrate on:

- Employees (working conditions, work safety, personnel development, monitoring of employee satisfaction and dialogue and collective bargaining);
- Stakeholders from the market environment (standards for suppliers and contractors, product and service quality and safety, corporate governance compliance for investors);
- The natural environment (reporting on greenhouse gas emissions, energy and water consumption, waste management and environmental protection and investment);
- Local communities (social projects, monitoring impact on local community, programmes and initiatives in the areas of education, sports, health care, national and regional heritage).

The analyzed companies emphasize their ethical conduct, adopting internal procedures for operations, non-discrimination policy, values and rules derived from the codes of ethics. The ethical stance is intended to be internalized by employees and remains the foundation for a strong corporate culture. Although it is difficult to estimate the degree of fulfilment of stakeholders' expectations, the CSR policies of the three analysed companies reveal high efficiency. PKN Orlen SA, KGHM SA and PGNiG SA remain among the best representatives of Polish companies in terms of their engagement in CSR, contribution to environmental protection, and reporting and disclosure standards. All analysed companies publish detailed reports on CSR and environmental activities, thus establishing an important benchmark for other companies in Poland. Interestingly, all three are included in the RESPECT Index; adopt GRI framework – the CSR and sustainability benchmark of the Warsaw Stock Exchange, which covers about 5 per cent of listed companies. Two are members of the Global Compact initiative. At the same time none of them adopts any stakeholder involvement model (e.g. AA1000) to address and monitor their impact on the environment and cooperation with their stakeholders. PGNiG, with support from PwC, developed its own framework for stakeholder involvement specifically tailored to the energy sector.

The social and environmental performance of the three analysed companies should also be related to the Polish post-transition specificity of social passivity and state weakness. These companies' involvement and transparency provide an important signal for individuals and firms on the company's responsibility and role in the society and the economy, the role of CSR and the environmental protection.

Conclusion

The paper has discussed the practical dimensions of CSR, addressing the question of the effectiveness of its activities and of the potential of CSR to fulfil stakeholders' expectations. The paper presents case studies of three of the largest companies listed on the Warsaw Stock Exchange. Companies were deliberately chosen for the study that operate in 'sensitive' sectors such as oil processing, gas extraction and copper mining, which pose a significant threat in terms of their negative impact on the natural environment and on stakeholders. The article presents detailed CSR initiatives undertaken by these companies and provides insights into the measurement and evaluation of selected efficiency criteria. Addressing the questions: What impact do businesses have on stakeholders? and How beneficial are these programmes to the stakeholders?, the paper delivers a positive notion of the CSR involvement of the three studied companies, as the analysis of their websites and CSR reports indicate that all of them integrate CSR into their strategies, perceiving stakeholder management as a core of their businesses. PKN Orlen SA, KGHM SA and PGNiG SA do identify their stakeholders and address their expectations and postulates. They adopt a wide range of programmes and undertake many initiatives in all CSR dimensions, formulating criteria for the measurement of its effectiveness. Although it is difficult to measure the efficiency of the companies' CSR policy, their stakeholders (employees, suppliers, customers, investors and local communities) seem to benefit from the actions and programmes undertaken. More importantly, the engagement in CSR initiatives and the social and environmental performance and transparency revealed in the analysis may serve as an important benchmark for other companies and contribute to the positive changes in the passive society of post-transition Poland.

References

Ackerman, R. (1973). How companies respond to social demands. *Harvard Business Review*, 51(4), 88–98.

Aluchna, M. (2010). Corporate social responsibility of the top ten: examples taken from the Warsaw Stock Exchange, *Social Responsibility Journal*, 6(4), 611–26.

Arevalo, J. and Aravind, D. (2010). The impact of the crisis on corporate responsibility: the case of UN global compact participants in the USA, *Corporate Governance*, 10(4) 406–420.

Benn, S. and Dunphy, D. (2007). New forms of governance, in Benn, S. and Dunphy, D. (eds), *Corporate Governance and Sustainability: Challenges for Theory and Practice*. London: Routledge, 9–35.

Birch, D. and Jonker, J. (2006). The CSR landscape: An overview of key theoretical issues and concepts, in Jonker, J. and de Witte, M. (eds), *The Challenge of Organizing and Implementing Corporate Social Responsibility*. New York: Palgrave Macmillan, 13–30.

Boni, M. (2009). Społeczna odpowiedzialność biznesu w budowaniu kapitału społecznego [CSR in the process of social capital development], Kompendium CSR, Niezależny Dodatek Tematyczny, *Gazeta Prawna*, 14 December, F4.

Carroll, A. (1979). A three-dimensional conceptual model of corporate performance. *The Academy of Management Review*, 4(4), 497.

Charan, R. and Freeman, R. (1980). Planning for the business environment of the 1980s. *Journal of Business Strategy*, 1(2), 9–19.

Charitoudi, G. Giannarakis, G. and Lazarides, T. (2011). Corporate social responsibility performance in periods of financial crisis, *European Journal of Scientific Research*, 63(3), 447–55.

Clement-Jones, T. (2004). Corporate social responsibility – bottom-line issue or public relations exercise?, in Hancock, J. (ed.) *Investing in Corporate Social Responsibility*. London: Kogan Page (2005), 5–14.

Crowther, D. and Jatana, R. (2005a). Overview, in Crowther, D. and Jatana, R. (eds), *International Dimensions of Corporate Social Responsibility*, I. Hyderabad: ICFAI University Press.

—— (2005b). Is CSR profitable?, in Crowther, D. and Jatana, R. (eds), *Representations of Social Responsibility*, I. Hyderabad: ICAFI University Press, 1–33.

Czapiński, J. (2009). Kapital ludzki [Social capital], in Czapiński, J. and Panek, T. *Diagnoza społeczna 2009* [Social Diagnosis 2009]. Ministry for Labour and Social Policy, Council for Social Monitoring, 270–80. Available at: http://www.diagnoza.com/pliki/raporty/Diagnoza_raport_2009.pdf.

Donaldson, T. (1982). *Corporations and Morality*. New York: Prentice-Hall.

European Commission (2001). *Promoting a European framework for Corporate Social Responsibility*. Green Paper (COM (2001) 366 final). Brussels: Commission of the European Communities. Available at: http://eur-lex.europa.eu/LexUriServ/site/en/com/2001/com2001_0366en01.pdf [accessed: 15 November 2013].

Freeman, R. (1984). *Strategic Management: A Stakeholder Approach*. Boston, MA: Pitman.

Freeman, R. E. (2005). A stakeholder theory of the modern corporation, in Allhof, F. and Vaidya, A. (eds), *Business Ethics*, 1. Los Angeles and London: SAGE Publications, 253–64.

Freeman, R. and Reed, L. (1983). Stockholders and Stakeholders: A new perspective on corporate governance. *California Management Review*, 25(3), 88–105.

Gasparski, W. (2005). Business expectations beyond profit, in Habisch, A. (ed.), *Corporate Social Responsibility Across Europe*. Berlin: Springer, 167–82.

Habisch, A. and Moon, J. (2006). Social capital and corporate social responsibility, in Jonker, J. and de Witte, M. (eds), *The Challenge of Organizing and Implementing Corporate Social Responsibility*. New York: Palgrave Macmillan, 63–77.

Hawkins, D.E. (2006). *Balancing Tomorrow's Sustainability and Today's Profitability*. London: Palgrave Macmillan.

Hillman, A. and Keim, G. (2001). Shareholder value, stakeholder management and social issues: What's the bottom line?, *Strategic Management Journal*, 22, 125–39.

Hollender, J. and Fenichell, S. (2004). *What Matters Most: Business, Social Responsibility and the End of the Era of Greed*. London: Random House Business Books.

Idemudia, U. (2011). Corporate social responsibility and developing countries: Moving the critical CSR research agenda in Africa forward. *Progress in Development Studies*, 11(1), 1–18.

Jamali, D. and Mirshak, R. (2007). Corporate social responsibility (CSR): Theory and practice in a developing country context. *Journal of Business Ethics*, 72, 243–62.

Kemper, A. and Martin, R. (2011). After the fall: The global financial crisis as a test of corporate social responsibility theories. *European Management Review*, 7, 229–39.

Kendall, B., Gill, R. and Cheney, G. (2007). Consumer activism and corporate social responsibility, in May, S., Cheney, G. and Roper, J., *The Debate Over Corporate Social Responsibility*. Oxford: Oxford University Press, 241–64.

Leisinger, K. (2011). Corporate responsibility for pharmaceutical corporations, in Crouch, C. and Maclean, C. (eds), *The Responsible Corporation in a Global Economy*. Social Trends Institute. New York: Oxford University Press, 95–117.

MacIagan, P. (1999). Corporate social responsibility as a participative process. *Business Ethics: A European Review*, 8(1), 43–49.

Maclean, C. and Crouch, C. (2011). Introduction: The economic, political and ethical challenges of corporate social responsibility, in Crouch, C. and Maclean, C. (eds), *The Responsible Corporation in a Global Economy*. Social Trends Institute. New York: Oxford University Press, 1–28.

Martin, R. (2002). The virtue matrix: Calculating the return on corporate responsibility. *Harvard Business Review*, 80(3), 68–75.

Matten, D. and Crane, A. (2005). Corporate citizenship: toward an extended theoretical conceptualization, *The Academy of Management Review*, 30(1), 166–79.

Mele, D. and Garriga, E. (2004). Corporate social responsibility theories: mapping the territory. *Journal of Business Ethics*, 53, 52–68.

Moir, L. (2001). What do we mean by corporate social responsibility? *Corporate Governance*, 1(2), 16–22.

Neal, A. (2008). Corporate social responsibility: Governance gain or laissez-faire figleaf? *Comparative Labor Law and Policy Journal*, 29, 459–74.

Oulton, W. and Hancock, J. (2004). Measuring corporate social responsibility, in Hancock, J. (ed.), *Investing in Corporate Social Responsibility*. London: Kogan Page, 39–48.

Palazzo, G. and Scherer, A. (2008). Corporate social responsibility, democracy, and the politicization of the corporation, Academy of Management Review, 33(3), 773–75.

PGNiG (2011). *CSR Report*. [Online.] Available at: http://www.pgnig.pl/binsource?docId=49751&language=PL&paramName=BINARYOBJ_FILE&index=0 [accessed: 16 November 2013].

Porter, M. and Kramer, R. (2002). The competitive advantage of corporate philanthropy. *Harvard Business Review*, 80(12), 56–68.

Prieto-Carron, M., Lund-Thomsen, P., Chan, A., Muro, A. and Bhushan, C. (2006). Critical perspectives on CSR and development: what we know, what we don't know and what we need to know. *International Affairs*, 82(5), 977–87.

Sethi, S. Prakash (1975). Dimensions of corporate social performance: An analytical framework. *California Management Review*, 17(3), 58.

Sternberg, E. (2011). How serious is CSR? A critical perspective, in Crouch, C. and Maclean, C. (eds), *The Responsible Corporation in a Global Economy*. Social Trends Institute. New York: Oxford University Press, 29–54.

Sułek, A. (2009). Doświadczenie i kompetencje obywatelskie Polaków [Citizen experience and competences of Poles], in Czapiński, J. and Panek, T. *Diagnoza społeczna 2009* [Social Diagnosis 2009]. Ministry for Labour and Social Policy, Council for Social Monitoring. Available at: http://www.diagnoza.com/pliki/raporty/Diagnoza_raport_2009.pdf, 265–70.

Warhurst, A. (2011). Past, present and future corporate responsibility: Achievement and aspirations, in Crouch, C. and Maclean, C. (eds), *The Responsible Corporation in a Global Economy*. Social Trends Institute. New York: Oxford University Press, 55–83.

Wood, D. (1991). Corporate social responsibility revisited. *Academy of Management Journal*, 16(4), 691–718.

12 *Livelihood Assets Financing as a CSR Initiative of Microfinance Banks in Nigeria*

ADEWALE ABIDEEN ADEYEMI

Abstract

The objective of this chapter is to provide a theoretical model that accentuates the imperatives of Nigerian microfinancial institutions' corporate social responsibility (CSR) activities aimed at ensuring that access to and use of financial services are maximized by the unbanked. Based on the extant literature, this chapter demonstrates that enormous opportunities that transcend philanthropy exist through which the Nigerian microfinance banks can be socially responsible. The conclusion and recommendation offered elicit the need for empirical studies that investigate the implications of the apparent social mission drift of the Nigerian microfinance banks for the accumulation of the requisite livelihood assets needed by the poor for a sustainable livelihood.

Introduction

Just as was the case in the transition from microcredit to microfinance, the variability of the vulnerability of the poor is perhaps a main reason for the call to transiting to livelihood finance Mahajan, 2005). Strandberg (2005; cited in Decker and Sale, 2009: 142) indicates the imperative of a sustainable financing arrangement that ensures the provision of financial capital and risk management in such a manner that economic, ecological, and societal concerns are not discounted. As such, it seems that the economic responsibilities of firms that provide financial services to the poor would have to be blended with socio-ecological considerations towards ensuring a sustainable livelihood and socio-economic development.

The interrelationship among the various livelihood assets[1] is such that each may be the cause, the effect, or both, in the livelihood framework. In most instances, however,

---

[1] These include: financial capital, social capital, natural capital, physical capital and human capital (see DFID, 2001).

financial capital is the pivot around which others rotate (Howell, 2005). Hence in this chapter, financial capital is viewed as a determining factor of other livelihood assets. Conceptually, in this study, financial capital is viewed as a combination of both the stock and the regular flow of money available to the poor. Such financial capital includes access to and use of savings, credit, remittances, credit transfers such as pensions, liquid assets such as jewellery and so on. It is envisaged that since the poor often lack financial capital they lack financial citizenship[2] due mainly to financial market friction (Galor and Moav, 2004). Accumulation of other capital assets in the sustainable livelihood assets (SLA) framework may therefore be impeded. Lack of financial citizenship in the context of this chapter is the gap in the demand for and supply of financial services. That is, demand by certain groups of people, usually the poor, and supply by the financial institutions. Although no distinction is made in most related studies among the classes of financial institutions,[3] this chapter focuses on the microfinance banks in Nigeria.

The main aim of this chapter is to conceptualize the implications of a social mission drift of microfinance banks in Nigeria. The thesis sponsored in the chapter is that the lack of livelihood assets accumulation and, by extension, the incidence of persistent poverty in Nigeria can be located within the relegation of the social responsibility of the microfinance banks meant to provide financial capital to the financially repressed poor.

The remainder of the chapter is structured as follows. A trend in the poverty incidence in Nigeria is presented in the next section of this chapter followed by a brief explanation of microfinance. Thereafter, financial citizenship as a social mission of the microfinance banks is explained, followed by microfinance banks' social mission drift and its implications for financial citizenship and livelihood assets acquisition in Nigeria. The theoretical framework underpinning the thesis sponsored in this chapter is also presented. The chapter ends with a conclusion and suggested recommendations.

The Social Menace of Poverty

Although there is no universally acceptable definition of poverty, a consensus among development researchers and scholars suggests that poverty is a terrible state of the human condition. According to the Nobel Laureate Yunus (1999; 2007), poverty is simply reflected in the inability of the poor to apply their latent talents to empower themselves due to the failure of institutions. According to Mathur (2008; cited in Daley-Harris, 2009:4), it is ironic that while a reasonably small number of people enjoy a life of unimaginable abundance, the majority live in poverty. He aptly describes this as 'Party in the Penthouse – Fire in the Basement'.

Today, almost 3 billion people – about half of the earth's inhabitants – live on less than $2 per day.[4] This category of people is referred to as those at the base of the pyramid

---

2   The failure of the formal banking system to offer a full range of depository and credit services, at competitive prices, to all households and/or businesses, especially the poor, thus compromising their ability to participate fully in the economy and to accumulate wealth (Dymski, 2005:2).

3   Howell (2005) classifies such financial institutions into mainstream, fringe and informal markets.

4   This threshold is universally acknowledged and adopted as defining the poor (Demirgüç-Kunt and Levine, 2007:2). However, in realization of the underestimation of the number of the poor in the world, a threshold of $1.25 was used in the most recent report of the World Bank (see WDI, 2013).

(BoP).[5] Currently, the majority of these poor people live in sub-Saharan Africa, Latin America and South Asia (Islam, 2006). According to Moore (2001), it is estimated that by 2015, when the international developments target are expected to be met, an estimated 900 million people, most of whom live in rural areas in sub-Saharan Africa and South Asia will be living in poverty.

In the case of sub-Saharan Africa, Nigeria plays a pivotal economic and political role, given its vast human and physical resources. It is, however, ironic that most Nigerians still live in poverty despite Nigeria being resource-rich.[6] More worrying, however, is the dimension of intergenerational transmission of poverty (ITP) as being experienced in Nigeria. In this case, unlike their cohorts from rich families who may inherit *properties*, the children of the poor may likely inherit *poverty*. For this latter group of children, and like their poor parents and grandparents who are trapped in poverty (Kimenyi, 2006) and live impoverished life (Demirguç-Kunt and Levine, 2007), breaking the poverty cycle is arduous. This seemingly unpleasant trend has attracted the attention of the government, development researchers and scholars alike. Obviously, there is the need for the evaluation of the social and economic development strategy pursued to alleviate poverty in Nigeria, especially via the provision of, among other options, financial capital.

According to Chowdhury, Ghosh, and Wright (2005), evidence abounds that the financial repression from both the formal and informal sources of finance interact with many other economic, social and demographic factors to cause the vicious circle of poverty and low level of economic development. The relative importance of an efficient and inclusive financial system cannot, therefore, be ignored. Such a system is needed for ensuring efficient allocation of resources and prevention of inequalities in outcome and opportunities, especially among the poor (Demirguç-Kunt, Beck and Honohan, 2008).

According to Isern et al. (2009), notwithstanding the global expansion in the financial sector, it is still below average in sub-Sarahan Africa. Specifically, without prejudice to the ongoing financial sector reforms in Nigeria, her financial sector is still considered very weak and shallow. Thus, most Nigerians still lack access to and use of financial services. In comparison to other African countries like Kenya, Tanzania and South Africa, Nigeria has the highest percentage of people who are financially excluded in absolute terms. Table 12.1 shows some key financial services access figures for Nigeria.

In recognition of the relative indispensability of an efficient financial sector to the development process, the Nigerian government also approved the Financial System strategy 2020 (FSS 2020) in September 2007. The aim of the FSS 2020 is to serve as a complement to the ongoing financial sector reform in Nigeria and ensure the greater stability, depth and diversity of the entire financial system, with particular regard to ensuring better access to financial services by all Nigerians through, among other means, microfinance.

---

5   According to Klein (2008:3), The BoPis a socio-economic group of people who form the 'underclass' of society and are prone to marginalization. Klein (2008:3) stated further that the world is often portrayed as a pyramid with three categories: the wealthy at the top, the middle class in the middle and the large numbers of poor making up the base.

6   Birdsall, Pinckney and Sabot (2004) and Roemer-Mahler (2006) linked the poverty incidence in Nigeria to the country's affliction with the 'Dutch Disease' and the 'staple trap'. The former relates to the negative economic consequences a country suffers due to the discovery of a natural resource like crude oil. The latter relates to the economic retardation a country experiences due to the rent-seeking attitude prevalent in its dominant economic resource sector.

Table 12.1 Key Nigerian financial services access and use figures

- 74 percent of adults (64 million) have never been banked
- 21 percent of adults (18 million) have bank accounts
- Men have better access to finance; only 15 percent of women currently have bank accounts
- 71 percent (9.6 million) of salaried workers vs. 15 percent (4.3 million) of farm employees have bank accounts
- 86 percent of rural adults are currently unbanked
- 80 percent penetration rate of mobile phones presents excellent opportunity for mobile banking

Source: FinScope Nigeria, 2008 conducted by EFinA, cited in Isern et al. (2009: 2).

Microfinance

The term 'microfinance' has been variously defined by many development scholars and researchers. Each definition reflects the purpose for the establishment, targeted beneficiaries and modus operandi of the institutions saddled with the responsibility of carrying out such financing endeavours. Moving a bit further from this strand of financial services definitions for the poor, some scholars argue that such financial services should be complemented with other ancillary, albeit non-financial services. This group of scholars note the inadequacy of access to financial services directed towards poverty alleviation.[7] Among the many proponents of this argument, Sarker and Singh (2006: 271) state that 'microfinance refers to the gamut of financial and non-financial services, including skill upgradation, and entrepreneurship development rendered to the poor for enabling them to overcome poverty'. Thus, notwithstanding the arguments for and against the efficacy of microfinance as a poverty alleviation tool, its potential for enhancing the financial citizenship of the financially repressed into the mainstream financial system is not in doubt. However, beyond its commercial sustainability, a microfinance firm should ideally also have a social mission (Prior and Argandona, 2009). This opinion aligns with the ethical theory of corporate social responsibility (CSR), which emphasizes both sustainable development and the common good of society (Garigga and Mele, 2004).

FINANCIAL CITIZENSHIP AND SOCIAL RESPONSIBILITY OF MICROFINANCE INSTITUTIONS

Lack of financial citizenship frustrates the ability to acquire livelihood assets. As succinctly stated by Dymski (2005: 2), lack of financial citizenship occurs due to 'the failure of the formal banking system to offer a full range of depository and credit services, at competitive prices, to all households and/or businesses, especially the poor'. This compromises the ability of the poor to participate fully in the economy and to accumulate wealth. Numerous voluntary and involuntary reasons may aggravate the incidence of lack of financial citizenship. As noted in Adewale, Pramanik, and MydinMeera (2012), in the

---

7   Notwithstanding their disagreement over which financial service provider is better, the Keynesian and the neoclassical economists and, more recently, the post-Washington Consensus proponents subscribe to the financial services inadequacy thesis towards poverty alleviation.

case of Nigeria such reasons may include religious consideration, debt phobia, cultural capital and financial complacency. Other reasons cited include affordability, eligibility and lack of awareness.[8]

The implications of lack of financial citizenship is well noted in the literature. A consensus is that financial exclusion can be a reason for persistent poverty and low economic development, albeit at varying degrees of severity. It therefore follows that beyond the economic philosophy that underlies the establishment of financial institutions they have a social obligation towards ensuring an inclusive financial service provision. As noted in Prior and Argandona (2009), although the social responsibility of any firm should be assessed within the context of its social function and operational environment, that of microfinance firms presents some peculiarities. This is because, right from inception microfinancing is motivated by the need to render social functions to the financially repressed. It is not surprising, therefore, that the efficacy of microfinance is now hinged on its ability to achieve the double-bottom or even the triple-bottom lines. While the former relates to microfinance institutions (MFIs) having both a financial and a social mission, the latter adds environmental considerations into the equation.

According to Prior and Argandona (2009), the main social responsibility of microfinance, therefore, would be to provide a platform whereby people in the active population would be integrated into the mainstream financial service provision with the aim of combating financial and social exclusion. They argue for what they refer to as 'bankization' of the core and marginally poor in a way that ensures best conditions of returns, costs and risks (Prior and Argandona, 2009: 5). However, the literature is awash with studies documenting the skewed attention paid to the economic mission at the expense of the social mission of microfinancing. Such mission drift (Hishigsuren, 2007), may lead to the unintended consequence that the very poor might no longer be reached in such instances. Consequently, the inequality gap in the social structure of a nation may be exacerbated.

NIGERIA MICROFINANCE INSTITUTIONS' SOCIAL MISSION DRIFT

Based on their service delivery, funding and target clients, most microfinance firms in Nigeria appear to have a leaning towards commercialization (Adewale, 2011). This is more so since most of the microfinance institutions were transformed from community banks that were established on the basis of commercial orientation. The argument, therefore, is that with these transformed microfinance institutions and the venturing into the microfinance business by some of the big banks in Nigeria, there would be increased competition. There would be more funds but at a commercial going rate, thus further discriminating against the core poor. The tendency towards what Hishigsuren (2007) calls a 'mission drift' is, therefore, imminent. The implication of this is that the socio-economic philosophy that underlies microfinancing may just have been relegated right from the inception of these relatively new microfinance institutions. In such a situation, the core poor are usually not the target clients, so that the scourge of poverty and, indeed, its intergenerational transmission may conveniently retain their perennial status.

---

8   See Leyshon (2007) for other classifications of barriers to financial citizenship.

As a distinction from previous similar studies that used traditional financial ratios,[9] Nawaz (2010) used Yaron (1992) Sustainability Dependence Index (SDI) based on a panel data of 179 MFIs in 54 countries including Nigeria.[10] One of the aims of the paper was to investigate the mission drift tendency in the MFIs studied. After controlling for endogeneity bias, the study found the MFIs have a tendency towards mission drift and that no trade-off exists between outreach and sustainability. Nawaz (2010), therefore concluded that though subsidization leads to cost inefficiency and low staff productivity, commercialization would also eventually lead to higher administration costs as MFIs scale up.

According to Hishigsuren (2007), this mission drift occurs by chance rather than by design. It is often consequent upon the microfinance institutions' quest for expansion and growth, especially where their mission is vague.[11] Duursman (2004) also acknowledged the increased competition and market saturation that these institutions have to grapple with, especially in the urban areas. He, therefore, posited that the rural areas should have been the alternative location for expansionary purposes. However, the incidences of high costs, risks and adaptation of products preclude these institutions from relocating or expanding to the rural areas. This further aggravates the mission drift phenomenon, as they tend to be more discriminatory in their lending to the poor. In this instance, Devine (2003) argues that the poor clients become the benefactors rather than the beneficiaries. This is in respect of the type and quality of relationship that exists between the clients and the microfinance institutions, which leaves the former with little or no room to manoeuvre.

The implication of the forgoing for the microfinance institutions in Nigeria is predictable. Most of them, apparently, are commercially oriented and in their bid to be sustainable, may exhibit commercial tendencies. This will erode their significance for social welfare. Not only are most of these institutions located in the urban areas but their client selection process may be an indication of their primary concern for profitability rather than their social philosophy. Quite apparently, most of them have neither clear-cut missions specifying their target beneficiaries nor the kind of impact they intend having on the lives of the poor they are meant to serve ab initio. As a result, their susceptibility to deliberate or circumstantial social mission drift is exacerbated. In this instance, the onus for the sustainability of these institutions is placed on the poor people through exorbitant charges, forced savings, etc.

As a sequel to the foregoing, it may be argued that, based on the theory of imperfect credit, the poor are unable to transform their native capacity into wealth. In such cases, their entrepreneurial efforts are not only frustrated but their inability to acquire livelihood assets is also further aggravated, thus making their poverty status persistent. A theoretical explanation of the forgoing is presented next.

---

9   See, for instance, Hudon and Traca (2008) and Cull et al. (2007).

10   Two leading MFIs in Nigeria, LAPO and SEAP, were included in the sample.

11   This is in the context of the targeted clients, and the impact they intend to have.

Theoretical Explanations

This study is based on a simple theoretical framework adapted from the study carried out by Demirguç-Kunt and Levine (2007). The framework is hinged on the assumption that financial exclusion impedes the acquisition of the requisite human and physical capital needed to ensure a sustainable livelihood. In particular, the theoretical framework explains how equality of opportunities is impeded by friction in the financial markets and the implications this has for persistent poverty.

Based on the conceptual framework, specific focus in this theoretical framework is on access to and use of financial capital and on human capital accumulation[12] (proxy by education). This is because they both relate to the theory of imperfect credit (Beck, Levine and Levkov, 2007:4). Also, given that theories of financial development (access and use of financial services), economic growth (microenterprise development) and persistent poverty (lack of capital accumulation) are often taken as conjoined (Osili and Paulson, 2007; Demirguç-Kunt and Levine, 2007, Demirguç-Kunt et al., 2008), occasional references are made to them in the developed framework. For ease of explanation, the sequencing used in Demirguç-Kunt and Levine (2007) is adopted in theorizing this framework.

ASSET ACCUMULATION AND PERSISTENT POVERTY

A basic explanation often provided in the extant literature for the intergenerational transmission of wealth or poverty from parents to children is the latter's inheritance of productive assets from the former. In the initial scenario, given Equation 1 below:

$$Y(i,t) = h(i,t)w(t) + a(i,t)r(t) \tag{1}$$

where $Y(i,t)$ is the total income of a given family i in generation t, $h(i,t)$ is human capital, $w(t)$ is wage rate, $a(i,t)$ is inherited assets as a function of parental income, and $r(t)$ is the return on assets. In this simple model, both the reward for labour and the return on assets are assumed to be immutable. It may, therefore, be expected that in their adulthood, the children of the rich will be richer than their cohorts from poor parents. This is because the rich parents have a high altruistic tendency, which makes them more interested in perpetuating dynastic wealth. They, therefore, would prefer to focus on nurturing successors and thus transferring knowledge and social networks across generation (Wong et al., 2007). It is further assumed that, as is usually the case, this altruistic inclination is automatically imbibed by the children of rich families. The implication is that in return, these children offer to contribute their best to sustain the dynastic dominance and affluence. Consequently, intergenerational correlation of income will be positive. This is shown by the first order partial derivative of inherited assets to parental income to be greater than zero (Equation 2):

$$a' = [\partial a(i,t)/ \partial Y(i,t-1)] > 0 \tag{2}$$

It should be stated that the persistence of the relative income differences among the poor and rich dynasties influenced by inherited income depends on whether or not such

---

12   Other livelihood assets such as physical capital, social capital, natural capital, and so on may also be included.

differences decline overtime. In this case, the second order partial derivative of inherited assets to parental income would either be positive or negative, implying persistent or declining intergenerational income inequalities respectively. That is, a'>0, a''>0 (convex function) and a'>0, a''<0 (concave function) respectively. In the case of the latter, average savings a/Y declines as the Y increases. Wong et al. (2007)provide plausible reasons for such a decline based on the unidirectional and asymmetric nature of the altruism paradigm. He argues that decline is often the result when younger generations lack the acumen and sense of responsibility to sustain the dynastic affluence inherited.[13]

The implication of this simple framework is provided in Demirguç-Kunt and Levine (2007). They state that in the absence of financial market imperfections, a convex function of the dynastic relative income differences across generations will perpetuate inequality and poverty. However, the limitation of this simple model in explaining the negative relationship between income inequality and economic growth is noted. Therefore, Demirguç-Kunt and Levine (2007) offer further illustration based on the Greenwood and Jovanovic (1990) model.

The Greenwood and Jovanovic (1990) model does not treat r(i,t) returns on assets in Equation 1 above as a constant. Rather, it assumes that there is a cross-dynasty difference in asset returns. This is because the return on assets is contingent upon access to information from a financial intermediary at a fixed cost about investable projects. It follows, therefore, that the difference in expected returns and, subsequently, the income of dynasties joining the intermediary will be higher than those of dynasties yet to join. This improves the resource allocation efficiency and, by extension, economic growth. This is due to the fact that return is tied to investment embarked upon based on information obtained at a cost.

At the low level of financial development, only a few can afford the high fixed cost to procure information about projects in which to invest. Therefore growth is also low and income is equal. As more people can afford the fixed costs and so join the financial intermediaries, the resultant improved financial development implies higher returns. Thus, growth and inequality will be increased in the process. This model assumes that persistence in the long run in dynasty assets returns is not feasible. This is because everyone will eventually be able to afford to join the financial intermediaries to get a higher return.

FINANCE, HUMAN CAPITAL ACCUMULATION AND PERSISTENT POVERTY

The simple model in Equation 1 explained thus far demonstrates the impact on dynastic wealth when human capital[14] is held constant. In this case, both inherited wealth and returns on assets as proxy for physical capital provide reasonable forecasts. They provide an indication of the likelihood of persistent relative poverty across generations. However, there is evidence of the relative indispensability of human capital in explaining dynastic differences in income in the intergenerational context and this necessitates its choice among other sustainable livelihood capitals (Bhukuth, 2005; Ferguson, 2006; Minnis, 2006;

---

13   Wong et al. (2007) argue further that the emphasis on direct transfer of wealth and resources to younger generations at the expense of entrepreneurial venturing spirit accounts for the decline in family businesses, even in the developed economies.

14   Human capital can also be substituted by any other capital among the sustainable livelihood assets.

Cull et al., 2007; Beck, Levine and Levkov, 2007; Demirgüç-Kunt and Levine, 2007; and Demirgüç-Kunt, et al., 2008).

Demirgüç-Kunt and Levine (2007:11) argue for the need to treat the physical and human forms of capital as non-symmetrical. This is notwithstanding the fact that they are both diminishable across generations.[15] Following this line of argument, a new model showing the influence of human capital based on Demirgüç-Kunt and Levine (2007:12) is introduced as follows in Equation 3 below.

$$h(i,t) = h\{e(i,t), s(i,t)\} \tag{3}$$

where $e(i,t)$ is dynastic endowment of ability, $s(i,t)$ is investment in human capital accumulation proxy by schooling. A logical assumption is that it is most socially efficient to have the most endowed children getting most schooling. This helps to optimize aggregate economic growth given that $\partial h/\partial e > 0$ and $\partial h/\partial s > 0$. Also, assuming further that the second order partial derivative of 'h' to both variables 'e' and 's' is positive, that is, $\partial^2 h/\partial e \partial s > 0$. In this scenario, the absence of financial market friction would mean that $s(i,t)$ in Equation 3 is held constant. As such, only $\partial h/\partial e > 0$ explains an individual's economic opportunities. Regardless of the dynastical affluence or poverty, an individual would have same opportunity to human capital accumulation determined by dynastical endowment ability, which though may be enhanced; is exogenous.

Decomposing $e(i,t)$ in order to express it as a function of some variables, Demirgüç-Kunt and Levine (2007: 13) specified (Equation 4):

$$e(i,t) = \rho e(i,t-1) + \varepsilon(i,t) \tag{4}$$

where ρ is the intergenerational correlation of abilities, and $\varepsilon(i,t)$, represents the random component of individual abilities. Since ability can only be inherited partially, it follows further that $0 \le \rho < 1$. Citing Becker and Tomes (1986), Demirgüç-Kunt et al. (2008:13) argue that such intergenerational ability endowment regresses to the mean subject to the random shock component $\varepsilon(i,t)$.

Of particular interest, therefore, may be the rate at which such ability regressing to the mean affects intergenerational outcome of opportunities. In a perfect financial market, this impact will be quicker. This is because regardless of dynastic wealth everybody can borrow to finance their investment in schooling. That is, $h(i,t) = h\{e(i,t)\}$. However, in a credit market friction scenario, such a rate of regression to the mean would be much slower. This is because, as noted in Ferguson (2006), financial market imperfection limits the acquisition and accumulation of human capital proxy by education.[16] This means that $h(i,t) = s(i,t)$ also holds. But from Equation 1, if $a(i,t)$ represents parental wealth, and investment in schooling is influenced by it in an imperfect market scenario, then $s(i,t)$ is a function $a(i,t-1)$. Therefore, Equation 1 can be rewritten as:

---

15   Human capital, unlike physical capital, is inherently embodied in humans. Its accumulation at the individual level is subject to diminishing returns due to human physiological constraints. The aggregate stock of human capital would be larger, therefore, if its accumulation were widely spread among individuals in society. However, the aggregate productivity of the stock of physical capital is largely independent of the distribution of its ownership in society. This asymmetry between the accumulation of human and physical capital suggests, therefore, that as long as credit constraints are largely binding, equality is conducive to human capital accumulation, whereas provided that the marginal propensity to save increases with income, inequality is conducive to physical capital accumulation (Galor and Moav, 2004:1002).

16   The poor often lack the resources to invest in their children's schooling.

$$h(i,t) = h[e(i,t), a(i,t-1)] \tag{5}$$

The implication in Equation 5 is that the tendency for an endowed child from a poor family to receive less schooling than a relatively less endowed child from rich dynasty is very high. The implication of this, according to Demirguç-Kunt and Levine (2007: 14), includes that it: (i) increases the cross-dynasty persistence of relative incomes; (ii) reduces the economic opportunities of individuals born into poor dynasties; and (iii) lowers the socially efficient allocation of schooling resources.

Given that ρ, ability endowment is exogenously determined,[17] and that it is mean reverting across generations, other views are warranted. In order to capture the impact of dynastic capital accumulation on persistent wealth distribution, Demirguç-Kunt and Levine (2007: 15) cite the Galor and Tsiddon (1997) long-growth model. The model assumes an identical innate ability of endowment, thus modelling human capital accumulation as:

$$h(t+1) = \Phi\{d(t),s(t)\} \tag{6}$$

where $d(t)$ is dynastic human capital and $s(t)$ investment in schooling. It is assumed in the model expressed in Equation 6 that $\Phi_1 = \partial h/\partial d > 0$ and $\Phi_2 = \partial h/\partial s > 0$. That is, both are positive even when it is further assumed that they diminish overtime: $\Phi_{11} = \partial^2 h/\partial d < 0$, and $\Phi_{12} = \partial^2 h/\partial s < 0$. Therefore, the second order partial derivative of h to both variables d and s is positive, that is, $\partial^2 h/\partial d \partial s > 0$ thus indicating that they are complements.[18]

In a frictionless financial market, differences in human capital accumulation, therefore, would be determined solely by the dynastic human capital. This is because all individuals can have access to the financial market to fund schooling investment. The implication is that at a low level of development, inequality in wealth distribution would exist. This is so as long as there is motivation for the rich dynasties to invest in schooling given the complementary relationship between dynastic human capital and investment in schooling. This is good for economic growth. It will arouse the interest of the poor dynasties to invest more in schooling to reduce the inequality, given that $\partial^2 h/\partial d < 0$. As this trend continues, the returns on human capital investment would enhance aggregate economic growth through global externality. This is in the sense of increased technological advancement and output. Consequently, differentials in wealth distribution are reduced in the long run. This model becomes stymied, however, by policies that accentuate equality of outcomes rather than opportunities. In such cases, Demirguç-Kunt et al. (2008) argue that incentives to invest in human capital may be less stimulating.

In reality, the assumption of the existence of a frictionless financial market is bogus. Therefore, viewing human capital accumulation as explained by dynastic human capital and investment in schooling in an imperfect financial market scenario is appropriate. An alternative model in this regard, cited in Demirguç-Kunt and Levine (2007: 17) is the Galor and Zeira (1993) model. Unlike Galor and Tsiddon (1997), who assume human capital is a smooth concave function of dynastic human capital, this model assumes a concave function of creating human capital. Although individual innate abilities are

---

17   Humans have no influence on its initial value.

18   The tendency that educated and non-financially constrained parents will send their children to school is very high.

identical, investment in schooling will be exclusively for the rich dynasties. Due to financial market friction, rich dynasties can, therefore, invest more in human capital to perpetuate relative differences in wealth distribution across generations. The implication is that the pivotal role of financial market friction in explaining long-term growth and wealth distribution is made discernible. It follows, therefore, that the ability of the poor to reduce such inequality in the long term is dependent on the causes of the inequality in the first instance, that is: financial market development. Hence, as concluded in Demirguç-Kunt and Levine (2007), Beck, Demirguç-Kunt and Levine (2007) and Demirguç-Kunt et al. (2008), financial market development enhances growth and reduces inequality. This is especially through effective financial sector reforms that help reduce friction and discourage indolence and poor savings attitudes synonymous with redistributive policies.

Demirguç-Kunt and Levine (2007) argue that without sufficient public investment in education, the human capital requirement may not be met. This may cause the economy to stagnate, because inequality persists. According to Minnis (2006), in acknowledgement of their acceptance of the human capital theory, governments in sub-Saharan Africa place a high priority on formal education. For instance, in Nigeria the government's Universal Basic Education (UBE) scheme is commendable. However, the government misses the point that only the privileged few have the means to send their children to high-class private primary schools.[19] Thus, the intergenerational gap in opportunities between the children of the poor and those of the rich can only get wider. This is due to lack of means to arouse the latent talents of the children of the poor via qualitative education (Ferguson, 2006). In this situation, he argues, persistent structural poverty may be inevitable.

Demirguç-Kunt and Levine (2007) also note that due to financial market imperfections, the poor and their progeny are highly susceptible to social isolation. As a result, they live in segregated environments relative to the rich dynasties[20] and so they miss the opportunity to leverage on the positive externalities such as social amenities, security and other livelihood opportunities that might accrue to them were they to live in the usually serene and orderly environs of the rich. Demirguç-Kunt and Levine (2007: 23) thus state that 'such local externalities can make market equilibria Pareto inefficient. This is by impeding the human capital accumulation of comparatively poor dynasties, which perpetuates cross-dynasty income differences.'

Implications of Microfinance Institutions' Social Mission Drift

Evidence from the literature suggests that lack of access to finance impedes accumulation of the various types of capital needed for a sustainable livelihood.[21] This is because the financially repressed, who, though talented, lack collateral assets, credit histories and social connections, need to exit the poverty trap they are immersed in (Yunus, 2007).

---

19   Parents who can afford to often do so to lay the right foundation for the accumulation of the requisite human capital. Plausible reasons may include the rot in the general educational system in Nigeria, particularly at the elementary level (Adewale, 2007). Based on personal observation, Adewale (2007) discovered that children of teachers of most public schools he sampled attend private primary schools. A case of not consuming what you sell!

20   Given financial market friction, the poor dynasties do not have access to mortgages or other financial assets to build houses in rich neighbourhoods, where the affluent dynasties have made an exclusive precinct.

21   Lack of access impedes accumulation of human capital in terms of investment in schooling. Also, accumulation of financial capital to transform the latent talents and entrepreneurial capacity of the poor into a source of livelihood is affected (Kimenyi, 2006; Cull et al., 2007; Demirguç-Kunt and Levine, 2007).

The pivotal role of access to finance in development issues can, therefore, not be overemphasized.

Some early theories of development such as the Kuznet's inverted U hypothesis hold that a trade-off exists between early stages of development and inequality. Modern theories have, however, shown that this does not always hold, especially for developing nations. For instance, the Galor and Zeira (1993) and Banerjee and Newmann (1993) models cited in Demirguç-Kunt et al. (2008) underlines the fact that the Kuznet's hypothesis do not always hold. They assert that inequality, whether of outcomes or opportunities, persists due to financial market friction.

A discernible fact arising from these issues is that if not rooted in financial market imperfection, they have a link to it. Unfortunately, financial market frictions have always been taken as a rite of passage in the early stages of economic development and so are treated as unchanging in financial policy reforms (Demirguç-Kunt and Levine, 2007). According to Demirguç-Kunt et al. (2008), imperfections in the financial markets impede the various efforts at both societal and individual levels towards the alleviation of poverty, for example, depriving the poor of the financial support (physical, human, social) they need to escape poverty and its persistence across generations. In the case of microfinance, whose mode of delivery is essentially group-oriented, reductions in transaction and monitoring costs, negotiations, litigation and the enforcement of contracts are some of the benefits of social capital. In agreement with Corr (2006: 27), the term 'financialization' of social relationships presupposes a link between financial inclusion and social capital, and this has significant implications for microentrepreneurial fortune or misfortune.

Conclusion

To address the problems related to persistent inequality and poverty, considerable efforts were made by the Central Bank of Nigeria (CBN) (2005) to identify the world's best practices as far as microfinancing is concerned. While it may be worthwhile replicating some of these practices, reforms to make such practices effective must be based on local realities (Van Horen et al., 2004; Adewale, 2007).[22] Unfortunately, the current development paradigm championed by the Washington Consensus (WC) and apparently adopted in Nigeria makes certain unrealistic assumptions. The WC treats the poor as a homogeneous lot having similar development aspirations, whereas the converse is also a fact (Misra, 2005).

Moreover, it has to be understood that to poor households, credit is not the only or in many cases the priority financial service they need. The provision for good savings and payments services (including international remittances) and insurance may deserve even higher priority.[23] For example, one of the reasons why the poor may not save financial assets is the lack of appropriate products offered by savings institutions

---

22   In this context, a study carried out by Porter (2003:134) in Ghana reiterated the importance of local realities, 'local confidence in home-grown perceptions and ideas about poverty and ways to tackle it are undermined by external ideas about development, causing grounded knowledge about poverty to be devalued and distorted'.

23   Overemphasis on microcredit at the expense of other microfinancial services required by the poor has magnified the inefficiency of microfinance banks (MFBs) in Nigeria. For instance, the microcredit funds (MCFs) provided by state governments as partners in microfinancing was ₦20 billion or $172 million as at 2007, representing 80 percent of total deposits in MFBs as at June 2008. This amount is expected to quadruple in 2010, therefore magnifying the MFBs' poor deposit mobilization.

rather than their inability to save, as such. In fact, the poor may prefer to save, as this represents their most patronized and cheapest cushion in the event of financial shock or stress.[24]

Building inclusive financial systems requires a focus much broader than microcredit. Even in Bangladesh, where there appears to be a very successful microfinance programme, Chowdhury et al. (2005) argues that emphasizing microcredit only does not provide long-lasting poverty alleviation. They found that the effect of microcredit on poverty does not last beyond six years, with some levelling off thereafter.

As for the availability of funds, most micro and small enterprises – even those owned by the non-poor – have limited or no access to formal finance. According to Nissanke and Aryeetey (1998), these firms are often too small to transact with the formal lending institutions and are also too big for the informal sources of finance. The recent consolidation of the banking industry in Nigeria might even have worsened the matter. This is because of scaling up in Nigerian banks' activities as big banks are subjected to the bank barrier hypothesis (Berger, Klapper and Udell, 2001) having implications for the poor via the microenterprises. Currently, some of these big banks in Nigeria; as an extension of their commercialization philosophy and disposition, quite contrary to the assumed social development inclination to microfinancing, have been making efforts to penetrate the microfinance market. According to Demirgüç-Kunt et al. (2008: 30) 'Researchers are reconsidering whether it might be possible to make profits while providing financial services to some of the world's poorest. Indeed, mainstream banks have begun to adopt some of the techniques used by the microfinance institutions to enter the financial markets.'

Moreover, while these banks may be able to easily demonstrate the 'mechanics' of microfinancing, they may also lack the 'spirit' of it, given their commercial orientation (Ahmed, 2004). This may further exacerbate the financial exclusion problem.

Recommendations

An all-inclusive financial system is a sine qua non for the development efforts in Nigeria. This is, however, not prejudicial to the fact that 'financial levers of development can never substitute for the nonfinancial ones' (Zekeri, 2006: 327). Hence, discerning the non-financial needs of the poor entails their active participation to achieve sustainable development and poverty alleviation in Nigeria. As Sarker and Singh observe: 'without this active participation by all, credit schemes run the risk of becoming mechanical, rigid, dehumanizing operations which fail to meet the needs of the poor and fail to galvanize the talents and spirit so essential for self-sustaining development' (2006: 21).

As dictated by their social philosophy, it is important that microfinance in Nigeria is viewed as a platform rather than, as at present, as a product meant for the poor.[25]

---

24   Shocks are unexpected occurrences such as death or accidents; stress events refer to anticipated events requiring large expenditures, such as weddings, payment of school fees, purchase of a house, etc. (Cohen and Young, 2007: 3).

25   According to Isern et al. (2009: 13), 'the motivation of most Nigerian MFBs investors has to do with opportunism and regulatory arbitrage, given that banking has long been perceived as a lucrative business in Nigeria. The banking sector reform and the new requirements for establishing a bank in Nigeria somewhat impeded investments in the sector. For some investors, the community bank license was the more accessible option. The performance of the community banks suggests that few of these investors entered the business with the interest or capacity for developing financial services for poorer income segments. This history provokes the more relevant question about the motives and talent of the MFB sector, since many of the same institutions transformed into MFBs, and their perceptions and opportunities exist today.'

As such, the replication of the best global practices by Nigerian microfinance banks (MFBs) should include social-oriented practices such as measuring social performance based on the Progress out of Poverty Index (PPI) so as to reduce their tendency towards mission drift.[26]

It is also suggested, therefore, that Nigerian MFBs are innovative enough to render affordable services to the poor and with less stringent eligibility criteria. Their target clients should therefore ideally include poor households and microenterprises.[27] Furthermore, it is suggested that a variety of financial products should be designed that suit the varying interests of the poor.[28] For instance, microinsurance is important to assuage the vulnerabilities of the poor. In this regard, big MFBs may be encouraged to either stand alone or partner existing insurance companies to provide microinsurance services to the poor.[29]

The adoption of the Grameen Bank model of microfinance as the baseline for microfinancial practices in Nigeria is essential. However, a modification of the standard practices of the Grameen Bank model in the context of Nigerian peculiarities is required. For instance, when group lending is necessary at the start of a loan cycle, individual liability may be introduced subsequently. This practice is currently being experimented with in the Grameen Bank and has yielded positive results.

Moreover, an aggressive campaign would have to be carried out by the government and MFBs to arouse the interest of the poor in the financial arrangements once again. The need for such massive awareness stems from the fact that the poor in Nigeria lack awareness of the various financing alternatives they can access. The cultural capital of Nigeria's poor, reflected in their voluntary financial exclusion and occasioned by distrust in the financial system, necessitates this recommendation.

References

Adewale, A.A. (2007, February). *Poverty Alleviation through Microenterprise Development and Access to Microcredit. A Case of Households in the Inner City of Ilorin Metropolis Enterprises in Ilorin, Nigeria*. Paper Presented at the Second National Conference on Nigeria and Beyond 2007: Issues, Challenges and Prospects, University of Ilorin, Ilorin, Kwara State, Nigeria.

Adewale, A.A. (2011). *Financial Citizenship Barriers among Muslim Micro-entrepreneurs in Ilorin, Nigeria: A Factorial Invariance Analysis*. A Paper presented at The Second International Conference on Inclusive Islamic Financial Sector Development Jointly organized by the Sudanese Academy for Banking and Financial Science and Islamic Research and Training Institute (IRTI) between 9 and 11 October 2011.

Adewale, A.A., Pramanik, A.H. MydinMeera, A.K (2012). A measurement model of the determinants of financial exclusion among Muslim micro-entrepreneurs in Ilorin, Nigeria. *Journal of Islamic Finance*, 1(1), 030–043.

---

26   The MFBs rent very expensive buildings in high-rent areas, and use very expensive cars. It is improbable that they transact their business with the core poor, if, at all, any poor.

27   According to Isern et al. (2009), most of the MFBs in Nigeria are located in Lagos and Abuja in apparent manifestation of their commercial orientation. Isern et al. (2009) also note the intense competition among the MFBs in these cities, whereas the rural areas have the largest percentage of the unbanked poor.

28   Ibiwoye and Adewunmi (2008) noted the relative indispensability of the insurance sub-sector to the Nigerian financial system. They argue that poor ethical practices and lack of corporate governance are the causes of the low patronage of the sub-sector by Nigerians. This perhaps explains the findings in Isern et al. (2009) that only 2 percent of Nigerian adults have an insurance policy.

29   Various tested collaboration options for microinsurance can be found in Churchill (2007).

Ahmed, H. (2004, September). *Islamic Alternative to Finance Poverty Focused Group-Based Micro-financing*. Paper presented at the Twenty-Sixth Annual Meeting of IDB with NDFIs, Tehran, Iran.

Aryeetey, E. (1999). *Informal Finance for Private-Sector Development*. A Background Paper prepared for African Development Report. N.p.

Beck, T., Levine, R. and Levkov, A. (2007). *Bank Regulation and Income Distribution. Evidence from Branch Deregulation*. Available at: http://www.worldbank.org [accessed: 2 May 2008].

Berger, N.A., Klapper, L.F. and Udell, G.F. (2001). The Ability of Banks to Lend to Informationally Opaque Small Businesses. *Journal of Banking and Finance*, 25, 1–47.

Bhukuth, A. (2005). *Child Labour and Debt Bondage: A Case Study of Brick Klin Workers in Southern India*. Available at: http://www.sagepublications.com [accessed: 1 May 2008].

Birdsall, N., Pickeney, T. and Sabot, R. (2004). Natural resources, human capital, and growth, in M. Auty (ed.) *Resource Abundance and Economic* Development. Oxford: Oxford University Press, 56–73.

Central Bank of Nigeria (CBN) (2005). *Microfinance Policy, Regulatory and Supervisory Framework for Nigeria*. Abuja: Central Bank of Nigeria.

Chowdhury, A.J., Ghosh, D. and Wright, R.E. (2005). The impact of microcredit on poverty. Evidence from Bangladesh. *Progress in Development*, 5, 298.

Cohen, M. & Young, P. (2007). Using microinsurance and financial education to protect and accumulate assets. Reducing global poverty: the case for asset accumulation. Downloaded on June 28, 2008 from www.microfinancegateway.org/.../Monique%Cohen%20-%20Brookin.

Corr, C. (2006). Financial exclusion in Ireland: an exploratory study and policy review. *Combat Poverty Agency Research Series*, 39.

Cull. R., Demirguç-Kunt, A. and Morduch. J. (2007). Financial performance and outreach: a global analysis of leading microbanks. *The Economic Journal*, 117, 107–133.

Daley-Harris, S. (2009). *State of the Microcredit Summit Campaign Report 2009*. Washington DC: Microcredit Summit Campaign.

Decker. S. and Sale, C. (2009). An analysis of corporate social responsibility, trust and reputation in the banking profession, in Idowu, S.L. and Filho, W.L (eds), *Professionals' Perspectives of Corporate Social Responsibility*. London: Springer, 135–56.

Demirguç-Kunt, A., Beck, T. and Honohan, P. (2008). *Finance For All: Policies and Pitfalls in Expanding Access*. A World Bank Policy Research Report. Washington DC: World Bank. Available at: http://www.worldbank.org [accessed: 2 May 2008].

Demirguç-Kunt, A. and Levine, R. (2007). *Finance and Opportunity: Financial Systems and Intergenerational Persistence of Relative Income*. Washington DC: World Bank. Available at: http://www.worldbank.org [accessed: 2 May 2008].

Devine, J. (2003). The paradox of sustainability: reflections on NGOs in Bangladesh. *The ANNALS of the American Academy of Political and Social Science*. 590, 227.

DFID (2001). *Sustainable Livelihoods Guidance Sheets*. London: UK Government Department for International Development.

Duursma, M. (2004). *Community-Based Financing Models in East Africa*. The Netherlands: FACET BV.

Dymski, G.A. (2005). Financial globalization, social exclusion, and financial crisis. *International Journal of Applied Economics*, 19(4), 439–57.

Ferguson, K.M. (2006). Responding to children's street work with alternative income-generation strategies. *International Social Work*. 49(6), 705–717.

Galor, O. and Moav, O. (2004). From physical to human capital accumulation: inequality and the process of development. *Review of Economic Studies*, 71(4), October, 1001–1026.

Galor, O. and Tsiddon, D. (1997).The distribution of human capital and economic growth. *Journal of Economic Growth*. 2(1), March, 93–124.

Galor, O. and Zeira. J. (1993). Income distribution and macroeconomics. *The Review of Economic Studies*. 60(1), January, 35–52.

Garriga, E. and Mele, D. (2004). Corporate social responsibility theories: mapping the territory. *Journal of Business Ethics*, 53: 51–71.

Greenwood, J. and Jovanovic, B. (1990). Financial development, growth, and the distribution of income. *The Journal of Political Economy*. 98(5), Part 1, 1076–1107.

Hishigsuren, G. (2007). Evaluating mission drift in microfinance: lessons for programmes with social mission. *Evaluation Review*, 31, 203.

Howell, N. (2005, June). *Financial Exclusion and Microfinance: An Overview of the Issues*. Paper presented to the QCOSS Seminar Opportunity Knocks: Microfinance as a Pathway to Financial and Social Exclusion, Brisbane, Australia.

Hudon, M. and Traca, D. (2008). On the Efficiency Effects of Subsidies in Microfinance: An Empirical Inquiry. *Working Paper CEB 06020*. Solvay Business School, Brussels, Belgium.

Ibiwoye, A. & Adewunmi, A. (2008). Repositioning the Insurance Industry: Insurance Practice, Ethics and Corporate Governance. *The Nigerian Banker*. Journal of the Chartered Institute of Bankers of Nigeria, April-June.

Isern, J., Agbakoba, A., Flaming, M., Mantilla, J., Pellegrini, G. and Tarazi, M. (2009). *Access to Finance in Nigeria: Microfinance, Branchless Banking, and SME Finance*. CGAP.

Islam, R. (ed.) (2006). Introduction, in Islam R. (ed.), *Fighting Poverty: The Development–Employment Link*. London: Lynne Rienner Publishers.

Kimenyi, S.M. (2006). *Economic Reform and Pro-Poor Growth: Lessons for Africa and Developing Regions in Transition*. Department of Economic Working Papers 2006-02. Storrs, CT: University of Connecticut, USA.

Klein, H.M. (2008). *Poverty Alleviation through Sustainable Strategic Business Models: Essays on Poverty Alleviation as a Business Strategy*. Rotterdam, The Netherlands: Erasmus University of Rotterdam. [Online: ERIM] Available at: httip://www.erim.eur.nl [accessed: 30 November 2009].

Leyshon, A. (2007). Financial exclusion, in Rob Kitchin and Nigel Thrift (eds), *International Encyclopaedia of Human Geography* (2009). The Netherlands: Elsevier. [Online.] Available at: andrewleyshon.files.wordpress.com/2007/11/financial-exclusion_iehg_final-draft.pdf.

Mahajan, V. (2005). From Microcredit to Livelihood Financing. [Online.] Available at: http://www.microfinancegateway.org/gm/document-1.9.25359/34431_file_06.pdf [accessed: 15 November 2013].

Minnis, J.R. (2006). Non-formal education and informal economies in Sub Sahara Africa: Finding the right match. *Adult Education Quarterly*. 56, 119.

Misra, A. (2005, November). *Why Microfinance Needs Participatory Impact Assessment: Case Analysis of SHG-Bank Linkage programme in India*. Paper presented at the Asia Workshop on Next Generation Participatory Monitoring and Evaluation, PRIA, New Delhi, India.

Moore, K. (2001). *Framework for Understanding Intergenerational Transmission of Poverty and Wellbeing in Developing Countries*. Chronic Poverty Research Centre Working Paper 8. IDPM, University of Manchester, UK.

Nawaz, A. (2010). *Issues in Subsidies and Sustainability of Microfinance: An Empirical Investigation*. CEB Working Paper Number 10/010. Centre Emile Bernheim Research Institute in Management Sciences, Solvay Brussels School of Economics and Management.

Nissanke, M. & Aryeetey, E. (1998). *Financial Integration and Development, Liberalization and Reform in Sub-Sahara Africa*. London: Routledge.

Paulson, A. and Osili, U.O. (2006). What Can We Learn about Financial Access from U.S. Immigrants? FRB of Chicago Working Paper No. 2006–25. Available at: http://www.chi.frb.org [accessed: 2 May 2008].

Porter, G. (2003). NGOs and poverty alleviation in a globalizing world: perspectives from Ghana. *Progress in Development*, 3, 131.

Prior, F. and Argandona, A. (2009). Credit accessibility and corporate social responsibility: the case of microfinance. *Business Ethics: A European Review*, 18, 4.

Roemer-Mahler, Anne (ed.) (2006). Drivers of change in government behavior: Adding public value: the limits of corporate responsibility: *OPI-NCBS-ESRC Workshop Series OPI*, Oxford.

Sarker, A.N. and Singh, J. (2006). Savings-led microfinance to bank the unbankables: sharing of global Experiences. *Global Business Review*, 7, 271.

Van Horen, B., Leaf, M. and Pinnawal, S. (2004). Localizing a global discipline: designing new planning in Sri Lanka. *Journal of Planning Education and Research*. 23, 255.

Wong, Y., Ahmed, P. and Farquhar, S. (2007). Founders versus descendants: the profitability, growth and efficiency characteristics comparison in the UK small and medium sized family businesses. *Journal of Entrepreneurship*. 16; 173.

WDI (2013).World Development Indicators. Washington DC: World Bank. [Online – World Bank Database.] Available at: http://www.worldbank.org/data-catalog/world-development-indicators [accessed: 16 November 2013].

Yaron, J. (1992). What makes rural microfinance institutions successful? *The World Bank Research Observer*, 9(9), 49–70.

Yunus, M. (1999). *Banker to the Poor: Micro-lending and the Battle against World Poverty*. New York: Public Affairs.

Yunus, M. with Weber, K. (2007). *Creating a World without Poverty: Social Business and the Future of Capitalism*. New York: Public Affairs.

Zekeri, A.A. (2006). Toward a sustainable rural development in Africa: a sociological case study of a World Bank agricultural project in Nigeria, in G.M. Mudacumura, D. Mebratu and M. Shamsul Haque (eds), *Sustainable Development Policy and Administration*. London: Taylor & Francis, 3.

13 Environmental Management Accounting: An Overview

SIRIYAMA KANTHI HERATH AND
LAKSITHA MAHESHI HERATH

Abstract

Environmental reporting as an important element of corporate social responsibility (CSR) has received much attention in recent years and many companies attempt to adopt practices that promote sustainable development. Organizations should align their economic development activities with CSR behaviour. Motivated by the lack of research on environmental management accounting (EMA), in this chapter we examine the development of EMA research and discuss several empirical research studies. It is believed that there is a lack of empirical evidence on the practice of EMA adoption, especially among developing countries. Investigation of various aspects of business management and environmental performance will provide a better understanding of EMA adoption. Also, research on various types of organizations will reveal better information for environmental management and CSR.

Introduction

This chapter presents an overview of environmental management accounting (EMA), which is a subsection of environmental reporting. Environmental reporting as an important element of corporate social responsibility (CSR) has received much attention in recent years and many companies attempt to adopt practices that promote sustainable development. CSR can positively contribute to the social, cultural and environmental aspects of corporation activities, and in recent years, social and environmental accounting research has received increased interest from researchers and practitioners across the globe. With the growing awareness of global warming and the resultant environmental issues, there is a need to conduct EMA research to assist businesses in resource allocation and decision-making (Ferreira et al., 2010). Many researchers have paid much attention to better understanding the environmental reporting practices and their contribution (Gray, 2002; Parker, 2005). Research reveals that by recognizing, measuring and allocating environmental costs, EMA can assist corporate managers to solve their existing environmental problems, to identify alternative actions for cost savings and to improve overall environmental performance. EMA can provide many benefits to organizations in their attempt to reduce waste and improve social responsibility. The use of environmental accounting information is also considered an important aspect of the process of organizational change.

In the past few decades, a series of environmental changes has affected the practice of management accounting (Ferreira and Merchant, 1992). EMA is a prime example of an area of practice and research that has developed rapidly in recent years (Ferreira et al., 2010; Burritt, 2004). One reason for these changes is the increased community awareness and interest in social and environmental issues related to the activities of organizations and the 'increased community attention toward the identification of approaches to deal more effectively with environmental concerns' (Wilmshurst and Frost, 2000: 10). As a result, many organizations have developed EMA systems and have increased their disclosure practices related to activities with an impact on the environment (Adams, 2004, Larrinaga et al., 2001; Guthrie and Parker, 1989). EMA is attempting to promote CSR aspects of economic development.

Although there has been considerable growth in EMA in the last few decades (Schaltegger and Burritt, 2000; Gray and Bebbington, 2001; Bennett and James, 1997), as 'a growing area of research, environmental management accounting (EMA) has received relatively little attention from accounting researchers' (Ferreira et al., 2010: 920). Many researchers highlight the need for more research on theoretical aspects of EMA (Bouma and van der Veen, 2002; Burritt, 2004). Similarly, Qian et al. (2011) and Parker (2005) emphasize the need for more empirical research on EMA. Qian et al. argue that although the concepts of environmental accounting emerged in the 1990s, 'very little interest has been placed in environmental management accounting practices' (2011: 95). Published research indicates a lack of empirical research in the public sector and developing economies. It has also been noted that there is even less research on EMA in the public sector (Qian et al., 2011: 95) and this calls for more research on EMA. Also, many researchers accept that there is a lack of empirical evidence for the contribution of management accounting research to social and environmental issues (Adams and Larrinaga-González, 2007; Parker, 2005; 2008).

Motivated by the lack of research into EMA, in this chapter we examine the development of EMA research and discuss several empirical research studies. We believe that a review of empirical research will guide accounting researchers and corporate managers to better understand the nature and current issues in the EMA field in their attempt to promote CSR behaviour.

Environmental Accounting Research

Environmental accounting is a branch of accounting that deals with social and environmental reporting of organizational activities (Schaltegger and Burritt, 2000). Environmental accounting relates to the recording of past and future environmental information and costs in the body of the financial statements (Gibbon and Joshi, 1999: 6). Similar to accounting in general, environmental accounting can be divided into two parts – environmental management accounting (EMA) and environmental financial accounting (EFA) (Jalaludin et al., 2011: 540). EMA falls under the broad body of literature labelled social and environmental accounting research (SEAR) (Deegan, 2002). In the last few decades, SEAR researchers have paid much attention to a better understanding of reporting practices and their contribution to the environmental agenda (Albelda, 2011; Gray, 2002; Mathews, 1997).

This subject area has been discussed in the literature under different names: corporate social reporting (Belal and Roberts, 2010) and social and environmental accounting (Cooper et al., 2005. It is difficult to determine the frontiers between social accounting and environmental accounting (Eugénio et al., 2010: 287). A historical view suggests that social accounting became an active area of research and practice during the 1970s (Gray and Bebbington, 2001: 275). As a result of the increasing understanding that sustainability and sustainable development have changed the business environment (IFAC, 2011; UNGC, 2010) numerous voluntary initiatives to integrate social and environmental issues into business are emerging nowadays (Albelda, 2011: 77). As sustainability is recognized as an important source of competitive advantage, organizations are moving into achieving sustainable economic, social and environmental performance while achieving economic growth (Albelda, 2011; Porter and Kramer, 2006). Jalaludin et al. claim that '[m]ost importantly, escalating concerns regarding the environment, as well as progress in accounting itself, provide signals for the substantial need for an accounting system that explicitly addresses environmental issues' (2011: 541).

Social and environmental accounting research therefore developed through the recognition of CSR which explored the relations between the accounting, the organization and the society (Eugénio et al., 2010). As a result, many corporations began to report information on both environmental performance and societal performance to the general public (Othman and Ameer, 2009; Adams, 2004). As Deegan points out 'in recent times, there has been substantial growth in the research attention being devoted to social and environmental accounting issues' (2002: 283).

Eugénio et al. state that '[t]he increase of legislation, requiring companies to report environmental information, probably contributed to this situation' (2010: 288). The increased attempts to provide more information have thus increased the trust embedded in financial reports. Othman and Ameer argue '[t]here are many stakeholders who use these environmental and societal performance indicators to gauge the social and environmental responsiveness of corporations' (2009: 298). Many researchers have revealed that companies strive to utilize what tools they have to their fullest extent. Othman and Ameer claim that '[v]arious social circles have profound interest in corporations' environmental and social responsibility disclosures, idealizing corporate social and environmental responsibility as the foundations for business ethics in the new millennium' (2009: 299). This increasing interest in social and environmental reporting has generated an increase in academic research (Ferreira et al., 2010; Parker, 2005; Deegan, 2002; Gray, 2002). Researchers have used a variety of research methods and approaches in explaining why and how corporations disclose social and environmental information. Deegan explains, 'However, reflecting the fact that we do not have an "accepted" theory for social and environmental accounting, there is much variation in the theoretical perspectives being adopted' (2002: 288).

Gibbon and Joshi state that 'Today, the impetus for research and action with regard to environmental reporting not only comes from the academic but also from the accounting profession' (1999: 7). The need for accountants to meet the challenge that the environment raises has resulted in an enormous amount of information through various academic publications. As noted by Gray (2002: 691): 'The business and management literature which had generated the basic terms of debate about "social responsibility" was increasingly interested in the accounts, audits and metrics of social accounting.'

With the increasing interest in environmental reporting related to the environmental impact of corporations, this subject area has been evolving continuously. Themes like social auditing (Owen et al., 2000, Elkington, 1997), sustainability reporting (O'Dwyer et al., 2005) labour and environmental intentions and performance (Gray, 2002) have received much attention from researchers. Research into social audits is especially thriving and interesting as explained by Deegan (2002:288): 'In relation to recent research efforts, amongst the many areas, there appears to be a particular increasing focus being given to a type of community engagement practice, often labeled as social auditing.'

According to Elkington (1997), a social audit is a process that enables an organization to assess its performance in relation to society's requirements and expectations. As Deegan argues (2002: 289):

> *Their use can be explained as a managerial device aimed to take various social pressures away from an organisation. For example, the international sportswear company Nike was criticised internationally for the labour practices imposed on its workforces in certain parts of Asia (in particular). As part of the response, a social audit was implemented with the assistance of the Global Alliance for Workers and Communities. If community suspicion or concern had not been demonstrated, would such a practice have been implemented? The results of the social audit are provided on Nike's Web site.*

As noted above, during the past few decades, a diverse body of research has been accumulated on the area of environmental accounting and the researchers' interest on this area is continuing as increasing numbers of stakeholders are interested in CSRs. According to Gray, 2002: 303):

> *The increasing concern with stakeholders, growing anxiety about business ethics and CSRs and the increasing importance of ethical investment have all raised the need for new accounting and accounting methods through which organisations and their participants can address such matters. But probably the most important of all the influences has been the dawning realisation that environmental issues – especially when examined within the framework of sustainability – cannot be separated from social issues and the accompanying questions of justice, distribution, poverty, and so forth. Social accounting, in all its guises, is designed to deal exactly with these issues.*

Albelda states (2011: 77):

> *Many organizations are nowadays trying to improve their contributions towards sustainability and sustainable development and report more and more environmental related information. Within the wide scope of voluntary initiatives which organizations participate in to show their commitment to sustainable development, the implementation of an environmental management system is increasingly a widespread tool.*

The European Community's Eco-Management and Audit Scheme (EMAS) is a good example of a widely accepted environmental voluntary certification scheme (Wätzold, 2009).

Even though a considerable amount of research has been conducted suggesting that accounting systems should be designed to incorporate social and environmental issues to encourage positive impacts on sustainability and sustainable development, ESAR has paid less attention to innovations and development in accounting related to social and environmental decision-making and control purposes (Albelda, 2011; Parker, 2005).

Environmental Management Accounting

Management accounting is 'the provision of accounting information for a company's internal users. It is the firm's internal accounting system and is designed to support the information needs of managers' (Mowen et al., 2009: 4). Information produced by a management accounting system 'guides management action, motivates behavior, and supports and creates the cultural values necessary to achieve an organization's strategic, tactical, and operating objectives' (Atkinson et al., 2001: 577). Unlike financial accounting which is bound by the generally accepted accounting principles (GAAP), the design of management accounting systems is determined by the information needs of internal managers. In other words, managerial accounting is socially constructed and it is designed to meet unique decision-making needs of managers in specific organizations.

The focus of EMA is to provide information to managers about environment-related activities. This information is expected to support enhanced managerial decisions which lead to improved environmental and financial performance. Previous studies have defined EMA in a variety of ways. For example, Bennett and James (1998: 33) defined EMA as '[t]he generation, analysis and use of financial and non-financial information in order to optimize corporate environmental and economic performance and to achieve sustainable business'. Hyršlová and Hájek (2006: 455) defined EMA as an important instrument that aims 'to minimize the total costs or environmental costs and mitigate the environmental impact of their activities, products and services'. According to Bartolomeo et al. (2000), EMA is concerned with the generation, analysis and use of environment-related financial information to support business decision-making. All of these definitions point out the need for EMA, as conventional management accounting did not provide enough information to support managerial decisions.

For many organizations, sustainable development has become an important strategic initiative leading to greater adoption and use of EMA systems (Figge et al., 2002) and EMA is supposed to provide data to support managerial decisions. Aras and Crowther argue (2009: 286):

> For sustainability accounting there is a need for costs and benefits of environmental and social matters to be identified, for measurement and quantification of these where appropriate, for provision of qualitative data when intangible costs and benefits arise, for the use of commonly accepted physical and monetary performance indicators, and for recognition that many impacts of companies take a long time to eventuate.

Traditionally, organizations have paid much attention to measuring their financial performance 'but ignored the ways to monitor the use and value of environmental resources, both in terms of raw materials consumed and the damage inflicted upon the environment by their commercial activities' (Gibbon and Joshi, 1999: 6).

EMA researchers recognize that EMA is expected to provide physical information on the use of environmental resources and also monetary information such as environment-related costs, earnings and savings (Hansen and Mowen, 2005; IFAC, 2005; Bartolomeo et al., 2000). Ferreira et al. argue that 'In seeking to achieve sustainable practices and eco-efficiency, organisations are led to develop new products and to improve existing processes in order to reduce their use of resources and the environmental damage caused by their activities' (2010: 922).

With the increasing understanding that social and environmental information play an important role in sustainability and sustainable development (Albelda, 2011) many organizations have integrated environmental aspects such as adopting EMA into their information systems. EMA provides economic information about an organization's activities and their impact on society and the environment (Schaltegger and Burritt, 2000). According to Burritt (2004: 13), 'EMA is concerned with the accounting information needs of managers in relation to corporate activities that affect the environment as well as environment-related impacts on the corporation'. Burritt et al. (2002) claim that by adopting EMA, accountants can track and treat environmental costs and revenues thus establishing a link between environment-related business activities and the firm's past, present and future financial performance.

Prior literature on EMA has recognized numerous economic and environmental benefits related to EMA reporting. Deegan (2002), reviewing prior research, discusses a variety of reasons for managers to voluntarily report social and environmental information. Some of these reasons are: to comply with legal requirements, to comply with borrowing requirements, to appear to do the right thing, to comply with community expectations, to attract investment funds and to win particular reporting awards. Deegan (2002: 291) argues: 'Of course, there could be several motivations simultaneously driving organisations to report social and environmental information and expecting that one motivation might dominate all others would be unrealistic.'

Through the adoption of EMA, firms can achieve better environmental and economic decision-making in the production process as a result of recording more accurate environmental costs (Jasch, 2006). Deegan (2002: 291) further argues 'one factor that has in recent times been embraced by many researchers as motivation behind corporate social and environmental disclosures is the desire to legitimise an organization's operations'. In this way, EMA aims to provide various benefits to organizations in carrying out their operations and fulfilling their social responsibilities. Jalaludin et al. explain that '[i]n addition to complying with the current environmental legislation and regulations, many companies now incorporate environmental issues into their strategic planning and project evaluation, provide external environmental reports, implement energy efficiency and waste minimisation programmes' (2011: 540).

Discussing the developments in sustainability accounting, Burritt and Schaltegger (2010: 829) recognized that the 'management orientated path to sustainability accounting, gives recognition to the importance of management decision making and views corporate sustainability accounting as a set of tools that provide help for managers dealing with different decisions'. These tools are intended to help managers make environmentally sound decisions while achieving organizational goals and objectives.

Burritt explains that 'environmental management accounting (EMA) is concerned with the accounting information needs of managers in relation to corporate activities that affect the environment as well as environment-related impacts on the corporation'

(2004: 13). Through EMA, both monetary and physical information that has an impact on the environment is identified, collected, estimated, analysed and used for decision making within the organization (Burritt et al., 2002). Ferreira et al. point out that '[i]ncreased awareness regarding environmental issues has encouraged organizations to use environmental management accounting (EMA) which has been said to deliver many benefits to users, including an increase in innovation' (2010: 920). Some of these benefits include cost reduction, process and product innovation and improvements in corporate image (Ferreira et al., 2010; Hansen and Mowen, 2005; Adams and Zutshi, 2004). Another important objective of EMA is to ensure management gets sufficient information to enhance the decision-making process (Bennett and James, 1997). EMA is an important component of sustainability accounting that helps organizations 'to minimize the total costs or environmental costs and mitigate the environmental impact of their activities, products and services' (Hyršlová and Hájek, 2006: 455).

EMA can also provide many benefits to organizations in their attempt to reduce waste and improve social responsibility. Failure to meet environmental responsibilities, however, can create serious consequences for organizations. Schaltegger and Burritt (2000) argue that corporate environmental impacts and incidents lead to larger monetary consequences for organizations. Ferreira et al. state that '[w]ith a growing awareness of environmental issues, mainly as a product of the now generally accepted global warming phenomenon, there is a need for this type of research to assist businesses in relation to resource allocation and decision-making' (2010: 921).

EMA is said to deliver considerable benefits to various user groups. Empirical evidence will play an important role in establishing an association between the use of EMA information and various benefits such as improved decision-making and environmental efficiencies. Thus, this paper also aims to investigate the issue by looking at recent empirical studies. In the next section, a review of recent empirical studies of EMA from different parts of the globe is conducted in order to recognize the benefits of EMA.

EMA Empirical Research and Environmental Performance

EMA is concerned with the integration of sustainability issues in the managerial decision-making process. Organizations can change the way they operate their business by incorporating environmental aspects with economic performance. Hopwood recognizes three roles that accounting can play in the context of organizational change: firstly, accounting provides visibility to things. Secondly, accounting functions as 'a calculative practice' and, accordingly, it 'is implicated in [...] making appear real and seemingly precise those things that would otherwise reside in the abstract' (1990: 9). Finally, accounting creates 'a domain of economic action' through which certain values and beliefs are incorporated into organizational culture (1990: 10).

Researchers have attempted to investigate organizational change in different ways. Sustainability development and managerial decision-making is one such aspect. Integration of sustainability issues with strategic management and performance measurement can be considered as a way of changing organizations. Analysis of environmental performance is another new area of investigation in accounting research. Organizational change has been 'examined in terms of the environmental impacts generated in the conduct of business, such as hazardous waste recycling, toxic releases, pollution level in discharged water, non-compliance with environmental statutes, or environmental ratings of firms developed by external groups' (Kihn, 2010: 476).

Several research studies conducted in recent periods have attempted to observe various aspects of EMA. One such study attempts to provide cross-sectional evidence of the relationship between strategy, EMA and innovation for the first time. Ferreira et al. (2010: 921) claim that 'there is limited academic research that attempts to either explore EMA empirically or focus on its potential effects on internal processes and outcomes within organisations, such as the development of innovations'. Ferreira et al. (2010), using statistical analysis, examine the notion of innovation as a problem-solving situation in sustainability accounting and the role of strategy with EMA use. They use a survey of large Australian businesses to examine the relationships between sustainability-related management accounting systems as a driver for product and process innovations. They want to see if there were economic benefits as well as environmental benefits of the use of EMA. Based on structural equation modelling, their analysis finds a significant positive association between the use of EMA accounting information and process innovation. No such association was found between the use of EMA information and product innovation or long-term strategy. Ferreira et al. (2010) contribute to the understanding of decision-making processes in which EMA information could provide benefits to the organization and the environment. Their study is also the first to propose a research instrument to examine EMA use as a multi-item construct.

According to the Ferreira et al. (2010) findings, managers can be expected to achieve enhanced environmental performance and economic performance through the use of EMA tools. The most evident limitation of the study is the small sample size. Investigations using similar multi-variable instruments may produce evidence that is more widely accepted.

Recent studies have used the input–output method for approaching sustainability as a system-based concept. For example, Henri and Journeault (2010) addressed the effect of eco-control in the environmental area. Eco-control is the application of financial and strategic control methods to environmental management (Henri and Journeault, 2010: 63). More specifically, Henri and Journeault (2010) examined the influence of management control systems on sustainability accounting and reporting. Using a sample of Canadian manufacturing firms, they investigated the extent to which eco-control systems influence the economic and environmental performance of organizations. They used a matrix which ranked environmental performance on two scales: (a) process versus results; and (b) internal versus external dimensions. They argued that these two scales provide a framework for organizing various aspects of environmental performance. They discussed four aspects of environmental performance: regulatory compliance; process and product improvements and innovations; financial impacts; and stakeholder relations. This study recognizes four major areas where environmental performance indicators can be used:

1. To monitor legal compliance with environmental policies and regulations;
2. To motivate continuous improvements;
3. To provide data for internal decision-making;
4. To provide data for external reporting. (Henri and Journeault, 2010)

Henri and Journeault (2010) observed a mediating effect of environmental performance on the link between eco-control and economic performance. Their research results revealed no direct relationship between eco-control and economic performance. Instead, their results indicate that environmental performance is indirectly affected by four situational variables: the level of environmental exposure, the level of public visibility, the level of environmental concern and the size of organization. They provide valuable insights for managers to integrate environmental related issues into the control system. They are:

- developing specific performance indicators (e.g. inputs of energy, outputs of solid waste, financial impact);
- frequently using those indicators to monitor compliance, to support decision-making, to motivate continuous improvement and for external reporting;
- fixing specific goals in the budget for the environmental expenses, incomes and investment; and
- linking environmental goals and indicators to rewards. (Henri and Journeault, 2010: 75)

This research contributed to EMA research by establishing a better link between control systems and sustainability accounting. Staniskis and Stasiskiene (2006) observe the implementation of EMA in Lithuania. They discuss the responsibility of the organization towards ecological, social and economic aspects of the environment and the importance of safe, environmentally sound and economically viable energy production and supply. Staniskis and Stasiskiene claim that '[s]ound energy and environmental accounting must be the basis of any strategic decision making in order to keep up with the increasing complexity of energy and environmental problems' (2006: 71). Using a sample of 38 cleaner production investment projects, they revealed that the use of EMA information helps companies to reduce their operating costs and achieve better prices, as well as save natural resources.

According to Staniskis and Stasiskiene (2006), the companies they surveyed utilized total cost assessment (TCA), flow cost accounting and other types of comprehensive, long-term financial analyses of cleaner production to recognize financial indicators of cleaner product investment. Staniskis and Stasiskiene (2006) identify efficiency, equity, ecological integrity and technological change as the fundamental aspects in a comprehensive sustainable energy production and supply framework. They recognize that EMA acts as a link between environmental aspects and shareholder value. They conclude that EMA enables companies to uncover hidden environmental costs, commonly included in overhead costs, which are very often neglected by managers.

These empirical research studies reveal very important aspects of EMA issues. As a growing area of accounting, EMA has many uncertainties and questions that are yet to be addressed. Recognizing environment-related liabilities and costs are important aspects of EMA reporting.

Conclusion

Growing attention and awareness of environmental issues by various stakeholders indicates that organizations have to pay much attention to their activities with an impact on the environment. Organizations should align their economic development activities with CSR behaviour. The use of EMA information may provide useful implications to address environmental related issues. EMA can be used to provide better information about the use of scarce resources and reduce waste and pollution. Also, the use of environmental accounting information is considered an important aspect of the process of organizational change.

It is believed that there is a there is a lack of empirical evidence on the practice of EMA adoption especially among developing countries. Investigation of various aspects of business management and environmental performance will provide a better understanding of EMA adoption. It is believed that case studies from different countries will provide differing perspectives on the use of EMA information. Also, research on various types of organizations will reveal better information for environmental management.

References

Adams, C. (2004). The ethical, social and environmental reporting–performance portrayal gap. *Accounting, Auditing & Accountability Journal*, 17(5), 731–57.

Adams, C.A. and Larrinaga-González, C. (2007). Engaging with organisations in pursuit of improved sustainability accounting and performance. *Accounting, Auditing & Accountability Journal*, 20(3), 333–55.

Adams, C. and Zutshi, A. (2004). Corporate social responsibility: why business should act responsibly and be accountable. *Australian Accounting Review*, 14(3), 31–40.

Albelda, E. (2011). The role of management accounting practices as facilitators of the environmental management: Evidence from EMAS organisations. *Sustainability Accounting, Management and Policy Journal*, 2(1), 76–100.

Aras, G. and Crowther, D. (2009). Corporate sustainability reporting: a study in disingenuity? *Journal of Business Ethics Supplement*, 87, 279–88.

Atkinson, A.A., Banker, R.D., Kaplan, R.S. and Young, S.M. (2001). *Management Accounting*. 3rd edition. Upper Saddle River, NJ: Prentice Hall.

Bartolomeo, M., Bennett, M., Bouma, J., Heydkamp, P., James, P. and Wolters, T. (2000). Environmental management accounting in Europe: current practice and future potential. *The European Accounting Review*, 9(1), 31–52.

Belal, A.R. and Roberts, R.W. (2010). Stakeholders' perceptions of corporate social reporting in Bangladesh, *Journal of Business Ethics*, 97, 311–24.

Bennett, M. and James, P. (1997). Environment related management accounting: current practices and future trends. *Greener Management International*, 17, 33–51.

Bennett, M. and James, P. (1998). The green bottom line, in Bennett, M. and James, P. (eds), *The Green Bottom Line: Current Practice and Future Trends in Environmental Management Accounting*, Sheffield, UK: Greenleaf Publishing, 30–60.

Bouma, J. and van der Veen, M. (2002). Wanted: a theory for environmental management accounting, in Bennett, M., Bouma, J. and Wolters, T. (eds), *Environmental Management Accounting: Informational and Institutional Developments*. Dordrecht: Kluwer Academic, 279–90.

Burritt, R.L. (2004). Environmental management accounting: roadblocks on the way to a green and pleasant land. *Business, Strategy and the Environment*, 13, 13–32.

Burritt, R.L. and Schaltegger, S. (2010). Sustainability accounting and reporting: fad or trend? *Accounting, Auditing & Accountability Journal*, 23(7), 829–46.

Burritt, R., Hahn, T. and Schaltegger, S. (2002). Towards a comprehensive framework for environmental management accounting – links between business actors and environmental management accounting tools. *Australian Accounting Review*, 12(2), 39–50.

Cooper, C., Taylor, P., Smith, N. and Catchpowle, L. (2005). A discussion of the political potential of social accounting. *Critical Perspectives on Accounting*, 16(7), 951–74.

Deegan, C. (2002). The legitimising effect of social and environmental disclosures: a theoretical foundation. *Accounting, Auditing & Accountability Journal*, 15(3), 282–311.

Elkington, J. (1997). *Cannibals with Forks: The Triple Bottom Line of 21st Century Business*. Oxford: Capstone Publishing.

Eugénio, T., Lourenco, I.C. and Morais, A.I. (2010). Recent developments in social and environmental accounting research. *Social Responsibility Journal*, 6(2), 286–305.

Ferreira, A., Moulang, C. and Hendro, B. (2010). Environmental management accounting and innovation: an exploratory analysis. *Accounting, Auditing & Accountability Journal*, 23(7), 920–48.

Ferreira, L.D. and Merchant, K.A. (1992). Field research in management accounting and control: a review and evaluation. *Accounting, Auditing & Accountability Journal*, 5, 3–34.

Figge, F., Hahn, T., Schaltegger, S. and Wagner, M. (2002). The sustainability balanced scorecard: linking sustainability management to business strategy, in *Business Strategy and the Environment*, Vol. 11, pp. 269–84. [Online: Wiley InterScience.] Available at: http://www.interscience.wiley.com [accessed 26 October 2013].

Gibbon, J. and Joshi, P.L. (1999). A survey of environmental accounting and reporting in Bahrain. *Journal of Applied Accounting Research*, 5(1), 4–36.

Gray, R. (2002). The social accounting project and Accounting, Organizations and Society: privileging engagement, imaginings, new accountings and pragmatism over critique? *Accounting, Organizations and Society*, 27(7), 687–708.

Gray, R. and Bebbington, J. (2001). *Accounting for the Environment*. London: Sage Publications,

Guthrie, J. and Parker, L. (1989). Corporate social reporting: a rebuttal of legitimacy theory. *Accounting and Business Research*, 19(76), 343–52.

Hansen, D.R. and Mowen, M.M. (2005). Environmental cost management. *Management Accounting*. Mason, OH: Thomson-South-Western, 490–526.

Henri, J-F. and Journeault, M. (2010). Eco-control: the influence of management control systems on environmental and economic performance. *Accounting, Organizations and Society*, 35(1), 63–80.

Hopwood, A.G. (1990). Accounting and organisational change. *Accounting, Auditing & Accountability Journal*, 3(1), 7–17.

Hyršlová, J. and Hájek, M. (2006). Environmental management accounting in Czech companies that have implemented environmental management systems, in Schaltegger, S., Bennett, M. and Burritt, R. (eds), *Sustainability Accounting and Reporting*, Dordrecht: Springer, 433–56.

IFAC (2005). *Environmental Management Accounting*, International guidance document. New York: International Federation of Accountants. Available at: www.ifac.org/members/Downloads/IFAC_Guidance_doc_on_EMA_FINAL.pdf [accessed 26 October 2013].

—— (2011). Sustainability Framework 2.0. Professional Accountants as Integrators. New York: International Federation of Accountants.

Jalaludin, D., Sulaiman, M., and Nik Ahmad, N.N. (2011), Understanding environmental management accounting (EMA): A new institutional sociology perspective, *Social Responsibility Journal*, 7(4), 540–57.

Jasch, C. (2006). Environmental management accounting (EMA) as the next step in the evolution of management accounting. *Journal of Cleaner Production*, 14, 1190–1193.

Joshi, P.L. and Ramadhan, S. (2002). The adoption of international accounting standards by small and closely held companies: evidence from Bahrain, *The International Journal of Accounting*, 37(4), 429–40.

Kihn, Lili-Anne (2010). Performance outcomes in empirical management accounting research: Recent developments and implications for future research, *International Journal of Productivity and Performance Management*, 1.59(5), 468–92.

Larrinaga, C., Carrasco, F., Caro, F., Correa, C. and Páez, J. (2001). The role of environmental accounting in organizational change: an exploration of Spanish companies. *Accounting, Auditing & Accountability Journal*, 14(2), 213–39.

Mathews, M.R. (1997). Twenty-five years of social and environmental accounting research Is there a silver jubilee to celebrate?, *Accounting, Auditing & Accountability Journal*, 6(4), 481–531.

Mowen, M.M., Hansen, D.R. and Heitger, D.L. (2009). *Cornerstones of Managerial Accounting*. 3rd edition. Mason, OH: South-Western Cengage Learning.

O'Dwyer, B., Unerman, J. and Hession, E. (2005). User needs in sustainability reporting: perspectives of stakeholders in Ireland. *The European Accounting Review*, 14(4), 759–87.

Othman, R. and Ameer, R. (2009). Corporate social and environmental reporting: where are we heading? A survey of the literature. *International Journal of Disclosure and Governance*, 6(4), 298–320.

Owen, D.J., Swift, T., Bowerman, M. and Humphreys, C. (2000). The new social audits: accountability, managerial capture or the agenda of social champions? *European Accounting Review*, 9(1), 81–98.

Owen, D.L. (2008). Chronicles of wasted time? A personal reflection on the current state of, and future prospects for, social and environmental accounting research. *Accounting, Auditing & Accountability Journal*, 21(2),240–67.

Parker, L. (2005). Social and environmental accountability research: a view from the commentary box. *Accounting, Auditing & Accountability Journal*, 18(6), 842–61.

Porter, M. and Kramer, M. (2006). Strategy and society: the link between competitive advantage and corporate social responsibility. *Harvard Business Review*, 82(12), 78–92.

Qian, W., Burritt, R. and Monroe, G. (2011). Environmental management accounting in local government: a case of waste management, *Accounting, Auditing & Accountability Journal*, 24(1), 93–128.

Schaltegger, S. and Burritt, R. (2000). *Contemporary Environmental Accounting: Issues. Concepts and Practice*. Sheffield, UK: Greenleaf Publishing.

Staniskis, J.K. and Stasiskiene, Z. (2006). Environmental management accounting in Lithuania: exploratory study of current practices, opportunities and strategic intents. *Journal of Cleaner Production*, 14, 1252–1261.

UNGC (2010). A New Era of Sustainability. *CEO Reflections on Progress to Date, Challenges Ahead and the Impact of the Journey toward a Sustainable Economy, Study 10*. New York, NY: UN Global Compact–Accenture.

Wätzold, F. (2009). Explaining differences in EMAS participation rates across Europe: the importance of institutions, incomplete information and path dependence. *European Journal of Law and Economics*, 28, 67–82.

Wilmshurst, T. and Frost, G. (2000). Corporate environmental reporting: a test of legitimacy theory. *Accounting, Auditing & Accountability Journal*, 13(1), 10–26.

CHAPTER 14

CSR: Global Perspective, Competitiveness, Social Entrepreneurship and Innovation

MANOJ JOSHI, S.P. TIWARI AND VINDHYALAYA JOSHI

Abstract

'Profit making and Social Responsibility' is an oxymoron and can be strongly debated. Profit-making is the most important reason for an enterprise to exist and grow. Social responsibility is the fundamental duty of the state, which must focus upon bringing up its stakeholders within a milieu of social justice. This includes proactive participation by government in elevating quality in the working lives of its citizens. Thus, to attempt to balance wealth and social justice/empowerment is to invite cooperation between people and business in a public–private partnership to enhance the competitive existence and growth of the national economy.

'The state is a necessary evil.' Its primary responsibility is to govern and to bring order from disorder. The city-states of Ancient Greece portrayed high levels of self governance and self-sustenance. Besides this, for a nation to be healthy and prosperous the state must not hinder liberty. Our world has witnessed social unrest caused by economic disparity, inequality, social injustice and other ills resulting in cross-border disputes, civil wars, battles and regional and world wars. It follows that there should be continuous efforts to reduce the economic disparity between the citizens of a state, but the irony is that a state may be unable to execute its primary duties – that is, carryout its social responsibilities – because (i) it is not able to mobilize funds; (ii) the funds available are not adequate for the requirement; (iii) it is not able to utilize the funds and/or (iv) there is lack of governance and willpower. As a result, the entrepreneurs in a corporation – which is a micro-community – emerge as entrepreneur–consortiums to carry out their critical task using innovative methods. They participate as social entrepreneurs and emerge as drivers of the engine of economic and social growth.

Introduction

The world has witnessed – over short and extended periods of time– provocations leading to battles and wars that took place as a result of economic disparity, social injustice and inequality. Innumerable movements and organizations such as apartheid, racism, the Ku Klux Klan have appeared and operated as a result of strong social disparity. The USSR, although based on far-reaching social reforms, could not retain its stability and in its latter days it saw internal resistance. As a result, after the fall of the Berlin Wall, which unfortunately created economic as well as political disparities, the USSR disintegrated and reformed as the Commonwealth of Independent States.

Criminal entrepreneurship, which has emerged in many parts of the world, has facilitated the amassing of wealth through despicable means. Conflicts from world wars to cross-border terrorism have been a consequence of extreme hopelessness. Research reveals that most of the movements and organizations behind these events have or are being led by socially unfit individuals, criminal minds engaged in fighting what they perceive as injustices done to them or to the societies they claim to represent. Adolf Hitler was one: in *Mein Kampf* he claimed that extreme poverty influences and corrupts the mind surreptitiously, giving birth to a vengeful personality. Clearly there is a need for us to combine our efforts and generate enough will to curb these menaces by reducing economic and social disparity before other catastrophes occur.

Many of the inequalities of today arose during the period of industrialization, among them child labour, the exploitation of women, severe labour conditions, as in mines, industrial hazards, pollution of all kinds, the dumping of chemical wastes, the deforestation of hills and the exploitation of rainforests; collectively these have opened up new social and environmental imbalances. Mountain terrains have become dumping grounds for human waste, rivers have started eroding faster, and global warming has fuelled disturbing climatic conditions. Cities are emerging with sensitive issues: beside every high-rise building one can sight 'children of a lesser god' – a term commonly used for those near or below the poverty line. Makeshift houses put up beside canals and railway tracks and on wastelands expand into shanty towns whose inhabitants make a living out of debris. This is just a trailer of a reality that bites and that could not fail to disturb and visibly shake any human being with rational ideas about the dignity of human life. How can we arrest the unequal distribution of wealth? Or, if this is unachievable, what innovative means can be find to reduce the gap between the rich and those with the most basic needs for their survival? The wealthy must desist from competitive bickering and engage their efforts towards social responsibility.

We must recognise that it is imperative to awaken our understanding and ask ourselves whether we should discuss how to create and maximize wealth for those who are already wealthy or how to elevate the quality of life for those – many of whom surround us – who are needy.

Profit-making is the fundamental activity that enables an enterprise to perform and grow, which means wealth maximization and mobilization; whereas social responsibility is the fundamental accountability of the state to focus on social issues in their totality.

Plato in his famous work *The Republic* defined the just state and the just man (Sabine, 1957). According to the Swiss jurist and politician Johann Kaspar Bluntschli, 'the state is a combination or association of men in the form of government and governed on a definite territory, united together into a moral organized masculine personality or, more shortly, the state is the politically organized national person of a definite country' (quoted in Gilchrist, 1950).The English idealist philosopher, Thomas Hill Green stated that will, not force, is the basis of a state.

Perennial topics of debate are the proposals that 'the state is a necessary evil' and 'the state is the obstruction of obstructions'. The primeval responsibility of the state is to bring order from disorder. The city states of Ancient Greece achieved high levels of self-governance and self-sustenance; while in modern times Abraham Lincoln in the Gettysburg Address of 1865 extolled the freedom of 'government of the people, by the people, for the people' afforded by democracy. An important role of the state is to balance the power of the executive, the judiciary and the legislature; yet the state must not hinder liberty – in its entirety, that is: natural liberty, civil liberty, political liberty and national liberty (Laski, 1954). Since value (i.e. marketable value) is the cornerstone of the economic structure (Marx, 1847), it is of crucial importance for the state to monitor growth as well as balance and to deliver social responsibility, but the irony is that the state is unable to execute its primary duties of social responsibility for the following reasons:

1. States may be unable to mobilize funds.
2. The funds available may not be not adequate for what the state is required to do.
3. The state may be unable to utilize available funds.
4. Lack of effective governance and willpower may weaken the state's ability to exercise social responsibility.

Consequently, entrepreneurs in the state may emerge as 'entrepreneur consortia' to exercise social responsibility. After all, there must be a driving force to keep consumers brand-loyal and alive. It is economic disparity, the inequality of wealth, income and property disparity that compel the corporation to grudgingly act as driver of the engine of economic and social growth.

What is Corporate Social Responsibility?

The Sanskrit saying, *atithi devo bhav*, meaning 'the guest is God', is considered to express the highest order of responsibility, be it to an individual or to society. Thus, the term 'social responsibility' has its roots in an Indian context. This term has long been used in the context of the growth of industries and corporations. It not only reflects the passage of time in its impact on and potential for transformation but its meaning has also been affected by the growth of society and of nations and by changes in the appreciation of cultural heritage and background (Gupta and Saxena, 2006).

Corporate Social Responsibility (CSR) is also concerned with treating the stakeholders of the firm ethically or in a responsible manner. 'Ethical' or 'responsible' treatment means treating stakeholders in a manner deemed acceptable in civilized societies. Stakeholders exist both within a firm and outside it. The wider aim of social responsibility for a corporation is to create higher and higher standards of living, while preserving the profitability of the corporation, for peoples both within and outside the corporation (Hopkins, 2004). Some companies use the term 'corporate citizenship', some 'the ethical corporation', while others use 'good corporate governance' or 'corporate responsibility'.

CSR, the Driving Force

Companies engaged in making profits also contribute to some, although obviously not all, aspects of social development. Every company should not be expected to be involved in every aspect of social development. There will be increased costs to implement CSR, but the benefits are likely to far outweigh the costs. Global concerns have been given an additional edge by the awful events of 11 September 2001. The collapse of Enron and WorldCom, and their auditor Arthur Andersen, due to uncertain accounting practices, has raised the level of scrutiny of large companies, as well as their auditors (Hopkins, 2004).

Enterprises operate around seven areas:

1. Shareholders and potential investors
2. Managers
3. Employees
4. Customers
5. Business partners and contractors or suppliers
6. The natural environment
7. The communities, within which they operate, including national governments.

Over US$1 trillion in assets are under management in the United States in socially and environmentally responsible portfolios. In the United Kingdom, pension fund trustees are required to incorporate their policy on socially responsible investment (SRI) in their statement of investment principles (Hopkins, 2004).

The Global Reporting Initiative (GRI) is currently the industry leader in providing a set of voluntary principles for companies in the area of CSR. It was established in 1997 with a mission to elevate sustainability reporting. CSR is a concept whereby companies incorporate social and environmental concerns in their business operations while interacting with their stakeholders on a charitable foundation.

Incorporating CSR into the main agenda should ensure that enterprises would be able to address issues such as excessive exploitation of labour, or bribery and corruption. There would be a certain level playing field creating a competitive environment for the firms to engage in a healthy battle for their profitable existence, as well as their duties towards the environment in which they operate. This would further deter rogue companies from engaging themselves in the business battle through nefarious means. Ultimately, the people and their society would emerge victorious with distributed wealth and congenial living.

In the longer term, more affluent customers and enhanced wide-reaching income distribution is clearly excellent for business and a socially good environment. What is not clear is the question of whether business should be directly involved in these issues, or simply pay taxes and rely on governments and public organizations to use their taxes astutely?

For enterprises, reputation is built around trust, reliability, quality, transparency, integrity, dependability and interrelationships. Investment in people as an asset is the most important criterion for an enterprise's useful existence. Firms must retain quality employees too, and CSR becomes as a visible tool in achieving this aim. Innovation and creativity become a vital tool for the strategy employed in implementing CSR. CSR aids in complying with governments, communities and other stakeholders in enhancing a company's reputation.

Good corporate citizenship can provide business benefits in eight areas (Hopkins, 2004):

1. reputation management
2. risk profile and risk management
3. employee recruitment, motivation and retention
4. investor relations and access to capital
5. learning and innovation
6. competitiveness and market positioning
7. operational efficiency
8. licence to operate.

Thus the issue of corporate sustainability has become an important topic of debate.

The United Nations Environment Programme (UNEP) focuses on ten measures for business performance. They are:

1. human and intellectual capital
2. customer attraction
3. brand value and reputation
4. risk profile
5. licence to operate
6. operational efficiency
7. shareholder value
8. access to capital
9. revenue
10. innovation. (UNEP, 2001)

These are linked to:

a) ethics, principles and values
b) triple bottom line commitment
c) environmental process focus
d) accountability and transparency
e) focus on environmental product
f) socio-economic development
g) workplace conditions
h) engaging business partners
i) human rights
j) engaging non-business partners. (UNEP, 2001)

CSR as a Need

Currently, enterprises have little or no choice but to speedily engage in CSR activities that must be reflected in their social report. This report is audited and must conform to industrial norms if the firm wishes to comply and compete globally. Thus the effort will lead to protecting and enhancing a company's reputation. In addition, this will establish the management's obligation to promote ethical behavior, which will raise stakeholder confidence.

However the firm engaging in CSR must restrain itself intelligently and bring about a rational balance between its profitability, an essential prerequisite to its survival, and its attempts at social responsiveness. It would therefore be advisable for the firm to create shareholder value in an ethically yet socially conscientious way. It must adhere to the norms established by the International Labour Organization (ILO), which include issues such as the right to organize and collective bargaining; a minimum age for employing children; an embargo on forced labour; and an assurance of acceptable working conditions (maximum number of hours per week, weekly rest period, minimum wage, minimum workplace safety and health standards and the abolition of prejudice in employment).

The Outcomes and our Query

CSR makes a difference as it connects stakeholders and human resource policies. It also takes into account the impact it has on those inside and outside the enterprise. Public awareness has strongly increased as a result of many industrial disasters, unethical and malign business practices, and other issues that have either resulted in human and environmental catastrophe or caused irrecoverable loss of property and wealth. There is eventually no escape. All concerned are answerable in a court of law and may have to face other, more dangerous consequences from those who have been affected by such issues.

We must be able to address certain issues: Who are the key stakeholders of a firm? Does a firm engaged in business and CSR adapt to standards set by the governing bodies? Does the core culture of a firm reflect its positive attitude towards addressing issues concerning labour, human rights and environmental concerns? To what extent do ethics, principles and value govern a business? Will sustainability and social accountability remain at the top of a firm's agenda? Does CSR really address an enterprise's brand and its reputation?

These issues are more baffling but cannot be ignored. The responses form an important guiding force for the survival of a profitable enterprise in the society in which it operates. It follows that management must evolve some formula with respect to their industry, the nature of their firm, the economic and social environment in which it operates, legal presence, mandatory systems etc. to act as a link to their profitable–socially responsive existence.

COMPETITIVENESS AND CSR

Thus we need to understand what the relationship between competitiveness and CSR is and the new meaning of competitiveness in the light of CSR. Zadek and his colleagues state that

> *some of the measures demanded of companies in the name of corporate responsibility are incompatible with current business models and markets. Pharmaceutical companies cannot alone provide affordable drugs to the poor, and the footwear companies cannot just decide to pay workers in Mexico or Vietnam a wage comparable to that earned by workers in London or New York. (Zadek et al., 2003)*

Opportunistic CSR is always counter-productive (Zsolnai, 2006). A Green Paper published in 2001 defines CSR as 'a concept whereby companies integrate social and environmental concerns in their business operations and in their interaction with their stakeholders on a voluntary basis' (Zsolnai, 2006).

COMPETITIVE PROWESS

Ethical conduct will always be a driving force that will bring gains to any enterprise. The pressure will be on firms to fit into the ecological, social and cultural positions required of them. Typically, many global firms have strategically positioned themselves by producing or engaging in activities in which the competition is minimal, enabling themselves to be market leaders in their area of expertise. Their products are environmentally safe and recyclable, or they engage in ethical practices that result in a harmonious existence. Social responsiveness elevates their status among their stakeholders. These enterprises should therefore adhere to their core values and remain committed to creating a congenial and healthy socio-economic environment based on mutual trust, interdependence and profitability, or face the results of disproportion in business dealings. Hence, an important element termed 'social entrepreneurship' is emerging as a key initiative among individuals or groups engaged in business.

Conclusion

Social entrepreneurs endeavour to create social value through innovative, entrepreneurial business models. The potential market for these entrepreneurs is huge because of the wide range of social needs that remain unsatisfied by existing markets and institutions. Social entrepreneurs often create tremendous value when they cater to very basic humanitarian needs; for example, by providing medicines or food, which can be a matter of life or death for those who receive them. However, the challenges these entrepreneurs face are severe. Their customers may be willing, but are often unable, to pay even a small portion of the cost of the products and services provided. Many social entrepreneurs operate in developing countries that have no structures or resources that would enable and support traditional entrepreneurship (Seelos and Mair, 2004).

As a consequence these social entrepreneurs must create fresh business models and organizational structures that connect profitable existence to social value. Social entrepreneurship may provide some enthralling new insights and supplement designs for more socially suitable and sustainable business strategies. They discover new and competent ways to create products, services or structures, thus enabling them to cater to social needs to accomplish sustainable development. Entrepreneurship is the consequence of recognition of opportunity by highly-motivated individuals. Conventionally, most people would connect entrepreneurship with the quest for a business opportunity in order to make a living; and in the case of social entrepreneurship this business opportunity is a social need that cannot be fulfilled by markets or social systems. Entrepreneurs are determined to do no matter what it is in their influence to do to accomplish their goals. Their very flexibility, creativity and inventiveness produce tremendous performance in turning their ideas into outcome.

Social entrepreneurs distinguish themselves from other individuals by the very nature of their concerns for serving a social cause. They possess entrepreneurial quality and have respect for the environment in which they operate. At times social entrepreneurs do not even recognize themselves as such until they are recognized by people or organizations.

Major global issues that attract social responsibility are the eradication of poverty and hunger, universal primary education, the promotion of equality, the empowerment of women, the reduction of child mortality, and child and bonded/forced labour, the promotion of health, the combating of HIV/AIDS, malaria and other diseases, ensuring environmental sustainability and a green presence, and forging global partnerships for interdependent development.

Areas in which enterprises around the globe are actively engaged in CSR initiatives in addition to their core business are:

1. Water conservation
2. Revival of traditional arts and crafts
3. Culture and heritage
4. Environmental protection
5. Greening the environment
6. Transforming and managing wastes, and garbage handling
7. Good health for all
8. Providing means for a better livelihood
9. Rural welfare
10. Primary and adult education
11. Disaster management and relief
12. Sports.

Hence to carry forward this mammoth task, enterprises will have to evolve innovative processes or systems that will perhaps give them an edge over their competition. Such processes and systems have to evolve and cannot be replicated. Thus it is necessary to research into why some enterprises are able to create more value than others! How do some sectors create more wealth than others? Why do confident nations do better than others and what is the underlying cause for such successes in the creation of wealth? (Joshi et al., 2007).

Strategic innovation is the answer. It is termed 'strategic' because such innovation has an everlasting impact on the survival of an enterprise. CSR with an innovative approach will create a brand that will ensure success and growth for any enterprise.

References

Gilcrist, R.N. (1950). *Principles of Political Science*. India: Orient Longmans.

Gupta, D.K. and Saxena, K. (2006).*Corporate Social Responsibility in Indian Service Organisations: An Empirical Study, International Conference on CSR-Agendas for Asia*. Organised jointly by ICCSR, Nottingham University Business School, UK; Business School, University of Nottingham in Malaysia; CSR-Asia and Corporate Citizenship Research Unit (CCRU). Deakin University, Australia.

Hopkins, M. (2004).*Corporate Social Responsibility: An Issue Paper, Policy Integration Department World Commission on the Social Dimension of Globalisation*, Working paper 27 (May). Geneva: ILO.

Joshi, M., Joshi, N. and Joshi, V. (2007).*Business War: Competitive Innovation Velocity*. Kansas, USA: Ewing Marion Kauffman Foundation, USA. Lucknow, India: Amity University Business School.

Laski, H.J. (1954). *Liberty the Modern State*. London: George Allen and Unwin.

Marx, K. (1847). *The Poverty of Philosophy*. Moscow: Foreign Languages Publishing House.

Sabine, G.H. (1957). *A History of Political Theory*. London: Harrap.

Seelos, C. and Mair, J. (2004). *Social Entrepreneurship. The Contribution of Individual Entrepreneurs to Sustainable Development*. Working Paper 553. Navarra, Spain: Universidad de Navarra.

UNEP (2001). *Buried Treasure: Uncovering the Business Case for Corporate Sustainability*. Paris: UNEP/ Sustainability.

Zadek, S., Sabapathy, A., Døssing, H. and Swift, T. (2003). *Responsible Competitiveness. Corporate Responsibility Clusters in Action*.Copenhagen: The Copenhagen Centre/Accountability.

Zsolnai, L. (2006).*Competitiveness and Corporate Social Responsibility*. CSR paper 2.2006 (December). Fondazione Eni Enrico Mattei Series. Budapest: Corvinus University of Budapest, Business Ethics Centre.

15 CSR: A Modern Tool for Building Social Capital

SAMUEL O. IDOWU

Introduction

The American economist Harold Rothmann Bowen posited in his book *Social Responsibilities of the Businessman* (1953) that business people have some social responsibilities towards society; and his definition of corporate responsibility as 'the obligations of businessmen to purse those policies, to make those decisions, or to follow those lines of action which are desirable in terms of the objectives and values of our society' was in fact the genesis of modern corporate social responsibility (CSR). But many counter arguments have been put forward by scholars such as Levitt (1958), Friedman (1962), Lippke (1996) and Henderson (2001), who see things differently from Bowen. Despite that, one cannot help but acknowledge that Bowen's book marks the evolution of serious discussion of the field of CSR and the advancements we have made globally to date in the field.

It is therefore easy to argue without being rhetorical that CSR has drastically changed our world and how we conduct business. There is evidence everywhere, in theory and in practice, to back up this assertion; the chapters of this book are probably the latest addition to the many proofs around which confirm that CSR has transformed and reoriented the way corporate entities of our time behave and conduct their operational practices.

Social Capital and CSR

It is not exactly easy to affirm that CSR has improved our social capital but that there is enough evidence to suggest that social capital (SC) continues to improve year on year in the Scandinavian countries, while in countries such as the UK, the USA and France the reverse is the case (Halpern, 2009). According to the OECD, SC consists of the links, shared values and understandings in society that enable individuals and groups to trust each other and, as a consequence, work together to achieve desired objectives. SC could take many forms but the OECD has divided it into three categories:

1. **Bonds** – links to people based on common identity ('people like us'), such as family close friends and people who share our culture and ethnicity.

2. **Bridges** – links that stretch beyond a shared sense of identity, for example to distant friends, colleagues and associates.
3. **Linkages** – links to people further up or down the social ladder.

One supposes that CSR should be practised in an environment where there is a high degree of trust between business and society; and that if this were not to be the case for whatever reason, then CSR would facilitate trust between corporate entities and their stakeholders. This is because markets work more efficiently when oiled with high levels of trust, enabling transactions to occur at lower costs – that is without the need for incurring legal, insurance and other hedging instruments' costs (Halpern, 2009). Lower costs inevitably mean improved bottom lines and consequently more opportunities for socio-economic progress to be facilitated, which perhaps suggests why sociologists have argued that higher SC results in increased social and financial benefits to individuals and communities.

Some Lessons Learned

It would be an irresponsible waste of resources and, of course, socially irresponsible of everyone connected with this book if there were no obvious lessons to be learned from the contributions in the fourteen preceding chapters. The first lesson of the book, in Chapter 1 and the five following chapters of Part I, which discuss multinational corporations (MNCs), relates to environmental reporting. MNCs of the twenty-first century are contributing immensely to the socio-economic progress of their home and host nations in diverse ways. Asaolu and Ayoola writing on the oil and gas sector in Nigeria (a high profile sector on environmental issues globally) expose the fragmented, cosmetic and disconnected from business strategy, corporate disclosure practices of oil and gas corporations operating in Nigeria. They took a bold step in suggesting how this problem could be resolved by putting in place a mandatory CSR framework for companies operating in the oil and gas sector of this oil-rich nation, which might be used by oil and gas corporations operating in other parts of the world. Another lesson from Part I is highlighted by Professor Zaharia in Chapter 6, which compares the CSR of MNCs and indigenous Romanian corporations. While applauding the many benefits MNCs bring to their host nations, she does not hide her disgust at some occasional double standards of many of these MNCs in their host nations, which have the propensity to erode trust and consequently lower the effectiveness of the SC. If these practices were followed by all MNCs everyone would undoubtedly be worse off at the end of the day, a great lesson indeed.

Moving swiftly on to Part II, Professor Muranda elaborates in Chapter 7, on the significance of diamond mining in the Southern African state of Botswana. She suggests that the diamond, a very valuable resource to any economy, is the main product which holds the economy of Botswana together. Professor Muranda espouses the view that the practice of CSR in Botswana (which is mainly discretionary (philanthropic) CSR) and socio-economic advancement are inseparable. It is the 'licence to operate' in the mining communities of Botswana. The practice of CSR plays an integral part in operationalizing the existence of SC in Botswana's social and business environment.

Further lessons are discernible from the chapters 10–14, each focusing on a different country, of Part III. Chapters 11 and 14 are highlighted for the purposes of espousing these lessons. In Chapter 11, Dr Aluchna, writing on the effectiveness of CSR initiatives and how they impact the stakeholders in Poland, notes that a real understanding of how CSR has advanced in the Polish context requires reference to the country's political, economic and social past prior to the fall of Iron Curtain. One would probably not be far from being correct to suggest that a lesson other emerging nations could learn from the Polish experience would be to avoid the following ills, which, Dr Aluchna notes, befell that country's economy:

- high social costs
- a massive increase in social inequalities
- a high level of unemployment
- weak institutions (e.g. an inefficient legal system)
- the emergence of aggressive capitalism
- liberal but ineffective economic policies.

From Chapter 11, one could not help but notice the presence of a generally weak and ineffective system of governance within the economy of this promising emerging nation.

In Chapter 14 Dr Joshi and others, writing from India – an emerging economic world power classed as one of the BRICS nations (Brazil, Russia, India, China and South Africa) – on CSR, observe that global perspective, competitiveness, social entrepreneurship and innovation have brought to the fore many pertinent lessons which emerging economies of the future would find useful when their processes of development begin. The following lessons highlighted by Dr Joshi et al. are noteworthy:

- CSR has increased as a result of many industrial and environmental disasters.
- weak corporate governance has resulted in corporate scandals.
- unethical and maligned business practices are common.

All these have led to human and environmental catastrophe and irrecoverable losses to society, they argue. These scholars also affirm that CSR makes a difference, as it connects stakeholders and human resource policies.

Understandably, India is still emerging as a world class economy and so it still has a number of issues to address, but there is still plenty of time for it to go through this period of transformation if the will to install a sound and problem immune economic mechanism is there.

Our world continues to transform from various standpoints and CSR continues to evolve, along with other useful management concepts of value to corporate entities of today and tomorrow. Sustainability and sustainable development, sustainable entrepreneurship and social entrepreneurship, and social innovation have all reoriented thoughts and practices. They have kept both scholars and practitioners busy. All these innovative concepts of our time should hopefully assist us in finding solutions to many of our social, economic and environmental problems as and when they emerge.

References

Bowen, H.R. (1953). *Social Responsibilities of the Businessman*. New York: Harper & Row.

Friedman, M. (1962). *Capitalism and Freedom*. Chicago, IL: University of Chicago.

Halpern, D. (2009). Capital gains. *RSA Journal*, Autumn 10–15.

Henderson, D. (2001). The case against corporate social responsibility. *Policy*, 17(2), 28–32.

Levitt, T. (1958). The dangers of social responsibility. *Harvard Business Review*, 36, 41–50.

Lippke, R.L. (1996). Setting the terms of the business responsibility debate, in Larmer, R.A. (ed.), *Ethics in the Workplace, Selected Readings in Business Ethics*. St Paul, MN: West Publishing Co.

Index

Page numbers in **bold** refer to figures and tables.

For Product Safety Concerns and Information please contact our EU
representative GPSR@taylorandfrancis.com Taylor & Francis Verlag GmbH,
Kaufingerstraße 24, 80331 München, Germany

Printed and bound by CPI Group (UK) Ltd, Croydon, CR0 4YY
01/05/2025
01858361-0001